The Art of Oratory

Selected, edited and introduced by
Charles Mosley

WORTH
PRESS

Concept, editorial, layout, design and panel sequence © Worth Press Ltd 2007

Text © Charles Mosley
The author has asserted his rights under the Copyright Designs and Patents Act 1988
to be identified as the author of this work.

First published 2007 by Worth Press Limited, Cambridge, UK
www.worthpress.co.uk

The images used in this book come from either the public domain or
from the public commons.

The publishers would like to thank Connie Robertson for arranging the necessary permissions.

British Library Cataloguing in Publication Data
A catalogue record for this book is available from the British Library.

ISBN 978-1-903025-42-0

Designed and edited by Bookcraft Limited, Stroud, Gloucestershire, UK
Printed and bound in Malaysia by Imago

Contents

Acknowledgements

Crown copyright material is reproduced under the terms of the Click-Use Licence with the permission of the Controller of HMSO and the Queen's Printer for Scotland.

We are also grateful for permission to reprint the following speeches that are in copyright:

David Ben-Gurion Extract from Statement to the Elected Assembly of Palestine Jewry, from State of Israel *Historical Documents Vols. 1 & 2: 1947–1974, II, From Mandate to Independence.*

Winston Churchill Extracts from his speeches reprinted with permission of Curtis Brown Ltd, London, on behalf of The Estate of Winston Churchill.

Tim Collins Extract from address to the Royal Irish Regiment, 20 March 2003, reprinted with permission.

Diana, Princess of Wales Extract from speech given at the Royal Geographical Society, 12 June 1997, reprinted with permission of the Princess of Wales Memorial Fund.

Elizabeth II Extracts from speech given in Capetown, 21 April 1947, and from Christmas message, 25 December 1952, reprinted with permission.

Mahatma Gandhi Extract from speech addressed to the Indian National Congress Committee, 8 August 1942, reprinted with permission of the Mahatma Gandhi Centre, Bombay.

John Paul II Extract from homily published on the Vatican website, copyright © Libreria Editrice Vaticana, 2007, reprinted with permission of the Vatican Publishing House.

Dr Martin Luther King Jr. Extract from 'I have a Dream', copyright © 1963 Martin Luther King Jr., copyright renewed 1991 by Coretta Scott King, reprinted by arrangement with the heirs of the Estate of Martin Luther King Jr., c/o Writers House as agent for the Proprietor, New York, NY.

Nelson Mandela Extracts from inaugural speech given at Pretoria, 10 May 1994, reprinted with permission.

Mao Zedong Extract from 'Talk with the American Correspondent Anna Louise Strong', August 1946, in *Selected Works*, Vol IV (Lawrence & Wishart).

George S. Patton Jr Extract from *The Unknown Patton* by Charles M. Province (CMP Productions, 1992), copyright © 1983, 1992, 1998 by Charles M. Province, reprinted with permission of the author. All rights reserved.

Harold Pinter Extract from the Nobel Lecture given when awarded the Nobel Prize for Literature 2005, reprinted with permission.

Enoch Powell Extract from speech given on 20 April 1968, reprinted with permission of the Executors of the Estate of Enoch Powell.

Ronald Reagan Extracts from speeches written by Peggy Noonan from *Speaking My Mind: Selected Speeches* (Hutchinson, 1990), reprinted with permission of the Random House Group Ltd and Janklow & Nesbit Associates, Inc.

Earl Spencer Extract from eulogy given at the funeral of Diana, Princess of Wales, reprinted with permission of Earl Spencer.

Although every effort has been made to trace and contact copyright holders before going to print, this has not been possible in every case. If notified, the publisher will be pleased to rectify any errors or omissions at the earliest opportunity.

The Speeches

Introduction

The speech is an odd literary genre. It has a life of its own, independent of whether or not it is delivered. What could be more pregnant — to continue this midwife imagery — than the Japanese Emperor Hirohito's apology for World War II, composed yet destined never in its author's lifetime to comfort the ears of others?

So a speech is not still-born simply because not given utterance. And like a changeling it can have many parents. It may be composed by someone other than the person who delivers it, as famously in the 1980s for Ronald Reagan by Peggy Noonan. It may be inadvertently plagiarised by a different speaker to the original upon a wholly different occasion, as Disraeli once did with a speech of his contemporary's, the French statesman Thiers, and as the US politician Joe Biden did more recently with a speech of Neil Kinnock's. At a more sublime level, a speech may be delivered many times, over many years, by many different people under many different 'interpretations', as are speeches in plays, though not only that sort.

The original draft text may be delivered with so many ad hoc interpolations, excisions and changes, the better to ram a particular point home to an audience you have unexpectedly aroused on a circumambient topic, that the spoken version is in effect an entirely different body of words. Anyone who has ever compared *Hansard* with the version of a parliamentary speech given in a political biography, however diligently researched, can observe numerous discrepancies.

Sir Jock Colville, Sir Winston Churchill's secretary and much relied upon by this author because of it, speaks in his diaries of 'correcting' the official report of his master's words to improve such elements as the grammar, since Churchill had when speaking inserted much that sounded well but read badly. In any case, the acoustics of parliamentary chambers were not so good, until microphones, that even the *Hansard* reporters took down every word of a politician's speech correctly. And during World War II, as early as November 1940, the Commons met at Church House rather than the Palace of Westminster, later being bombed out of their regular Palace of Westminster chamber altogether. In new surroundings the acoustics may have been worse; or, if adequate, speakers may have been unaccustomed to them and have thrown their voices maladroitly in consequence. Similar considerations apply elsewhere and in other eras.

Then there are the censored 'official' versions, such as Reagan's 'Evil Empire' speech, which offer posterity only an emasculated account of what was actually spoken. All the same, it is usually the 'official' version that is published, though sometimes not for decades, as with Khrushchev's 1956 denunciation of Stalin.

The speech is primarily a political instrument. As such it can at its best elevate; more often, since it is not at its best, it debases. The late-19th-century Prime Minister Lord Rosebery saw even the best speeches as firework displays or bravura operatic performances: elaborately scripted, choreographed and presented, certainly, but essentially one-offs. 'No one reads old speeches any more than old sermons … ', he wrote. 'The more brilliant and telling they were at the time, the more dolorous the quest. The lights are extinguished; the flowers are faded; the voice seems cracked across the empty space of years, it sounds like a message from a remote telephone; one wonders if that can really be the scene that fascinated and inspired … It all seems as flat as decanted champagne … Genuine political speeches that win the instant laurels of debate soon lose their savour. All the accompaniments have disappeared — the heat, the audience, the interruptions, and the applause; and what remains seems cold and flabby.'

Rosebery had a great gift of words. But he was as perverse in his judgement of old speeches as in his conduct of the premiership, which he took up unenthusiastically and resigned a year later when feeling under the weather. It is one reason he was not included in this book. He was of course thinking only of political speeches. Perhaps he found them unsympathetic. He was a very good speaker himself, if over-rehearsed. But when he resigned the Liberal leadership, which he did some time after stepping down as Prime Minister, it was because of a speech, one of Gladstone's (*qv*) last. And this despite Rosebery's showman flair nearly 20 years earlier in organising Gladstone's Midlothian Campaign, arguably the greatest triumph of serial oratory of all time. Besides, in Rosebery's day old speeches *were* read — avidly, as numerous published collections of them testify. George Eliot, for instance, used to read aloud in the evenings from a selection of John Bright's.

The speech also has a literary function, independent of politics. There is the speech as erotic wallpaper: that at the Yonville agricultural fair in *Madame Bovary*, used by Flaubert in what critics call the first 'cinematic' cross-cutting exercise to act as back-drop to Rodolphe's seduction of Emma. There is the speech egotistic: that by Toad of Toad Hall on celebrating the retaking of his country seat from squatter weasels and stoats — 'there will be other speeches by TOAD during the evening', he promises us in the programme. But we never encounter the first speech, let alone the others. Toad's clutch of panegyrics on himself remains one of the great lost texts of civilisation, along with the entire library at Alexandria, Byron's memoirs and Carlyle's first MS of *The French Revolution*, used by a house-maid to kindle a fire. Coincidentally Barack Obama Sen., father of the youngest speaker in this anthology, was likened by a family friend to Toad of Toad Hall.

There is the speech traumatic: much used by P.G. Wodehouse as a device to show up his heroes' panic when called on to make one — if Bertie Wooster and Gussie Fink-Nottle can be called heroes. There is the speech as instrument of tyranny: Lord Copper droning to his victims at his ghastly banquet in Waugh's *Scoop* (forerunner of Castro's (*qv*) four-hour speeches?).

Speeches, even if as much fiction as fact, portray human beings in each age just as faithfully as does portraiture. They convey what was thought important, what was not; what might be said, what mightn't; what had huge, sometimes unintended, effect; what didn't. Even when misused, they have interest as showing the speaker's darker side. Exaggerations, half truths and outright lies indicate areas he (or she) thought worth obfuscating.

And mention of Castro's prolixity necessitates a word about the length of speeches excerpted here. Most have been abridged to roughly 500 words, or five minutes-worth of speaking. Though varying with climate, this is marginally longer than the time it would take before a lump of ice held in the hand melted — a good criterion adopted in ancient times, though often breached in practice, to wit by Socrates (*qv*).

I make no apology for most of the cuts to 500 words or so. Very few speakers needed longer to get their essential points across. The two chief exceptions were Burke and, to my surprise, Daniel Webster. Their speeches were so cohesive and dovetailed, like a Chippendale cabinet, that editing resembled vandalism. The most pleasurable discovery, to me at any rate, has been Lloyd George. Churchill, with whom, as will be seen, Lloyd George was often subject to a 'compare and contrast' process, is as great as ever, but like Olivier perhaps over-rich for our austere post-modern tastes. Or so I take Harold Pinter's soft impeachment of Churchill to indicate.

I would only add that, as far as I know, I am no kin to Sir Oswald Mosley.

CHARLES MOSLEY

To his fellow fallen angels

Belial, Paradise Lost
John Milton
Book I

• Biography

Belial is the thinking man's devil: specious, persuasive, artful, flattering. Belial is clearly something of a double agent or *agent provocateur* in the struggle between God and Hell's demons, one moment the instrument of God's punishment, the next the arch-rebel. He may, like the young Stalin (*qv*), who allegedly combined the callings of revolutionary and police informer, have worked both sides of the street.

• Context of speech

Milton shows us the fallen angels gathered together in debate over what to do after they have rebelled against God and been expelled from heaven.

Eloquent Belial may be. Bold he is not. His is the voice of appeasement down the ages. Just because he is a devil and the appeasement he proposes is of God is no reason to view his defeatism as any the less craven. But it is eloquent.

The lines of blank verse have been recast in continuous prose to emphasise the forensic force. This may seem presumptuous but not, it is submitted, on a Luciferian scale.

> **I should be much for open war ..., as not behind in hate, if what was urged main reason to persuade immediate war did not dissuade me most, and seem to cast ominous conjecture on the whole success ...**

The towers of Heaven are filled with armed watch, that render all access impregnable ... 'Wherefore cease we, then?' say they who counsel war; 'we are decreed, reserved, and destined to eternal woe; whatever doing, what can we suffer more, what can we suffer worse?'

Is this, then, worse — thus sitting, thus consulting, thus in arms? ...

War ... open or concealed, alike my voice dissuades; for what can force or guile with Him, or who deceive His mind, whose eye views all things at one view? He from Heaven's height all these our motions vain sees and derides, not more almighty to resist our might than wise to frustrate all our plots and wiles.

Shall we, then, live thus vile — the race of Heaven thus trampled, thus expelled, to suffer here chains and these torments? Better these than worse, by my advice; since fate inevitable subdues us, and omnipotent decree, the victor's will.

To suffer, as to do, our strength is equal; nor the law unjust that so ordains. This was at first resolved, if we were wise, against so great a foe contending, and so doubtful what might fall.

I laugh when those who at the spear are bold and venturous, if that fail them, shrink, and fear what yet they know must follow — to endure exile, or ignominy, or bonds, or pain, the sentence of their Conqueror.

This is now our doom; which if we can sustain and bear, our Supreme Foe in time may much remit His anger, and perhaps, thus far removed, not mind us not offending, satisfied with what is punished; whence these raging fires will slacken, if his breath stir not their flames.

Our purer essence then will overcome their noxious vapour; or, inured, not feel; or, changed at length, and to the place conformed in temper and in nature, will receive familiar the fierce heat; and, void of pain, this horror will grow mild, this darkness light; besides what hope the never-ending flight of future days may bring, what chance, what change worth waiting — since our present lot appears for happy though but ill, for ill not worst, if we procure not to ourselves more woe."

To his sons

Jacob
The Bible
Genesis XLIX

• Biography

The Jacob of the Old Testament was the junior of Isaac and Rebecca's twin sons. His elder brother Esau first traded away to Jacob his expectations for some soup, being too weary after a day's hunting to safeguard his business interests. Jacob then connived with Rebecca to impersonate Esau, thus tricking from Isaac the blessing meant for Esau.

When Esau discovered the swindle he exploded. Jacob ran away to his uncle Laban, who in turn tricked him into taking in marriage Leah, the older of his two daughters. Jacob preferred Rachel and had worked seven years for Laban on the understanding he would win her.

Jacob now offered to work for Laban an extra seven years but was allowed to marry after only another week. With his two wives Jacob returned home. En route he had a wrestling bout with an angel, lost the contest, was renamed Israel and made his peace with Esau.

His twelve sons became ancestors of the tribes of Israel.

66 **1** ... **Gather yourselves together, that I may tell you that which shall befall you in the last days.**

2   Gather yourselves together, and hear, ye sons of Jacob; and hearken unto Israel your father.

3   Reuben, thou art my firstborn, my might, and the beginning of my strength, the excellency of dignity, and the excellency of power:

4   Unstable as water, thou shalt not excel; because thou wentest up to thy father's bed; then defiledst thou it: he went up to my couch.

5 Simeon and Levi are brethren; instruments of cruelty are in their habitations.

6 O my soul, come not thou into their secret; unto their assembly, mine honour, be not thou united: for in their anger they slew a man, and in their selfwill they digged down a wall.

7 Cursed be their anger, for it was fierce; and their wrath, for it was cruel: I will divide them in Jacob, and scatter them in Israel.

8 Judah, thou art he whom thy brethren shall praise: thy hand shall be in the neck of thine enemies; thy father's children shall bow down before thee.

9 Judah is a lion's whelp: from the prey, my son, thou art gone up: he stooped down, he couched as a lion, and as an old lion; who shall rouse him up?

10 The sceptre shall not depart from Judah, nor a lawgiver from between his feet, until Shiloh come; and unto him shall the gathering of the people be.

11 Binding his foal unto the vine, and his ass's colt unto the choice vine; he washed his garments in wine, and his clothes in the blood of grapes:

12 His eyes shall be red with wine, and his teeth white with milk.

13 Zebulun shall dwell at the haven of the sea; and he shall be for an haven of ships; and his border shall be unto Zidon.

14 Issachar is a strong ass couching down between two burdens:

15 And he saw that rest was good, and the land that it was pleasant; and bowed his shoulder to bear, and became a servant unto tribute.

16 Dan shall judge his people, as one of the tribes of Israel.

17 Dan shall be a serpent by the way, an adder in the path, that biteth the horse heels, so that his rider shall fall backward.

18 I have waited for thy salvation, O Lord.

19 Gad, a troop shall overcome him: but he shall overcome at the last.

20 Out of Asher his bread shall be fat, and he shall yield royal dainties.

21 Naphtali is a hind let loose: he giveth goodly words.

22 Joseph is a fruitful bough, even a fruitful bough by a well; whose branches run over the wall:

23 The archers have sorely grieved him, and shot at him, and hated him:

24 But his bow abode in strength, and the arms of his hands were made strong by the hands of the mighty God of Jacob; (from thence is the shepherd, the stone of Israel:)

25 Even by the God of thy father, who shall help thee; and by the Almighty, who shall bless thee with blessings of heaven above, blessings of the deep that lieth under, blessings of the breasts, and of the womb:

26   The blessings of thy father have prevailed above the blessings of my progenitors unto the utmost bound of the everlasting hills: they shall be on the head of Joseph, and on the crown of the head of him that was separate from his brethren.

27   Benjamin shall raven as a wolf: in the morning he shall devour the prey, and at night he shall divide the spoil."

To the Trojans

Hector, The Iliad
Homer
Book VIII

• Biography

Homer is the name given by the Ancient Greeks to an individual who around the late 8th century BC is thought to have worked up various oral narratives about much earlier events into epic poems. The two of these that have survived we know as the *Iliad* and *Odyssey* and they were committed to writing soon after Homer assembled them. The *Odyssey* need not concern us here. The *Iliad* tells of a single episode in a ten-year struggle known as the Trojan War between the citizens of Troy, thought to have been situated in what is now northwest Turkey, and an expeditionary force of Greeks. The latter had come to recover Helen, wife of one of their kings, from the clutches of a Trojan prince, Paris, who had (with little apparent reluctance on her part) persuaded her to run away with him.

• Context of speech

This excerpt is the Trojan hero Hector's speech to his comrades. It follows their sortie on the Greeks' ships, which the latter had pulled up on the sea shore. The operation had come within an ace of success.

The Dardanians are sometimes identified as just another name for Trojans, Dardanus being Troy's founder in myth. But archaeological finds on the site of Troy (which is now thought to have fallen *c.* 1180 BC) may have been used by an Illyrian people called the Dardanians, settled in the Balkans.

A cubit was the length of a man's forearm, roughly one-and-a-half to nearly two feet. A spear 11 cubits long would thus have extended some 17 to 24 feet. It would surely have been much too unwieldy for throwing, even by a hero of legend. It must have more resembled a pike. If so, it would have been the forerunner of the highly formidable sarissa of Alexander the Great's (*qv*) time, the 4th century BC.

The sarissa, arguably more than any other single device, was what enabled Alexander the Great to conquer the Persian Empire, distant successor to Troy in controlling the Aegean coast of Asia Minor. This is in one way apt, since Alexander identified with the Greek hero Achilles, but in another way odd, since the implication in Homer is that the proto-sarissa 11 cubits long was a Trojan weapon. Perhaps the Greeks adopted it.

'Then Hector led the Trojans back from the ships and summoned a meeting near the river on open space which was clear of corpses. The Trojans left their chariots and sat on the ground to listen to him. He grasped a spear. It was 11 cubits long, its gleaming point bronze, the ring round its neck gold. He said:

"**Trojans, Dardanians and other allies. I had supposed that by now I would have destroyed the Greeks' ships — the Greeks too — and then returned to Troy. But night fell too soon. It was night that saved the Greeks, them and their transports along the shore. So to the night let us now give way, and get ready our evening meal.**

Unharness your horses from the chariots and give them their corn. Bring sheep and cattle from the city. Bring wine too — and more corn, that your horses may further feed. Then gather much wood, so that till dawn itself we may stoke fires to watch by, great fires whose flare will flicker to within reach of Heaven.

For under cover of this self-same night the Greeks may try to re-embark, make a run for it in abject flight by sea. If so, they must be harried. They must not escape unharmed.

See to it that, as far as possible, each Greek takes home a grievous wound; a wound to torment him as he stretches by his hearth; stricken by arrow or spear as he scuttles to clamber aboard his boat. This done, no other race will dare to afflict the Trojans, whether by blood or tears.

Further, let our heralds proclaim throughout Troy that our menfolk who do not bear arms, whether from tender youth or sere old age, must keep watch upon its sacred walls. And let our women kindle fires in their houses, so that a watch be kept at home. All this lest Troy be broken in upon by stealth while its fighting troops defend it from without its walls.

See to it, brave Trojans. Let this be enough for now. At dawn I will issue fresh orders ...

Tonight we must keep watch. But at sunrise let us both buckle on our armour and loose unbridled war upon the Greeks. Then shall I know if brave Diomed the son of Tydeus will drive me back from the ships to the very walls of Troy, or whether I shall manage to overcome him, killing him and carrying off his bloody arms and armour as spoils of war. Tomorrow let him show his mettle, and confront my spear if he dare.

It is my belief that, come the dawn, he shall be among the first of the Greeks to fall. Would that I were as sure of ageless immortality and the reverence that befits a god, as I am that tomorrow will bring disaster to the Greeks.'"

To the Greeks

Achilles, The Iliad
Homer
Book XXII

• Context of speech

Hector was the Trojans' only real hero, whereas the Greeks possessed several. Chief among them was Achilles, their best fighter. This arose partly from his physical strength and skill, but mostly from his near-total invulnerability, conferred by his mother Thetis's dipping him in magic waters when an infant. But she had held him by a heel to do so, hence that part of his body was as easy to wound as anyone else's.

The *Iliad* deals with Achilles's pique at being deprived by a superior officer of a slave girl, his withdrawal from combat in consequence and his rejoining the fray to avenge the death at Hector's hands of Patroclus, his best friend and probable lover. When Achilles kills Hector, Troy's eventual doom is set in motion. Yet Achilles then postpones a follow-up strike to indulge his own homoerotic preoccupation with the dead Patroclus. An almost invincible expert in single combat, yes; a master of tactics, no. That was Achilles' true heel.

'When Achilles had finished stripping his victim, the dead Hector, of his armour, he took his place among the Greeks and said:

"**Comrades in arms, chieftains among the Greek host and strategists in our counsels, now that Providence has granted us victory over this man, who did us more harm than all the rest of the Trojans put together, consider whether we should not immediately launch an all-out assault on Troy.**

If we do, we can assess the morale of its citizens. They may, it is true, still struggle on, even though Hector no longer lives. But it may be that they will evacuate the city now that their hero is dead.

But why am I saying this? Why am I eating up precious moments weighing the arguments for and against further action while Patroclus still lies by our ships, lies there unhallowed by funeral rites and unmourned by his fellows – he who in memory is with me forever while I breathe and can wield a spear?

Most men forget the dead when once they sink down to the Underworld. Not I. Not even when I end there myself, will I forget the companion I have lost.

So now, fellow Greeks, let us together strike up a song of triumph and return to our ships, taking this man with us. For we have brought off a splendid victory and have killed the noble Hector, whom Trojans revered throughout their city as if he had been a god."'

Funeral oration

Pericles (*c.* 495–429 BC)
Thucydides
Peloponnesian War, II 34–46 _____

● Biography

General, orator and statesman, Pericles dominated Athens for 30 years. During that period Athens's old enemy, the Persians, were replaced by fellow Greeks, chiefly the Spartans. Inasmuch as Pericles hastened the change of the anti-Persian alliance of Athens and her neighbours called the Delian League to an empire dominated by Athens alone, he was in part to blame. Yet he also fostered advances in thought, democracy and the arts, notably public works of surpassing beauty, that made Athens one of the jewels of civilisation. (Some, though not Athens' slaves or imperial victims, would say *the* jewel.) Thucydides (*c.* 460–399BC), the historian from whose works the speech below is taken, called Pericles Athens's first citizen.

Pericles's family connexions helped launch his career. By the late 460s Pericles was leading Athens' democratic faction. His conservative enemies called him a populist. Pericles certainly wooed the masses: free theatre seats for the poor; a lowered property qualification for senior magistrates; attendance allowances for jurors. This sometimes involved subordinating equity to chauvinism, for instance by restricting citizenship to those with Athenian parents.

During the first phase (459–444) of the struggle between Athens and Sparta for supremacy in Greece called the Peloponnesian War, Pericles was involved in several expeditions, though with indifferent success. As the 440s wore on, he did better. But Athens' hinterland was vulnerable to Spartan attacks and lesser cities nearby became increasingly hostile. By the Thirty Years' Peace (concluded 446/5) Athens renounced most of her territorial acquisitions of the last fifteen years and agreed with Sparta that neither would try to detach the other's allies.

• Context of speech

In autumn 431 Pericles led a sortie against the nearby city of Megara, whose defiance of Athens had sparked the second phase of the Peloponnesian War in 432. It was the casualties of this operation that in the winter of 431–430 he commemorated in the speech below. It is the earliest funeral panegyric we possess, though Pericles's calling it a tradition shows the genre already flourished, possibly from *c.* 470.

The following summer Athens was hit by a pestilence, which modern DNA tests have shown was typhoid. Next year Pericles himself succumbed. His gathering Attica's population behind Athens' walls may have begun the epidemic through overcrowding.

Pericles's speeches were not written down and Thucydides's versions may therefore be more the historian's words than the orator's, even if, as is generally agreed, Thucydides reconstructed the speeches from memory, having presumably been present when they were delivered.

That winter the Athenians gave a funeral at public expense to the first casualties of the war. Pericles was chosen to deliver the address. He said:

"**Tradition favours public panegyrics like this. I only wish brave men's reputations were not at the mercy of a single person's oratory. It is hard to speak properly where it is difficult to convince hearers you tell the truth. The friend who knows the story may think some vital point is overlooked; strangers may suspect exaggeration. Men endure praise of others only if they think they can equal the actions recounted; beyond that envy obtrudes, and with it incredulity** …

Our constitution does not ape the laws of neighbouring states. We are the pattern to others, not imitators. With us, government favours the many, not the few. That is why it is called a democracy. Our laws offer equal justice to all. Advancement in public life falls to those with capacity. Class does not stifle merit, nor poverty prove a hindrance … The freedom we enjoy in our government extends to our daily existence. There, far from prying into each other's lives, we feel at ease with our neighbour, who may do what he likes. We do not even give way to frowns or pursed lips, those disapproving expressions which are never not offensive, though they impose no specific penalty.

This easiness in our private relations does not make us lax as citizens. There apprehension is our safeguard, teaching us to obey the laws, particularly those that protect the weak, whether written or stemming from that code of honour which when broken brings disgrace.

Further, we give the opportunity for refreshment of the spirit following hours of business. We organise games and sacrifices all year round. The elegance of our private establishments is a daily source of pleasure and keeps discontent at bay. The size of our city draws the produce of the world, so that to the Athenian the best that other lands have to offer is as familiar a luxury as that of his own.

In defence we also differ from our foes. We throw open our city to the world. We do not bar outsiders from the chance to learn or observe, even though an enemy may exploit our liberality. We put faith less in system and policy than in the native spirit of our citizens.

In education, where our rivals from their cradles are led by painful discipline to manliness, at Athens we live as we please, yet are alert to every proper danger. Observe as proof of this how the Spartans do not invade our land alone, but drag with them their confederates. We Athenians advance unsupported upon the territory of a neighbour, and though fighting on foreign soil tend to vanquish with ease even those who are defending their homes.

We cultivate refinement without extravagance and knowledge without effeminacy. Wealth we deploy more for use than show. We hold that the true disgrace of poverty lies not in admitting it but in declining to fight it. Our public men have, besides politics, their private affairs. Our ordinary citizens, though occupied with earning a living, are still good judges of state matters. We look on him who takes no part in public life not as unambitious but as useless ... We look on discussion not as hampering action but as vital prelude to any wise action at all. We present the singular spectacle of daring and deliberation, each carried to its highest point, and united in the same persons. Too often decision is the fruit of ignorance, hesitation of reflection. Courage more properly applies to those who distinguish hardship from pleasure yet are not tempted to shrink from danger.

In generosity we are equally singular, acquiring our friends by conferring, not by receiving, favours. Yet he who confers the favour is the firmer friend of the two ... It is the Athenians alone, who, fearless of consequences, confer their benefits not from calculations of expediency, but in the confidence born of liberality ...

Athens alone of her contemporaries is found when tested to be greater than her reputation. To be worsted by Athens is alone an occasion when attackers fall back yet have no cause for shame ... The veneration of the present and future ages will be ours, since we lack no witnesses to our power. Yet far from needing a Homer for panegyrist, whose verses may move hearers for a spell yet enchantment vanish at a touch of fact, we have impressed every sea lane and land highway into bearing the footprint of our boldness. Everywhere, whatever the outcome, we have left imperishable monuments behind us.'"

Defence at his trial

Socrates (469–399 BC)
Plato
Apologia

• Biography

Few thinkers have been commemorated in an entire branch of dialectics. Socrates, with the Socratic Method, is one.

The Socratic Method involved dispelling other people's illusions, often cherished ones, by a series of questions requiring mostly yes/no answers, interspersed with palpably reasonable propositions. These the victim agreed with, being lured ever deeper into a forensic quagmire. The upshot was supposedly enlightenment but, human nature being what it is, in practice often humiliation, despite the questioner's gentle approach.

Socrates left no writings, or none that survive. Our knowledge of him comes nearly all from Plato, Socrates's junior by 40 years, also his fervent admirer, and hence a partial source. Moreover, Plato was an idealist philosopher, and only fully developed his position years after Socrates's death. The end to which he portrays Socrates's investigations as tending, namely the development of virtue, may have been much less apparent to Socrates's contemporaries. And only Plato's early dialogues are reckoned to depict Socrates's position anywhere near faithfully.

Socrates came from a village outside Athens but lived all his adult life in Athens, bar military service during the Peloponnesian War (*see* Pericles). He was a brave soldier. His only official position was when in 406 he was chosen by lot to chair the committee preparing the agenda for Athens' popular assembly.

His father, a sculptor, seems to have left him a modest competence. Alternatively, he may himself have accumulated enough to live on, perhaps as mason or sculptor working on the Acropolis statuary (*see* Pericles). His *rentier* status allowed him to forgo charging fees to his followers, unlike most disputational pundits. And when Socrates transformed sacred cows to aunt sallies, he set up no new sacred cows to comfort his more woolly-minded listeners with. Such intellectual austerity will not have increased his popularity.

His appearance hampered him. He lacked the classic Greek profile, being instead snub-nosed. Rightly or wrongly, such a physiognomy to many people denotes impudence. Had Socrates resembled some hawk-visaged proto-F.E. Smith (*qv*) terror of the law courts, being worsted by him would have been less galling. He was not even notably learned in the law. It is significant that in the speech below he says he is a stranger to the courts.

• Context of speech

At the time of Socrates's trial Athens, once the glory of Greece, had lost a war to the loutish Spartans. Oligarchic tyranny had followed. Democracy was soon restored, but Athenian self-confidence was shaken. Someone on whom to vent popular frustration came in handy.

One of Socrates's accusers, Meletus, had already suborned the comic playwright Aristophanes into lampooning Socrates in *The Clouds* (first performed 423). The trial that finished Socrates was therefore the climax to years of gunning for him.

Trials lasted a single day and the jury, always large by our standards, was in this case 500-strong. State prosecutors and defence advocates pleading in return for fees were unknown. A prosecutor acted as an individual. The defendant conducted his case himself.

The speech excerpted below is from the beginning of Socrates's defence.

> **I have no idea, men of Athens, how much the prosecution has swayed you. Speaking for myself, I nearly forgot my name, so powerful a spell did the prosecution oratory cast. The trouble is, almost none of it was true. Of the many distortions, one in particular astounded me: the warning to you to be on your guard, not to let yourselves be tricked by my silver tongue, as if I were an artful juggler with words. To imply this, when I have only to part my lips to prove myself anything but a polished speaker, seems to me a shameless attack.**
>
> Or does the prosecution mean by my silver tongue a devotion to the sterling qualities of truth? If so, I plead guilty to the charge of eloquence. But it is not eloquence as the prosecution understands it. To the prosecution, eloquence is a way of concealing the truth. To me it is truth. Not from me, so help me God, will you get an elaborate oration, tricked out with high-flown sentiments and fancy phrases. From me you will get whatever arguments lie to hand. I am sufficiently confident in the justice of my cause not to have to scrabble around in dictionaries.

Besides, at my age I would do better not to appear before you in the character of a clever undergraduate debater. I am too old a dog to learn new tricks and when I defend myself with everyday expressions, the same many of you have heard me utter in the marketplace and other public spots, please do not be surprised and please do not interrupt me. The fact is, I am over seventy and unaccustomed to court rooms, not least their jargon.

So look on me as if I were a backwoodsman, someone you would make allowances for because he spoke a sort of dialect, after the fashion of his locality. Is this unreasonable? Anyway, forget the manner of my speaking. Whether it is any good or not is neither here nor there. Concentrate on whether I am telling the truth. In short, let the speaker speak straightforwardly and the jury make up its mind justly."

To his reluctant troops

Alexander the Great (356–323 BC)
Arrian
Anabasis V 28.1–29.1

• Biography

Son of King Philip of Macedon; his assassinated father's successor aged 19; master of Greece thereafter; conqueror of the Persian Empire by 25 — Alexander was the marvel of the ancient world, which regarded global domination more highly than is thought proper today.

He also overran most of the rest of the Middle East, thrust successfully into Central Asia and invaded northwest India. He achieved all this between epic drinking sessions with his officers, after one of which he killed a foster-brother and after another of which he allegedly torched Persepolis, one of Persia's greatest cities.

His only defeat was at the hands of his troops, who as recorded below effectively mutinied. Theirs was a bloodless victory but galling. Perhaps through pique, Alexander then led them back to Persia across deserts, a trek as exhausting as it was militarily unsound.

Technically bisexual though probably more persistently attracted to men than women, Alexander nonetheless took two wives, the Sogdian wildcat Roxana then the gentle Stateira, daughter of his old adversary the Persian Emperor Darius.

His failure was political. He omitted to beget a full-grown heir or appoint a successor before his early death, one that for a campaigner who so often and so conspicuously led his troops in battle was always on the cards. These oversights brought the swift break-up of his empire.

• **Context of speech**

Arrian (in full Lucius Flavius Arrianus, *c.* AD 87–after 145) was born in Nicomedia, a Greek city of northwest Asia Minor (modern Turkey). He served in the Roman Army till the reign of the Emperor Hadrian (117–138), a friend of his, probably from their having been at school together. Through Hadrian's influence he became a provincial governor and both senator and consul in Rome. He retired to Athens.

Much of his work is lost. His *Anabasis* means literally 'journey into the interior' and is sometimes — inadequately — rendered as 'Journey Up Country', as if describing a jaunt by a leisured travel writer. It was in fact deliberately so entitled to remind readers of the much earlier Greek writer Xenophon's work of the same name. The latter describes a march to the sea by Greek soldiers stranded in what was then the Persian Empire a couple of generations before Alexander the Great's time.

Arrian's *Anabasis*, also written in Greek, recounts Alexander's push across southwestern Asia. (A further work, *Indikē*, deals with his invasion of India.) Both are enormously valuable since Arrian, even though writing four centuries after Alexander's time, drew on eye-witness accounts now lost. He fails to examine Alexander's motives and is largely uninterested in character study, but he did aim at a factual narrative untainted by legend. Having both fought for and run an empire at a very senior level, he knows his subject. Moreover his tours of duty in the East may well have allowed him to visit several of the chief places connected with Alexander's life.

Alexander had in May 326 defeated the local Indian King Porus. Two months later, on the banks of the River Hyphasis (modern Beas, near Kashmir), his troops refused to push any further east. Arrian identifies their spokesman as one Coinos, the Greek for 'in common', from which one is tempted to infer that he is a symbolic figure representing the generality of Alexander's troops. Arrian further relates that after the speech below Alexander retired to his tent, waiting for his words to effect a change of heart. This they failed to do. Alexander is then said to have made a sacrifice to the gods to ensure a successful river crossing (the Hyphasis was hugely wide at that point). The omens proving unfavourable, Alexander announced that he would turn west again.

66 **I have asked you to meet me that we may decide together: are we, as I advise, to proceed, or, as you prefer, to turn back? If you have any complaint as to the outcome of your efforts hitherto, or about myself as your commander, there is no more to say.**
But let me remind you: through your courage and endurance you have conquered Ionia, the Hellespont, both Phrygias, Cappadocia, Paphlagonia, Lydia, Caria, Lycia, Pamphylia, Phoenicia and Egypt.

The Greek part of Libya is now yours, together with much of Arabia, lowland Syria, Mesopotamia, Babylon and Susa.

Persia and Media … are in your hands. You have made yourselves masters of the lands beyond the Caspian Gates, beyond the Caucasus, beyond the Tanais, of Bactria, Hyrcania and the Hyrcanian Sea.

We have driven the Scythians back into the desert. The rivers Indus and Hydaspes, Acesines and Hydraotes flow now through lands which are ours.

With all that accomplished, why do you hesitate to extend the power of Macedon — *your* power — to the Hyphasis and the tribes on the other side? Do you fear that the few natives left there will offer opposition? Come, come. These natives either surrender without a blow, are caught on the run or leave their country undefended for the taking — *your* taking.

And when we take it, we make a present of it to those who have joined us of their own free will and fight on our side …

The area still before us, from here to the Ganges and the Eastern Ocean, is comparatively small.

You will assuredly find that this ocean connects with the Hyrcanian Sea. For the great Stream of Ocean encircles the earth. Moreover I shall prove to you that the Indian and Persian Gulfs and the Hyrcanian Sea are all three connected and continuous.

Our ships will sail from the Persian Gulf to Libya as far as the Pillars of Hercules, whence all Libya eastward will soon be ours, and all Asia too. And to this empire there will be no limit but what God Himself has set for the whole world …

Come, then. Add the rest of Asia to what you already possess, a small addition to the vast sum of your conquests …

I would not blame you for loss of heart had I, your commander, not shared in your forced marches and arduous campaigns. I would not blame you, had you done all the work while others reaped the reward. But it is not so. You and I have shared both the labour and the danger. The rewards are for us all. The conquered territory belongs to you. From your ranks its governors are chosen. Already the greater part of its treasure has passed into your hands.

And when all Asia is overrun, then indeed will I go beyond the mere satisfying of our ambitions. The utmost hopes of wealth or power which each of you may cherish will then be far surpassed. Whoever wishes to return home will be

Funeral panegyric on Caesar

Marc Antony
Shakespeare (1564–1616)
Julius Caesar

• Biography

The Ancient Roman politician and soldier Marc Antony is most famous for turning the tables on Caesar's assassins in a single speech.

By the time he delivered it he had held a series of major offices under the Roman Republic and suggested Caesar's elevation as Emperor. This prompted Brutus and his co-conspirators to assassinate Caesar.

On 14 March 44 BC Marc Antony, now consul, was warned of a threat to Caesar's life. On the fifteenth, the Ides, he tried unsuccessfully to prevent Caesar appearing in public. Subsequently he divided control of the known civilized world with Octavian (Caesar's great-nephew and adopted son) and a nonentity, Lepidus. His dalliance with the Egyptian Queen Cleopatra led to his destruction.

• Context of speech

Following Caesar's murder Marc Antony fled Rome but returned and initially let matters rest. At Caesar's funeral he accused Brutus's faction of murder, pulling the shroud from Caesar's corpse to reveal the stab wounds, pointing at each assassin and identifying him by name. He also read out Caesar's will. This bequeathed vast sums to the people. That evening a mob attacked the conspirators' houses and they in turn fled Rome.

The anti-Caesar conspirators numbered only about 60 and were drawn from the aristocracy. Caesar had been the hero of the whole Roman world. The best known version of the speech given below is Shakespeare's. But some similarly powerful address was delivered in actuality.

riends, Romans, countrymen, lend me your ears;
I come to bury Caesar, not to praise him.
The evil that men do lives after them;
The good is oft interred with their bones;
So let it be with Caesar. The noble Brutus
Hath told you Caesar was ambitious:
If it were so, it was a grievous fault,
And grievously hath Caesar answer'd it.
Here, under leave of Brutus and the rest —
For Brutus is an honourable man;
So are they all, all honourable men —
Come I to speak in Caesar's funeral.
He was my friend, faithful and just to me:
But Brutus says he was ambitious;
And Brutus is an honourable man.
He hath brought many captives home to Rome
Whose ransoms did the general coffers fill:
Did this in Caesar seem ambitious?
When that the poor have cried, Caesar hath wept:
Ambition should be made of sterner stuff:
Yet Brutus says he was ambitious;
And Brutus is an honourable man.

You all did see that on the Lupercal
I thrice presented him a kingly crown,
Which he did thrice refuse: was this ambition?
Yet Brutus says he was ambitious;
And, sure, he is an honourable man.
I speak not to disprove what Brutus spoke,
But here I am to speak what I do know.
You all did love him once, not without cause:
What cause withholds you then, to mourn for him?
O judgment! thou art fled to brutish beasts,
And men have lost their reason. Bear with me;
My heart is in the coffin there with Caesar,
And I must pause till it come back to me."

On admitting non-Romans to the Senate

Emperor Claudius (AD 41–54)
Tacitus (c. AD 55–120)
To the Senate c. AD 48

• Biography

The fourth Roman Emperor, Claudius ascended the throne at the age of 50. This was old given the life expectancy of most imperial kin. If healthy, hence the current Emperor's potential rivals, they often died young and unexpectedly. Claudius was thought simple-minded, hence survived. Actually, his drooling and stammer suggest something like cerebral palsy rather than idiocy.

His first official post was as consul in the summer of 37. His nephew Caligula, then Emperor, maliciously procured him the job to highlight his frailties. When four years later Caligula was murdered, Claudius in one account hid from the ensuing pandemonium behind a curtain, was discovered by some soldiers and acclaimed emperor, being swiftly accepted everywhere. But he may have been chosen in advance by a group of Praetorian Guards anxious to maintain their privileges.

Once in power, he proved a reasonably competent chief executive, though overly swayed by his freedmen ministers and wives. His first empress, Messalina, was formerly thought a mere nymphomaniac but is now increasingly portrayed as using sex to attain power. Claudius had her executed after her sexual games got out of hand. He then married his niece Agrippina, who engineered the succession of Nero, her son by an earlier husband, over Claudius's own son Britannicus. She may have poisoned Claudius.

• Context of speech

The complete version of the speech excerpted below is particularly interesting since it includes heckling. Claudius certainly antagonised the Senate by broadening its composition to include even Gauls, and by purging its reactionaries. But he was not the only emperor to sideline it. Would later ones have been so insulted?

66 **The Divine Augustus, my great-uncle, and Tiberius Caesar, my uncle, both desired that the flower of the colonies and municipal towns … should be admitted to this assembly.**
… I do not think we should reject provincials who can honour the Senate. Take the splendid and powerful colony of Vienna [*not the Austrian capital but Vienne, in France's Rhone Valley*] … From it hails Lucius Vestinus, one of the glories of the equestrian [*middle class*] order, my personal friend, who I get to manage my private affairs. Let his sons be allowed, I beseech you, to work their way up to a similarly exalted position …

You surely cannot object to seeing such young men as these, of respectable rank already, numbered among those who hold the high honour of senator, any more than Persicus, that high-born gentleman (and friend of mine), is ashamed when among the gallery of his various ancestors he comes upon the name Allobrogius [*a Gaul from the mountainous region of what is now southeast France*].

If you do still object, what policy would you prefer? Meanwhile, do I have to point out to you the reasonableness of what I propose? Take even a territory so far away as that beyond Gallia Narbonnensis [*roughly modern South of*

France]. Has it not already sent you senators? And surely we cannot regret going as far afield for members of our order as Lugdunum [*modern Lyons, France; also Claudius's birthplace, hence his citing it*].

I assure you, it is not without hesitation that I reach beyond the limits of the provinces familiar to you. But the moment has come when I must plead openly the cause of Further Gaul [*roughly what is now northern France*]. It will be objected that Gaul made war against the Divine Julius [*Caesar*] for ten years. But against this let us weigh the memory of a century of steadfast fidelity, and a loyalty tested in many trying circumstances.

My father, Drusus, could campaign in Germany because behind him reigned a profound peace ensured by the tranquillity of the Gauls. Bear in mind, too, that just when he was called on to begin that campaign, he was busy instituting a census in Gaul, an innovation to its inhabitants and contrary to their customs. The difficulty and danger attending this business of the census … we have learned by all too much experience."

Deathbed apology for oppressing the English

William the Conqueror (1027–87)
Orderic
Ecclesiastical History 1130–33
Book VII

• Biography

Bastard-born, genocidal and in later life so paunchy the King of France compared him to a pregnant woman, William the Conqueror is nonetheless the only successful organiser in history of a full-scale, wholly opposed invasion of England.

He was sired on Arlette/Herleve, daughter of a tanner (or even corpse-dresser; *see* below) in the Norman town of Falaise, by Robert I 'the Devil' Duke of Normandy (reigned 1027–35). Robert never married Arlette/Herleve but did find her a husband, one Herlouin. William later created him Vicomte de Conteville.

William was a fighter most of his life: first to establish his succession to Robert as Duke of Normandy, then to repulse Normandy's enemies, then to strengthen its frontiers, then to invade England and finally to consolidate his hold on it. His is not a particularly attractive personality, but in its dogged, grim and painstaking fortitude it commands respect.

William died at Rouen, capital of Normandy, in the early hours of 9 September 1087, probably from an internal rupture sustained six weeks before when his horse stumbled, thrusting William's paunch down on the pommel of his saddle.

The word 'genocidal' above refers to William's laying waste the north of England in the winter of 1069–70. Resistance to the new regime had continued longer and stronger there than elsewhere. William's response was to destroy all means of subsistence and kill, either by butchering or starvation, as many of the inhabitants as he could. Perhaps 150,000 succumbed, or 15 percent of the national population. England has known nothing like it since. In modern Europe only the famine forced on the Ukraine by Stalin (*qv*) in 1932–33 can compare with it for 'free-range' mass murder rather than in a confined space, such as a concentration camp.

• Context of speech

Orderic Vitalis is the leading chronicler of the end of William's reign. He was a boy at the time but may have later met some of the leading figures. It is he who first mentions Herleve as Duke Robert's kept woman and her father as little more than an undertaker.

The translation below is from the original Latin, which was probably written in the period 1130–33. The language William used would have been Norman French, a dialect now more or less confined to administrative circles in the Channel Islands.

The bequeathing of England to God reflects the awkward fact that the kingdom in question was a conquered one. Accordingly, it did not under the custom predominant in England pass automatically to William's eldest son, Robert (*c.* 1054–1134), who had quarrelled with William and was absent when he died. Robert did inherit Normandy. Yet there may well have been no formal making over of England to William Rufus (*b.* between 1056 and 1060, reigned 1087–1100), the second son, either. William Rufus simply made straight for England even before his father breathed his last and mounted there what was in effect a *coup d'etat*.

66 "I have cruelly persecuted the natives of England beyond all reason, and irrespective of whether they were of gentle or low birth. Many I have unjustly disinherited.

Huge numbers have perished through me, either by famine or the sword. I fell upon the English of the northern counties like a ravening lion. I directed that their houses and their corn, their tools and chattels, be burnt without distinction. I ordered vast herds of cattle and beasts of burden to be butchered wherever they were found. In this way I took revenge on multitudes of both sexes by inflicting on them the most savage famine, thus becoming the murderer of thousands of that fine race of people, both young and old. Having gained the throne of that kingdom by so many crimes, I dare not leave it to anyone but God."

To Commissioners enforcing the oath denying papal supremacy

St. Sir Thomas More (1478–1535)
Political martyr (1516)
1534

• Biography

In autumn of the year 2000 Pope John Paul II (*qv*) declared Thomas More the patron saint of politicians and statesmen. It was an odd choice. More's fame rests on his martyrdom. This was so far from the role of a typical politician, who to fulfil his aims places survival above consistency and compromise above straightforwardness, that when he was destroyed it was by truly professional politicians, whole-hearted practitioners of that sordid craft.

More was certainly interested in political theory, his chief book being *Utopia* (1516). But the society it portrays is uncomfortably totalitarian. Writing in the first person, More disassociates himself from this, the key aspect of his Utopia (a word he coined, meaning not an ideal place but a non-existent one). And he advocates discretion and tact, those twin nutrients of 'the art of the possible'. But in the end he found them inadequate against reasons of state. Logically, he should be the patron saint of the victims of politicians, a group that needs all the help it can get. Indeed his end testifies to the impossibility in the long run of a public figure reconciling conscience and expedience, a dilemma that has bedeviled many scrupulous statesmen, not excluding popes.

The paradox extends further. He was an able lawyer and a distinguished Lord Chancellor (1529–32), the first layman in the post. Yet at his Chelsea home he illegally detained suspected dissidents (a group that in his day comprised both religious and political mavericks), then had them imprisoned without trial and even tortured. When hearing cases he was celebrated for his fairness, charity and incorruptibility. But his role as martyr was combined so little with that of a lawyer, in the sense of a diligent but narrowly-focused researcher into a canon of man-made rules, then paid proponent of a case resting on them, that he set a supernaturally derived authority above the duly enacted statutes of a government of which he had till recently been an ornament.

And when John Paul II said, in discussing More and politics, that "the basis of ... values cannot be provisional and changeable 'majority' opinions", he overlooked the way More's defence during interrogation rested on the majority opinion of all the bishops and Christian councils that had ever been.

More was born in London, his father, Sir John More, being a judge. He was well educated and became an accomplished, though not meticulous, classicist in the new humanist spirit. Yet he never quite lost a medieval outlook. As such he wore hair shirts, scourged himself and in youth contemplated becoming a priest. As Chancellor he ardently promoted the burning of heretics and with distressingly crude invective anathematised them, notably William Tyndale (*d.* 1536), chief early translator of the Bible into English. What can only be called his bigotry was noted in his own time, and not just by Protestant polemicists.

More became a barrister in 1501, an MP in 1504 and married his first wife, Jane Colt, the next year. His best-known child, his daughter Margaret, married Will Roper, More's earliest biographer.

More was drawn into the service of Henry VIII, who initially offered personal friendship. More saw through the *faux bonhomme*. He nonetheless helped Henry with his anti-Lutheran tract *Defence of the Seven Sacraments*, which won Henry the title 'Defender of the Faith' from the Pope.

• Context of speech

More resigned as Lord Chancellor in 1532 because he opposed Henry's detaching the English Church from papal control, though he did not then state this. He boycotted the coronation of Anne Boleyn (*qv*) and when in 1534 Henry altered the succession he refused to swear a confirmatory oath, not because he opposed altered successions but because the oath entailed denying papal supremacy.

After over a year in the Tower of London he was executed for treason. Henry VIII feared a scaffold speech damaging to the regime, so pressured More into making his last words short. More's treatment in prison was scarcely harsher, though more malevolent, than what he had once imposed on himself. He was now much older, however, and so weak that when led to the scaffold he stumbled. He quipped to the Governor, "I pray you, Master Lieutenant, see me safe up, and for my coming down, let me shift for myself." (He had originally been sentenced to hanging, but Henry VIII commuted this to beheading, then a more up-market death.)

More requested that the spectators pray for him and testify that he died for his faith, that of the Holy Catholic Church. He finished with "I die as the King's true servant, but as God's servant first." After being cut off, his head was stuck up on London Bridge for several weeks to edify the people, a common practice then. He was beatified in 1886 and canonised in 1935, the 400th anniversary of his death.

> 66 Seeing that I see ye are determined to condemn me (God knoweth how), I will now in discharge of my conscience speak my mind plainly and freely touching my indictment and your statute withal.
>
> And foreasmuch as this indictment is grounded upon an Act of Parliament directly repugnant to the laws of God and his Holy Church, the supreme government of which, or any part whereof, may no temporal prince presume by any law to take upon him, as rightfully belonging to the See of Rome, a spiritual pre-eminence by the mouth of our Saviour himself, personally present upon earth, only to Saint Peter and his successors, bishops of the same see, by special prerogative granted; it is therefore in law, amongst Christian men, insufficient to charge any Christian man."
>
> More was told that ecclesiastical and academic authorities differed from him. He riposted:
>
> "If there were no more but myself upon my side, and the whole Parliament upon the other, I would be sore afraid to lean to mine own mind only against so many. But if the number of bishops and universities be so material as

your lordships seemeth to take it, then see I little cause, my lord, why that thing in my conscience should make any change. For I nothing doubt but that, though not in this realm, yet in Christendom about, of those well learned bishops and virtuous men that are yet alive, they be not the fewer part that are of my mind therein. But if I should speak of those that are already dead, of whom many be now holy saints in heaven, I am very sure it is the far greater part of them that, all the while they lived, thought in this case that way that I think now, and therefore am I not bounden, my Lord, to conform my conscience to the council of one realm against the general council of Christendom. For of the aforesaid holy bishops I have for every bishop of yours above one hundred, and for one council or parliament of yours (God knoweth what manner of one), I have all the councils made these thousand years. And for this one kingdom, I have all other Christian realms."

Scaffold speech

Anne Boleyn (c. 1501–36)
Edward Hall, Lancastre and Yorke/
John Stow, Annales
19 May 1536

• Biography

The second, but best known, of the six wives of Henry VIII (1509–47), Anne Boleyn was daughter of Sir Thomas Boleyn, a courtier of long standing. Her mother, Lady Elizabeth Howard, was sister of the 3rd Duke of Norfolk, the man who presided at Anne's trial and announced the verdict.

The Boleyns had 'arrived' with Sir Thomas's grandfather Sir Geoffrey Boleyn, Lord Mayor of London 1457–58. Sir Thomas's father, Sir William Boleyn, had married a descendant of Edward I. When Anne married Henry VIII she was marrying a distant cousin twice over, since she also descended from Edward I through her mother.

In addition, her grandmother Margaret's aunt was mother through Edward IV of a bastard son. Accordingly, Anne's career as royal consort had an almost hereditary element to it.

Anne was educated at the Burgundian and French courts before joining the English one. Around 1526 she caught Henry VIII's eye. She seems to have refused fully to consummate physical relations with Henry unless they involved marriage. Henry had despaired of getting a male heir by his first wife, Catherine of Aragon, and on 25 January 1533 replaced her with Anne. By him she was mother of the future Queen Elizabeth I (*qv*). The baby was conceived by mid-December 1532, so that Anne must have relied on Henry's promise of marriage. Her trust in him was not always to be so well placed.

She was crowned Queen on 1 June 1533 and for two years held her husband's interest, meanwhile promoting the new Protestant doctrines, to which Henry was relatively hostile. By January 1536 Henry had fallen in love with Jane Seymour. Two specific events that month finished Anne. One, the death of Catherine of Aragon on the seventh. Henry could hardly repudiate his second wife while his first still lived. Two, Anne's failure to produce a male heir: she had a stillborn and very premature son on or around the twenty-ninth.

• Context of speech

On 2 May 1536 Henry had Anne taken to the Tower of London. She was tried on trumped up charges of treason and multiple adultery, including incest with her brother, and sentenced to death.

On the nineteenth she was up at 2 am. The site of the execution was Tower Green, inside the fortress precincts, rather than Tower Hill, thus excluding the general public and frustrating any demonstrations of support.

She was beheaded with a single stroke of a sword wielded by an executioner brought over from Calais, then still English-held. Sword strokes rather than axe hackings were the mode of execution in France.

The first version is Hall's; the second version comes in the 1631 edition of the *Annales*, being added by a continuator.

1 "Good Christian people, I am come hither to die, for according to the law, and by the law, I am judged to die, and therefore I will speak nothing against it. I am come hither to accuse no man, nor to speak anything of that whereof I am accused and condemned to die. But I pray God save the King and send him long to reign over you, for a gentler nor a more merciful prince was there never. And to me he was ever a good, a gentle and sovereign lord. And if any person will meddle of my cause, I require them to judge the best. And thus I take my leave of the world and of you all, and I heartily desire you all to pray for me. O Lord have mercy on me. To God I commend my soul."

2. "Masters, I here humbly submit me to the law, as the law hath judged me, and as for mine offences, I here accuse no man. God knoweth them. I remit them to God, beseeching him to have mercy on my soul; and I beseech Jesus save my Sovereign and master the King, the most godly, noble and gentle Prince that is, and long to reign over you."

To Parliament on choosing a husband

**Elizabeth I (1558–1603)
Queen of England
9 August 1588**

• Biography

Elizabeth I enjoyed the longest and most glorious reign of three successive English queens. This arose partly from her prudence, which, however, often mutated to stinginess; partly from her procrastination; partly from her celibacy. Mostly, unlike the other two, she had very good luck.

She was the only child of Henry VIII by Anne Boleyn (*qv*). She survived the latter's downfall but was declared illegitimate and was never properly rehabilitated in that regard. But she was placed in line to the throne.

She was excellently educated, becoming in particular a fluent linguist. Her stepmother Catherine Parr's last husband, Thomas Seymour, brother of that Duke of Somerset who dominated Edward VI's reign, was familiar with her to the point of molestation. He had in any case proposed marriage to her before wedding Catherine. Elizabeth's lifelong judiciousness and abstinence from sex may arise from this episode.

She was not above flirtations, however, notably with the courtier Robert Dudley (*c.* 1532–88), who she created Earl of Leicester and appointed to military commands, including the troops at Tilbury in 1588 when she addressed them (*see* below). This was misjudged since he was incompetent.

The main foreign threat to England in the early years of her reign was France. Later, Spain replaced it. Spain's king, Philip II, was Europe's leading Catholic monarch. In 1588 he sent a massive seaborne expedition against Elizabeth, Europe's arch-Protestant. This was the Armada. It was destroyed, though more by bad weather than English seamanship.

• Context of speech

The speech below covers Elizabeth's choice of husband, by whom she was expected to bear successors, and, if she did not marry, then her choice of heir.

There had been an earlier petition by Parliament over her marriage. That had been in 1559. Her response then had been much more temperate. By 1566 she was 33, old for motherhood by contemporary standards.

Her vehemence on this second occasion may derive from more than irritation at being badgered or regret that she could not make a free choice (if she did regret this). Experience had taught her how little royal marriages brought happiness. She had seen her mother and three of her stepmothers (Catherine of Aragon, Anne of Cleves and Catherine Howard) repudiated by a capricious husband. She had seen two other stepmothers (Jane Seymour; Catherine Parr) die in childbirth. She had seen her sister Mary first overborne then neglected by an unsympathetic husband. She now saw her cousin Mary Queen of Scots risking her throne through a personal rather than political choice of second husband.

In addition, she knew how dangerous it was both for the incumbent sovereign and the heir for the latter to be named.

The speech seems not to have been delivered directly to Parliament but to have been transmitted. For the Commons, Elizabeth's Chief Secretary of State Lord Burghley had a more tactful version prepared, needing no fewer than three rewrites to strike the appropriate note.

"Was I not born in the realm? Were my parents born in any foreign country? Is not my kingdom here? Whom have I oppressed? Whom have I enriched to others' harm? What turmoil have I made in this commonwealth that I should be suspected to have no regard to the same? How have I governed since my reign [began]? … I need not to use many words, for my deeds do try [i.e., *speak as character witnesses in favour of me*].

Well, the matter whereof they would have made their petition (as I am informed) consisteth in two points: in my marriage, and in the limitations of the succession of the crown, wherein my marriage was first placed, as for manners' sake. I did send them answer by my council, I would marry (although of mine own disposition I was not inclined thereunto) but that was not accepted nor credited, although spoken by their Prince [i.e., *by herself, the Queen, 'prince' applying to either sex then*].

I will never break the word of a prince spoken in a public place, for my honour's sake. And therefore I say again, I will marry as soon as I can conveniently, if God take not him away with whom I mind to marry, or myself, or else some other great let happen. I can say no more except the party were present. And I hope to have children, otherwise I would never marry. A strange order of petitioners that will make a request and cannot be otherwise assured but by the prince's word, and yet will not believe it when it is spoken.

The second point was for the limitation of the succession of the crown, wherein was nothing said for my safety, but only for themselves. A strange thing that the foot should direct the head in so weighty a cause …

I am sure there was not one of them that ever was a second person, as I have been and have tasted of the practices against my sister, who I would to God were alive again …

There were occasions in me at that time, I stood in danger of my life, my sister was so incensed against me. I did differ from her in religion and I was sought for divers ways. And so shall never be my successor. I have conferred with those that are well learned, and have asked their opinions touching the limitation of succession …

I am your anointed Queen. I will never be by violence [i.e., *force*] constrained to do anything. I thank God I am indeed endowed with such qualities that if I were turned out of the realm in my petticoat I were able to live in any place in Christendom.

Your petition is to deal in the limitation of the succession. At this present it is not convenient, nor never shall be without some peril unto you, and certain danger unto me. But as soon as there may be a convenient time and that it may be done with least peril unto you, although never without great danger unto me, I will deal therein for your safety and offer it unto you as your prince and head without requests. For it is monstrous that the feet should direct the head."

To troops at Tilbury when Armada threatened

• Context of speech

England had no standing army. National defence rested with a locally raised militia. In 1588, when the Armada threatened, contingents were gathered together where they might strike hardest. Tilbury, in Essex, was easily fortified, hence its selection. On 9 August 1588 Elizabeth, who had put off spending money to supply the fleet and who supplied far too little even when she did get going, partly atoned for this disgraceful negligence by addressing her soldiers there. They numbered about 4,000. The only trouble was, they were barely needed by now. The Armada had passed by several days before. That the speech was long seen as one of history's great morale-boosting exercises owes much to Tudor propaganda.

66 **My loving people, we have been persuaded by some that are careful of our safety, to take heed how we commit ourselves to armed multitudes, for fear of treachery. But I assure you I do not desire to live to distrust my faithful and loving people. Let tyrants fear. I have always so behaved myself that, under God, I have placed my chiefest strength and safeguard in the loyal hearts and goodwill of my subjects. And therefore I am come amongst you, as you see, at this time, not for my recreation and disport, but being resolved, in the midst and heat of the battle, to live and die amongst you all; to lay down for my God, and for my kingdom, and my people, my honour and my blood, even in the dust.**

I know I have the body but of a weak and feeble woman. But I have the heart and stomach of a king, and of a king of England too, and think foul scorn that Parma [*Duke of Parma and son of Margaret, Regent of the Netherlands, a territory then under Spanish control*] or Spain, or any prince of Europe, should dare to invade the borders of my realm; to which rather than any dishonour shall grow by me, I myself will take up arms, I myself will be your general, judge, and rewarder of every one of your virtues in the field.

I know already, for your forwardness you have deserved rewards and crowns. And we do assure you in the word of a prince, they shall be duly paid you. In the mean time, my lieutenant-general shall be in my stead, than whom never prince commanded a more noble or worthy subject; not doubting but by your obedience to my general, by your concord in the camp, and your valour in the field, we shall shortly have a famous victory over those enemies of my God, of my kingdom, and of my people."

On relations between gentlemen and sailors at sea

Sir Francis Drake (*c.* 1540–96)
Circumnavigator
13 December 1577

• Biography

One of England's legendary heroes, Drake was an explorer and, less politely, a bandit. As such, he became an unusually sharp thorn in the side of Spain, with whom England went to war in part because of his buccaneering provocations. In circumnavigating the world he became the first man to do so while continuously commanding an expedition.

It took nearly three years, starting from Plymouth on 13 December 1577 and returning there on 26 September 1580. His chief activity during it consisted of raids on the Spanish possessions in the Pacific, by which he amassed considerable loot.

On his return home Elizabeth I (*qv*) knighted him. Drake was increasingly given official positions at sea. He was one of the leading commanders against the Armada in 1588 (*see* also Elizabeth I), being the senior officer present at the action off Gravelines, the only major engagement, as opposed to skirmishing, that took place.

He kept up raids against Spain proper and its possessions in the Americas till his death from dysentery off Puerto (called by the English Porto) Bello, on the Isthmus of Panama.

• Context of speech

Drake's world cruise appears to have been underwritten by a business syndicate which included Elizabeth I, though such embarrassing details were long kept secret. By this account, the court interest had representatives aboard whose gentlemanly, amateur approach to seamanship antagonised Drake's more experienced but relatively low-born sailors. The chief troublemakers, however, were not just gentlemen but friends of Drake's, brothers Thomas and John Doughty. Thomas was switched by Drake from command of one ship, a captured Portugese merchantman, to another after he was accused of pilfering part of the merchantman's cargo.

At Port St. Julian, on what is now the coast of Argentina, Drake presided as judge over an ad hoc court that tried Thomas Doughty for mutiny and treason. The verdict was in one account not guilty on the charge of treason but guilty on that of mutiny, and in another account guilty on both charges, together with guilty on a third, that of raising adverse storms by sorcery.

Either the next day or two days later Drake had Doughty beheaded. Unrest continued, chiefly the old class animosity and quarrels about how to manage the enterprise. After a few weeks Drake held a church service then said:

> ❝ I am a very bad orator, for my upbringing was not in learning. But what I say now let every man take good note. Let him write it down, for I will say nothing I am not prepared to answer for to England. Yes, and before Her Majesty.
>
> Wherefore we must have these mutinies and discords that are grown amongst us redressed … here is such a controversy betwixt the sailors and the gentlemen and such stomaching between the gentlemen and sailors that it doth

even make me mad [i.e., '*angry*', *a meaning that survives in American English*] to hear it. But, my masters, I must have it left. For I must have the gentleman to haul and draw with the mariner, and the mariner with the gentleman. What! Let us show ourselves to be of one company and let us not give occasion to the enemy to rejoice at our decay and overthrow. I would know him that would refuse to set his hand to a rope, but I know there is not any such here …

As gentlemen are very necessary for government's sake in the voyage, so I have shipped them for that … and yet, though I know sailors to be the most envious people of the world and unruly without government, yet may I not be without them …

Consider what we have done, my masters. We have set by the ears three mighty princes, Her Majesty and the Kings of Spain and Portugal. If this voyage does not succeed we should not only be a scorning and a scoffing stock to our enemies but also a great blot to our whole country for ever."

Scaffold speech

Sir Walter Rale(i)gh (*c.* 1552–1618)
Courtier, explorer and literary figure
29 October 1616 _____

• Biography

Drake (*qv*) and Raleigh are often seen as something like twin Elizabethan adventurers. But Raleigh was, as well as a man of action, a poet, political essayist, topographical writer and historian.

After education at Oxford, Raleigh between the springs of 1578 and 1579 participated in a voyage of exploration, probably to the West Indies, captaining one of the smaller ships. He then attended court, where he caught the attention of

Elizabeth I. Whether he really spread a cloak for her to walk upon over a muddy thoroughfare is uncertain, though perfectly possible.

Elizabeth showered lucrative trading monopolies on him. She also made him Captain of her Guard. But this involved court attendance, which irked him. It was he who in 1584 launched the expedition which resulted in the establishment of the first English North American colony of Virginia. It was as a result of his enterprise that the potato was first planted in England and, still more importantly, in Ireland, where Raleigh accumulated much land. He was the first man of fashion to take up smoking.

When the Armada (*see* also Drake) threatened England, Raleigh helped oversee land defences. He later became fascinated by the legend of Eldorado, the South American city of vast reputed wealth. In 1595 he went to look for it, exploring the interior of what is now Venezuela. He lacked supplies for a long stay and soon returned to England, though with gold-bearing mineral samples, suggesting he nearly stumbled on a gold mine.

When James I succeeded Elizabeth in 1603 he imprisoned Raleigh in the Tower for treason, of which Raleigh was barely guilty other than failing to inform on a friend who had corresponded seditiously with the Spanish Ambassador. In the Tower he wrote his *History of the World*. His masterpiece, it delighted among others Oliver Cromwell (*qv*) but irritated James I, who in the words of a contemporary thought it 'too saucy in censuring princes'. Though long superseded purely as history, it emphasised the importance of geography to human developments, something Raleigh knew at first hand.

• Context of speech

In early 1616 Raleigh was allowed to return to South America, but only on condition that he struck gold, otherwise his death sentence stood. Bad weather, disease, disaffected crews and Spanish hostility frustrated him from the first. He reluctantly returned home and re-entered the Tower. When at his execution he had lain his head on the block ready for the axe, it was proposed that it be turned to the East (*i.e.*, the Holy Land). He answered, "What matter how the head lie, so the heart be right?" His wife had his head pickled and kept it in a red leather bag till she died. The rest of Raleigh was buried in St Margaret's Westminster. His scaffold speech ran thus:

> 66 I thank my God heartily that He hath brought me into the light to die, and not suffered me to die in the dark prison of the Tower, where I have suffered a great deal of adversity and a long sickness …

There are two main points of suspicion ... His Majesty hath conceived against me ... which I desire to clear and resolve you in. One ... that I have had some plot with France ... one reason [being] ... that when I came back ... to Plymouth I endeavoured to go to [La] Rochelle ... [since] I did intend to fly to France for saving of my life ...

I ... call the Lord to witness, as I hope to be saved, and as I hope to be seen in His kingdom (which will be within this quarter of an hour), that I never had any commission from the King of France ...

The second suspicion was, that His Majesty hath been informed that I should speak dishonourably and disloyally of him. But my accuser was a base Frenchman, a kind of chemical fellow — one whom I knew to be perfidious; for ... he being sworn to secrecy overnight, he revealed it in the morning ...

But in this I speak now, what have I to do with kings? I have nothing to do with them, neither do I fear them. I have now to do with God ... I confess I did attempt to escape, and I did dissemble, and made myself sick at Salisbury [*on his way up from Plymouth to London to re-enter the Tower*], but I hope it was no sin. The prophet David did make himself a fool, and did suffer spittle to fall upon his beard, to escape the hands of his enemies, and it was not imputed to him as sin, and I did it to prolong time till His Majesty came, hoping for some commiseration from him ...

And now I entreat you all to join with me in prayer, that the great God of Heaven, whom I have grievously offended, being a man full of all vanity, and having lived a sinful life, in all sinful callings, having been a soldier, a captain, a sea captain, and a courtier, which are all places of wickedness and vice; that God, I say, would forgive me, cast away my sins from me, and receive me into everlasting life. So I take my leave of you all, making my peace with God."

Scaffold speech

Charles I (1625–49)
King of England, of Scots and of Ireland
29 January 1649

• Biography

Charles was an unlucky king in ascending the throne after his father James I (*see* Raleigh) had weakened royal prestige. His financial problems started the moment he did so. But his constantly breaking faith with his subjects was his own fault. After an uneasy beginning to his relations with Parliament, he ruled without it from 1629 to 1640. The Scots were his undoing. He tried to impose his own brand of liturgy and church government on them. They rebelled. He was forced to summon Parliament to vote him money. He lost control of it and, through indecision, the ensuing civil war. He then repeatedly tried to double-cross his Parliamentary captors. Cromwell (*qv*) and Charles's other leading opponents decided the only way to deal with him was to try then execute him.

• Context of speech

Around 10 am on the day of the execution, 29 January 1649, Charles was escorted on foot from St James's Palace through St James's Park to Whitehall. His attendant troops comprised an infantry regiment, their colours flying and drums beating. In Whitehall he was taken into Whitehall Palace. He consumed no meal bar a glass of claret and a bit of bread. He had previously taken Communion. It was now around midday.

He passed to the scaffold through the Inigo Jones-designed Banqueting House (all that today survives of the 17th-century palace). He prefaced his speech by saying he would have been content to keep silent but that people might have thought he submitted not just to the punishment but to the charge. He spoke from notes he had jotted down on a scrap of paper.

He was separated by soldiers from the main onlookers in Whitehall proper, hence was inaudible to them. His true audience was the knot of people immediately surrounding him on the scaffold. Chief among these were the two senior Army officers presiding, Colonels Matthew T(h)omlinson and Francis Hacker, the latter's name having a melancholy appositeness. There were also soldiers of lower rank and short-hand reporters, while Charles had as attendants William Juxon, Bishop of London, and one Thomas Herbert.

After the main speech, Bishop Juxon intimated to Charles that he ought to say something more about religion, which Charles duly did. He then turned to Hacker and said "Take care that they do not put me to pain." He then addressed the executioner: "I shall say but very short prayers, and when I thrust out my hands … " He then asked Juxon for his night-cap, donned it and asked the executioner "Does my hair trouble you?" The executioner told him to tuck his hair under the cap. Having done so, Charles said to Juxon "I go from a corruptible to an incorruptible crown; where no disturbance can be, no disturbance in the world". To the executioner he said "Is my hair well?", doffed his cloak and doublet, put his cloak on again and told the executioner "You must set it fast." The executioner told him it was fast(ened) already. Charles said "It might have been a little higher." The executioner told him it could not be.

Charles repeated the words "When I put out my hands this way, then … " and stooped to lay his head on the block. The executioner again tucked his hair under his cap (it having presumably fallen loose) and presently Charles stretched his hands forward. The executioner cut off his head with a single blow, held it up and showed it to the onlookers.

Charles's death gave an immense propaganda boost to royalism through the concept of 'Charles the Martyr'.

66 **The world knows … I never did begin a war with the two Houses of Parliament. And I call God to witness, to whom I must shortly make an account, that I never did intend for to encroach upon their privileges. They began upon me, it is the Militia they began upon, they confessed that the Militia was mine, but they thought it fit for to have it from me …**
God forbid that I should lay it upon the two Houses of Parliament; there is no necessity of either, I hope … they are free of this guilt …

God forbid that I should be so ill a Christian as not to say that God's judgments are just upon me. Many times he does pay justice by an unjust sentence …

I will only say this, that an unjust sentence [*the execution in 1641 at Parliament's hands, though with Charles's reluctant acquiescence despite promising to save him, of Thomas Wentworth Earl of Strafford, one of Charles's two chief ministers*] that I suffered for to take effect is punished now by an unjust sentence upon me …

I have forgiven all the world, and even those in particular that have been the chief causes of my death. Who they are, God knows. I do not desire to know. God forgive them. But this is not all. My charity must go further. I wish that they may repent, for indeed they have committed a great sin in that particular …

Now, sirs, I must show you both how you are out of the way and will put you in a way; first, you are out of the way, for certainly all the way you have ever had yet … is by way of conquest … Conquest, in my opinion, is never just, except that there be a good just cause … and then if you go beyond it … that makes … unjust at the end that was just at the first …

If it be … conquest, there is … great robbery; as a pirate said to Alexander [*the Great; qv*], that he was the great robber, he was but a petty robber … Sirs, I do think the way that you are in, is much out of the way.

Now sirs, for to put you in the way, believe it you will never do right, nor God will never prosper you, until you give God his due, the King his due (that is, my Successors) and the People their due. I am as much for them as any of you: You must give God his due by regulating rightly His Church (according to the Scripture) which is now out of order …

For the King [i.e., *for the King his due*], indeed I will not … The laws of the land will clearly instruct you for that; therefore, because it concerns my own particular, I only give you a touch of it.

For the people, truly I desire their liberty and freedom as much as anybody whosoever. But I must tell you, that their liberty and freedom consists in having of government those laws by which their life and their goods may be most their own. It is not for having share in government, that is nothing pertaining to them. A subject and a sovereign are clean different things, and therefore until they do that … they will never enjoy themselves …

If I would have given way to an arbitrary way, for to have all laws changed according to the power of the sword, I needed not to have come here. And therefore, I tell you, and I pray God it be not laid to your charge, that I am the Martyr of the People."

To Parliament when closing it down

Oliver Cromwell (*b.* 1599)
Lord Protector (1653–58)
19 April 1653 _____

• Biography

Britain's only military dictator (to date), Oliver Cromwell united the legislatures of the three kingdoms of England, Ireland and Scotland; extended higher education; reformed the legal system; welcomed back the Jews (expelled by Edward I nearly four centuries earlier); and helped impoverished debtors. But he was able to do this only because he led a professional standing army.

The name Cromwell was only assumed by Oliver's paternal line three generations earlier. Before that they had been called Williams. (They were of Welsh origin.) The mother of Oliver's great-grandfather Sir Richard Williams, later Cromwell (*c.* 1495–1545/6), was sister of Henry VIII's minister Thomas Cromwell.

Oliver was from a junior branch of the family. It was one which, after initially prospering (mostly through Henry VIII's dissolving the monasteries), had slightly sunk in the world. He shot to prominence in the Civil War. By 1645 he was a Lieutenant-General commanding the New Model Army's cavalry. By the early 1650s, having defeated the Scots supporters of Charles II in the Second Civil War and reduced Ireland, he controlled the British Isles.

• Context of speech

Parliament was supposed on 19 April 1653 to be debating a motion to dissolve itself. It had earlier been called the 'Long' Parliament since it had sat since 1640 but through death and expulsions was now so reduced that it numbered little more than 50 members and was known as the 'Rump' Parliament. By the next day the MPs had started talking about a further extension of the life of their Parliament. Cromwell came down to the House accompanied by a detachment of musketeers, who he left outside the chamber. On entering the chamber he at first listened quietly to the proceedings. Just as the motion was about to be voted on, he began to speak, stamping on the floor from time to time to emphasise a point.

After speaking, he gave the Mace to a musketeer. The MPs, demoralized by the speech (and perhaps the soldiers too), left the chamber, though at least one, Sir Harry Vane the younger (1613–62), protested. "Oh Sir Harry Vane!" said Cromwell. "The Lord deliver me from Sir Harry Vane!" When every MP had left, Cromwell left too, locking the door behind him.

66 **It is high time for me to put an end to your sitting in this place, which you have dishonoured by your contempt of all virtue and defiled by your practice of every vice.**
Ye are a factious crew and enemies of all good government. Ye are a pack of mercenary wretches and would, like Esau, sell your country for a mess of pottage [*see* Bible]; and, like Judas, betray your God for a few pieces of money.

Is there a single virtue now remaining amongst you? Is there one vice that you do not possess? Ye have no more religion than my horse! Gold is your God. Which of you have not bartered your conscience for bribes?

Is there a man amongst you that has the least care for the good of the Commonwealth?

Ye sordid prostitutes! Have you not defiled this sacred place, and turned the Lord's temple into a den of thieves by your immoral principles and wicked practices? Ye are grown intolerably odious to the whole nation. Ye, who were deputed here by the people to get grievances redressed, are yourselves become the greatest grievance.

Your country therefore calls upon me to cleanse the Augean Stable [*referring to one of the Labours of the mythical Ancient Greek hero Hercules*], by putting a final period to your iniquitous proceedings in this House, and which by God's help, and the strength He has given me, I am now come to do.

I command ye, therefore, upon the peril of your lives, to depart immediately out of this Place. Go! Get out! Make haste, ye venal slaves, begone! So, take away that fool's bauble there [*referring to the Mace*] and lock up the doors. Ye have sate here too long for the good you do. In the name of God, go!"

Against the Stamp Act

Pitt 'the Elder'
1st Earl of Chatham (1708–78)
14 January 1766

- ## Biography

Like Sir Winston Churchill (*qv*), Pitt the Elder was a great war leader and orator but remained in office past his best. Paternally grandson of an opulent nabob, he in 1735 he became MP for the family-owned constituency of Old Sarum, Britain's most notorious rotten borough. In 1746 George II reluctantly gave him minor office. George had been enraged by Pitt's maiden speech congratulating him on the Prince of Wales's marriage, thinking it satirical since everyone knew that George hated his son. In 1755 he sacked Pitt, but in 1756 reinstated him. By now Britain and France were struggling for control of North America and India. George could not stomach Pitt as Prime Minister, so made him Secretary of State, as which Pitt effectively led the wartime government.

Pitt's strength lay in appointing British military commanders on their merits, not family connexions. Numerous victories followed, also the capture of various French posts in North America, including Fort Duquesne, renamed in his honour Pittsburgh. George III acceded in 1760. He wanted peace. In 1761 Pitt resigned. He refused invitations to return till 1766, when he was made Prime Minister with a seat in the House of Lords as Earl of Chatham to save him having to face the more turbulent House of Commons. His ennoblement damaged his standing. He bullied his ministers and many resigned. From early in 1767 till late 1768, when he too resigned, he virtually ceased to see his Cabinet colleagues. Little in the way of Pitt's directly reported speeches survives. And since he was better at extempore orations than prepared ones, we have no textual versions of the cream of them. We do know that he was reckoned better at attack than conciliation or defence.

- ## Context of speech

The Stamp Act taxed American colonists without giving them any say in the matter, *e.g.*, through representation in Parliament. It was later repealed but the principle of taxation without representation was continued, fatally for Britain. The 'gentleman' is George Grenville, Prime Minister 1763–65.

" **I have been charged with giving birth to sedition in America … Sorry I am to hear the liberty of speech in this house imputed as a crime. No gentleman ought to be afraid to exercise it. It is a liberty by which the gentleman who calumniates it might have profited, and by which he ought to have profited.**

The gentleman tells us, America is obstinate. America is almost in open rebellion. I rejoice that America has resisted. Three million of people so dead to all feelings of liberty as voluntarily to submit to be slaves would have been fit instruments to make slaves of the rest.

I come not here armed at all points, with law cases and Acts of Parliament, with the statute book doubled down in dog's-ears, to defend the cause of liberty … I would not debate a particular point of law with the gentleman. I know his abilities. I have been obliged to his diligent researches. But, for the defence of liberty … it is a ground on which I stand firm; on which I dare meet any man …

The gentleman boasts of his bounties to America. Are not those bounties intended finally for the benefit of this kingdom? If they are not, he has misapplied the national treasures. I am no courtier of America. I stand up for this kingdom. I maintain that the Parliament has a right to bind, to restrain America. Our legislative power over the colonies is sovereign and supreme. When it ceases to be sovereign and supreme, I would advise every gentleman to sell his lands, if he can, and embark for that country. When two countries are connected together, like England and her colonies, without being incorporated, the one must necessarily govern; the greater must rule the less; but so rule it, as not to contradict the fundamental principles that are common to both …

The gentleman asks, when were the colonies emancipated? But I desire to know, when were they made slaves? But I dwell not upon words. When I had the honour of serving His Majesty I availed myself of the means of information which I derived from my office. I speak, therefore, from knowledge. My materials were good. I was at pains to collect, to digest, to consider them. And I will be bold to affirm, that the profits to Great Britain from the trade of the colonies, through all its branches, is two millions a year. This is the fund that carried you triumphantly through the last war …. You owe this to America. This is the price America pays you for her protection …

A great deal has been said without doors of the power, of the strength of America. It is a topic that ought to be cautiously meddled with. In a good cause, on a sound bottom, the force of this country can crush America to atoms. I know the valour of your troops. I know the skill of your officers. There is not a company of foot that has served in America out of which you may not pick a man of sufficient knowledge and experience to make him governor of a colony there. But on this ground, on the Stamp Act, when so many here will think a crying injustice, I am one who will lift up my hands against it.

In such a cause, your success would be hazardous. America, if she fell, would fall like a strong man. She would embrace the pillars of the state, and pull down the constitution along with her. Is this your boasted peace? Not to sheathe the sword in its scabbard, but to sheathe it in the bowels of your countrymen? Will you quarrel with yourselves, now the whole House of Bourbon [i.e., *France*] is united against you ...?

The Americans have not acted in all things with prudence and temper. They have been wronged. They have been driven to madness by injustice. Will you punish them for the madness you have occasioned? Rather let prudence and temper come first from this side. I will undertake for America, that she will follow the example ...

I will beg leave to tell the House what is really my opinion. It is, that the Stamp Act be repealed absolutely, totally and immediately; that the reason for the repeal should be assigned, because it was founded on an erroneous principle. At the same time, let the sovereign authority of this country over the colonies be asserted in as strong terms as can be devised, and be made to extend every point of legislation whatsoever, that we may bind their trade, confine their manufactures and exercise every power whatsoever — except that of taking money out of their pockets without their consent."

On the American War

• Context of speech

As early as 1778 some men in Britain feared the Americans would succeed in overthrowing British rule. Pitt was not among them, and when he heard that the 3rd Duke of Richmond, an old enemy, was going to propose recognising American independence, he put in an appearance in the House of Lords, being led into the chamber by his second son William (the future Prime Minister Pitt the Younger, *qv*). After the Duke's speech and a Government reply Pitt rose slowly and stiffly. Leaning on his son, he was able to let go of his crutch and raise his hand. His voice, though weak to start with, soon resumed its old power.

On finishing, Pitt sat down. The Duke of Richmond then spoke again, asserting that Britain could not continue the war even if Pitt were still Prime Minister. Pitt evidently disagreed and when the Duke sat down tried to rise but sank back, felled by a seizure. His son William leapt to catch him. Pitt was taken unconscious to his country seat in Kent, where he died a month later.

" **I** thank God that I have been enabled to come here today to perform my duty ... I am old and infirm. I have one foot — more than one foot — in the grave. I have risen from my bed to stand up in the cause of my country, perhaps never again to speak in this House ...

My Lords, I rejoice that ... I am still alive, to lift up my voice against the dismemberment of this ancient and most noble monarchy. Pressed down as I am by the hand of infirmity, I am little able to assist my country in this most perilous conjuncture. But, my Lords, while I have sense and memory, I will never consent to deprive the offspring of the royal house of Brunswick, the heirs of the Princess Sophia [i.e., *the Hanoverian Dynasty that then reigned in Britain*] of their fairest inheritance. I will first see the Prince of Wales, the Bishop of Osnaburgh [*Frederick Duke of York, George III's second son*] and the other rising hopes of the royal family brought down to this committee, and assent to such an alienation.

Where is the man who will dare to advise it? My Lords, His Majesty succeeded to an empire as great in extent as its reputation was unsullied. Shall we tarnish the lustre of this nation by an ignominious surrender of its rights and fairest possessions? Shall this great nation, that has survived, whole and entire, the Danish depredations, the Scottish inroads, the Norman Conquest — that has stood the threatened invasion of the Spanish Armada, now fall prostrate before the House of Bourbon [i.e., *France, America's ally*]? Surely, my Lords, this nation is no longer what it was. Shall a people that seventeen years ago was the terror of the world now stoop so low as to tell its ancient inveterate enemy 'Take all we have, only give us peace'? It is impossible.

I wage war with no man or set of men. I wish for none of their employments; nor would I co-operate with men who still persist in unretracted error, or who, instead of acting on a firm, decisive line of conduct, halt between two opinions, where there is no middle path. In God's name, if it is absolutely necessary to declare either for peace or war, and the former cannot be preserved with honour, why is not the latter commenced without delay? I am not, I confess, well informed as to the resources of this kingdom, but I trust it has still sufficient to maintain its just rights, though I know them not. But, my Lords, any state is better than despair. Let us at least make one effort, and, if we must fall, let us fall like men."

'Liberty or Death'

Patrick Henry (1736–99)
Virginia's first post-colonial Governor
23 March 1775

• Biography

Like other legends of American history, notably Lincoln (*qv*), Patrick Henry failed in lesser careers before succeeding in a hugely demanding one. Again like Lincoln, he made his name as a lawyer, then (as now) America's best springboard into politics. But he preferred prominence at state level to high office at a national one and died before the United States leaders could persuade him otherwise.

He made his name when in 1763 he pleaded so persuasively for his church vestry clients against an Anglican clergyman who had already won from them an increased stipend, that the jury fixing the sum awarded only a penny extra. In his speech Henry attacked not just the Anglican established church, whose privileges derived from British colonial authority, but British colonial authority itself, which had overruled local legislators on the original stipend question.

Two years later, when Britain had just passed the Stamp Act, Henry outflanked the moderate opposition to it as a specific tax by suggesting that Britain should not tax Americans at all.

He helped draft Virginia's Declaration of Rights, articles 5 and 16 of which may have been his unaided work. He was elected Virginia's first post-colonial Governor in 1776, re-elected each of the next two years and served a further two terms from 1784 to 1786. He developed into an Anti-Federalist, or supporter of states' rights against what he saw as an overmighty Federal Government.

But by the mid-1790s he was coming round to Federalism, being concerned at the excesses both of the French Revolution and of the more extreme Anti-Federalists.

• Context of speech

The speech excerpted below, more than anything else, allegedly swung Virginia behind the struggle for independence. On Henry's finishing it, his audience apparently rose to its feet and exclaimed "To arms! To arms!" This alarmed the British-appointed governor, Lord Dunmore. He seized munitions stored in Williamsburg and only a march on Williamsburg by Henry and his newly formed militia made Dunmore back down. But the version of the speech we possess today was not set down in textual form till 1817.

66 **We have done everything that could be done to avert the storm which is now coming on. We have petitioned; we have remonstrated; we have supplicated; we have prostrated ourselves before the throne, and have implored its interposition to arrest the tyrannical hands of the [*British*] ministry and Parliament.**

Our petitions have been slighted. Our remonstrances have produced additional violence and insult. Our supplications have been disregarded. And we have been spurned, with contempt, from the foot of the throne. In vain, after these things, may we indulge the fond hope of peace and reconciliation.

There is no longer any room for hope. If we wish to be free — if we mean to preserve inviolate those inestimable privileges for which we have been so long contending — if we mean not basely to abandon the noble struggle in which we have been so long engaged, and which we have pledged ourselves never to abandon until the glorious object of our contest shall be obtained — we must fight! I repeat it, sir, we must fight! An appeal to arms and to the God of hosts is all that is left us.

They tell us, sir, that we are weak, unable to cope with so formidable an adversary. But when shall we be stronger? Will it be the next week, or the next year? Will it be when we are totally disarmed, and when a British guard shall be stationed in every house? Shall we gather strength by irresolution and inaction? Shall we acquire the means of effectual resistance by lying supinely on our backs and hugging the delusive phantom of hope, until our enemies shall have bound us hand and foot?

Besides, sir, we shall not fight our battles alone. There is a just God who presides over the destinies of nations, and who will raise up friends to fight our battles for us. The battle, sir, is not to the strong alone; it is to the vigilant, the active, the brave.

Besides, sir, we have no election [i.e., *choice*]. If we were base enough to desire it, it is now too late to retire from the contest. There is no retreat but in submission and slavery. Our chains are forged. Their clanking may be heard on the plains of Boston. The war is inevitable — and let it come. I repeat it, sir, let it come.

It is in vain, sir, to extentuate the matter. Gentlemen may cry 'Peace, peace' — but there is no peace. The war is actually begun. The next gale that sweeps from the north will bring to our ears the clash of resounding arms. Our brethren are already in the field. Why stand we here idle? What is it that gentlemen wish? What would they have? Is life so dear, or peace so sweet, as to be purchased at the price of chains and slavery? Forbid it, Almighty God! I know not what course others may take; but as for me, give me liberty or give me death!"

On an MP's responsibilities

Edmund Burke (1729–97)
Parliamentarian
Autumn 1774

• Biography

An Irishman from a predominantly Catholic minor gentry family, Burke was nonetheless reared as a Protestant. This was common then, Catholics being barred from public office.

He studied but never practised law. Politics he first studied then practised, writing a book on political theory then becoming private secretary to Lord Rockingham (Prime Minister 1765–66 and 1782) and in 1765 MP for the pocket borough of Wendover, in Buckinghamshire.

Burke held office only twice. His fame was as a parliamentarian, but one of uncommon eloquence and ability to think deeply on constitutional matters.

He was in his lifetime a member of Rockingham's Whig group. By the 20th century he had become an oracle to Conservatives. His arguments in favour of institutions and the importance of maintaining them proved especially influential almost from the time of his death.

The content of Burke's oratory was vastly superior to his delivery. The former is immediately grasped from the printed page. The latter was rapid, sometimes too much so for his ideas. His tone was harsh — oddly, since he spoke with an Irish accent, which most hearers find soft. His gestures were often awkward. But in his early days as an MP he could move the House to tears or laughter. Later he lost his ascendancy and was much heckled.

• Context of speech

By 1774 Lord Verney, who owned Burke's seat of Wendover, needed someone who would pay him for the privilege of representing it. A group of Bristolians put up Burke as candidate for their city and on 3 November he was elected. Bristol, in common with other constituencies then, was represented by two members. Burke's fellow Bristol MP, a Mr Cruger, announced that in Parliament he would toe any line his constituents demanded of him. Burke took the contrary view.

66 **C**ertainly, gentlemen, it ought to be the happiness and glory of a representative to live in the strictest union, the closest correspondence and the most unreserved communication with his constituents. Their wishes ought to have great weight with him; their opinion, high respect; their business, unremitted attention.**

It is his duty to sacrifice his repose, his pleasures, his satisfactions, to theirs; and above all, ever, and in all cases, to prefer their interest to his own. But his unbiased opinion, his mature judgment, his enlightened conscience, he ought not to sacrifice to you, to any man, or to any set of men living.

These he does not derive from your pleasure; no, nor from the law and the constitution. They are a trust from Providence, for the abuse of which he is deeply answerable. Your representative owes you, not his industry only, but his judgment; and he betrays, instead of serving you, if he sacrifices it to your opinion.

… If government were a matter of will upon any side, yours, without question, ought to be superior. But government and legislation are matters of reason and judgment, and not of inclination; and what sort of reason is that, in which the determination precedes the discussion; in which one set of men deliberate, and another decide; and where those who form the conclusion are perhaps three hundred miles distant from those who hear the arguments?

Parliament is not a *congress* of ambassadors from different and hostile interests; which interests each must maintain, as an agent and advocate, against other agents and advocates; but Parliament is a *deliberative* assembly of *one* nation, with *one* interest, that of the whole; where, not local purposes, not local prejudices, ought to guide, but the general good, resulting from the general reason of the whole.

You choose a member indeed; but when you have chosen him, he is not member of Bristol, but he is a member of *Parliament …* ”

On impeaching Warren Hastings

• Context of speech

Warren Hastings (1732–1818) had been Governor-General of Bengal from 1773 to 1784. His high-handedness and ensuing quarrels with various other leading figures among the British in India led to his impeachment back home. Impeachment involved a trial before the House of Lords, members of the House of Commons being the prosecutors. Burke, who had long had profitable dealings with the East India Company, which in effect ran much of India, led the Commons team of five. The trial took seven years. Hastings was acquitted but ruined by the legal costs of his defence. The East India Company later reimbursed him. Burke delivered his opening speech on 13 February 1787.

66 My lords, you have now heard the principles on which Mr Hastings governs the part of Asia subjected to the British Empire. Here he has declared his opinion that he is a despotic prince; that he is to use arbitrary power; and, of course, all his acts are covered with that shield. 'I know', says he, 'the Constitution of Asia only from its practice.'

Will your lordships submit to hear the corrupt practices of mankind made the principles of government? *He* have arbitrary power? My lords, the East India Company have not arbitrary power to give him. The King has no arbitrary power to give him. Your lordships have not; nor the Commons; nor the whole Legislature.

We have no arbitrary power to give, because arbitrary power is a thing which neither any man can hold nor any man can give. No man can lawfully govern himself according to his own will — much less can one person be governed by the will of another. We are all born in subjection — all born equally, high and low, governors and governed, in subjection to one great, immutable, pre-existent law, prior to all our devices and prior to all our contrivances, paramount to all our ideas and to all our sensations, antecedent to our very existence, by which we are knit and connected in the eternal frame of the universe, out of which we can not stir.

This great law does not arise from our conventions or compacts. On the contrary, it gives to our conventions and compacts all the force and sanction they can have. It does not arise from our vain institutions. Every good gift is of God. All power is of God. And He who has given the power, and from whom alone it originates, will never suffer the exercise of it to be practised upon any less solid foundation than the power itself ...

Arbitrary power is not to be had by conquest. Nor can any sovereign have it by succession, for no man can succeed to fraud, rapine and violence. Those who give and those who receive arbitrary power are alike criminal. And there is no man but is bound to resist it to the best of his power, wherever it shall show its face to the world.

Law and arbitrary power are in eternal enmity. Name me a magistrate, and I will name property. Name me power, and I will name protection. It is a contradiction in terms, it is blasphemy in religion, it is wickedness in politics, to say that any man can have arbitrary power. In every patent of office the duty is included. For what else does a magistrate exist? To suppose for power, is an absurdity in idea. Judges are guided and governed by the eternal laws of justice, to which we are all subject. We may bite our chains, if we will, but we shall be made to know ourselves, and be taught that man is born to be governed by *law*, and he that will substitute *will* in the place of it is an enemy to God.

My lords, what is it that we want here, to a great act of national justice? Do we want a cause, my lords? You have the cause of oppressed princes, of undone women of the first rank, of desolated provinces and of wasted kingdoms. Do you want a criminal, my lords? When was there so much iniquity ever laid to the charge of any one? No, my lords, you must not look to punish any other such delinquent from India. Warren Hastings has not left substance enough in

India to nourish such another delinquent. My lords, is it a prosecutor you want? You have before you the Commons of Great Britain as prosecutors. And I believe, my lords, that the sun, in his beneficent progress round the world, does not behold a more glorious sight than that of men, separated from a remote people by the material bounds and barriers of nature, united by the bond of a social and moral community — all the Commons of England resenting, as their own, the indignities and cruelties that are offered to all the people of India.

I impeach Warren Hastings, Esquire, of high crimes and misdemeanors. I impeach him in the name of the Commons of Great Britain in Parliament assembled, whose parliamentary trust he has betrayed. I impeach him in the name of all the Commons of Great Britain, whose national character he has dishonoured. I impeach him in the name of the people of India, whose laws, rights and liberties he has subverted; whose properties he has destroyed; whose country he has laid waste and desolate. I impeach him in the name and by virtue of those eternal laws of justice which he has violated. I impeach him in the name of human nature itself, which he has cruelly outraged, injured and oppressed, in both sexes, in every age, rank, situation and condition of life."

On terror

Maximilien Robespierre (1758–94)
French revolutionary
5 February 1794

• Biography

A decidedly dressy, yet at the same time prim, lawyer is a strange person to conduct the bloodiest phase of a revolution. Such a figure was Robespierre. But then one recalls Lenin (*qv*), a trained lawyer, tooling around in a Silver Ghost Rolls-Royce (he owned no fewer than nine), and Mao (*qv*), wearer of silk-lined versions of the eponymous suit. So the de luxe despot is a historic type.

Robespierre was electeded to the Estates General (so called since they comprised the three estates of the realm: nobility, church and people) that in 1789 were summoned, for the first time in well over 150 years, to extricate the monarchy from its financial mess. The Estates General were soon displaced by the National Constituent Assembly and it in its turn by the National Convention. Robespierre was elected to them too but made his name in the Jacobin Club, a talking shop which he eventually led and which nurtured other radical revolutionaries.

• Context of speech

Revolutionary France was attacked by *ancien régime* countries determined to crush democracy. A Committee of Public Safety was formed with sweeping powers to safeguard the Revolution and on 27 July 1793 Robespierre had been elected to it. He eliminated both his ultra-leftist and leading moderate rivals through a reign of terror in which some 15,000 to 17,000 people were guillotined. But France recovered militarily. The need for terror became for Robespierre's surviving colleagues less pressing. Besides, they might be his next victims.

He was denounced at a session of the Convention on 27 July 1794 (called 9 Thermidor in the new revolutionary calendar) and guillotined next day. His cult of 'virtue' was in practice an obsession with civic responsibility carried to absurd lengths. The choice in his time of 'safety' as an end so desirable that in its 'Public' form it needed an oppressive 'Committee' to effect foreshadows the Health and Safety regulations that frustrate everyday existence in the 21st century, and in particular the way curbs on liberty are always announced over public address systems with the preludial phrase 'For your safety ...'.

Robespierre is said to have had a high-pitched and metallic voice, though whether this means tinny or brass is unclear (it presumably did not mean silvery, other than of tongue).

> 66 **Virtue is natural to the people, notwithstanding aristocratic prejudices. A nation is truly corrupted when, having ... lost its character and its liberty, it passes from democracy to aristocracy or to monarchy. That is the decrepitude and death of the body politic ...**

[The] purity of the French Revolution ... , the ... sublimity of its objective, ... causes both our strength and our weakness. Our strength, because it gives to us truth's ascendancy over imposture, and the rights of the public interest over private interests. Our weakness, because it rallies all vicious men against us, all those who in their hearts contemplate despoiling the people and all those who intend to let them be despoiled with impunity, both those who have rejected freedom as a personal calamity and those who have embraced the Revolution as a career and the Republic as prey.

Hence the defection of so many ambitious or greedy men who ... have abandoned us ... because they did not begin ... with the same aim in view. The two opposing spirits that ... struggle to rule nature may be said to be fighting in this great period of human history to fix irrevocably the world's destinies. France is the scene of this fearful combat. Without, tyrants encircle you; within, tyranny's friends conspire. They will conspire until hope is wrested from crime. We must smother the internal and external enemies of the Republic or perish with it. The first maxim of your policy ought now to be to lead the people by reason and the people's enemies by terror.

If the spring of popular government in time of peace is virtue, the springs of popular government in revolution are at once virtue and terror. Virtue, without which terror is fatal; terror, without which virtue is powerless. Terror is nothing other than justice, prompt, severe, inflexible. It is therefore an emanation of virtue. It is not so much a special principle as it is a consequence of the general principle of democracy applied to our country's most urgent needs.

It has been said that terror is the principle of despotic government. Does your government resemble despotism? Only as the sword that gleams in the hands of the heroes of liberty resembles that with which the henchmen of tyranny are armed. Let the despot govern by terror his brutalised subjects; he is right, as a despot. Subdue by terror the enemies of liberty, and you will be right, as founders of the Republic. The government of the Revolution is liberty's despotism against tyranny. Is force made only to protect crime? And is the thunderbolt not destined to strike the heads of the proud? ...

Society owes protection only to peaceable citizens. The only citizens in the Republic are the republicans. For it, the royalists, the conspirators are only strangers or, rather, enemies. This terrible war waged by liberty against tyranny — is it not indivisible? Are the enemies within not the allies of the enemies without? The assassins who tear our country apart, the intriguers who buy the consciences that hold the people's mandate; the traitors who sell them; the mercenary pamphleteers hired to dishonour the people's cause, to kill public virtue, to stir up the fire of civil discord and to prepare political counterrevolution by moral counterrevolution — are all those men less guilty or less dangerous than the tyrants whom they serve?"

Farewell address

George Washington (1732–99)
1st President of the USA 1789–97
September 1796

• Biography

George Washington was not only the fledgling USA's first chief executive and head of state, he was the man who made the USA possible in the first place. He did this by beating the British in war then by holding together in peace a completely new form of government. That Washington succeeded in both tasks bespeaks his chief talent, which was essentially managerial.

He trained first as a surveyor then as a soldier, serving (technically as an officer of the King) in what Americans call the French and Indian War (1754–63); the British know it as the Seven Years War and date it from 1756.

In 1775 war with Britain looked inevitable and the Second Continental Congress, representing all 13 states, appointed him Commander-in-Chief of the colonial insurgents' forces, known as the Continental Army. As an ex-militia officer who had experienced two defeats by the French, Washington knew the risk of engaging regular troops in direct action. Instead he waged a more or less guerilla war. Even this might not have succeeded but for British incompetence and the intervention of the French.

Initially, independent America was a confederation. But central government was too weak, and when the much better-designed Constitution was adopted, Washington was the unanimous choice for President.

• Context of speech

Judged by the passage below, the peroration to his farewell address, Washington seems verbose. Its interest lies in two quite different things: its taking place at all and its warning.

There was then no convention, let alone a 22nd Amendment, which was brought in after Franklin D. Roosevelt's (*qv*) four-term presidency, restricting a President to two terms at most. Had Washington not retired when he did he might have died in office and the presidency might thereafter have been held for life.

He advised Americans to preserve the Union, particularly given the contrast between the North and South; the Constitution; and sound public finances. Also to eschew faction, overmighty government and foreign entanglements. Apart from his distaste for faction (as an ex-soldier he confused healthy party political tussles with military insubordination), it is a wish list as valuable today as when he issued it, though less observed.

This farewell address was not delivered orally. Washington had it published, first in a Philadelphia newspaper on 19 September 1796, then in a Boston one a week later.

66 **The acceptance of ... the office to which your suffrages have twice called me [has] ... been a uniform sacrifice of inclination to ... duty ... I constantly hoped ... that it would have been much earlier in my power ... to return to that retirement from which I had been reluctantly drawn. The strength of my inclination to do this, previous to the last election, had even led to the preparation of an address to declare it to you ...**

In looking forward to the [end] ... of my public life, [I cannot] suspend ... acknowledgment of [the] ... gratitude ... I owe ... my beloved country for the many honors it has conferred upon me; still more for the steadfast confidence with which it has supported me; and for the opportunities I have thence enjoyed of manifesting my inviolable attachment, by services faithful and persevering, though in usefulness unequal to my zeal.

If benefits have resulted to our country from these services, let it always be remembered to your praise, and as an instructive example in our annals, that under circumstances in which the passions, agitated in every direction, were liable to mislead, amidst appearances sometimes dubious, vicissitudes of fortune often discouraging, in situations in which not unfrequently [*sic*] want of success has countenanced the spirit of criticism, the constancy of your support was the essential prop of the efforts, and a guarantee of the plans by which they were effected.

Profoundly penetrated with this idea, I shall carry it with me to my grave, as a strong incitement to unceasing vows that Heaven may continue to you the choicest tokens of its beneficence; that your union and brotherly affection may be perpetual; that the free constitution, which is the work of your hands, may be sacredly maintained; that its administration in every department may be stamped with wisdom and virtue; that, in fine, the happiness of the people of these States, under the auspices of liberty, may be made complete, by so careful a preservation and so prudent a use of this blessing, as will acquire to them the glory of recommending it to the applause, the affection, and adoption of every nation, which is yet a stranger to it."

Against the slave trade

William Wilberforce (1759–1833)
House of Commons
12 May 1789

• Biography

The chief parliamentary campaigner against the slave trade in late 18th-century Britain, Wilberforce was born into a mercantile family at Hull, for which he became MP in 1780, though from 1784 he sat for Yorkshire. In 1787 he embarked on his struggle to abolish through legislation the slave trade. In his day it involved overwhelmingly the export to the Americas by Europeans and North and South Americans of blacks from West Africa with the co-operation of other blacks there.

• Context of speech

In its entirety the speech lasted three hours and technically involved passing 12 resolutions. But the West Indian plantation interest got the immediate business held over till the next parliamentary sitting. Further progress was delayed till 1807. The chief obstacles were obstructionism by vested interests, chiefly in the House of Lords, and alarm over the French Revolution, particularly in the mind — or what passed for one — of George III, who thought that to outlaw slaving would encourage Jacobinism.

Wilberforce in later life agitated to abolish slavery itself and died jut as the second reading of the Bill to do so took place in Parliament. His quoting the loathsome Mr Norris, forerunner of today's slimiest sort of PR executive, must have won support that no amount of straightforward condemnation could have done. (Perhaps Jane Austen borrowed the name for Fanny Price's cruelly unfeeling aunt in *Mansfield Park*, particularly as Fanny's uncle Sir Thomas Bertram must have run his West Indian plantations on slave labour.)

> 66 **I mean not to accuse any one, but to take the shame upon myself, in common, indeed, with the whole Parliament of Great Britain, for having suffered this horrid trade to be carried on under their authority. We are all guilty — we ought all to plead guilty, and not to exculpate ourselves by throwing the blame on others** ...
>
> I ... speak of the transit of the slaves in the West Indies ... I will not accuse the Liverpool merchants. I will allow them, nay, I will believe them to be men of humanity. And I will therefore believe, if it were not for the enormous magnitude and extent of the evil which distracts their attention from individual cases, ... they would never have persisted in the trade.
>
> I verily believe ... if the wretchedness of any one of the many hundred negroes [*the word 'negro' then lacked the pejorative overtones it has now*] stowed in each ship could be brought before their view, and remain within the sight of the African merchant, that there is no one among them whose heart would bear it.
>
> Let anyone imagine to himself 600 or 700 of these wretches chained two and two, surrounded with every object that is nauseous and disgusting,

diseased and struggling under every kind of wretchedness. How can we bear to think of such a scene as this? One would think it had been determined to heap upon them all the varieties of bodily pain, for the purpose of blunting the feelings of the mind.

And yet, in this very point ... the situation of the slaves has been described by Mr Norris, one of the Liverpool delegates, in a manner which ... will convince the House how interest can draw a film across the eyes, so thick, that total blindness could do no more; and how it is our duty therefore to trust not to the reasonings of interested men, or to their way of colouring a transaction.

'Their apartments', says Mr Norris, 'are fitted up as much for their advantage as circumstances will admit. The right ankle of one, indeed, is connected with the left ankle of another by a small iron fetter, and if they are turbulent, by another on their wrists. They have several meals a day; some of their own country provisions, with the best sauces of African cookery; and by way of variety, another meal of pulse, etc., according to European taste.

After breakfast they have water to wash themselves, while their apartments are perfumed with frankincense and lime-juice. Before dinner, they are amused after the manner of their country. The song and dance are promoted', and, as if the whole was really a scene of pleasure and dissipation, it is added that games of chance are furnished. 'The men play and sing, while the women and girls make fanciful ornaments with beads, which they are plentifully supplied with.'

Such is the sort of strain in which the Liverpool delegates, and particularly Mr Norris, gave evidence before the Privy Council."

Against the slave trade

Pitt 'the Younger' (1759–1806)
House of Commons
2 April 1792

• Biography

Britain's longest-serving Prime Minister, and its youngest ever on taking office, Pitt the Younger was also the first to shoulder something like the modern burden of the office. It eventually killed him.

He was Pitt the Elder's (*qv*) second boy, and it was in part to vindicate his father, whose reputation late in life had sunk, that Pitt the Younger entered national politics at all.

To improve his supposedly delicate health he was prescribed port from as early as fourteen. He became very fond of it, taking far more than was good for him. He was even fonder of mathematics than port, but turned it to better use, becoming a master of finance.

In 1780 Pitt entered Parliament. A year later he was offered a junior government post but declined, being determined to take a Cabinet post or nothing — an extraordinarily audacious attitude.

He had not long to wait. The Prime Minister, Lord Rockingham, died. Many Rockinghamites disliked his replacement, Lord Shelburne, and went into opposition. Shelburne needed good debaters and made Pitt Chancellor of the Exchequer. He was barely 23.

He defended the peace terms with America so adroitly that although Shelburne's administration fell, he, Pitt, managed to escape the obloquy, indeed seemed the natural successor to his father's position. George III offered him the premiership four times in 1783. Pitt accepted the fourth time, won the ensuing election and held power for the next 17 years.

He was reckoned less brilliant and as having less presence than his father, but as using superior language and reasoning. He was particularly good at clarifying for his audience public finance. Yet he could rise to great emotional heights too.

Though he avoided scripts, he did use notes. But his phenomenal memory made such aids almost superfluous. The harmoniousness of his voice was remarked on. It seems to have been quite deep and was likened by one hearer to a bell. His fluency was another asset, a characteristic Pitt claimed to have learnt from his father. He enunciated superbly. It has been said that his mere whisper was audible in the farthest corners of the chamber. He could be highly sarcastic (samples can be found in the second speech below). Contemporaries thought it demeaning in a Prime Minister. On at least two occasions he was evidently so offensive that he was challenged to a duel.

• Context of speech

It resulted in a vote for gradual abolition of the slave trade.

66 **There was a time ... when the very practice of the slave trade prevailed among us. Slaves ... were formerly an established article in our exports ...**
But it is the slavery in Africa which is now called on to furnish the alleged proofs that Africa labours under a natural incapacity for civilisation; that Providence never intended her to rise above ... barbarism; that Providence has ... doomed her to be ... a nursery for slaves for us ... Europeans.

Allow of this ... applied to Africa, and I should be glad to know why it might not also have ... applied to ancient ... Britain. Why might not some Roman Senator, ... pointing to British barbarians, have predicted ... 'There is a people that will never rise to civilisation; there is a people destined never to be free.'

We ... have long ... emerged from barbarism. We have almost forgotten that we were once barbarians. There is ... one thing wanting to ... clear us ... from the imputation of acting ... as barbarians; ... we continue ... to this hour a barbarous traffic in slaves.

... I trust we shall no longer continue this commerce, to the destruction of every improvement on that wide continent; and shall not consider ourselves as conferring too great a boon in restoring its inhabitants is too liberal, if, by abolishing the slave trade, we give them the same ... chance of civilisation with other parts of the world; and that we shall now allow ... Africa the opportunity

— the hope — the prospect — of attaining ... the same blessings which we ourselves ... have been permitted at a ... more early period to enjoy.

If we listen to the voice of reason and duty ... some of us may live to see a reverse of that picture from which we now turn our eyes with shame and regret. We may live to behold the natives of Africa engaged in the calm occupations of industry, in the pursuits of a just and legitimate commerce. We may behold the beams of science and philosophy breaking in upon their land ...

Then may we hope that even Africa, though last of all quarters of the globe, shall enjoy at length, in the evening of her days, those blessings which have descended so plentifully upon us in a much earlier period of the world ... "

On peace with France

• Context of speech

War with revolutionary France erupted in 1793. Most of Britain's ruling class feared France's example might spark revolution at home and Pitt felt obliged to curb civil liberties. By 1800 the two countries had reached something like stalemate. Pitt felt that as long as France was a revolutionary power she would continue a threat, and the danger of the Continental Channel coast's staying in French hands was obvious. So when Napoleon (*qv*) made peace proposals, he was rebuffed. The speech below needs to be read in conjunction with that by Fox, which immediately followed it.

66 **The all-searching eye of the French Revolution looks to every part of Europe, and every quarter of the world, in which can be found an object either of acquisition or plunder. Nothing is too great for the temerity of its ambition, nothing too small ... for the grasp of its rapacity ...**
Bonaparte and his army proceeded to Egypt. The attack was made, pretences were held out to the natives of that country in the name of the French King,

whom they had murdered; they pretended to have the approbation of the Grand Signior [i.e., *the Ottoman Sultan*], whose territories they were violating; their project was carried on under the profession of a zeal for Mahometanism; it was carried on by proclaiming that France had been reconciled to the Mussulman faith, had abjured that of Christianity, or, as he [i.e., *Bonaparte*] in his impious language termed it, of 'the sect of the Messiah'.

... This attack against Egypt was accompanied by an attack upon the British possessions in India made on true revolutionary principles. In Europe the propagation of the principles of France had ... prepared the way for ... its arms. To India the lovers of peace had sent the messengers of Jacobinism for the purpose of inculcating war in those distant regions on Jacobin principles, and of forming Jacobin clubs, which they actually succeeded in establishing, and which in most respects resembled the European model but which were distinguished by this peculiarity, that they were required to swear in one breath hatred to tyranny, ... love of liberty and ... destruction of all ... sovereigns — except the good and faithful ally of the French Republic, Citizen Tippoo [i.e., *Tipu Sultan (1749–99), Sovereign ruler of Mysore, in southern India, who had long been a hindrance to British domination in India but who was finally defeated and killed the year before this speech*]...

This is the ... acting spirit of the French Revolution; this is the spirit which animated it at its birth, and this is the spirit which will not desert it till the moment of its dissolution, ... which has not abated under its misfortunes nor declined in its decay; ... it has been inherent in the Revolution in all its stages, ... and to every one of the leaders of the Directory [*see* Napoleon], but to none more than ... Bonaparte ...

Groaning under every degree of misery, the victim of its own crimes, ... France ... retains (while it has neither left means of comfort, nor almost of subsistence to its own inhabitants) new and unexampled means of annoyance and destruction against all the other powers of Europe.

Its first ... principle was to bribe the poor against the rich by proposing to transfer ... the whole property of the country ... It has been accompanied by an unwearied spirit of proselytism, diffusing itself over all ... the earth, ... which inspired the teachers of French liberty with the hope of alike recommending themselves to those who live under the feudal code of the German Empire; to the various states of Italy ... ; to the old republicans of Holland and to the new republicans of America; to the Catholic of Ireland, whom it was to deliver from Protestant usurpation; to the Protestant of Switzerland, whom it was to deliver from popish superstition; and to the Mussulman of Egypt, whom it was to deliver from Christian persecution; to the remote Indian, blindly bigoted to [*sic*] his ancient institutions; and to the natives of Great Britain, enjoying the perfection of practical freedom, and justly attached to their constitution, from … habit, … reason and … experience …

Thus qualified, thus armed for destruction, the genius of the French Revolution marched forth, the terror and dismay of the world … "

On peace with France

Charles James Fox (1749–1806)
Three times Foreign Secretary
3 February 1800

• Biography

On paper Fox's career does not impress. He was never Prime Minister and although he was thrice Foreign Secretary, it was only ever briefly and on the last occasion he was well past his prime.

His fame rests first on his liberalism, which contrary to most people's waxed with age; second, the cogency with which he expressed it; and third, his immense good nature. Contemporaries mention his capacity for friendship, high cultivation, fondness for the drama and participation in many sports despite his bulk. He appealed to the British love of gentleman amateurs for his habitually lurching tipsily down to Westminster from Brooks's, the great Whig club in St. James's, after having lost thousands of pounds at hazard (a forerunner of craps), only to electrify MPs with brilliant off-the-cuff oratory.

He was a younger son of Lord Holland, one of the leading Whig noblemen of the day (though of distinctly plebeian origins), by a sister of the 3rd Duke of Richmond (*see* also Pitt the Elder). He entered Parliament, aged only 19, for Midhurst, in Sussex, a pocket borough his family had bought him. He joined the Government in 1770 but became unpopular for supporting its curbs on press freedom.

Holding office curbed his own freedom of opinion and he resigned in 1772. He rejoined the Government ten months later and recommenced attacks on the press. George III disliked him for opposing the Royal Marriage Act, which restricted royal personages' choice of spouse, and got him sacked after only two months.

Fox now co-operated with the Whig followers of Lord Rockingham (*see* also Burke and Pitt the Younger), in which capacity he opposed Lord North's administration's handling of American unrest (*see* also Pitt the Elder and Patrick Henry). In March 1782 he became Foreign Secretary in Rockingham's administration. It was divided from the first between George III's stooges and a more independent element but foundered on rivalry between Fox and Lord Shelburne, particularly over peace terms with America. When Rockingham died and George III appointed Shelburne his successor, Fox resigned. He had been Foreign Secretary just over three months.

He now allied with Lord North, his former target. They ousted Shelburne's administration and in April 1783 Fox again became Foreign Secretary. His policy both times aimed at allying with Prussia (and possibly Russia) to counterbalance France.

Fox's skill as a speaker derived from his knowledge, quick mind, wit, excellent memory and simplicity of expression. His involvement in amateur dramatics was good training for a speaker, though his voice was not naturally sonorous (he tended to sound shrill when worked up). He was better at the cut and thrust of debate than the extended solo work of pure oratory.

• Context of speech

The passage below was delivered in response to a speech by Pitt the Younger (the second quoted in the section on him). Fox had rather welcomed the French Revolution, hence in the 1790s became politically isolated and for over five years had shunned the House of Commons. On 3 February 1800 he nevertheless appeared there to attack Pitt, who won the subsequent vote by 285 to 64 but soon resigned. Peace was made with France shortly after. When Pitt died in 1806, Fox became Foreign Secretary a third time, but died eight months later.

66 **Were we not told five years ago that France was not only on the brink and in the jaws of ruin, but that she was actually sunk into the gulf of bankruptcy? Were we not told, as an unanswerable argument against treating [i.e., *making a***

peace treaty], **that she could not hold out another campaign — that nothing but peace could save her — that she wanted only time to recruit her exhausted finances — that to grant her repose was to grant her the means of again molesting this country, and that we had nothing to do but persevere for a short time, in order to save ourselves forever from the consequences of her ambition and her Jacobinism?** …

After having gone on from year to year upon assurances like these, and after having seen the repeated refutations of every prediction, are we again to be gravely and seriously assured, that we have the same prospect of success on the same identical grounds? … If the Right Honourable gentleman [*Pitt, then Prime Minister*] shall succeed in prevailing on Parliament and the country to adopt the principles … he has advanced this night, I see no possible termination to the contest …

I continue to think, and … shall continue to … say, that this country was the aggressor in the war … With regard to Austria and Prussia — is there a man who, for one moment, can dispute that they [*too*] were the aggressors? … The unfortunate monarch, Louis XVI [*guillotined in 1793*], himself, as well as those who were in his confidence, has borne decisive testimony to the fact that between him and the Emperor [*Leopold of Austria*] there were an intimate correspondence and a perfect understanding.

Do I mean by this that a positive treaty was entered into for the dismemberment of France? Certainly not. But … [*there*] was not merely an intention, but a declaration of an intention, on the part of the great powers of Germany, to interfere in the internal affairs of France for the purpose of regulating the government against the opinion of the people.

This, though not a plan for the partition of France, was, in the eye of reason and common sense, an aggression against France …

Did they not declare to France that it was her internal concerns, not her external proceedings, which provoked them to confederate against her? … They did not pretend to fear her ambition — her conquests — her troubling her neighbours … They accused her of new-modelling her own government. They said nothing of her aggressions abroad. They spoke only of her clubs and societies at Paris …

I am not justifying the French. I am not trying to absolve them from blame, either in their internal or external policy. I think, on the contrary, that their successive rulers have been as bad and as execrable … as any of the most despotic and unprincipled governments … the world ever saw … Men bred in the school of the house of Bourbon could not be expected to act otherwise. They could not have lived so long under their ancient masters without imbibing the restless ambition, the perfidy and the insatiable spirit of the race. They have imitated the practice of their great prototype, and, through their whole career of mischiefs and … crimes, have done no more than servilely trace the steps of their own Louis XIV.

If they have overrun countries and ravaged them, they have done it upon Bourbon principles. If they have ruined and dethroned sovereigns, it is entirely after the Bourbon manner. If they have even fraternised with the people of foreign countries, and pretended to make their cause their own, they have only faithfully followed the Bourbon example. They have constantly had Louis, the Grand Monarch, in their eye … "

On the Louisiana Purchase

Thomas Jefferson (1743–1826)
3rd President of the USA 1801–9
17 October 1803 _____

• Biography

Understatement is more a British trait than an American one, and among politicians is rare whatever their nationality. Jefferson was the exception. His triple accomplishments, as recorded on his gravestone in words chosen by him, remind us only that he drafted both the Declaration of Independence and the Virginia state law establishing religious freedom, also that he founded the University of Virginia. The first is undeniably earth-shattering. The last two make him sound another Patrick Henry (*qv*) — keener on local than national prominence.

Jefferson of course accomplished much more. He was, as well as a statesman at national, indeed international, level, an architect, author, inventor, musician and scientist. Yet if he left a complete list of his accomplishments off his gravestone it was not just because there was insufficient room. The fact is, he had his impish side. Witness his ambiguous remarks on his family's ancestry ('they trace [it] ... far back ... , to which let everyone ascribe the ... merit he chooses'). Literal-minded biographers infer he was indifferent to pedigree. Not quite so. He instituted enquiries at the English Heralds' College as to a coat of arms.

Further, his love of liberty stopped short of the pure hostility to slavery of men like Wilberforce (*qv*) across the Atlantic. Jefferson was undoubtedly prejudiced towards blacks. And the augmentation of US territory that he alludes to in the speech below was managed by him without the Amendment that a strict interpretation of the Constitution required — exactly the sort of high-handed large-scale Federal action he opposed as an Anti-Federalist.

He was born into a landowning family. In 1774 he published a pamphlet arguing that loyalty to George III was limited by God-given rights, including liberty. He sat in the Second Continental Congress and with four other delegates, including Benjamin Franklin (1706–90) and the future President John Adams (1735–1826), composed the Declaration of Independence, most of it his unaided work.

Following Independence he sat as a congressman, and after a relatively fruitless time as envoy to France (1784–89) became Washington's (*qv*) Secretary of State. He quarrelled with the Secretary of the Treasury Alexander Hamilton (*see* also Washington), whose Federalist (*i.e.*, relatively strong central government) vision he distrusted. In 1793 he resigned and led the new Anti-Hamilton Party, or Republicans as they soon dubbed themselves. The term was deliberate since Jefferson suspected Hamilton of planning a monarchical restoration.

In 1796 he ran for President against Adams on a party basis and lost narrowly. But in 1800, having been Adams' Vice-President, he still more narrowly defeated him. As President he let Adams' more authoritarian laws expire, proposed paying off the public debt and did cut domestic taxes and defence expenditure.

• Context of speech

The one skill Jefferson lacked was peculiarly political, namely public speaking. Almost alone of orators in this book, he accomplished political ends wholly in other ways. The background to the speech below is thus unusually important. Jefferson's defence cuts might have proved disastrous in war, especially one with France or Britain, and in his second term they did indeed hamper America's resistance to British and French bullying, chiefly the abduction of American seamen. But they also obliged him to act promptly after Spain ceded the Louisiana territory to France.

How to prevent this buffer, now under Napoleon's vigorous regime, from endangering America's westward expansion? Luckily, Napoleon was happy to sell. For a paltry 60 million francs (roughly $175–200 million [£82.5–100 million] today) the US more than doubled its size. The speech below, which was delivered to Congress on 17

October 1803, should therefore be read as a kind of corporate M&A (mergers and acquisitions) report — a notoriously dully worded sort of communication — rather than as a flight of eloquence. That does not lessen its importance. Three days after it, the Senate ratified the purchase by 24 votes to 7.

> 66 **In calling you together, fellow citizens, at an earlier day than was contemplated by the act of the last session of Congress, I have not been insensible to the personal inconveniences necessarily resulting ... But matters of great public concernment have rendered this call necessary ...**

We had not been unaware of the danger to which our peace would be perpetually exposed while so important a key to the commerce of the western country [as New Orleans] remained under foreign power ... Propositions had, therefore, been authorized for obtaining, on fair conditions, the sovereignty of New Orleans, and of other possessions in that quarter ... and the provisional appropriation of two millions of dollars, to be applied and accounted for by the President of the United States, intended as part of the price, was considered as conveying the sanction of Congress to the acquisition proposed.

The enlightened government of France saw, with just discernment, the importance to both nations of such liberal arrangements as might best and permanently promote the peace, friendship and interests of both; and the property and sovereignty of all Louisiana, which had been restored to them [i.e., *the French*], have on certain conditions been transferred to the United States by instruments bearing date the 30th of April last. When these shall have received the constitutional sanction of the Senate, they will without delay be communicated to the Representatives also, for the exercise of their functions as to those conditions which are within the powers vested by the Constitution in Congress.

While the property and sovereignty of the Mississippi and its waters secure an independent outlet for the produce of the western states, and an uncontrolled navigation through their whole course, free from collision with other powers and the dangers to our peace from that source, the fertility of the country, its climate and extent, promise in due season important aids to our treasury, an ample provision for our posterity and a wide-spread field for the blessings of freedom and equal laws.

With the wisdom of Congress it will rest to take those ulterior measures which may be necessary for the immediate occupation and temporary government of the country; for its incorporation into our Union; for rendering the change of government a blessing to our newly-adopted brethren; for securing to them the rights of conscience and of property: for confirming to the Indian inhabitants their occupancy and self-government, establishing friendly and commercial relations with them, and for ascertaining the geography of the country acquired. Such materials for your information, relative to its affairs in general, as the short space of time has permitted me to collect, will be laid before you when the subject shall be in a state for your consideration."

Against the death penalty for Luddites

Lord Byron (1788–1824)
House of Lords
27 February 1812

• Biography

Popularly known as a Regency rake rendered even more glamorous by his calling of poet, Byron is in literary circles admired nowadays for his letters and, almost alone of his specifically creative works, the late-period verse satire 'Don Juan'. His emotional existence, seesawing between melancholy romanticism and cynical debauch, is what most makes him irresistible, both to his own age and ours. In domestic politics he was at heart a liberal. In foreign politics he tended to hero-worship Napoleon (*qv*), though by no means blind to the man's despotism. On the other hand he died helping the Greeks win independence, though he never saw action. He is the precursor of today's celebrity with a conscience, though a lot less vacuous.

George Gordon Byron, later Noel-Byron, 6th Baron Byron of Rochdale (the full title, usually abbreviated), inherited his peerage from a great-uncle aged 10. He was born lame and in childhood was mocked for it by his widowed mother. He therefore did not dance, though he became an accomplished swimmer and dogged boxer, often dieting to keep his weight down. He also played cricket for his school, Harrow.

He was further educated at Trinity College Cambridge, where (as at Harrow) he contracted intense friendships, some of which were probably homosexual. He was the first author whose sex life is better known than his works. This was less because the poetry was duller, though some of it is shockingly slapdash, than because he made sure the sex life was widely discussed. Today's vogue of bisexuality and heterosexual sodomy owes much to his pioneering promotional work, though his relationship with his half-sister Augusta Leigh has yet to make incest acceptable.

His breakthrough as a poet came in 1812, when he was taken up by high society. In 1815 he married a puritanical blue-stocking heiress. The marriage foundered on his heterodox sexual activities, as touched on above. He left Britain in 1816 and thereafter lived mostly in Italy, becoming something of a tourist curiosity to visiting Britons.

• Context of speech

The excerpt below is from Byron's maiden effort in the House of Lords and was delivered on 27 February 1812. The occasion was the second reading of the Frame-work Bill, which imposed death for anyone sabotaging machines. Nottinghamshire, Byron's home county, contained thousands of textile workers. They had in recent years begun to produce their goods on primitive knitting machines, called 'frames', which were much more productive than hand-made methods, though quality suffered.

Most 'frames' belonged to capitalists, who hired them out to the weavers and in general exercised a stranglehold on the industry. The Napoleonic Wars led to trade restrictions between Britain and Continental Europe, hence to falling wages, soaring prices and the hiring of unskilled operatives. This angered the regular weavers, who took it out on the 'frames'. They got called 'Luddites', after 'General Ned Ludd' (also called 'Captain' or 'King Ludd'), an imaginary folklore figure whose name was affixed to threatening letters aimed at Nottingham capitalists from early 1811 on. (Luddism spread later to other cities in the Midlands and North of England.)

Despite Byron's eloquence, the Bill passed. Twelve thousand troops were despatched to enforce it locally. Mass executions and transportations to Australia ensued. In March 1812, the month after his speech, Byron published 'Childe Harold', the poem that overnight made him famous, and thereafter he promoted his cultural rather than political celebrity. He only ever spoke in the Lords twice again, the last time being to introduce a petition by someone else. His public oratory was considered even in his day rather laboured and his manner histrionic, while his intonation seemed to observers too sing-song, though his voice was apparently very clear. But the House of Lords, more than most forums, preferred restraint. At Harrow he on at least one occasion won praise for his delivery, both of set speeches and a passage he introduced into one of them.

" **I** have traversed the seat of war in the Peninsula, I have been in some of the most oppressed provinces of Turkey; but never under the most despotic of infidel governments did I behold such squalid wretchedness as I have seen, since my return, in the very heart of a Christian country ...

Setting aside the palpable injustice and the certain inefficiency of the Bill, are there not capital punishments sufficient in your statutes? Is there not blood enough upon your penal code, that more must be poured forth to ascend to Heaven and testify against you?

How will you carry the Bill into effect? Can you commit a whole county to their own prisons? Will you erect a gibbet in every field, and hang up men like scarecrows? Or will you proceed ... by decimation; place the county under martial law; depopulate and lay waste all around you; and restore Sherwood Forest as an acceptable gift to the Crown in its former condition of a royal chase and an asylum for outlaws?

Are these the remedies for a starving and desperate populace? Will the famished wretch who has braved your bayonets be appalled by your gibbets? When death is a relief, and the only relief it appears that you will afford him, will he be dragooned into tranquillity? Will that which could not be effected by your grenadiers be accomplished by your executioners? If you proceed by the forms of law, where is your evidence? Those who have refused to impeach their accomplices when transportation only was the punishment, will hardly be tempted to witness against them when death is the penalty ...

Sure I am, from what I have heard, and from what I have seen, that to pass the Bill under all the existing circumstances, without inquiry, without deliberation, would only be to add injustice to irritation, and barbarity to neglect ...

But suppose it passed. Suppose one of these men, as I have seen them, meagre with famine, sullen with despair, careless of a life which your Lordships are perhaps about to value at something less than the price of a stocking-frame; suppose this man surrounded by the children for whom he is unable to procure bread at the hazard of his existence, about to be torn for ever from a family which he lately supported in peaceful industry, and which it is not his fault that he can no longer so support; suppose this man — and there are ten thousand such from whom you may select your victims — dragged into court, to be tried for this new offence, by this new law; still, there are two things wanting to convict and condemn him and these are, in my opinion, twelve butchers for a jury and a Jeffreys for a judge."

Farewell to his Old Guard

Napoleon B(u)onaparte (1769–1821) Emperor of the French (1804–14 and March–June 1815) Château de Fontainebleau 20 April 1814

• Biography

The symbol for his contemporaries of successful nationalist revolt against the selfish, short-sighted and over-privileged monarchs of a decayed feudal past, Napoleon was certainly a master of the art of war. But he also initiated many of the bossier aspects of the modern state, including police snooping, an intrusive legal code, religion subordinated to the civil power and heavy taxation. More creditably, he set up a secure financial system for France, created the Legion of Honour (first of the national- as opposed to class-based orders) and improved the judiciary.

He was born into a Corsican family of the minor nobility, educated in France and in 1785 became an artillery officer. During the Revolution he won fame by his skilful gunnery in 1793 at the Siege of Toulon against royalists and their foreign allies. The next year he got into trouble through links with the recently toppled Robespierre (*qv*) but survived and first in Italy (1796) then in the Middle East (1798–99) won a string of spectacular victories. He overthrew the regime called the Directory and became France's First Consul, an executive position loosely modelled on Ancient Rome's (*see* also Marc Antony). In 1804 he made himself Emperor.

He failed to invade Britain but regularly defeated Austria and various German states and usually Russia too. But when he invaded Russia in 1812 he was defeated, the Allies formed yet another coalition against him, this time successful, and he was beaten back to France. His occupying forces in the Iberian Peninsula were also defeated, allowing invasion of France from the south as well.

• Context of speech

The Château de Fontainebleau lies about 35 miles southeast of Paris. It was the seat chiefly of François I (1515–47) before being chosen by Napoleon as his main residence outside Paris and as the chief architectural symbol of his regime. (Versailles he rejected as too much associated with the Bourbons.)

When the Allies invaded France in 1814 Napoleon made his headquarters at Fontainebleau. On 2 April he paraded his troops there. By now they were reduced to 18,000, far fewer than the Allied armies. He told his men that Paris had surrendered and said:

"I have offered the Emperor Alexander [*I of Russia (1801–25)*] peace at the price of great sacrifices such that France would be confined to her ancient limits and would renounce all her conquests since the Revolution.

Not only has he refused, but he has listened to the suggestions of a faction composed of émigrés [i.e., *ancien régime aristocrats*] whom I have pardoned and persons whom I have enriched. These men on his entering Paris encircled him and by their perfidious insinuations obtained his permission to assume the white cockade [*the Bourbon symbol*]. But we will preserve our own. In a few days I will march upon Paris. I count on you. Or am I wrong to do so?"

The troops shouted "Paris! Paris! Paris!" but Napoleon's senior officers were horrified at the prospect of Paris's destruction, especially as further success was unlikely. Next day the men cooled towards the idea too. Napoleon tried unsuccessfully to negotiate an abdication in favour of his son rather than a restoration of the Bourbons. On the 6th the Allies told Napoleon he must abdicate unconditionally.

Nicolas Oudinot, one of his Marshals, now marched the bulk of the army away lest it be influenced by the Imperial (or 'Old') Guard, 6,000–7,000 strong and still loyal to Napoleon. On the 11th Napoleon abdicated. On the 20th, having spent several days in relative inaction (during which he allegedly contracted syphilis, presumably from a female camp follower, his wife being absent), he addressed the Guard for what he and they thought would be the last time. He was not much of an orator before a civilian audience, going by his coup against the Directory in 1799, when he was heckled then lost his nerve. But he knew how to inspire his troops, even though his French was encumbered by a heavy Italian accent.

After his speech, General Petit, the Old Guard's commander, grasped a standard and stepped forward. Napoleon clasped it in his arms and kissed it. According to different accounts a sigh or a moan went up from the soldiers. Another account says there was silence broken only by their sobs. In addition, it is said that Napoleon himself broke down. He pulled himself together and added loudly: "Once again, adieu, my old companions. May this last kiss pass to your hearts."

He was then escorted to Elba, off the northwest coast of Italy, which he had been granted as sovereign. Early in 1815 he escaped back to France. At Grenoble on 7 March 1815 he gave further evidence of his simple but powerful way with fighting men. A detachment of the 5th Regiment of the Line had been sent to arrest him. He addressed them with the words "Soldiers of the Fifth, you recognise me. If any man would shoot his Emperor, he may do so now." They joined him forthwith.

He rallied many more of the French but was defeated on 18 June at Waterloo, near Brussels, by the British and Prussians. This time he was exiled to St. Helena, in the South Atlantic, one of the remotest spots on earth. There he died six years later from what in January 2007 was conclusively shown to be stomach cancer. Arsenic poisoning was at one time suggested too since high arsenic levels were found in his hair. Arsenic was then used to treat syphilis.

"**Officers, non-commissioned officers and soldiers of the Old Guard, I bid you goodbye. For twenty years I have been able to count on your support. I have ever found you steady upon the road to glory. The allied powers have armed all Europe against me, much of my army has failed in its duty and France herself has given way to selfish desires.**

With you and the other heroic troops who have stayed faithful to me I could have kept civil war going for three years. But France would have been made wretched and this is not an outcome I would even consider. I must therefore sacrifice my personal interest to France's well-being. This I now do.

Be faithful to the new sovereign whom France has chosen. Do not forsake this dear land for too long plunged in misery. Do not lament my fate. I will be happy once I know you accept it. I could have embraced death. Nothing would have been easier. But I prefer to live so that I can maintain my affection for you all. I intend to write the history of what we have done together.

I cannot embrace you all. But I shall embrace your commander. Come, General [*General Petit*]. Let someone bring me the eagle [*the standard, depicting that bird*] that I may embrace it also. Adieu, my children. Be always gallant and good. Do not forget me."

On the New–Old World balance

George Canning (1770–1827)
House of Commons
12 December 1826

• Biography

Canning is something of a bohemian among British Prime Ministers. He had a sprightliness of character that ran counter to the increasing seriousness of the age. He dashed off quite good verse. He was a practical joker. He at one point helped run and was one of the main contributors to a satirical newspaper, the *Anti-Jacobin*, a forerunner in many ways of *Private Eye*.

He was born into a Protestant Ascendancy family from Northern Ireland and was taken up by Pitt the Younger (*qv*), who so promoted him that he entered Parliament and married an heiress.

Canning needed not just wealth but the consequence such a wife conferred. His quick-wittedness, short temper and impudence had made him enemies. Later in life his speeches became more temperate. At the height of his forensic powers, roughly from the death of Pitt, he could sway the Commons like no one else.

His first major post was as Foreign Secretary in 1807, as which he confiscated the Danish fleet to keep it from Napoleon. He also persuaded the Portuguese to seek British protection when the French threatened their independence, thus making Wellington's Peninsular Campaign possible. From 1809 to 1822, when he became Foreign Secretary again, he was out of office.

When Lord Liverpool resigned as Premier in early 1827, Canning was by no means certain to be his successor. Most of his Cabinet colleagues opposed his support for Catholic emancipation. When he did take office, it was only after bringing a number of Whigs into his administration, for seven of his former ministerial colleagues had resigned. Canning did not live long afterwards. He died on 8 August, having been Prime Minister just under four months. But his real career stretched back a generation.

He was less liberal than he was subsequently given credit for. But he opened the way to two crucial developments in parliamentary democracy. The first was a good, solid, argumentative opposition (previously it was thought bad form for oppositions to be too contentious). The other was his introducing policy to the public by making speeches up and down the country rather than in parliamentary debates or Cabinet sessions. In that respect he remained true to his early calling as a journalist.

• Context of speech

From 1822 on, Canning intensified the policy of disentangling Britain from the gang of reactionary monarchs that dominated mainland Europe. He secured Portugal's continuing independence of Spain. But his chief feat was to extend British recognition of the South American countries that were establishing their independence of Spain, formerly their imperial master. It won Britain a major share of Latin American trade that survives to some extent today.

It was in defending his Spanish policy, which at this point concerned his acquiescing in a renewed French occupation of Spain, that he delivered his famous tag (quoted below) about calling the New World into existence to redress the balance of the Old. Canning reckoned it was better received than any announcement of a French withdrawal from Spain would have been.

Canning's mother had been an actress, though a very undistinguished one, but clearly he inherited some of her theatrical temperament when it came to making speeches. He got very nervy before an important debate and after his performance confessed to feeling limp with exhaustion.

Byron (*qv*) thought him Britain's best, indeed only orator, but by the time Byron was old enough to judge, the older generation (Burke, Fox and Pitt the Younger, *qqv*) had passed away. In composition, power and vocabulary they are usually rated higher than Canning. (Delivery is another matter; *see* in particular accounts of Burke's.)

The immediate occasion of the speech below was a message of George IV of 12 December 1826 pledging Britain's support for her old ally Portugal in any conflict with Spain.

---

66 **Is the Spain of the present day the Spain of which the statesmen of the times of William [*III*] and [*Queen*] Anne were so much afraid? Is it indeed the nation whose puissance was expected to shake England from her sphere? No, sir, it was quite another Spain. It was the Spain within the limits of whose empire the sun never set. It was the Spain 'with the Indies' that excited the jealousies and alarmed the imaginations of our ancestors.**

But then, Sir, the balance of power! ...

I have already said, that when the French army entered Spain, we might, if we chose, have resisted or resented that measure by war. But were there no other means than war for restoring the balance of power? Is the balance of power a fixed and unalterable standard? Or is it not a standard perpetually varying, as civilisation advances, and as new nations spring up, and take their place among established political communities?

The balance of power a century and a half ago was to be adjusted between France and Spain, the Netherlands, Austria and England. Some years afterwards, Russia assumed her high station in European politics. Some years after that again, Prussia became not only a substantive, but a preponderating monarchy. Thus, while the balance of power continued in principle the same, the means of adjusting it became more varied and enlarged ...

To look to the policy of Europe, in the times of William and Anne, for the purpose of regulating the balance of power in Europe at the present day, is to disregard the progress of events, and to confuse dates and facts which throw a reciprocal light upon each other.

It would be disingenuous, indeed, not to admit that the entry of the French army into Spain was in a certain sense a disparagement, an affront to the pride, a blow to the feelings of England. And it can hardly be supposed that the Government did not sympathise, on that occasion, with the feelings of the people. But I deny that, questionable or censurable as the act might be, it was one which necessarily called for our direct and hostile opposition. Was nothing then to be done? ...

What if the possession of Spain might be rendered harmless in rival hands, harmless as regarded us and valueless to the possessors? ...

If France occupied Spain, is it necessary, in order to avoid the consequences of that occupation, that we should blockade Cadiz? No. I looked to another way, sought materials of compensation in another hemisphere. Contemplating Spain, such as our ancestors had known her, I resolved that if France had Spain, it should not be Spain 'with the Indies'. I called the New World into existence, to redress the balance of the Old."

Pilgrim Fathers' commemoration

Daniel Webster (1782–1852)
Plymouth, Massachusetts
22 December 1820 _____

• Biography

Like Charles James Fox (*qv*), Webster was often in debt and over-convivial (his death was caused partly by cirrhosis of the liver). Again like Fox, he was thrice appointed his country's foreign minister, died in office and failed to become chief executive, despite widespread support.

Webster was born in New Hampshire and briefly educated at its chief school, Phillips Exeter Academy. His parents, being hard-up, removed him after nine months. Its traditional sporting rivalry with Phillips Academy at Andover, Mass., which educated both Bush (*qv*) presidents, resembles the Eton–Harrow one in England.

Webster became a lawyer, making his name in 1816 by a case he won against the state of New Hampshire through establishing as unconstitutional its interference with the running of his old college, Dartmouth.

After moving to Boston he became Massachusetts's most powerful voice nationally. For much of his career he sat in Congress, first as Representative then as Senator. Politically he started as a Federalist (*see* Patrick Henry, Washington and Jefferson) but later helped form the Whig Party, essentially opponents of President Andrew Jackson (1829–37). He was the Whig presidential candidate in 1836.

He was Secretary of State 1841–43. As such he brokered the Webster-Ashburton Treaty of 1842, which settled a US–British dispute over the Canadian border.

He was Secretary of State again from 1850 to 1852. This involved supporting the 1850 Compromise (*see* also Calhoun), which restricted slavery in new parts of the US but allowed Southern slave-owners to round up runaways, even in the North. It helped destroy the Whigs, but did postpone civil war and the break-up of the Union.

Webster had studied declamation at Dartmouth, where it formed part of the curriculum, and practised it as member of a literary society before becoming a lawyer. Even so, he had initially suffered from stage fright. He nonetheless developed a solid but impressive rhetorical style. His ability to compose his rolling periods in advance then hone them for delivery in his head made him arguably the foremost speaker of his age, and by no means just in America.

• Context of speech

This excerpt was delivered two centuries and a day after the Pilgrim Fathers had reached the spot. It was also widely read when disseminated in print.

66 **We have come to this rock to record here our homage for our Pilgrim Fathers; our sympathy in their sufferings; our gratitude for their labors; our admiration of their virtues; our veneration for their piety; and our attachment to those principles of civil and religious liberty which they encountered the dangers of the ocean, the storms of heaven, the violence of savages, disease, exile and famine to enjoy and to establish** ...

There is a local feeling connected with this occasion, too strong to be resisted; a sort of genius of the place, which inspires and awes us ...

We cast our eyes abroad on the ocean, and we see where the little bark, with the interesting group upon its deck, made its slow progress to the shore. We look around us, and behold the hills and promontories where the anxious eyes of our fathers first saw the places of habitation and of rest. We feel the cold which benumbed, and listen to the winds which pierced them.

Beneath us is the Rock, on which New England received the feet of the Pilgrims. We seem even to behold them, as they struggle with the elements, and, with toilsome efforts, gain the shore. We listen to the chiefs in council; we see the unexampled exhibition of female fortitude and resignation; we hear the whisperings of youthful impatience, and we see, what a painter of our own has also represented by his pencil, chilled and shivering childhood, houseless, but for a mother's arms, couchless, but for a mother's breast, till our own blood almost freezes ... "

Against nullification by South Carolina

US Senate
26–27 January 1830

• Context of speech

Webster was not above wordiness, but with him it was skilfully deployed. He saw its undesirability in lesser orators, among them President William H. Harrison. Webster tried to get Harrison to shorten his Inaugural speech, the length of which (delivered coatless, out of doors and in bitter cold) proved fatal to its author. Webster eventually resigned from the Cabinet of Harrison's successor Tyler over the latter's persistent vetoing of tariff bills. He was replaced by John C. Calhoun (*qv*), whose nullification doctrine Webster eloquently opposed.

'Nullification' argued that a state was sovereign, hence could cancel inconvenient Federal statutes. This clearly risked secession. To prevent such a catastrophe President Jackson, with Webster's support, was prepared in 1832 to invade South Carolina, which opposed the high tariffs that helped manufacturing states like Massachusetts at the expense of the agrarian South.

But the argument over nullification had already surfaced in 1828, with the first of the high tariffs. It was over the two days of 26–27 January 1830 that Webster in the Senate delivered the anti-nullification speech below. Nominally it was in riposte to Robert Y. Hayne, Senator from South Carolina. Actually it answered the much better-known South Carolinian Calhoun, who as Vice-President presided over the Senate, hence was excluded from speaking.

‟**Let me remind you that, in early times, no states cherished greater harmony, both of principle and feeling, than Massachusetts and South Carolina ... Shoulder to shoulder they went through the Revolution, hand in hand they stood round the administration of Washington ... Unkind feeling, if it exist, alienation, and distrust are the growth, unnatural to such soils, of false principles since sown. They are weeds, the seeds of which that same great arm never scattered ...**

I shall enter on no encomium upon Massachusetts; she needs none ...

There yet remains to be performed ... the most ... important duty ... It is to state, and to defend, what I conceive to be the true principles of the Constitution ...

I understand the honorable gentleman from South Carolina to maintain, that it is a right of the state legislatures to interfere, whenever, in their judgment, this government transcends its constitutional limits, and to arrest the operation of its laws.

I understand him to maintain this right, as a right existing *under* the Constitution, not as a right to overthrow it on the ground of extreme necessity, such as would justify violent revolution.

I understand him to maintain an authority, on the part of the states, thus to interfere, for the purpose of correcting the exercise of power by the general government, of checking it, and of compelling it to conform to their opinion of the extent of its powers.

I understand him to maintain that the ultimate power of judging of the constitutional extent of its own authority is not lodged exclusively in the general government, or any branch of it, but that, on the contrary, the states may lawfully decide for themselves, and each state for itself, whether, in a given case, the act of the general government transcends its power.

I understand him to insist, that, if the exigency of the case, in the opinion of any state government, require it, such state government may, by its own sovereign authority, annul an act of the general government which it deems plainly and palpably unconstitutional.

This is the sum of what I understand from him to be the South Carolina doctrine, and the doctrine which he maintains. I propose to consider it, and compare it with the Constitution. Allow me to say ... that I call this the South Carolina doctrine only because the gentleman himself has so denominated it. I do not feel at liberty to say that South Carolina, as a state, has ever advanced these sentiments. I hope she has not, and never may ...

If the government of the United States be the agent of the state governments, then they may control it, provided they can agree in the manner of controlling it. If it be the agent of the people, then the people alone can control it, restrain it, modify, or reform it. It is observable enough, that the doctrine for which the honorable gentleman contends leads him to the necessity of maintaining, not only that this general government is the creature of the states, but that it is the creature of each of the states severally, so that each may assert the power for itself of determining whether it acts within the limits of its authority.

It is the servant of four-and-twenty masters [*then the number of states in the Union*], of different will and different purposes and yet bound to obey all. This absurdity (for it seems no less) arises from a misconception as to the origin of this government and its true character. It is, Sir, the people's Constitution, the people's government, made for the people, made by the people, and answerable to the people. The people of the United States have declared that the Constitution shall be the supreme law. We must either admit the proposition, or dispute their authority ...

No state law is to be valid which comes in conflict with the Constitution, or any law of the United States passed in pursuance of it. But who shall decide this question of interference? To whom lies the last appeal? This, Sir, the Constitution itself decides ... by declaring 'That the judicial power shall extend to all cases arising under the Constitution and laws of the United States.'

These two provisions cover the whole ground. They are, in truth, the keystone of the arch. With these it is a government; without them it is a confederation. In pursuance of these clear and express provisions, Congress established, at its very first session, in the judicial act, a mode for carrying them into full effect, and for bringing all questions of constitutional power to the final decision of the Supreme Court. It then, Sir, became a government ...

While the Union lasts, we have high, exciting, gratifying prospects spread out before us and our children. Beyond that I seek not to penetrate the veil ... When my eyes shall be turned to behold for the last time the sun in heaven, may I not see him shine on the broken and dishonored fragments of a once glorious Union; on states dissevered, discordant, belligerent; on a land rent with civil feuds, or drenched, it may be, in fraternal blood.

Let their last feeble and lingering glance rather behold the gorgeous ensign of the republic, now known and honored throughout the earth, still full high advanced, its arms and trophies streaming in their original luster, not a stripe erased or polluted, not a single star obscured, bearing for its motto, no such miserable interrogatory as 'What is all this worth?', nor those other words of delusion and folly, 'Liberty first and Union afterwards'; but everywhere, spread all over in characters of living light, blazing on all its ample folds, as they float over the sea and over the land, and in every wind under the whole heavens, that other sentiment, dear to every true American heart, Liberty *and* Union, now and for ever, one and inseparable."

'Ireland shall be free'

Daniel ('The Liberator') O'Connell (1775–1847)
Mullaghmast, Co. Kildare
September 1843

• Biography

The two leading 19th-century Irish nationalist parliamentarians were O'Connell and Parnell (*qv*). Both as MPs were obliged to operate at Westminster since Pitt the Younger (*qv*) had by the 1801 Act of Union abolished the old Irish Parliament. Both demanded its restoration. But O'Connell was forced by circumstances to proceed cautiously and made his mark as much outside Parliament as in it, notably by speeches to mass but peaceful open-air meetings, in this respect anticipating Gladstone (*qv*). Parnell, who lived two generations later, could afford to be more aggressive and won his successes as a parliamentary tactician.

O'Connell started his career as a barrister, becoming known for his acute cross-examining in criminal cases. Politically he became the chief lay Catholic spokesman, at one point nearly getting involved in a duel with Sir Robert Peel (*qv*), then resident in Dublin as Chief Secretary for Ireland.

In 1828 he was elected MP for Co. Clare on such a wave of popular enthusiasm that the Government was obliged to repeal the anti-Catholic laws. O'Connell himself was barred from taking his Parliamentary seat through refusal to swear the oath acknowledging the King as head of the Church — the same rock on which Sir Thomas More (*qv*) had foundered. A new election for Co. Clare was ordered. O'Connell won it and in 1830 took his seat unopposed.

• Context of speech

O'Connell usually spoke spontaneously and in simple language, but in tone ranged between sarcastic vilification and what his critics called cringing servility. His speeches to open-air meetings began in 1843, during which he addressed no fewer than thirty-one. Attendance was usually around 100,000, though it has been claimed that on one occasion it reached 1,000,000.

The meetings were to have culminated in one at Clontarf, Co. Dublin, on 8 October, but the authorities panicked, banned it at the last minute and later had O'Connell arrested, although he had cooperated fully in the ban. Life in prison, together with other troubles led in 1847 to his going abroad for his health, hoping to reach Rome. He died at Genoa.

> " **I declare solemnly my ... conviction as a constitutional lawyer that the Union is totally void in ... principle and ... constitutional force.**
>
> I tell you that no portion of the Empire had the power to traffic on the rights and liberties of the Irish people. The Irish people nominated them [*sic*] to make laws, and not legislatures. They were appointed to act under the Constitution, and not annihilate it. Their delegation from the people was confined within the limits of the Constitution, and the moment the Irish Parliament went beyond those limits and destroyed the Constitution, that moment it annihilated its own power ...
>
> My friends, I want nothing for the Irish but their country, and I think the Irish are competent to obtain their own country for themselves ... This is our land, and we must have it ... Oh, what a scene surrounds us! It is not only the countless thousands of brave and active and peaceable and religious men that are here assembled, but nature herself has written her character with the finest beauty in the verdant plains that surround us ...
>
> The richest harvests that any land can produce are those reaped in Ireland ... Here are the sweetest meadows, the greenest fields, the loftiest mountains, the purest streams, the noblest rivers, the most capacious harbours — and her water power is equal to turn the machinery of the whole world.
>
> Oh my friends, it is a country worth fighting for. It is a country worth dying for. But, above all, it is a country worth being tranquil, determined, submissive and docile for ... I will see every man of you having a vote, and every man protected by the ballot from the agent or landlord ...
>
> I will see prosperity in all its gradations spreading through a happy, contented, religious land. I will hear the hymn of a happy people go forth at sunrise to God in praise of His mercies. And I will see the evening sun set down among the uplifted hands of a religious and free population. Every blessing that man can bestow and religion can confer upon the faithful heart shall spread throughout the land.
>
> Stand by me — join with me — I will say be obedient to me, and Ireland shall be free."

Resignation as Prime Minister

Sir Robert Peel (1788–1850)
House of Commons
29 June 1846

• Biography

Peel was a superb administrator and the first British politician to lead his party in a thoroughly professional fashion. He was not one of the land-owning aristocrats who still dominated politics in his day but from an industrialist background, hence lacked their prestige. His father bought him a seat in Parliament and in 1810 he delivered his maiden speech. Many considered it the best since Pitt the Younger's (*qv*).

As Chief Secretary for Ireland he clashed with Daniel O'Connell (*qv*), who may have coined the nickname 'Orange Peel', referring to Peel's Protestant outlook and perhaps the colour of his hair.

Peel next undertook purely parliamentary business, including the move to return to the gold standard, which when enacted brought reasonably stable prices till World War I.

In 1822 he became Home Secretary, as which he simplified and humanised the tortuous criminal code. Canning (*qv*) thought him the best Home Secretary ever. In 1829 he founded the Metropolitan Police, long called after him 'Peelers' and 'Bobbies'.

Appointed Prime Minister in late 1834 Peel called a general election. But first he issued a policy statement called the *Tamworth Manifesto*, now regarded as the document that launched the Conservative Party.

It was endorsed by the rest of the Cabinet, then disseminated nationally. Conservative candidates up and down the country referred to it, quoted from it, pledged themselves to abide by it — unremarkable now, but novel then.

By stressing cautious and piecemeal, not root-and-branch, reform Peel transformed his party from a reactionary organisation to the moderately progressive one which, despite claims to the contrary, it has arguably remained ever since.

As Conservative leader he in his early days regularly briefed backbenchers, circulated a whips' bulletin on coming events, put pairing under the whips' control and ensured regular attendance in Parliament. He stressed the importance of a party machine in the constituencies and maintained good relations with the press.

He became Prime Minister a second time in 1841. In the 1842 budget he re-introduced the principle of taxing incomes. (Pitt the Younger had tried it half a century earlier, but only as a temporary measure.) Peel also reduced many tariffs. This stimulated demand, so that in only a few years the state benefited financially and the average citizen saw the cost of living drop.

But he had to cope with mounting backbench unrest, much of it fomented by Disraeli (*qv*). By 1845 Peel concluded that the protectionist Corn Laws were more trouble than they were worth. He initially failed to convert his Cabinet to repeal, but eventually hung onto most of the Party's talent. The rank-and-file deserted. He resigned on 29 June 1846.

When he died, four years later, more than 400,000 artisans contributed to a working men's memorial of gratitude. No other Prime Minister has generated such a testimonial.

• Context of speech

The excerpt below is from his resignation speech. Peel was a logical rather than mesmerising orator. 'Facts', he once declared, 'are ten times more valuable than declamation'. He had a strong voice and spoke with a Lancashire accent but dropped his aitches.

"Within a few hours, probably, that power which I have held for a period of five years will be surrendered into the hands of another — without repining, without complaint on my part, with a more lively recollection of the support and confidence I have received during several years, than of the opposition which during a recent period I have encountered.

In relinquishing power, I shall leave a name, severely censured I fear by many who, on public grounds, deeply regret the severance of party ties — deeply regret that severance, not from interested or personal motives, but from the firm conviction that fidelity to party engagements — the existence and maintenance of a great party — constitutes a powerful instrument of government.

I shall surrender power severely censured also by others, who, from no interested motive, adhere to the principle of protection, considering the maintenance of it to be essential to the welfare and interests of the country. I shall leave a name execrated by every monopolist who, from less honourable motives, clamours for protection because it conduces to his own individual benefit.

But it may be that I shall leave a name sometimes remembered with expressions of good will in the abodes of those whose lot it is to labour, and to earn their daily bread by the sweat of their brow, when they shall recruit their exhausted strength with abundant and untaxed food, the sweeter because it is no longer leavened by a sense of injustice."

'Civis Romanus sum'

Henry John Temple, 3rd Viscount Palmerston (1784–1865)
House of Commons
25 June 1850

• Biography

Palmerston has long been admired as championing not just Britishness but what we now call human rights. Actually, when he supported foreign liberal and nationalist movements it was chiefly to avoid revolution. Even domestically, he was as much reactionary as reformer. But his adroit manipulation of the press and appeal to jingoistic passions tend to obscure these facts.

He was born before the French Revolution and first held office during the Napoleonic Wars, though his career only really took off 50 years later. His lack of respect for the monarchy suggests something even more anachronistic — the Whig magnifico of 1688–89 vintage, replacing one king with another as if they were unsatisfactory butlers.

He made no great mark in Parliament till 1829, when a speech of his condemning the Government's foreign policy brought him almost overnight success. It was due less to a good reception in Parliament than his distributing copies to the press.

He became a skilled propagandist, timing his constituency speeches so journalists could rush copy up to London for tomorrow's edition; more or less drafting leaders for papers to print as their own; and ingratiating himself with all editors across all shades of political opinion. Standard practice nowadays, but unusual then.

In 1830 he became Foreign Secretary and by his policies won radical support, an important factor in sustaining Whig administrations till the emergence of the Liberal Party proper a quarter of a century later. Nationally he dominated foreign affairs till his death.

Though nominally supporting liberal trends in Western Europe, his main aim there was to hamper France. His technique — threatening armed intervention — was stigmatised even in his day as 'gunboat diplomacy'; today it would constitute 'brinkmanship'. His run-ins were not all with foreigners. From the later 1840s on he clashed with Queen Victoria, who eventually had him sacked.

• Context of speech

Perhaps his most notable triumph as the British Lion standing up to foreign bullying was over Don Pacifico. The latter, an obscure Jewish merchant, was originally a British subject, having been born in Gibraltar. He had settled in Athens, his unhappy experiences there in 1847 being described in the speech extract below. Palmerston did not actively press his case till over two-and-a-half years later. When he did, he acted decisively, blockading Athens early in 1850. This caused an uproar back in Britain, where the Opposition won a vote of censure against the Government. Palmerston hit back on 25 June.

Right up to his death, two days short of his eighty-first birthday, Palmerston attended Commons debates regularly, though he sometimes dozed. By then his speeches tended to be set-piece affairs, since he could no longer read even notes, let alone gauge the expression on his audience's faces. Even in his early days he had been better at reading from a text. When he improvised he often stopped in mid-sentence till he could hit on the right word, extending his hands and making clutching motions..

66 “Stories have been told, involving imputations on the character of M. Pacifico. I know nothing of the truth … of these stories. All I know is, that M. Pacifico, after the time to which those stories relate, was appointed Portuguese Consul, first to Morocco and afterwards at Athens. It is not likely that the Portuguese Government would select … a person whose character they did not believe to be above reproach. But I … don't care what M. Pacifico's character is …

It is an abuse of argument to say that you are not to give redress to a man because in some former transaction he may have done something which is questionable. Punish him … if he is guilty, but don't pursue him as a pariah through life …

In … Athens … M. Pacifico, living … within forty yards of the great street, within a few minutes' walk of a guard-house, where soldiers were stationed, was attacked by a mob. Fearing injury, … he sent an intimation to the British Minister, who immediately informed the authorities. Application was made to the Greek Government for protection. No protection was afforded. The mob … employed themselves in gutting the house … , carrying away or destroying every single thing the house contained, and left it a perfect wreck …

The Greek Government neglected its duty, and did not pursue judicial inquiries, or institute legal prosecutions as it might have done … The sons of the Minister of War were pointed out to the Government as actors in the outrage. The Greek Government … declined to prosecute the Minister's sons …

This was a case in which we were justified in calling on the Greek Government for compensation … M. Pacifico having … been treated either with answers wholly unsatisfactory, or with a positive refusal, or with pertinacious silence, it came at last to this, either that his demand was to be abandoned altogether, or that … we were to proceed to use our own means of enforcing the claim.

'Oh, but', it is said, 'what an ungenerous proceeding to employ so large a force against so small a power!' Does the smallness of a country justify the magnitude of its evil acts? …

Was there anything … uncourteous [sic] in sending … a force which should make it manifest … that resistance was out of the question? Why, it seems to me … that it was more consistent with the honour and dignity of the [Greek] Government … that there should be placed before their eyes a force [to] which it would be … no indignity to yield …

I contend that we have not in our foreign policy done anything to forfeit the confidence of the country … I maintain that the principles which can be traced through all our foreign transactions, as the guiding rule and directing spirit of our proceedings, are such as deserve approbation.

I therefore fearlessly challenge the verdict which this House, as representing a political, a commercial, a constitutional country, is to give on the question now brought before it; whether the principles on which the foreign policy of Her Majesty's Government has been conducted, and the sense of duty which has led us to think ourselves bound to afford protection to our fellow subjects abroad, are proper and fitting guides for those who are charged with the Government of England; and whether, as the Roman, in days of old, held himself free from indignity, when he could say '*Civis Romanus sum*' ['I am a Roman Citizen']; so also a British subject, in whatever land he may be, shall feel confident that the watchful eye and the strong arm of England, will protect him against injustice and wrong."

'The Angel of Death'

John Bright (1811–89)
House of Commons
23 February 1855

• Biography

Lord John Russell, Prime Minister 1846–52 and 1865–66, in 1854 called Bright the House of Commons's most powerful speaker. A much later Prime Minister, Lord Salisbury, thought him the greatest master of English oratory in generations. One ordinary MP reckoned Bright the only man in the House of Commons — bar Gladstone (*qv*) — who ever changed his hearers' voting intentions by eloquence alone.

The subject of all this praise was a Lancashire mill-owner's son who got involved in speaking against the Corn Laws (*see* Peel), soon after which he started promoting Free Trade generally. He became an MP, avowedly as a Free Trader, in 1843 and remained in Parliament for over 40 years, eventually serving in several Liberal administrations.

• Context of speech

It was during the Crimean War (1954–6), that Bright made his 'Angel of Death' speech excerpted below. He delivered it at one o'clock in the morning while suffering from a nasty cold. It was an important part of his campaign to force Palmerston (*qv*), then Prime Minister, to make peace. He even offered to refrain from parliamentary speeches for 15 years if Palmerston would cease hostilities.

Bright has other accomplishments to his credit. During the American Civil War (*see* Lincoln) he was one of the chief British supporters of the North, helping in the 1863 Parliamentary session to defeat a motion to recognise the Confederacy. In old age he saw off a challenge by Lord Randolph Churchill (*qv*) during the 1885 general election.

In his very early days he learned his speeches by heart. But after on one occasion 'drying' he used notes, albeit full ones, writing out only the opening sentence and the winding up passage. In the early 1870s ill health weakened his speaking powers. By 1879 some of his oratorical strength had returned and he helped bring down the Disraeli administration following its inept conduct of foreign policy. In the 1880s his strength declined again, this time irreparably. He died partly, but appositely, of Bright's Disease.

66 **I should like to see any man get up and say that the destruction of 200,000 human lives lost on all sides during ... this unhappy conflict is not a sufficient sacrifice. You are not pretending to conquer territory. You are not pretending to hold ... towns. You have offered terms of peace which, as I understand them, I do not say are not moderate ...**

Breathes there a man in this House or in this country whose appetite for blood is so insatiable that, even when terms of peace have been offered and accepted, he pines for that assault in which of Russian, Turk, French and English ... 20,000 corpses will strew the streets of Sebastopol? ...

I am not now complaining of the war. I am not now complaining of the terms of peace ... But I wish to suggest to this House what, I believe, thousands and tens of thousands of the most educated and ... most Christian ... people of this country are feeling upon this subject, although, indeed, in the midst of a certain clamour in the country, they do not give public expression to their feelings.

Your country is not in an advantageous state at this moment. From one end of the kingdom to the other there is a general collapse of industry ... An increase in the cost of living is finding its way to the homes and hearts of ... the labouring population.

At the same time there is growing ... a bitter and angry feeling against that class which has ... long ... conducted ... public affairs ... I like political changes ... made as the result, not of passion, but ... deliberation and reason ...

I cannot but notice ... that an uneasy feeling exists as to the news which may arrive by the ... next mail from the East. I do not suppose ... your troops are to be beaten in actual conflict ... or that they will be driven into the sea. But I am certain that many homes in England in which ... now exists a fond hope that the distant one may return ... may be rendered desolate when the next mail shall arrive.

The Angel of Death has been abroad throughout the land. You may almost hear the beatings of his wings ... He takes his victims from the castle of the noble, the mansion of the wealthy and the cottage of the poor and ... lowly ... It is on behalf of all these classes that I make this solemn appeal."

Against slavery

Abraham Lincoln (1809–65)
16th President of the USA 1861–65
Peoria, Illinois
16 October 1854 _____

• Biography

Many historians consider Lincoln the greatest of the US Presidents. Nobody can deny that he was one of the greatest. He was certainly the greatest orator President.

Lincoln was Kentucky-born but from 1830 made Illinois his home state. He was long a lawyer, and his political career at national level took off relatively late. It coincided with and benefited from a mass shift in party allegiance, chiefly the decline of the Whigs. Originally a group united by little more than hostility towards President Andrew Jackson (*see* also Calhoun and Webster), they never really found better common ground even after Jackson's retirement.

Lincoln himself was long a Whig, remaining so till 1856. But he failed to get any Whig nomination in the 1842 Congressional elections. He failed in his bid as a Whig for the Senate in 1855. He failed to win the Whig Vice-Presidential nomination in 1856. Even after joining the new Republican Party, he failed in 1858 to win election to the Senate against Stephen A. Douglas.

But he had immense grit. It paid off. In 1860, having attracted national fame through his debates with Douglas two years earlier, he won the Republican presidential nomination and then the Presidency, Douglas being one of two Democratic candidates such that the Democratic vote was split. As President, Lincoln went on to win one of the bloodiest civil wars ever.

That done, he re-established the supremacy of the Union, to reassert which that war had in essence been fought. Along the way he freed America's slaves, having long realised how much slavery poisoned not just America's public life but its claim to democracy. He had just started his second term as President when he was gunned down by John Wilkes Booth, first cousin to the great-great-great grandfather of Cherie Booth, wife of the early-21st century British Prime Minister Tony Blair (*qv*).

Lincoln was largely self-taught, reading anything he could about American and British history and becoming particularly familiar with the Bible (*qv*) and

Shakespeare (*see* also Marc Antony and Olivier). He taught himself law from Blackstone's *Commentaries* (in full *Commentaries on the Laws of England* (1765–69), by the British jurist Sir William Blackstone). Blackstone was essentially a lecturer rather than writer, much as the Bible and Shakespeare are best appreciated when declaimed rather than read silently. It is not surprising to find in Lincoln's speeches distinct echoes of the latter two sources, but a glance at Blackstone shows how much his style influenced Lincoln too.

• Context of speech

This is from Lincoln's reply to Douglas on 16 October 1854. Douglas had been Senator from Illinois since 1847. Lincoln was not only relatively unknown, he had also given up full-time politics five years earlier. Douglas as Chairman of the Senate Committee on Territories had been instrumental in repealing the Missouri Compromise of 1820, which limited the spread of slavery in new states. And it was Douglas who now proposed the Kansas-Nebraska Act, which allowed potentially new states to adopt slavery much more easily. This prompted Lincoln to re-enter public life.

On 3 October 1854 at Springfield (the Illinois state capital and later Lincoln's place of burial) Douglas rallied his supporters. Lincoln, as part of his ultimately successful campaign for the State Legislature, replied against Douglas the next day, reading from a text. But the speech was not taken down by reporters till he gave it again nearly a fortnight later on 16 October, this time in Peoria, Illinois.

In the next century the expression 'will it play in Peoria?' became current. At its bluntest it meant 'is this act corny enough to fetch the rubes in your typical Mid-West backwater?' However unsophisticated Peorians may have become by then, they were in 1854 sufficiently discerning to appreciate Lincoln, repeatedly cheering him to the rafters throughout his four-hour performance.

66 **The Kansas-Nebraska Act's declared indifference, but, as I must think, covert real zeal for the spread of slavery, I cannot but hate.**
I hate it because of the monstrous injustice of slavery itself. I hate it because it deprives our republican example of its just influence in the world — enables the enemies of free institutions, with plausibility, to taunt us as hypocrites — causes the real friends of freedom to doubt our sincerity, and especially because it forces so many really good men amongst ourselves into an open war with the very fundamental principles of civil liberty …

Near eighty years ago we began by declaring that all men are created equal. But now from that beginning we have run down to the other declaration, that for some men to enslave others is a 'sacred right of self-government'. These principles cannot stand together …

Fellow countrymen — Americans South as well as North — shall we make no effort to arrest this? … In our greedy chase to make profit of the Negro, let us beware lest we 'cancel and tear to pieces' even the white man's charter of freedom.

Our republican robe is soiled and trailed in the dust. Let us repurify it. Let us turn and wash it white, in the spirit if not the blood of the Revolution. Let us turn slavery from its claims of 'moral right' back upon its existing legal rights and its argument of 'necessity'.

Let us return it to the position our fathers gave it, and there let it rest in peace. Let us readopt the Declaration of Independence and with it the practices and policy which harmonise with it.

Let North and South — let all Americans, let all lovers of liberty everywhere — join in the great and good work.

If we do this, we shall not only have saved the Union but we shall have so saved it as to make and to keep it forever worthy of the saving. We shall have so saved it that the succeeding millions of free happy people the world over shall rise up and call us blessed … "

'A house divided against itself cannot stand'

Springfield, Illinois
16 June 1858

• Context of speech

In June 1858 Lincoln, the Republican nominee for election to the Senate, debated against his old adversary Douglas, representing the Democrats. The excerpt below is from his acceptance speech on the sixteenth of the month at the state convention, held in Springfield. The speech itself was committed to paper before he spoke, but he apparently used scraps of the stuff rather than sheets. This suggests he elaborated on notes, however full, rather than read out an entire text. If so, such relative improvisation was uncharacteristic.

---

66 **If we could first know where we are, and whither we are tending, we could better judge what to do, and how to do it. We are now far into the fifth year since a policy was initiated with the avowed object and confident promise of putting an end to slavery agitation [*the Kansas-Nebraska Act of 1854*; see *above*]. Under the operation of that policy, that agitation has not only not ceased, but has constantly augmented.**

In my opinion, it will not cease until a crisis shall have been reached and passed. 'A house divided against itself cannot stand.' I believe this government cannot endure permanently half-slave and half-free. I do not expect the Union to be dissolved — I do not expect the house to fall — but I do expect it will cease to be divided.

It will become all one thing, or all the other. Either the opponents of slavery will arrest the further spread of it, and place it where the public mind shall rest in the belief that it is in the course of ultimate extinction; or its advocates will push it forward till it shall become alike lawful in all the states, old as well as new, North as well as South ...

Our cause, then, must be entrusted to, and conducted by, its own undoubted friends — those whose hands are free, whose hearts are in the work, who do care for the result. Two years ago the Republicans of the nation mustered over thirteen hundred thousand strong. We did this under the single impulse of resistance to a common danger, with every external circumstance against us. Of strange, discordant, and even hostile elements, we gathered from the four winds, and formed and fought the battle through, under the constant hot fire of a disciplined, proud and pampered enemy.

Did we brave all then, to falter now — now, when that same enemy is wavering, dissevered and belligerent? The result is not doubtful. We shall not fail. If we stand firm, we *shall not fail.* Wise counsels may accelerate, or mistakes delay it, but sooner or later the victory is sure to come."

Gettysburg Address

Gettysburg, Pennsylvania
19 November 1863

• Context of speech

Gettysburg, fought between 1 and 3 July 1863, was the turning point of the Civil War in the Washington area. So it was an obvious spot at which to commemorate war dead.

The main speaker at the dedication was Edward Everett, then distinguished but now virtually forgotten. His speech lasted two hours. Lincoln's two-and-a-half-minute-long address completely eclipsed Everett's. Not that it seemed so that day. Everett's original audience of some 15,000 had dispersed, and although Lincoln was applauded five times he himself thought his speech a failure. So did *The Times* of London, not for the first (or last) time hopelessly misjudging things.

Lincoln had fine-tuned his draft repeatedly beforehand. He said afterwards he should have spent even more time on it. It is allegedly the most often quoted speech of all time.

Two textual versions survive and there may have been a third reading copy. Lincoln usually followed his written text closely and people present later testified that he read it out. But even the most slavish follower of a prepared text will modify it in speech if at the last minute he notices a clumsily expressed thought or a word repeated just one time too often.

The version given here is the most polished. A few points of difference are put in square brackets where their use would have involved minimal loss of impact.

66 **Fourscore and seven years ago our fathers brought forth, upon this continent, a new nation, conceived in liberty and dedicated to the proposition that 'all men are created equal'.**
Now we are engaged in a great civil war, testing whether that nation, or any nation so conceived, and so dedicated, can long endure. We are met here on a great battlefield of that war. We have come to dedicate a portion of it as a final resting place for those who here gave their lives, that the nation might live. This we may in all propriety do.

But, in a larger sense, we cannot dedicate, we cannot consecrate, we cannot hallow this ground. The brave men, living and dead, who struggled here, have consecrated [*the other version repeats* 'hallowed'] it, far above our poor power to add or detract. The world will little note, nor long remember, what we say here; but [it] can never forget what they did here.

It is for us the living, rather, to be here dedicated to the great task which they [who fought here] have thus far so nobly advanced — that from these honored dead we take increased devotion to that cause for which they [here] gave the last full measure of devotion — that we here highly resolve that these dead shall not have died in vain, that this nation, under God, shall have a new birth of freedom, and that government of the people, by the people, for the people shall not perish from the earth."

'With malice toward none'

Second Inaugural address, Washington, DC
4 March 1865

• Context of speech

Lincoln was re-elected President in 1864 by an overwhelming majority. It was much greater than his 1860 victory, when he had often not even featured on the ballot in southern states. This excerpt is from his Second Inaugural address, which he thought among his best speeches.

" **Now, at the expiration of four years, during which public declarations have been constantly called forth on every point and phase of the great contest which still absorbs the attentions, and engrosses the energies of the nation, little that is new could be presented. The progress of our arms, upon which all**

**else chiefly depends, is as well known to the public as myself ...
With high hopes for the future, no prediction in regard to it is
ventured.**

On the occasion corresponding to this four years ago, all thoughts were
anxiously directed to an impending civil war. All dreaded it. All sought to avert
it. While the inaugural address was being delivered from this place, devoted
altogether to saving the Union without war, insurgent agents were in the city
seeking to destroy it without war, seeking to dissolve the Union ... Both parties
deprecated war. But one of them would make war rather than let the nation
survive; and the other would accept war rather than let it perish. And the war
came.

One eighth of the whole population were colored slaves, not distributed
generally over the Union, but localized in the southern part of it. These slaves
constituted a peculiar and powerful interest. All knew that this interest was,
somehow, the cause of the war. To strengthen, perpetuate, and extend this
interest was the object for which the insurgents would rend the Union, even by
war; while the government claimed no right to do more than to restrict the territorial enlargement of it.

Neither party expected for the war the magnitude, or the duration, which
it has already attained. Neither anticipated that the cause of the conflict might
cease with, or even before, the conflict itself should cease. Each looked for an
easier triumph, and a result less fundamental and astounding. Both read the
same Bible, and pray to the same God, and each invokes His aid against the
other ...

If we shall suppose that American slavery is one of those offences which,
in the providence of God, must needs come, but which, having continued
through His appointed time, He now wills to remove, and that He gives to both
North and South this terrible war as the woe due to those by whom the offence
came, shall we discern therein any departure from those divine attributes
which the believers in a living God always ascribe to Him?

Fondly do we hope, fervently we do pray, that this mighty scourge of war
may speedily pass away. Yet if God wills that it continue, until all the wealth
piled by the bondman's two hundred and fifty years of unrequited toil shall be
sunk, and until every drop of blood drawn with the lash shall be paid by
another drawn with the sword, as was said three thousand years ago, so still it
must be said 'the judgements of the Lord are true and righteous altogether.'

With malice toward none, with charity for all, with firmness in the right
as God gives us to see the right, let us strive on to finish the work we are in; to

bind up the nation's wounds, to care for him who shall have borne the battle, and for his widow, and for his orphan — to do all which may achieve and cherish a just and a lasting peace, among ourselves and with all nations."

On America's 'Gilded Age'

Mark Twain (*né* Samuel Langhorne Clemens) (1835–1910) London 1873

• Biography

Humour is notoriously the literary genre that dates most. Of its 19th-century practitioners Mark Twain is virtually the only one still readable. He was more than just a humourist. *Huckleberry Finn* (1884), reckoned his masterpiece, has independent literary merit.

Like many of the best writers, especially in America, he had a multiplicity of other occupations and travelled widely. Specifically, he was a typesetter, journalist and printer in the Mid-West and back East; a river pilot up and down the Mississippi; a Confederate militiaman (and deserter); a functionary and silver prospector in the Wild West; a newspaper editor on both the East and West Coasts; a lecturer; and publisher (notably of General Grant's hugely successful *Memoirs*), amateur scientist and speculator in patent devices in New York and New England.

He first took the *nom de plume* Mark Twain in 1863. It derived from the Mississippi pilots' call 'by the mark twain' [*i.e.*, two (fathoms depth of clear water)].

• Context of speech

In 1873 Mark Twain was on his second visit to Britain and attended a Fourth of July celebration for Americans in London. He had prepared the speech below. After giving its essence in a book of reminiscences, he continued to his readers: 'At least the above is the speech which I was *going* to make, but our minister, General Schenck ... made a great, long, inconceivably dull harangue, and wound up by saying that inasmuch as speech-making did not seem to exhilarate the guests much, all further oratory would be dispensed with during the evening.'

66 **This is an age of progress, and ours is a progressive land** ... We have a criminal jury system which is superior to any in the world; and its efficiency is only marred by the difficulty of finding twelve men every day who don't know anything and can't read. And I may observe that we have an insanity plea that would have saved Cain. I think I can say, and say with pride, that we have some legislatures that bring higher prices than any in the world.

I refer with effusion to our railway system, which consents to let us live, though it might do the opposite, being our owners. It only destroyed three thousand and seventy lives last year by collisions, and twenty-seven thousand two hundred and sixty by running over heedless and unnecessary people at crossings. The companies seriously regretted the killing of these thirty thousand people, and went so far as to pay for some of them — voluntarily, of course, for the meanest of us would not claim that we possess a court treacherous enough to enforce a law against a railway company.

But I must not stand here and brag all night. However, you won't mind a body bragging a little about his country on the Fourth of July. It is a fair and legitimate time to fly the eagle. I will say only one more word of brag — and a hopeful one. It is this. We have a form of government which gives each man a fair chance and no favor. With us no individual is born with a right to look down upon his neighbor and hold him in contempt. Let such of us as are not dukes find our consolation in that. And ... unhappy as is the condition of our political morality today, England has risen up out of a far fouler since the days when Charles II ennobled courtesans and all political place was a matter of bargain and sale ... "

Attack on Peel

**Benjamin Disraeli, 1st and last Earl of
Beaconsfield (1804–81)
House of Commons
1846** _____

• Biography

The first and so far only wholly Jewish premier, Disraeli was personally the most exotic holder of the post ever, being a dandy in youth, histrionically mannered all his life and author of amusing novels that often caused a sensation, and once an uproar. Yet he pushed through more nuts-and-bolts social reform measures than any other premier his century.

He was also a major extender of popular voting rights, though somewhat accidentally, and founder of the Conservative tendency to make patriotism its special preserve. Lastly, he lured Queen Victoria from her seclusion following the death of Albert, a seclusion that had fed republicanism, and exercised a very personal fascination over her thereafter.

His Jewishness was familial not religious, his father having quarrelled with his synagogue and having Disraeli baptised an Anglican. Disraeli entered Parliament in 1837. He led a knot of party rebels and presently overthrew his chief, Peel (*qv*). This split the Conservative Party into a majority of protectionists under Disraeli and Lord Derby, while a rump of top talent, including Gladstone (*qv*), stuck with Peel.

Disraeli's major triumph in office was to outflank the Liberals when introducing the Reform Bill of 1867. He adroitly ensured that though it extended the suffrage, the Conservatives largely benefited. This, more than anything, secured him the party leadership on Derby's retirement in 1868.

He lost the 1868 election to Gladstone, by now his arch-foe, but in the 1874 election won an outright majority. His subsequent legislative programme improved matters as regards trades unions, public health, housing, agricultural tenancies, savings, the employment of women and children and standards in food and pharmaceuticals.

In foreign affairs his accomplishments were positively spectacular. He in 1875 acquired for Britain an interest in the Suez Canal Company. He made Queen

Victoria Empress of India. He faced down Russia when war seemed imminent over the decaying Ottoman Empire in the Middle East. His prestige at this point rose so high that Queen Victoria offered him a dukedom.

He lost his touch thereafter. The Zulu and Afghan Wars of 1879 went badly, agriculture declined and in the 1880 election the Conservatives were defeated.

• Context of speech

The excerpt below was the climax of Disraeli's attacks on Peel. His diction in his younger days was once described as 'lisping affectation' but warming to an implicitly more masculine delivery as he proceeded. Later he sometimes affected a stammer. He pronounced each syllable of words most people slur ('biz-y-ness' for 'biz-n'ss', *i.e.*, 'business', and 'Parlee-a-ment' for 'Parl'm'nt'). His voice was calm, low-pitched and sometimes monotonous, though at others well-modulated, and always clear. He pronounced his own peerage title 'Beeconsfield' rather than 'Beckonsfield', as if it were actually spoken the way it was written, something only the very unsophisticated normally do with proper names in British English usage.

"The Right Hon. Gentleman [*Peel*], has been accused of foregone treachery – of long meditated deception – of a desire unworthy of a great statesman, even if an unprincipled one – of always having intended to abandon the opinions by professing which he rose to power ...

I entirely acquit the Right Hon. Gentleman of any such intention. I do it for this reason: that when I examine the career of this minister ... I find that for between thirty and forty years ... that Right Hon. Gentleman has traded on the ideas and intelligence of others. His life has been one great appropriation clause. He is a burglar of others' intellect ...

And ... even now, in this last scene of the drama, when the party whom he unintentionally betrayed is to be unintentionally annihilated ... the Right Hon. Gentleman ... is going to pass a project which, I believe it is a matter of notoriety, is not of his own invention.

After the ... Right Hon. Gentleman made his first exposition of his scheme, a gentleman ... learned in all the political secrets behind the scenes[,] met me, and said 'Well, what do you think of your chief's plan?' Not knowing exactly what to say, but, taking up a phrase which has been much used in the House, I observed 'Well, I suppose it's a "great and comprehensive" plan.' 'Oh', he replied, 'we know all about it. It was offered to us. It is not his plan. It's Popkins's plan.'

And is England to be governed by 'Popkins's plan'? Will he go with it to that ancient and famous England that once was governed by statesmen — by Burleighs [*see* Elizabeth I] and by Walpoles, by a Chatham [*see* Pitt the Elder] and a Canning [*qv*] — will he go to it with this fantastic scheming of some presumptuous pedant?

I won't believe it. I have that confidence in the common sense … of our countrymen, that I believe they will not long endure this huckstering tyranny of the Treasury Bench — these political pedlars that bought their party in the cheapest market, and sold us in the dearest …

It may be vain now … to tell them that there will be an awakening of bitterness. It may be idle now, in the spring-tide of their economic frenzy, to warn them that there may be an ebb of trouble. But the dark and inevitable hour will arrive. Then, when their spirit is softened by misfortune, they will recur to those principles that made England great … "

Attack on Gladstone

Manchester
3 April 1872

• Context of speech

The excerpt below began Disraeli's 1874 return to power. The eloquence of the full speech is the more remarkable since he fortified himself during the three-and-a-quarter hours it took to deliver with two bottles of white brandy (so chosen because indistinguishable from water).

66 **I cannot pretend that our position either at home or abroad is … satisfactory. At home, at a period of immense prosperity, with a people contented and naturally loyal, we find to our surprise the most extravagant doctrines professed …**

… this … is accounted for … by the circumstances under which the present administration was formed[,] … the first instance … of a British Administration … formed on a principle of violence. Their specific was to despoil churches and plunder landlords, and what has been the result? Sedition rampant, treason thinly veiled and whenever a vacancy occurs in the representation a candidate is returned pledged to the disruption of the realm.

Her Majesty's new ministers proceeded in their career like a body of men under the influence of some delirious drug. Not satiated with the spoliation and anarchy of Ireland, they began to attack every institution and every interest, every class and calling in the country …

Let us look what they have done with the Admiralty … The Navy was not merely an instance of profligate expenditure, but of incompetent and inadequate management. A great revolution was promised in its administration. A gentleman [*Hugh Childers (1827–96)*], almost unknown to English politics, was strangely preferred to one of the highest places in the councils of Her Majesty [*First Lord of the Admiralty*]. He set to at his task with ruthless activity. The Consultative Council, under which Nelson had gained all his victories, was dissolved …

But, gentlemen, as time advanced it was not difficult to perceive that extravagance was being substituted for energy by the Government. The unnatural stimulus was subsiding. Their paroxysms ended in prostration. Some took refuge in melancholy, and their eminent chief alternated between a menace and a sigh. As I sat opposite the Treasury Bench the ministers reminded me of one of those marine landscapes not very unusual on the coasts of South America. You behold a range of exhausted volcanoes. Not a flame flickers on a single pallid crest. But the situation is still dangerous. There are occasional earthquakes, and ever and anon the dark rumbling of the sea… "

On the Congress of Berlin

The Mansion House, London
27 June 1878

• Context of speech

The third excerpt was delivered following Disraeli's return from the Congress of Berlin, which had met to settle affairs following the Russo-Turkish war of 1877–78. Britain had lent its not entirely disinterested assistance, acquiring as part of the Convention of Constantinople (an ancillary Turco-British defence pact) the island of Cyprus.

"**One of the results of my attending the Congress of Berlin has been to prove, what I always suspected ... , that neither the Crimean War [*see* Bright] nor this horrible, devastating war ... just terminated [*between Russia and Turkey*] would have taken place if England had spoken with the necessary firmness ...**

Suppose ... that my noble friend [*Lord Salisbury, Disraeli's Foreign Secretary*] and I had come back with the Treaty of Berlin, and had not taken the step [*negotiating the Convention of Constantinople*] which is to be questioned within the next eight-and-forty hours, could we with any self-respect have met our countrymen when they asked 'what securities have you made for the peace of Europe? ... Why', they could say, 'all we have gained by the Treaty of Berlin is probably the peace of a few years, and at the end of that time the same phenomenon will arise and the Ministers of England must patch up the affair as well as they could.'

That was not the idea of public duty entertained by my noble friend and myself. We thought the time had come when we ought to ... produce ... order out of the anarchy ... that had so long prevailed. We asked ourselves, was it absolutely a necessity that the fairest provinces of the world should be the most devastated ... and ... that there is no security for life or property so long as that country is in perpetual fear of invasion ...?

... Under these circumstances ... we recommended the course we have taken. And I believe ... the consequences ... will ... secure peace and order in a portion of the globe ... hitherto ... seldom blessed by these celestial visitants ...

But I am sorry to say that though we taxed our brains ... to establish a policy which might be beneficial to the country, we have not satisfied those who are our critics.

I was astonished to learn that the Convention [*of Constantinople*] ... has been described as 'an insane convention'. It is a strong epithet. I do not myself pretend to be as competent a judge of insanity as my Right Honourable opponent [*Gladstone* (qv), *whose sister Helen had been unbalanced, though whether Disraeli intended such a below-the-belt reference is doubtful; more probably he intended to imply Gladstone himself was unbalanced*].

I would put this issue to an English jury: which do you believe the most likely to enter into an insane convention — a body of English gentlemen honoured by ... their sovereign and the confidence of their fellow-subjects, managing your affairs for five years, I hope with prudence, and not altogether without success — or a sophistical rhetorician inebriated with the exuberance of his own verbosity, and gifted with an egotistical imagination that can at all times command an interminable and inconsistent series of arguments to malign an opponent and to glorify himself? ... "

Attack on Disraeli

W(illiam) E(wart) Gladstone (1809–98)
House of Commons
17 December 1852

• Biography

Gladstone was the youngest son of a self-made merchant, part of whose fortune came from slave-owning, a practice the merchant defended in print. Gladstone's fervent taking-up of causes, intensified by self-mortification, was arguably an attempt to sublimate these unattractive facts.

He entered Parliament in 1832 and in his maiden speech attacked too hasty a freeing of slaves in British-held territories, so any sublimation process had yet to start. He dissented from official policy in the 1840 Opium War, when the British were forcing narcotics on the Chinese, but even this may have owed more to his sister Helen's drug addiction than to liberal principles.

By 1843 he was in Peel's (*qv*) Conservative Cabinet. In 1845 he resigned over Peel's proposal to increase subsidies to Irish Catholic seminarists, though he then voted for it, having become horrified by the bigotry of his more Protestant supporters.

Yet in these years he established a reputation not just for oratory but tact. He was in short already the odd mixture of canniness and idealism that both fascinated and exasperated his contemporaries. The Liberal politician Henry Labouchère said 'I don't object to Gladstone always having the ace of trumps up his sleeve … merely to his belief that the Almighty put it there.'

Gladstone's ability made him indispensable, despite his idiosyncrasies. In late 1845, when Peel's administration began to crumble over his proposed rescinding of the protectionist Corn Laws, Peel made Gladstone Colonial Secretary. Under the then rules, Gladstone had to seek re-election to Parliament. But the ducal owner of the pocket borough for which he sat was a protectionist. Gladstone looked in vain for another seat, hence remained out of Parliament and was unable to counter Disraeli's (*qv*) attacks on Peel. He might otherwise have saved the Conservatives from splitting (and ended his future foe Disraeli's career).

• Context of speech

In 1852 Gladstone began his lengthy duel with Disraeli by demolishing Disraeli's budget. Gladstone was more than equal to this through his incomparable mastery of detail, phenomenal memory for facts and figures and prodigious powers of instant calculation, though he also said that the speech had been fermenting within him for days. The speech, delivered after one in the morning on 17 December, resulted in a 19–vote defeat for the Government, which forthwith resigned.

66 **I must tell the Right Hon. Gentleman [*Disraeli*] that whatever he has learned — and he has learned much — he has not yet learned the limits of discretion, of moderation and of forbearance that ought to restrain the … language of every Member of this House …**

After the deliberation of months, the Right Hon. Gentleman produces a plan [*the budget*] which … he might have as well given … us the first hour after he took office as after the six months during which he has remained in office …

I come now to the question which is vital … Has the Chancellor … included in his new scheme … the subversion of … those rules of prudence … necessary for the conduct of … financial affairs? Has he, in other words, presented … a budget without a surplus [*then considered gravely unorthodox*]? …

If I vote against the Government, I vote in support of those Conservative principles which I thank God are common in a great degree to all parties in the … House … , but of which I thought it was the peculiar pride and glory of the Conservative Party to be the champions … Are you not the Party of 1842 [see

Peel, who although then Premier had been the real author of the 1842 budget]? Are you not the Party who, in times of difficulty, chose to cover a deficit, and to provide a large surplus? And are you the same Party … united now in … prosperity, to convert a large surplus into a deficiency?

I appeal to you by what you were then. I appeal to you to act now as you did then. Us [*the Peelites*] you have cast off. I do not blame you for that. I … view with regret the rupture of party ties — my disposition is rather to retain them.

I confess that I look, if not with suspicion, at least with disapprobation, on anyone who is disposed to treat party connexions as … of small importance. My opinion is that party ties closely appertain to those principles of confidence which we entertain for the House …

But us you have cast off for inconsistency. Have we ever complained of that? Have we ever made it a matter of charge against you? No, certainly not. You owe us no grudge on that account. But you must remember that you also have a character to maintain — that you also are on your trial — that you also are bound to look with suspicion on those principles of financial policy which depart from those rules that not only all statesmen, but the common sense of the country, agree to be essential to the prosperity of this nation … "

Note

Because Gladstone's career is so long, some narrative of the years 1852 (the time of the first speech) and 1879 (the time of his second) is necessary.

Gladstone now became Chancellor, as which his chief virtue was his anxiety to lower income tax. But when the Crimean War forced him to raise it he typically shifted the responsibility onto God's shoulders, ample though these doubtless are. 'The expenses of war are a moral check', he said, 'which it has pleased the Almighty to impose upon … lust of conquest …'

He was still not a full Liberal. Parliamentary reform he opposed as late as 1857. In 1859 he accepted the new Premier Palmerston's (*qv*) offer of a Cabinet post, choosing the Chancellorship yet again. Gladstone's earlier opposition to Palmerston was well-known, but he ignored charges of inconsistency.

Nonetheless, every Cabinet meeting he attended, he took a letter of resignation with him, though it remained unused. He particularly opposed

Palmerston's high defence estimates. His Liberalism was now stronger in other respects. In an 1864 debate on extending the vote he accepted the idea of universal male suffrage. This alarmed Palmerston. Gladstone resorted to pamphleteering to get his point across nationally, in this respect anticipating 20th-century agitprop techniques.

He lost his seat in 1865 and partly in consequence embarked on speaking tours around Britain, another innovation of his. When Lord John Russell succeeded Palmerston in late 1865, he made Gladstone Leader of the Commons. When Russell retired as Liberal leader in 1867, Gladstone was his inevitable successor.

His new cause was to disestablish the Church of Ireland. During the 1868 general election he broadened his target to include the Protestant Ascendancy in Ireland. Ireland became not just a party political problem but affected his relations with Queen Victoria. Gladstone sensibly wanted the Royal Family to show their faces there more. Victoria refused, and came to detest Gladstone.

Gladstone nonetheless chipped away at the Irish problem. Had he attacked it root and branch, in the way he did trees (he was an energetic lumberjack at his country seat, Hawarden Castle; *see* also Lord Randolph Churchill), he might conceivably have got somewhere. As it was, his extending Irish tenant rights was undermined by depressed agricultural prices from the mid-1870s on.

On the rights of the savage

Dalkeith Corn Exchange, near Edinburgh
26 November 1879

• Context of speech

On losing the 1874 election, Gladstone resigned as Liberal leader. The 1876 massacre by the Turks of numbers of their Christian subjects in the Balkans inspired him to write a denunciatory pamphlet. It sold 200,000 copies in three and a half weeks. Gladstone had barely retained his English seat in 1874, so now looked further afield, alighting on Midlothian in Scotland.

The Dalkeith audience numbered some 3,500 and would seem, judging by Gladstone's choice of words, to have been mostly women. The Afghanistan reference denotes an unsuccessful episode in Disraeli's conduct of foreign affairs.

"Look back over ... history. Consider the feelings with which we now regard wars that our forefathers ... supported ... Consider ... the American War [*of Independence*], now condemned by 999 out of every 1,000 persons in this country, ... which [*yet*] for years was enthusiastically supported by the mass of the population ...

Do not suffer appeals to national pride to blind you to the dictates of justice. Remember the rights of the savage, as we call him. Remember that the happiness of his humble home, ... the sanctity of life in the hill villages of Afghanistan among the winter snows, is as inviolable in the eye of Almighty God as can be your own.

Remember that He who has united you ... as human beings ... has bound you by the law of mutual love; that that mutual love is not limited by the shores of this island, is not limited by the boundaries of Christian civilization; that it passes over the whole surface of the earth, and embraces the meanest along with the greatest ... "

Against the Zulu War

St Andrew's Hall, Glasgow
5 December 1879

• Context of Speech

The audience numbered almost twice the Dalkeith one – 6,000 to 6,500.

"We have finance in confusion. We have legislation in intolerable arrear. We have honour compromised by the breach of public law. We have public distress aggravated by the destruction of confidence. We have Russia aggrandised and yet estranged. We have Turkey befriended ... but mutilated, and sinking every day. We have Europe restless and disturbed ...

In Africa you have before you the memory of bloodshed, of military disaster, the record of 10,000 Zulus … slain for no other offence than their attempt to defend against your artillery with their naked bodies their hearths and homes, their wives and families.

You have the invasion of a free people [*the Boers*] in the Transvaal. And you have … in one quarter or another … prospects of further disturbance and shedding of blood.

You have Afghanistan ruined. You have India not advanced, but thrown back in government, subjected to heavy and unjust charges, subjected to what may well be termed … a system of oppression …

Amidst the whole of this pestilent activity, … this distress and bloodshed … not in one instance did we either do a deed, or speak an effectual word, on behalf of liberty …

To call this policy Conservative is, in my opinion, a pure mockery, and an abuse of terms. Whatever it may be in its motive, it is in its result disloyal. It is in its essence thoroughly subversive …

Is this the way … a free nation inhabiting these islands wishes to be governed? Will the people, be it now or be it months hence, ratify the deeds that have been done …? The whole humble aim … of my proceedings has been to bring home … this great question to the mind and to the conscience of the community at large.

If I cannot decide the issue — and of course I have no power to decide it — I wish at least to endeavour to make it understood by those who can. And I cherish the hope that … I have spared no effort to mark the point at which the roads divide — the one path which plunges into suffering, discredit and dishonour, the other which slowly … but surely leads a free and … high-minded people towards the blessed ends of prosperity and justice, of liberty and peace."

Opening the Home Rule debate

• Context of speech

When the size of the 1879–80 Liberal landslide was announced it was clear that no government was possible without Gladstone and that the only possible post in it for Gladstone was as leader, despite his standing down previously. A popular choice of chief executive had been foisted on not just the Sovereign but the aristocracy and the official leaders of the winning party — in effect, a presidential election, Britain's only one to date.

But in Parliament Gladstone's party members proved intractable. Luckily he encountered a weak Opposition. Many people were intimidated by his personality. It led to their suppressing criticism of his wilder pronouncements and explains how he got away with such extraordinary flights of rhetorical fancy.

He presently started throwing Britain's weight around overseas. Nearer home he faltered. The Irish MPs, under Parnell (*qv*), were becoming formidable in Parliament. Gladstone's response was in effect to alternate between coercion and conciliation.

He became increasingly convinced that nothing less for Ireland would suffice than Home Rule (what today would be called devolution). He became Prime Minister for the third time early in 1886. His Home Rule proposals split the Liberals permanently. The right wing eventually coalesced with Conservatives, meanwhile becoming known as Unionists.

Gladstone's speeches in support of his Home Rule Bill in spring 1886 were among the most powerful of his life. The Bill was defeated by 341 to 311. It was one of the best-attended divisions in Parliament's history, with only 18 MPs not voting out of a total of 670. Gladstone called a general election. It reduced his supporters to 191. The Conservatives formed a government but violence in Ireland continued. In the 1892 election the Liberals won 273 seats, the Conservatives 269, the Irish Nationalists 81, the Liberal Unionists 46 and the new Labour movement 1. The first group allied with the third and Gladstone became Prime Minister a fourth time.

The second Home Rule Bill resembled the first. But fighting erupted in Parliament. Irish-related stocks fell. The City of London grew restless. The Bill eventually passed the Commons, but failed in the Lords.

Gladstone proposed reintroducing a Home Rule Bill. What brought him down was his long-standing incomprehension of the country's defence needs. A Conservative motion to modernise the Navy was genuinely timely. Gladstone became isolated within his own Cabinet. In March 1894, after weeks negotiating with his ministers, he resigned.

Gladstone was reckoned by contemporaries best at off-the-cuff orations, in part because he spent little time in preparation, though he later edited such speeches for publication, chiefly as pamphlets. To that extent many versions of the non-Parliamentary speeches that have come down to us may not be verbatim, though the Midlothian Campaign speeches were more carefully thought out than most since they needed to vary and would be reported nationally. Conversely, on an occasion when Gladstone forgot to bring his spectacles along, hence could not read his notes, the speech he actually gave may have been the better for it.

His voice was rich and melodious. His flashing eye is frequently remarked on, also his graceful gestures. Clearly he was as much a master of deportment as of declamation. Perhaps more so: his prolixity and complex sentence structure now read poorly, though they enthralled audiences then. He avoided personalities, unlike Disraeli.

An 1888 recording of his voice exists in the National Sound Archive. It is of poor quality but a faint Liverpool accent is just discernible, while the authority of tone is unmistakeable. A Liverpudlian of Gladstone's generation, before mass Irish immigration, would, however, have lacked the nasal quality made famous by John Lennon.

Gladstone's Parliamentary speeches fill around 15,000 columns of *Hansard*, a record unlikely to be beaten.

---

66 **The two questions of land and ... Irish government are ... inseparably connected, for they are the ... channels ... to that question most vital of all – namely, ... social order in Ireland** ...

It is impossible to depend upon the finding of a jury in a case of agrarian crime according to the facts as they are viewed by the Government, ... judges and ... the public ...

It is not to be denied that there is great interference in Ireland with individual liberty in the shape of intimidation. Now, Sir, I am not about to assume the tone of the Pharisee on this occasion. There is a great deal of intimidation in England, too, when people find occasion for it; and if we, the English and the Scotch, were under the conviction that we had such grave cause to warrant irregular action, as is the conviction entertained by a very large part of the population in Ireland, I am not at all sure that we would not ... resort to the rude and unjustifiable remedy of intimidation ...

Law is discredited in Ireland, and discredited in Ireland upon this ground especially — that it comes to the people of that country with a foreign accent, and in a foreign garb ...

The case of Ireland, though she is represented here not less fully than England and Scotland, is not the same as that of England and Scotland. England, by her own strength, and by her vast majority in this House, makes her own laws just as independently as if she were not combined with two other countries.

Scotland — a small country, smaller than Ireland, [yet is] a country endowed with a spirit so masculine that never in the long course of history, excepting for two brief periods ... was the superior strength of England such as to enable her to put down the national freedom beyond the border.

The consequence is that the mainspring of law in England is felt by the people to be English; the mainspring of law in Scotland is felt by the people to be Scotch; but the mainspring of law in Ireland is not felt by the people to be Irish.

... What we seek is the ... establishment, by the authority of Parliament, of a Legislative Body sitting in Dublin, for the conduct of both legislation and administration under the conditions which may be prescribed by the Act defining Irish, as distinct from Imperial, affairs ... "

At the end of the same debate, exactly two months later (8 June 1886), Gladstone wound up with the following, which in its pathos and the way it personifies Ireland could almost have come from O'Connell (*qv*):

"Ireland stands at your bar, expectant, hopeful, almost suppliant. Her wounds are the words of truth and soberness. She asks a blessed oblivion of the past, and in that oblivion our interest is deeper than even here ...

So I hail the demand of Ireland for what I call a blessed oblivion of the past. She asks also a boon for the future, and that boon for the future, unless we are much mistaken, will be a boon to us in respect of honour no less than a boon to her in respect of happiness, prosperity and peace ... "

Attack on Gladstone

Lord Randolph Churchill (1849–95)
Blackpool
24 January 1884 _____

• Biography

Disraeli (*qv*) ran, as it were, a nicely judged race despite his early skittishness, cleverly jockeying Toryism to electability by clinging tightly to such elements of democratisation as a widened franchise, becoming Chancellor along the way and finishing as Prime Minister. At first Lord Randolph Churchill looked like following suit, particularly in his *ad hominem* attacks on Gladstone (*qv*). But he lacked Disraeli's staying power and, oddly for so capable a devotee of real-life racing, scratched from all further events shortly after winning the Chancellorship Stakes.

He was a younger son of a duke, specifically the 7th of Marlborough. Disraeli had a penchant for such creatures (three of his closest associates were ducal younger sons) and had first met Lord Randolph when the latter was in early manhood. Lord Randolph entered Parliament as a Conservative in 1874. But it was not till 1878, by which time Disraeli was a spent force, that he attracted attention. This he did by attacking the feebler among his party leaders, among them George Sclater-Booth, President of the Local Government Board.

But it was hard to take Lord Randolph seriously when, in his Sclater-Booth-baiting, he observed how often mediocrity bore a double-barrelled name. His own family, which had tacked 'Churchill' onto the patronymic 'Spencer' three generations back, sufficiently disproved the generalisation.

Indeed it was not till the 1880 Parliament that Lord Randolph begain to seem more than just a performing flea. The Conservatives had now lost power, were demoralised and weakly led. Lord Randolph effectively set up his own opposition and with a few followers constituted what came to be called the 'Fourth Party' (the first and second being Liberals and Conservatives, the third the Irish bloc (*see* also Parnell); oddly enough, 'the Fourth Party' was an Irish MP's coinage).

By intensive speech-making Lord Randolph and his followers did much to disrupt Parliamentary business. But he also improved grass-roots organisation among provincial Conservatives and supported their claim to a say in running the Party. His approach came to be known as 'Tory Democracy'. When Gladstone's administration fell in mid-1885, Lord Randolph became India Secretary, winning civil servants' respect as a very competent administrator. He also annexed Upper Burma.

When in spring 1886 Gladstone, now back in power, introduced his Irish Home Rule Bill, Lord Randolph was among its fiercest opponents. Some of his phrases at this time have become immortal: the term 'Unionist', the tag 'Ulster will fight, and Ulster will be right' and his calling Gladstone 'an old man in a hurry'.

The Conservatives won the July 1886 election and Lord Randolph was made Chancellor of the Exchequer and Leader of the House of Commons. He resigned five months later, specifically because he opposed higher defence expenditure. He then withdrew from full-time politics, becoming even more involved than hitherto in racing, also in social life, towards which, unlike racing, he was often equivocal.

By the early 1890s his speaking powers had deteriorated. He died aged 45 — from syphilis, it was long thought, but in 1997 Dr. John Mather, of the US Veterans' Administration, demolished this, suggesting instead circulatory problems induced by heavy smoking, exacerbated perhaps by a brain tumour.

• Context of speech

Lord Randolph had a somewhat guttural voice, also a noticeable lisp and a distorted delivery, as if his tongue was too big for his mouth. (Compare the alleged lisp and actual slurring of his son Winston.) He memorised his speeches, though he carried sheafs of notes, perhaps as a 'comfort blanket' rather than true *aide memoire*. In Parliament he comported himself with dignity. Before general audiences he waved his arms about vigorously.

66 **Gentlemen, we live in an age of advertisement, the age of Holloway's Pills, … Colman's Mustard … Horniman's Pure Tea. And the policy of lavish advertisement has been so successful in commerce that the Liberal Party, with its usual enterprise, has adapted it to politics.**

The Prime Minister [*Gladstone*] is the greatest living master of the art of personal political advertisement. Holloway, Colman and Horniman are nothing compared with him. Every act of his, whether it be for the purposes of health, or of recreation, or of religious devotion, is spread before the eyes of every man, woman and child in the United Kingdom on large and glaring placards…

For the purposes of recreation he has selected the felling of trees. And we may usefully remark that his amusements, like his politics, are essentially destructive. Every afternoon the whole world is invited to assist at the crashing fall of some beech or elm or oak [*one of the 'presidential' aspects of Gladstone's ascendancy at this time was the way mass deputations from Lancashire towns visited him at his country seat of Hawarden Castle, rather as US Presidential hopefuls in that age conducted 'front-porch' campaigns*]. The forest laments in order that Mr Gladstone may perspire ...

It has always appeared to me somewhat incongruous and inappropriate that the great chief of the Radical party should reside in a castle. But to proceed. One would have thought that the deputation would have been received in the house, in the study, in the drawing-room, or even in the dining-room.

Not at all. That would have been out of harmony with the advertisement 'boom'. Another scene had been arranged, The working men were guided through the ornamental grounds into the wide-spreading park, strewn with the wreckage and the ruin of the Prime Minister's sport.

All around them, we may suppose, lay the rotting trunks of once umbrageous trees. All around them, tossed by the winds, were boughs and bark and withered shoots. They come suddenly on the Prime Minister and Master Herbert [*Gladstone's son and Private Secretary*], in scanty attire and profuse perspiration, engaged in the destruction of a gigantic oak, just giving its last dying groan. They are permitted to gaze and to worship and adore and, having conducted themselves with exemplary propriety, are each of them presented with a few chips as a memorial of that memorable scene ...

To all who leaned upon Mr Gladstone, who trusted in him and who hoped for something from him — chips, nothing but chips; hard, dry, un-nourishing, undigestible chips."

On Tory democracy

St James's Hall, Manchester
6 November 1885

• Context of speech

Lord Randolph could be equally scathing about the Marquess of Hartington (later 8th Duke of Devonshire), nominally Gladstone's successor as Liberal leader following

Gladstone's resignation in 1874 but in the event supplanted by Gladstone on the latter's comeback in 1879–80.

The speech excerpted below was delivered to a vast throng, just before polling started in what turned out to be a dead heat general election (*see* Gladstone). Lord Randolph's American wife Jennie, *née* Jerome, was an assiduous canvasser, chiefly in the Radical leader Joseph Chamberlain's stronghold of Birmingham; as a result the Conservatives did very well in such places. Hartington was so wounded by the speech that he said he would never speak to Lord Randolph again. Two months later Lord Randolph wrote him an apology and the breach was healed.

"Did any of you ever go to the Zoological Gardens? If you go there ... you may ... observe the feeding of the boa constrictor, which is supplied with a great fat duck or a rabbit.

If you are lucky ... you are able to trace the progress of the duck or the rabbit down his throat and all along the convolutions of his body.

Just in the same way ... the British public can trace the digestion and deglutition by the Marquess of Hartington of the various morsels of the Chamberlain programme which from time to time are handed to him; and the only difference between the boa constrictor and the Marquess of Hartington is this — that the boa constrictor enjoys his food and thrives on it and Lord Hartington loathes his food and it makes him sick ...

I quite admit that there is nothing democratic about the Whig. He is essentially a cold and selfish aristocrat who believes that the British Empire was erected by Providence and exists for no other purpose than to keep in power a few Whig families ...

What is the Tory Democracy that the Whigs should deride it and hold it up to the execration of the people? It has been called a contradiction in terms; it has been described as a nonsensical appellation. I believe it to be the most simple and the most easily understood political denomination ever assumed. The Tory Democracy is a democracy which has embraced the principles of the Tory Party. It is a democracy which believes that an hereditary monarchy and hereditary House of Lords are the strongest fortification which the wisdom of man, illuminated by the experience of centuries, can possibly devise for the protection — not of Whig privilege — but of democratic freedom."

Call for a restored Irish Parliament

Charles Stewart Parnell (1846–91)
Cork city
21 January 1885 _____

• Biography

A Parliamentary tactician rather than orator, and inasmuch as he was obstructionist a somewhat negative tactician at that, Parnell nonetheless achieved what the more gentlemanly O'Connell (*qv*) never could — to make the British take Irish nationalism seriously.

His family were Protestant Ascendancy landowners rather than true Celts. His mother was American and from her he imbibed the Anglophobia, a sterile growth, that ultimately swayed him more than did love of Ireland, an altogether healthier plant.

Parnell first became politically aroused after three Irishmen were hanged in 1867 for killing a policeman while trying to rescue Irish nationalist prisoners from a Manchester gaol. He joined the (Irish) Home Rule Association and in 1875 entered the UK Parliament at Westminster for Co. Meath.

The next year he denied in Parliament that the Manchester killers had been murderers. This defiant attitude won him support from the more intransigent Irish nationalists and from 1877 he led other Irish MPs in systematically disrupting ordinary Parliamentary procedures, raising objections to each clause of a bill, proposing red herring amendments and tabling motions to adjourn business. All-night sittings and even 24–hour ones ensued. The obstructionism sometimes brought incidental benefits: he so hamstrung passage of one bill that flogging in the Army got abolished.

Following the 1880 general election, Irish Home Rule MPs numbered 68, all tightly under Parnell's control, though he mixed with them hardly at all socially. In response to increasing evictions of small tenants in rural Ireland, it was Parnell who invented the form of social ostracism called the boycott after its first main victim,

Captain Boycott, a Co. Galway land agent, or administrator of an estate for its owner. By late 1880 government in Ireland was paralysed.

Gladstone's seesawing response irritated now the Irish, now the landlords. Parnell thought Gladstone's concessions didn't go far enough, denounced him and got put in Dublin's Kilmainham Gaol.

Gladstone then started secret talks with Parnell, culminating in an agreement known from Parnell's place of imprisonment as the 'Kilmainham Treaty'. Under it, Parnell was in spring 1882 released provided he supported a new, more conciliatory Land Bill.

By the 1884 Reform Act the Irish electorate was greatly expanded. This was clearly going to increase Parnell's power. In mid-1885 he took advantage of the Conservatives' forcing a vote on a money bill to join them, thus toppling Gladstone's second administration.

In January 1886 he and his followers helped defeat the new Conservative administration. But five months later the Liberal Unionists split from the official Liberals and sided with the Conservatives, whereupon Parnell got his followers to support the official Liberals regularly. He himself now rather neglected Parliament.

Early in 1887 *The Times* published what turned out to be a bogus letter by Parnell condoning the murder by Irish nationalists of Gladstone's wife's nephew-in-law Lord Frederick Cavendish five years earlier. Parnell sued *The Times* for libel and the letter and others like it were proved in 1889 to be forgeries. But the next year the revelation of an adulterous affair involving Parnell outraged the Liberal Nonconformist conscience, not to mention the more strait-laced Catholics in Ireland. This and his slackened grip on his followers brought about his eclipse.

• Context of speech

Parnell was a second-rate orator (in his early days even tenth-rate, being intensely nervous and with an atrocious delivery). He was, however, a first-rate agitator. He despised Parliamentary speech-making. 'Speeches are not business', he once said. 'This fight cannot be fought ... by speeches.' Cork, where he delivered the speech excerpted below, was a famously nationalist city, hence Parnell's vagueness over the degree of independence he sought. He had to be neither too conciliatory to Britain to alienate his more extreme supporters, nor too extreme to alarm his moderate ones.

66 **In 1880 I ... pledged myself that I should form one independent Irish Party to act in opposition to every English Government which refused to concede the just rights of Ireland ...**

But we have not alone had that object in view. We have always been very careful not to fetter or control the people at home in any way — not to prevent them from doing anything by their own strength which it is impossible for them to do. Sometimes, perhaps, in our anxiety in this direction, we have asked them to do what is beyond their strength. But I hold that it is better even to encourage you to do what is beyond your strength, even should you fail sometimes in that attempt, than to teach you to be subservient or unreliant.

You have been encouraged to organise yourselves, to depend upon the rectitude of your cause for your justification and to depend upon that determination which has helped Irishmen through many centuries to retain the name of Ireland and to retain the nationhood of Ireland.

Nobody can point to any single action of ours in the House of Commons, or out of it, which was not based upon the knowledge that behind us existed a strong and a brave people; that without the help of that people our exertions would be as nothing and that with that help, and with their confidence, we should be ... unconquerable ...

I am convinced that the five or six hundred thousand Irishmen who within a year must vote for the man of their choice will be as true to Ireland as — even truer to Ireland than — those who have gone before them; and that we may safely trust to them the exercise of the great and important privilege — unequaled in its greatness ... in the history of any nation — which will shortly be placed before them.

I am convinced that when the reckoning comes after the general election of 1886 we in Ireland shall have cause to congratulate ourselves on the possession of a strong party which will bear down all opposition, and which, aided by ... our country behind us, will enable us to gain for our country those rights which were stolen from us ...

Every Irish politician must be driven back to the great question of national self-government for Ireland. I do not know how this great question will be eventually settled. I do not know whether England will be wise in time and concede the ... restitution of that which was stolen from us towards the close of the last century ...

We cannot ask for less than the restitution of Grattan's Parliament [*granted in 1782*]. But no man has the right to fix the boundary to the march of a nation. No man has a right to say to his country 'Thus far shalt thou go and no farther'. We have never attempted to fix the *ne plus ultra* to the progress of Ireland's nationhood, and we never shall ... "

Attack on the future Edward VIII

(James) Keir Hardie (1856–1915)
House of Commons
June 1894

• Biography

Early Socialism threw up two leaders born to unmarried mothers. Keir Hardie was the first, the other was Ramsay MacDonald (*see* Baldwin).

Hardie endured terrible childhood poverty and worked down a coal mine from age ten. He continued there for the next 12 years, meanwhile educating himself at night school, following long working shifts, moreover. He organised a union at his mine and in 1880 led a strike against wage cuts. It failed and he got sacked, but he extended his union activity, becoming in 1886 Secretary of the Scottish Miners' Federation, an organisation he had helped form. He supplemented his tiny income from union activity by journalism.

In 1888 he stood unsuccessfully for Parliament as a 'National Labour Party' candidate. The organisation he represented was minuscule, but the episode was nonetheless a milestone in the history of working-class Parliamentary representation. That year he helped found the Scottish Labour Party, becoming its first Chairman.

In 1892 he became an independent labour MP, though ultimately better known in Parliament as 'Member for the Unemployed'. In any case the word 'labour' at this point denoted the entire body of working people, not a party. The next year he became the first Chairman of the fledgling Independent Labour Party proper. He went on to be elected first leader of the extant Labour Party in the House of Commons after it won 29 seats in the 1906 general election, its first breakthrough.

• Context of speech

Keir Hardie was as radical in breaching Parliamentary tradition as had been Parnell (*qv*). Only in his case it was over etiquette not procedure. He appeared in the House in cloth cap and tweed suit rather than the topper and frock coat then in vogue.

Oddly enough this was exactly the garb which, when worn by Harold Macmillan (*qv*) out shooting in the early 1960s, was attacked by the then Labour leader Harold Wilson as typifying Tory 'grouse moor' remoteness from ordinary people. Thus do sartorial preoccupations come full circle.

In June 1894 the House was discussing a congratulatory address following the birth of the future Edward VIII (*qv*). Keir Hardie thought the families of over 250 miners recently killed in a mine explosion at Pontypridd deserved equal Parliamentary attention, and suggested that a message of condolence to them be added to the royal one. He was turned down, whereupon he delivered the speech excerpted below. It is thought to have lost him his seat in the general election the following year.

66 **I am unable to join in this public address. I owe no allegiance to any hereditary ruler, and [*but?*] I will expect those who do to allow me the ordinary courtesies of debate.**

The Resolution ... seeks to elevate to an importance ... it does not deserve an event of everyday occurrence ...

From his childhood onwards this boy will be surrounded by sycophants and flatterers by the score, and will be taught to believe himself as of a superior creation ... A line will be drawn between him and the people whom he is to be called upon some day to reign over.

In due course, following the precedent which has already been set, he will be sent on a tour round the world, and probably rumours of a morganatic alliance will follow. And the end of it all will be that the country will be called upon to pay the bill ...

The Government will not find an opportunity for a vote of condolence with the relatives of those who are lying stiff and stark in a Welsh valley. And if that cannot be done, the motion before the House ought never to have been proposed either.

If it be for rank and title only that time and occasion can be found in this House, then the sooner the truth is known outside the House the better for the House itself."

Eulogy on Queen Victoria

Edward VII (1901–10)
Accession Council, London
23 January 1901 _____

• Biography

Edward VII was nearly 60 when he succeeded his mother. He had long been the leader of society, however. He was not the most intelligent, cultivated or educated sovereign of Britain, but he had immense *savoir-faire* and geniality, while at the same time making those around him slightly afraid of him, an essential accomplishment in a constitutional sovereign, whose power is slight.

   Though greatly given to talks with the other crowned heads of Europe, Edward conducted himself as king with sufficient discretion to avoid diplomatic gaffes, prudently confining the talks to generalities. His last year was overshadowed by the obstructionism of the House of Lords towards Lloyd George's (*qv*) radical budget.

• Context of speech

The day after Queen Victoria's death on 22 January 1901 Edward as the new King came up to London from Osborne, on the Isle of Wight, where his mother had lived, to attend his Accession Council. This was where the death of the old sovereign and succession of the new was formally announced. He had mulled over the speech he was to deliver while travelling but had written down nothing, not even notes, and had consulted no one.

   On referring to his mother's death he was almost overwhelmed but pulled himself together and spoke eloquently for eight minutes. After he had finished, some of those present asked him for the manuscript of the speech to send a copy to the newspapers. The King told them he had spoken extempore. It turned out there had not even been a shorthand note taken of the speech. Some courtiers wrote down what they could remember of it, though they confessed their version was nowhere near as good as the original. The speech should be heard in the mind's eye as delivered with a strong guttural, virtually Germanic, accent, that being Edward's most notable characteristic when speaking.

"This is the most painful occasion on which I shall ever be called upon to address you. My first and most melancholy duty is to announce to you the death of my beloved mother, the Queen, and I know how deeply you, the whole nation, and I think I may say the whole world, sympathise with me in the irreparable loss we have all sustained.

I need hardly say that my constant endeavour will be always to walk in her footsteps. In undertaking the heavy load which now devolves upon me, I am fully determined to be a constitutional sovereign in the strictest sense of the word, and, as long as there is breath in my body, to work for the good and amelioration of my people.

I have resolved to be known by the name of Edward, which has been born by six of my ancestors*. In doing so I do not undervalue the name of Albert, which I inherit from my ever-lamented great and wise father, who by universal consent is I think deservedly known by the name of Albert the Good, and I desire that his name should stand alone.

In conclusion, I trust to Parliament and the nation to support me in the arduous duties which now devolve upon me by inheritance, and to which I am determined to devote my whole strength during the remainder of my life."

---

* This was not quite accurate. Edwards V and VI were not his ancestors, though Queen Victoria's father Edward Duke of Kent was. But the Duke of Kent was never king. Of one only of the pre-Conquest Anglo-Saxon King Edwards (Edward the Elder) was Edward VII a descendant, so the total score is five not six.

'Square Deal'

Theodore (Teddy) Roosevelt (1858–1919)
26th President of the USA 1901–9
Syracuse, NY
7 September 1903 _____

• Biography

One of only two US Presidents so far to win the Nobel Peace Prize (the other being Woodrow Wilson, *qv*), Teddy Roosevelt was by origin a New York patrician of predominantly Dutch ancestry, or 'Knickerbocker'.

His Nobel status sits oddly on a man who, as Assistant Navy Secretary 1897–98, did arguably more than any other American to foment the war with Spain of 1898. Once war was joined, Teddy led his own field force, the famous 'Rough Riders', to Cuba, then still a Spanish possession. The ensuing Battle of San Juan Hill was by no means a clear-cut American victory but Teddy, already a consummate politician, persuaded folks back home otherwise and partly on the strength of it won election first as Governor of New York State then as Vice-President. President McKinley was assassinated by a lunatic six months after his inauguration, and Teddy took over. He proved one of the greatest Presidents, notably for his reforming zeal, something which grew stronger with time.

Despite the braggadocio of Teddy's pronouncements on the strenuous life, he was at heart both a sensitive soul and an intelligent one. He was one of the first public figures to encourage conservation. He was so heartbroken by the early death of his first wife that he never mentioned her name to their daughter again, nor in his autobiography. He won the Nobel Peace Prize specifically for negotiating an end to the Russo-Japanese War of 1905 and generally for initiating use of the international Court of Arbitration at The Hague. Prior to his involvement, it had been a mere ornament.

He selflessly laid down the presidency in 1908, having served nearly eight years. Yet his atavistic love of a scrap would not die. He decided to re-enter the political fray, ran against his successor William H. Taft in 1912, split the Republican vote and so let in Woodrow Wilson.

• Context of speech

It was not the first time Teddy Roosevelt had used the term 'square deal' (nor was it to be the last). Two months earlier he had said in a speech to service veterans at Springfield, Ill., "A man who is good enough to shed his blood for his country is good enough to be given a square deal afterwards. More than that no man is entitled, and less than that no man shall have." This time the audience consisted of farmers at the New York State Agricultural Association.

66 **I**f ... **thrift, energy, industry and forethought enable the farmer, the tiller of the soil, on the one hand, and the wage-worker on the other, to keep themselves, their wives and ... children in reasonable comfort, then the state is well off... On the other hand, if there is in the long run a lack of prosperity among the two classes named, then all other prosperity is sure to be more seeming than real.**

It has been our profound good fortune as a nation that hitherto ... there has been ... a progressive betterment alike in the condition of the tiller of the soil and in the condition of the man who, by his manual skill and labor, supports himself and his family, and endeavors to bring up his children so that they may be at least as well off as, and, if possible, better off than, he himself has been ...

Side by side with this ... has gone on a great increase in prosperity among the businessmen and among certain classes of professional men... It cannot be too often repeated that in this country, in the long run, we all of us tend to go up or go down together. If the average of well-being is high ... the average wage-worker ... farmer, and ... businessman are ... well-off. If the average shrinks, there is not one of these classes which will not feel the shrinkage ...

Unfortunately, in this world the innocent frequently find themselves obliged to pay some of the penalty for the misdeeds of the guilty; and so if hard times come ...., the trouble once started is felt more or less in every walk of life ...

We can keep our government on a sane and healthy basis, we can make and keep our social system what it should be, only on condition of judging each man, not as a member of a class, but on his worth as a man. It is an infamous thing in our American life, and fundamentally treacherous to our institutions, to apply to any man any test save that of his personal worth, or to draw between two sets of men any distinction save the distinction of conduct, the distinction that marks off those who do well and wisely from those who do ill and foolishly ...

The failure in public and in private life thus to treat each man on his own merits, the recognition of this government as being either for the poor as such or for the rich as such, would prove fatal to our Republic, as such failure and such recognition have always proved fatal in the past to other republics. A healthy republican government must rest upon individuals, not upon classes or sections. As soon as it becomes government by a class or by a section, it departs from the old American ideal …

We must act upon the motto of all for each and each for all. There must be ever present in our minds the fundamental truth that in a republic such as ours the only safety is to stand neither for nor against any man because he is rich or because he is poor, because he is engaged in one occupation or another, because he works with his brains or because he works with his hands. We must treat each man on his worth and merits as a man. We must see that each is given a square deal, because he is entitled to no more and should receive no less … "

'The man in the arena'

Paris
23 April 1910

• Context of speech

The excerpt below was delivered at the Sorbonne during a visit by Teddy Roosevelt to France. The French newspaper *Le Temps* had 57,000 copies of the speech distributed throughout the country.

66 It is well if a large proportion of the leaders in any republic, in any democracy, are, as a matter of course, drawn from the classes represented in this audience today; but only provided that those classes possess the gifts of sympathy with plain people and of devotion to great ideals.

You and those like you have received special advantages; you have all of you had the opportunity for mental training; many of you have had leisure; most of you have had a chance for enjoyment of life far greater than comes to the majority of your fellows. To you and your kind much has been given, and from you much should be expected.

Yet there are certain failings against which it is especially incumbent that both men of trained and cultivated intellect, and men of inherited wealth and position should especially guard themselves, because to these failings they are especially liable; and if yielded to, their — your — chances of useful service are at an end.

Let the man of learning, the man of lettered leisure, beware of that queer and cheap temptation to pose to himself and to others as a cynic, as the man who has outgrown emotions and beliefs, the man to whom good and evil are as one. The poorest way to face life is to face it with a sneer. There are many men who feel a kind of twister pride in cynicism; there are many who confine themselves to criticism of the way others do what they themselves dare not even attempt. There is no more unhealthy being, no man less worthy of respect, than he who either really holds, or feigns to hold, an attitude of sneering disbelief toward all that is great and lofty, whether in achievement or in that noble effort which, even if it fails, comes to second achievement.

A cynical habit of thought and speech, a readiness to criticise work which the critic himself never tries to perform, an intellectual aloofness which will not accept contact with life's realities — all these are marks, not as the possessor would fain to think, of superiority but of weakness. They mark the men unfit to bear their part painfully in the stern strife of living, who seek, in the affection of contempt for the achievements of others, to hide from others and from themselves in their own weakness.

The rôle is easy; there is none easier, save only the rôle of the man who sneers alike at both criticism and performance.

It is not the critic who counts; not the man who points out how the strong man stumbles, or where the doer of deeds could have done them better. The credit belongs to the man who is actually in the arena, whose face is marred by dust and sweat and blood; who strives valiantly; who errs, who comes short again and again, because there is no effort without error and shortcoming; but who does actually strive to do the deeds; who knows great enthusiasms, the great devotions; who spends himself in a worthy cause; who at the best knows in the end the triumph of high achievement, and who at the worst, if he fails, at least fails while daring greatly, so that his place shall never be with those cold and timid souls who neither know victory nor defeat … "

Maiden speech as MP

F.E. Smith,1st Earl of Birkenhead (1872–1930)
House of Commons
11 March 1906

• Biography

Barristers' effusions may sound brilliant in court, less so out of it. F.E. Smith, so famous in his day that the initials 'F.E.' alone became instantly recognisable, sounded best of all in his own recounting of his exploits.

He was the son of an estate agent, now a frequently encountered calling among would-be Conservative MPs but then rather *infra dig.* His daughter Eleanor claimed that his grandmother, the splendidly named Bathsheba Green, had gipsy origins, and his son Freddie referred on one occasion to F.E.'s 'Romany' good looks. Certainly F.E. appeared just as quick at getting up a speech or a brief as a thimble-rigger trousering a greenhorn's fiver at a country fair — 'appeared', because actually he often toiled at preparing speeches and exaggerated his brilliant repartee afterwards. The story that F.E.'s 1895 Oxford First in Jurisprudence was gained after only six months, albeit intensive, study is therefore open to question.

He built a hugely successful and lucrative practice at the Bar and in 1906 entered Parliament. MPs still followed outside professions then. F.E. was no exception, claiming to earn as much as £40,000 a year at his peak (*c.* £1,300,000 now, and that omits property inflation). His sheer brilliance sometimes lost him trust but won him the friendship of political opponents such as Lloyd George and Churchill (*qqv*), as did also in Churchill's case his conviviality. (Lloyd George, hostile to topers, made an exception in F.E.'s case.)

He was an active Unionist (*see* Lord Randolph Churchill), especially in the negotiations over excepting Ulster from Irish Home Rule that preceded World War I. During the War he became in swift succession Solicitor-General, Attorney-General and Lord Chancellor. His end was hastened by alcohol. Baldwin (*qv*) in 1928 would not reappoint him Lord Chancellor lest he be seen drunk in public. His extravagance exacerbated matters, forcing him to write popular books while holding high office, for which he was much criticised.

• Context of speech

No other maiden speech in Parliament has matched F.E.'s. The circumstances were propitious. The Conservatives, massively defeated in the 1906 general election, were demoralised. F.E. knew he had little to lose and everything to gain. One of his most famous sayings was that glittering prizes are available to those with stout hearts and sharp swords.

The speech does not read (though it may well have sounded) spontaneous. Indeed he was overheard rehearsing it some days previously. The timing of its delivery was fixed on his behalf by one of his party chiefs for 10 pm, the best moment; the date was less than a month after the new House had first met.

F.E. had a pronounced Cheshire accent on going up to Oxford. This he seems to have 'cured' in about two years, speaking thereafter not just with an 'Oxford' (*i.e.,* plummy) accent but exaggeratedly so. Sir Oswald Mosley (*qv*), who only knew him later in his life, mentions his 'customary lisp', but that may be the drink. His forensic technique began with a clear setting out of the legal position (if in a law court), for he was not just a flashy word-smith but formidably learned, modulating to persuasive advocacy, deviating now into fantasy (less so in a law court), now into witty thrusts against his opponent, the whole delivered with lounging impudence. His tone was usually calm, getting louder when he wanted to emphasise an important point and climaxing with a blow of his fist on any surface in front of him, after which he became calm again.

There are four printed versions of the maiden speech. F.E.'s local paper in Liverpool gives the completest.

> 66 **It is far easier, if one is a master of scholarly irony and a charming literary style, to describe protection as a 'stinking rotten carcass' than to discuss scientifically whether certain limited proposals are likely to prove protective … It is far easier, if one has a strong stomach, to suggest to simple rustics, as the President of the Board of Trade (*Lloyd George*, qv) did, that, if the Tories came into power, they would introduce slavery on the hills of Wales.**
>
> [*Lloyd George here interposed 'I did not say that'.*]
>
> The Right Hon. Gentleman would, no doubt, be extremely anxious to forget it, if he could. But, anticipating a temporary lapse of memory, I have in

my hand the *Manchester Guardian* of January 16 1906, which contains a report of his speech. The Right Hon. Gentleman said: 'What would they say to introducing Chinamen at 1/- [*a shilling; 5p in decimal currency*] a day into the Welsh quarries? Slavery on the hills of Wales! Heaven forgive me for the suggestion!'

I ... have no means of judging how Heaven will deal with persons who think it decent to make such suggestions. The distinction drawn by the Right Hon. Gentleman is more worthy of the county court than of the Treasury Bench ...

The Free Church Council gave thanks publicly for the fact that Providence had inspired the electors with discrimination to vote on the right side. I do not in the least mind being cheated at cards; but I find it a trifle nauseating if my opponent then proceeds to ascribe his success to the favour of the Most High [*a variation of Labouchère on Gladstone*, qv].

What the future of this Parliament has in store for Right Hon. Gentlemen opposite I do not know, but I hear that the Government will deny to the Colonial Conference of 1907 free discussion on the subject which the House is now debating, so as to prevent the statement of unpalatable truths.

I know that I am the insignificant representative of an insignificant minority in this House, but I venture to warn the Government that the people of this country will never forget or forgive a party which, in the heyday of its triumph, denies to the infant Parliament of the Empire one jot or tittle of that ancient liberty of speech which our predecessors in this House vindicated for themselves at the point of a sword."

'Mr Balfour's poodle'

David Lloyd George, 1st Earl Lloyd George of Dwyfor (1863–1945)
House of Commons
26 June 1907

• Biography

The Welsh, arguably even more than the Irish, have been the poor relations among the peoples of the old United Kingdom. One of their compensations was to launch on the world Lloyd George.

He was a schoolmaster's son born in Manchester, though Welsh-speaking from childhood. When negotiating the Irish Free State Treaty in 1921 he communicated confidentially with his assistant in Welsh, baffling the Irish contingent.

He became a solicitor in North Wales, as which he won a case favouring Nonconformist burial services in Anglican churchyards. This in 1890 helped get him into Parliament. His hostility to Anglican influence in Wales, not just ecclesiastically but educationally, and to the Boer War won him national fame. In 1905 he became President of the Board of Trade and in 1908 was promoted Chancellor of the Exchequer. He pursued Welsh Disestablishment (*i.e.*, of the Anglican Church in Wales). The cause met firm House of Lords opposition. Worse, the Lords, with their in-built Conservative majority, initially rejected Lloyd George's attempt to fund old-age pensions and sickness and unemployment benefits — his 'People's' Budget of 1909. This sparked a constitutional crisis (*see* the second and third speeches). The Lords eventually submitted after threats that enough new peers might be created to pass the Bill.

In 1915, with World War I under way, a munitions shortage toppled the Liberal government. A Coalition was formed and Lloyd George became Minister for Munitions. The next summer he became War Secretary and in December Prime Minister. He ran the national war effort for the rest of the hostilities with great efficiency and almost presidential powers.

Following the 1918 Armistice, Lloyd George represented Britain in negotiating the Treaty of Versailles. At home the Coalition became dominated by the Conservatives. To build a political fund of his own (he was increasingly at odds with Liberals loyal to his predecessor as Premier, Asquith) he embarked on a sale of honours — an old practice in the hands of former premiers and even monarchs, but on a new scale in his. In 1922 the Conservatives ceased their support, chiefly over the honours-trafficking and his bringing Britain and Turkey to the brink of war. He thereupon resigned. He remained an MP another 23 years but never regained office.

Though from a very different background, Lloyd George has been much compared with Sir Winston Churchill (*qv*), both as a brilliant war Premier and as an orator. (The two were close friends and allies when fellow-Liberal ministers, Lloyd George having brought the younger man over from the Conservatives in 1904.) Lloyd George is reckoned to have been the better speaker in the Commons and at public meetings, but not over the wireless. Vocally he was more melodious (not surprisingly since he addressed many meetings in Welsh, an inherently musical language) and his style a lot more colloquial (not hard, given Churchill's 'sham Augustan' prose — as Evelyn Waugh once called it). That said, his Agadir speech of 1911 (*see* fourth speech below) reveals an uncharacteristic orotundity. Lloyd George memorised his speeches, though using notes to refresh his memory. As he became more famous he often dictated a speech to a reporter before delivering it, thus ensuring the press reported the 'correct' version.

• Context of speech

The Conservative-dominated House of Lords had already blocked or amended out of all recognition various Liberal measures within a year of the Liberal House of Commons landslide of 1906 (*see* also F.E. Smith). In 1907 Lloyd George made a famous speech likening the Lords to a poodle, specifically the pet of the then leader of the (Conservative) Opposition, Arthur Balfour.

The phrase 'Mr Balfour's poodle', though never uttered by Lloyd George in precisely those words, passed into history, to be resuscitated when used by the late Roy Jenkins as title of a book on the Lords–Commons relationship at that time. The speech excerpted below was made on 26 June 1907, the second day of a debate on the House of Lords. The original metaphor dreamed up by Lloyd George when preparing the speech was 'lapdog', more exact but less offensive.

66 **The House of Lords … is the leal [sic, i.e., *faithful*] and trusty mastiff who is to watch over our interests, but who runs away at the first snarl of the trade unions … A mastiff? It is the Right Hon. Gentleman's [*Arthur Balfour, Conservative Prime Minister 1902–6 but now Leader of the Opposition*] poodle. It fetches and carries for him. It barks for him. It bites anybody that**

he sets it on to. And we are told that this is a great revising Chamber, the safeguard of liberty in this country.

Talk about mockeries and shams. Was there ever such a sham as that? No wonder the Right Hon. Gentleman scolds the naughty boys who throw stones at it ...

[*Later in the debate, following contributions by other speakers*] there is nothing more disastrous to the effective criticism of measures in the House of Commons than the knowledge that, though a Bill may pass through this House, it is likely to be mangled or rejected elsewhere [i.e., *in the House of Lords*]...no revision, no check, when a Tory Government is in power, but every check when there is a Liberal Government in power ...

If there is a revolution, it is not the House of Lords that will arrest it. It will be the first institution that will vanish without a struggle. In the English Revolution [i.e., *the 17th-century Civil War*] it was the House of Commons that made the last fight. The House of Lords was abolished by a resolution. The House of Commons made the fight and when the time for a revolution comes — if it ever does come — the only share ... the House of Lords will have in the revolution will be in creating it ...

It is very remarkable that every great Liberal statesman ... for 50 years has always come to the same conclusion about the House of Lords ... Lord Rosebery ... came to the same conclusion, and the two greatest names of all — John Bright and Mr Gladstone (*qqv*) — who had given long service to the state and were no revolutionaries, were of the same opinion.

John Bright ... was a prudent, cautious and temperate man in action, and always essentially anti-revolutionary. Mr Gladstone had an almost exaggerated reverence for existing institutions, especially hereditary institutions. He was the last man to lift his powerful arm against them, and yet after the longest and most distinguished public career ... this country probably has known, when he had no further personal interest in the matter and when he had no responsibility for leadership of the Party, he said that practically progress was impossible until you had dealt with this barrier."

On the cost of dukes and dreadnoughts

Newcastle
9 October 1909

• Context of speech

By the end of the first week of October 1909 Lloyd George's 'People's Budget' had passed through its Committee Stage in the House of Commons. But it still had to encounter the Lords, where a mangling looked inevitable. Moreover, naval competition with Germany meant that many ordinary people thought guns were more important just now than butter. When Lloyd George spoke at Newcastle, his audience numbered a little over 5,000, the venue being the Palace Theatre. He mixed factual rebuttal of his opponents' allegations of the Budget's economic shortcomings with pure verbal fisticuffs. In particular he hit out, though obliquely, at the northeast's chief landlord, the Duke of Northumberland, who like most other big landowners opposed the Budget's land valuation element and had also just been ordered by magistrates to cease letting some insanitary miners' cottages in the district.

66 **It is ... remarkable that since this 'attack on industry' [*as his opponents had termed the Budget*] was first promulgated in the House of Commons, industry has improved. It is beginning to recover from the great crash which ... came from America ...** There has been, on the whole, an improvement even in brewery shares ...

Only one stock has gone down badly. There has been a great slump in dukes. They used to stand rather high in the market, especially in the Tory market, but the Tory press has just discovered that they are of no value.

They have been making speeches lately. One especially expensive duke made a speech, and all the Tory Press said 'Well now, really, is that the sort of thing we are spending £250,000 a year upon?' Because a fully-equipped duke costs as much to keep up as two Dreadnoughts — and they are just as great a terror — and they last longer.

As long as they were content to be mere idols on their pedestals, preserving that stately silence which became their rank and their intelligence, all went well and the average British citizen rather looked up to them ...

But then came the Budget. They stepped off their perch. They have been scolding like omnibus drivers purely because the Budget cart has knocked a little of the gilt off their old stage coach. Well, we cannot put them back again …

Who talks about … meddling with the Constitution? The Constitutional Party — the great Constitutional [i.e., *Conservative; Sir Winston Churchill (qv) at one point sat as a Constitutionalist MP, though in practice supporting the Conservatives*] Party. As long as the Constitution gave rank and possession and power to the Lords it was not to be interfered with. As long as it secured even their sports from intrusion and made interference with them a crime; as long as the Constitution enforced [*mineral*] royalties [e.g., *from coalmines*] and ground rents and fees and premiums and fines, and all the black retinue of exaction; as long as it showered writs and summonses and injunctions and distresses, and warrants to enforce them, then the Constitution was inviolate …

But the moment the Constitution … begins to discover that there are millions of people outside park gates who need attention, then the Constitution is to be torn to pieces.

Let them realise what they are doing. They are forcing a revolution, and they will get it. The Lords may decree a revolution, but the people will direct it. If they begin, issues will be raised which are now whispered in humble voices, and answers will be demanded then with authority. The question will be asked whether five hundred men, ordinary men chosen accidentally from among the unemployed, should override the judgement — the deliberate judgement — of millions of people … engaged in the industry which makes the wealth of the country … "

On the coming 1910 election

Caernarvon
December 1909

• Context of speech

The duel with the House of Lords took from 1909 to 1911 to resolve. This was partly because Edward VII (*qv*) died half way through. But in addition, Asquith's Liberal Government had lost the initiative even before that. Asquith himself was most at fault through failing to press on Edward VII before the January 1910 general election that Edward must behave in correct constitutional fashion and forward what was one of the central points of Liberal policy, *viz.*, ending the House of Lords veto on Liberal legislation. Edward was still reluctant to do so by any means as drastic as flooding the House of Lords with new creations.

The December phase of the campaign (general elections then took many weeks more than nowadays) saw Lloyd George at his most nostalgic, as well as metaphorical. He was addressing a crowd of 7,000 in the Pavilion at Caernarvon, his constituency. He began in Welsh, switched to English and delivered his peroration in Welsh again.

66 I understand that some people on this side and on the other of Offa's Dyke are desirous of reading what I have spoken, and for that reason I am going to deliver my address in English. I have not lost my Welsh yet [*indeed he hadn't, as the preceding words were in Welsh*]...

Yesterday I visited the old village where I was brought up. I wandered through the woods familiar to my boyhood. There I saw a child gathering sticks for firewood, and I thought of the hours which I spent in the same pleasant and profitable occupation, for I also have been something of a 'backwoodsman' [*this term had special reference to the sort of peer who rarely attended the House of Lords, and then only to oppose enlightened measures, e.g., the 'People's Budget'*].

And there was one experience taught me then which is of some profit to me today. I learnt as a child that it was little use going into the woods after a period of calm and fine weather, for I generally returned empty-handed; but after a great storm I always came back with an armful.

We are in for rough weather. We may even be in for a winter of storms which will rock the forest, break many a withered branch and leave many a rotten tree torn up by the roots.

But when the weather clears you may depend upon it that there will be something brought within the reach of the people that will give warmth and glow to their grey lives, something that will help to dispel the hunger, the despair, the oppression and the wrong which now chill so many of their hearths."

Agadir Crisis

The Mansion House, London
21 July 1911 _____

• Context of speech

One of the chief international crises culminating in World War I was when in 1911 a German warship, the *Panther*, visited the Moroccan port of Agadir. France was the preponderant foreign influence in Morocco. Indeed Morocco was what in those days was termed 'a [French] sphere of influence'. The *Panther*'s dropping anchor was seen by the British and French as sabre-rattling generally, and specifically as a German threat to that influence.

Lloyd George took advantage of an invitation to speak at the Mansion House to declare Britain's interest in the matter. The Mansion House, the official residence of the Lord Mayor of London, has like that other City venue the Guildhall (*see* ninth speech below) long been a forum where senior government ministers put forward major policy statements.

"Personally I am a sincere advocate of all means which would lead to the settlement of international disputes by methods such as those which civilisation has so successfully set up for the adjustment of differences between individuals. And I rejoice in my heart at the prospect of a happy issue to Sir Edward Grey's [*Liberal Foreign Secretary 1905–16, created Viscount Grey of Fallodon; see also Baldwin*] negotiations with the United States of America for the settlement of disputes which may occur in future between ourselves and our kinsmen across the Atlantic by some more merciful, more rational, and by a more just arbitrament than that of the sword.

But I am also bound to say this, that I believe it is essential in the highest interests, not merely of this country, but of the world, that Britain should at all hazards maintain her place and her prestige amongst the Great Powers of the world.

Her potent influence has many a time been in the past, and may yet be in the future, invaluable to the cause of human liberty. It has more than once in the past redeemed Continental nations, who are sometimes too apt to forget that service, from overwhelming disaster and even from national extinction.

I would make great sacrifices to preserve peace. I conceive that nothing would justify a disturbance of international good will except questions of the greatest national moment. But if a situation were to be forced upon us in which peace could only be preserved by the surrender of the great and beneficent position Britain has won by centuries of heroism and achievement, by allowing Britain to be treated where her interests were vitally affected as if she were of no account in the Cabinet of nations, then I say emphatically that peace at that price would be a humiliation intolerable for a great country like ours to endure.

National honour is no party question. The security of our great international trade is no party question. The peace of the world is much more likely to be secured if all nations realise fairly what the conditions of peace must be ... "

On the UK entering World War I

Queen's Hall, London
9 September 1914

• Context of speech

World War I began for the chief European belligerents on 4 August 1914. What forced Britain's participation was Germany's invading Belgium, which gave her possession of the European North Sea coast. Additionally, safeguarding the rights of small nations was one of the Allied aims.

"We are bound in an honourable obligation to defend the independence, the liberty, the integrity of a small neighbour that has lived peaceably. But she could not have compelled us, because she was weak. The man who declines to

discharge his debt because his creditor is too poor to enforce it is a blackguard. We entered into this treaty, a solemn treaty, a full treaty, to defend Belgium and her integrity. Our signatures are attached to the document. Our signatures do not stand alone there. This was not the only country to defend the integrity of Belgium. Russia, France, Austria, and Prussia — they are all there ...

It is now the interest of Prussia to break the treaty, and she has done it. Well, why? She avowed it with cynical contempt for every principle of justice. She says treaties only bind you when it is to your interest to keep them. 'What is a treaty?' says the German Chancellor. 'A scrap of paper.' Have you any £5 notes about you? I am not calling for them. Have you any of those neat little Treasury £1 notes? If you have, burn them. They are only 'scraps of paper'. What are they made of? Rags. What are they worth? The whole credit of the British Empire ...

Treaties are the currency of international statesmanship. Let us be fair. German merchants, German traders had the reputation of being as upright and straightforward as any traders in the world. But if the currency of German commerce is to be debased to the level of her statesmanship, no trader from Shanghai to Valparaiso will ever look at a German signature again ...

If there are nations that say they will only respect treaties when it is to their interest to do so, we must make it to their interest to do so for the future.

Belgium has been treated brutally ... She was one of the most unoffending little countries in Europe. She was peaceable, industrious, thrifty, hard-working, giving offence to no one; and her cornfields have been trampled down, her villages have been burned to the ground, her art treasures have been destroyed, her men have been slaughtered, yea, and her women and children, too.

What had she done? Hundreds of thousands of her people have had their quiet, comfortable little homes burned to the dust, and are wandering homeless in their own land. What is their crime? Their crime was that they trusted to the word of a Prussian King. I don't know what the Kaiser hopes to achieve by this war. I have a shrewd idea of what he will get, but one thing is made certain, that no nation in future will ever commit that crime again ...

The burning and massacring, the shooting down of harmless people, why? Because, according to the Germans, they fired on German soldiers. What business had German soldiers there at all? Belgium was acting in pursuance of a most sacred right, the right to defend your own home. But they were not in uniform when they shot.

If a burglar broke into the Kaiser's Palace at Potsdam, destroyed his furniture, shot down his servants, ruined his art treasures, especially those he made himself, burned his precious manuscripts, do you think he would wait until he got into uniform before he shot him down? ...

The world owes much to little nations — and to little men. This theory of bigness — you must have a big empire and a big nation, and a big man — well, long legs have their advantage in a retreat. Frederick the Great chose his warriors for their height, and that tradition has become a policy in Germany. Germany applies that ideal to nations; she will only allow six-feet-two nations to stand in the ranks ...

Have you read the Kaiser's speeches? If you have not a copy, I advise you to buy it; they will soon be out of print, and you won't have any more of the same sort again. They are full of the clatter and bluster of German militarists — the mailed fist, the shining armour.

That is what we are fighting, that claim to predominancy of a civilisation, a material one, a hard one, a civilisation which if once it rules and sways the world, liberty goes, democracy vanishes, and unless Britain comes to the rescue, and her sons, it will be a dark day for humanity. We are not fighting the German people. The German people are just as much under the heel of this Prussian military caste ... . It will be a day of rejoicing for the German peasant and artisan and trader when the military caste is broken.

You know his pretensions. He gives himself the airs of a demi-god. Walking the pavements — civilians and their wives swept into the gutter; they have no right to stand in the way of the great Prussian junker. Men, women, nations — they have all got to go. He thinks all he has got to say is 'We are in a hurry.' That is the answer he gave to Belgium. 'Rapidity of action is Germany's greatest asset', which means 'I am in a hurry. Clear out of my way.'

You know the type of motorist, the terror of the roads, with a 60-h.p. car. He thinks the roads are made for him, and anybody who impedes the action of his car by a single mile is knocked down. The Prussian junker is the road-hog of Europe. Small nationalities in his way hurled to the roadside, bleeding and broken; women and children crushed under the wheels of his cruel car. Britain ordered out of his road. All I can say is this: if the old British spirit is alive in British hearts, that bully will be torn from his seat ... "

To the American Club, London

12 April 1917

• Context of speech

On 6 April 1917 the US entered World War I (*see* also Woodrow Wilson). Lloyd George a week later congratulated expatriate Americans in Britain on their choice.

> " I am not at all surprised, when one recalls the wars of the past, that America took its time to make up its mind about the character of this struggle. In Europe most of the great wars of the past were waged for dynastic aggrandisement and conquest. No wonder when this great war started that there were some elements of suspicion still lurking in the minds of the people of the United States of America. There were those who thought perhaps that kings were at their old tricks — and although they saw the gallant Republic of France fighting, they some of them perhaps regarded it as the poor victim of a conspiracy of monarchical swashbucklers …
>
> They naturally did not know at first what we had endured in Europe for years from this military caste in Prussia. It never has reached the United States of America. Prussia was not a democracy. The Kaiser promises that it will be a democracy after the war. I think he is right. But Prussia not merely was not a democracy. Prussia was not a state — Prussia was an army. It had great industries that had been highly developed; a great educational system; it had its universities, it had developed its science.
>
> All these were subordinate to the one great predominant purpose, the purpose of all — a conquering army which was to intimidate the world. The army was the spear-point of Prussia; the rest was merely the shaft.
>
> That was what we had to deal with in these old countries. It got on the nerves of Europe. They knew what it all meant. It was an army that in recent times had waged three wars, all of conquest, and the unceasing tramp of its legions through the streets of Prussia, on the parade grounds of Prussia, had got into the Prussian head.
>
> The Kaiser, when he witnessed on a grand scale his reviews, got drunk with the sound of it. He delivered the law to the world as if Potsdam was another Sinai, and he was uttering the law from the thunder clouds …
>
> The most characteristic of Prussian institutions is the Hindenburg Line. What is the Hindenburg Line? The Hindenburg Line is a line drawn in

the territories of other people, with a warning that the inhabitants of those territories shall not cross it at the peril of their lives. That line has been drawn in Europe for fifty years ...

Europe, after enduring this for generations, made up its mind at last that the Hindenburg Line must be drawn along the legitimate frontiers of Germany herself ...

It was hard at first for the people of America quite to appreciate that Germany had not interfered to the same extent with their freedom, if at all. But at last they endured the same experience as Europe had been subjected to. Americans were told that they were not to be allowed to cross and re-cross the Atlantic except at their peril. American ships were sunk without warning. American citizens were drowned, hardly with an apology — in fact, as a matter of German right.

At first Americans could hardly believe it. They could not think it possible that any sane people should behave in that manner. And they tolerated it once, and they tolerated it twice, until it became clear that the Germans really meant it. Then America acted, and acted promptly.

The Hindenburg Line was drawn along the shores of America, and the Americans were told they must not cross it. America said 'What is this?' Germany said 'This is our line, beyond which you must not go', and America said 'The place for that line is not the Atlantic, but on the Rhine and we mean to help you to roll it up.' ... "

Rebuttal of charges of UK responsibility for World War I

June 1917

• Context of speech

By mid-1917 Britain was at a critical state. The German U-boat campaign had nearly cut off supplies. War weariness was exacerbated by propaganda against the war and all participants in it generally, whichever side they were on, some of it sparked by the Russian Revolution, some of it whipped up by Germany.

"We might imagine from declarations which were made by the Germans, aye!, and even by a few people in this country, who are constantly referring to our German comrades, that this terrible war was wantonly and wickedly provoked by England — never Scotland — never Wales — and never Ireland.

Wantonly provoked by England to increase her possessions, and to destroy the influence, the power and the prosperity of a dangerous rival.

There never was a more foolish travesty of the actual facts ... What are the main facts? There were six countries which entered the War at the beginning. Britain was last, and not the first.

Before she entered the War Britain made every effort to avoid it; begged, supplicated and entreated that there should be no conflict.

I was a member of the Cabinet at the time, and I remember the earnest endeavours we made to persuade Germany and Austria not to precipitate Europe into this welter of blood ...

We begged Germany not to attack Belgium, and produced a treaty, signed by the King of Prussia, as well as the King of England, pledging himself to protect Belgium against an invader, and we said 'If you invade Belgium we shall have no alternative but to defend it.'

The enemy invaded Belgium, and now they say 'Why, forsooth, you, England, provoked this war.'

It is not quite the story of the wolf and the lamb. I will tell you why — because Germany expected to find a lamb and found a lion."

'Land fit for heroes'

Grand Theatre, Wolverhampton
23 November 1918

• Context of speech

Once World War I was over Lloyd George called a general election to exploit popular enthusiasm over victory. His audience of about 2,000 on Saturday 23 November, not quite a fortnight after the Armistice, had gathered at the Grand Theatre, Wolverhampton. In his speech he launched his famous catch phase 'a land fit for heroes', though he did not use precisely those words. Unfortunately, the land the servicemen came home to turned out often to be not at all fit for heroes, or indeed anyone else above the level of those same half-starved, rickets-ridden wretches Lloyd George had declared to be such a scandal. The phrase blew up in Lloyd George's face like a land mine in the Flanders mud.

"**There is, as I never witnessed before, a new comradeship of classes, and I am glad, as an old political fighter — who has been hit hard and has been able to return the blows — always in a spirit of meekness — I am glad that we are approaching the new problems in a spirit of comradeship** ...

What is our task? To make Britain a fit country for heroes to live in. I am not using the word heroes in any spirit of boastfulness, but in the spirit of humble recognition of the fact. I cannot think what these men have gone through. I have been there at the door of the furnace and witnessed it, but that is not being in it, and I saw them march into the furnace ...

I want us to take advantage of this new spirit. Don't let us waste this victory merely in ringing joy bells. Let us make victory the motive power to link the old land up in such measure that it will be nearer the sunshine than ever before, and, at any rate, that it will lift those who have been living in the dark places to a plateau where they can get the rays of the sun.

We cannot undertake that without a new Parliament. The old Parliament has done its duty. I have not a word to say about it — but it has exhausted its mandate ...

What is the first thing the Great War has shown us? The appalling waste of human material in this country ... Those ... in charge of recruiting came to the conclusion that, if the people of this country had lived under proper conditions, ... properly fed and housed, ... you could have had a million more men ... fit to put into the Army ...

There are millions of men's lives ... lost as a result of the War, but there are millions more ... maimed lives in the sense of undermined constitutions through atrocious social conditions ... You must put that right ...

One of the ways of dealing with that is ... to deal with ... housing conditions. Slums are not fit homes for the men who have won this war, or for their children ... the housing of the people must be a national concern."

'Murder by the throat'

Guildhall, City of London
9 November 1920 _____

• Context of speech

The end of the War in Europe did not mean the end of the struggle for independence in Ireland. It took three more years to bring about an agreement. During that time the IRA in Ireland waged a guerilla war and the British and Irish authorities, many of the latter of whom still adhered to the idea of British rule, struggled to impose order. The use by Lloyd George of auxiliaries and the notorious Black and Tans (so named from their uniform of policeman's black trousers surmounted by tan-coloured army jackets), made matters worse since the latter in particular were ill-disciplined, often brutal and senselessly arbitrary about who they took it out on.

Lloyd George's veiled references to their deployment in the speech below suggests he was aware of their shortcomings. He was later to be discomfited by Sir Oswald Mosley (*qv*) over their use. Britain eventually became a master of psychological warfare and the quelling of insurgenc. But in Ireland the necessary subtlety of approach was long lacking.

The occasion was the Lord Mayor of London's banquet on 9 November 1920. Lloyd George's point about firing from men not in uniform had been used by him in defending Belgium back in 1914, only he now turned it on its head. For from the Irish nationalists' point of view the forces of Anglo-Welsh imperialism were no more welcome, whether in 1920 or as far back as Strongbow's incursion in the 12th century, than 'Prussian' soldiers had been to Belgians in 1914.

> " **B**efore I sit down, if you will bear with me, I must say one word about one disturbed corner of the Empire …
>
> I hope soon it will be less disturbed. There we have witnessed the spectacle of organised assassination, of the most cowardly character. Firing at men who were unsuspecting, firing from men who were dressed in the garb of peaceable citizens, and who are treated as such by the officers of the law; firing from behind — cowardly murder.
>
> Unless I am mistaken, by the steps we have taken we have murder by the throat.

I ask you not to pay too much heed to the distorted accounts by partisans, who give detailed descriptions of horrors in what they call reprisals, and slur over the horrors of murder …

There will be no real peace in Ireland, there will be no conciliation, until this murder conspiracy is scattered. I am told that the result of the steps we are taking is that you have had more murders than ever in the last few weeks. Why? Before this action was taken, in vast tracts of Ireland the police were practically interned in their barracks. They dared not come out. Terror was triumphant …

If it is necessary to have further powers we shall seek them — because civilisation cannot permit a defiance of this kind to the elementary rule of its existence. Those men who indulge in these murders say it is war. If it is war, they, at any rate, cannot complain if we apply some of the rules of war. In war, if men come in civilian clothes behind your lines, armed with murderous weapons, intending to use them whenever they can do so with impunity — in war they are summarily dealt with … If it is war, the rules of war must apply …

There is no man in Ireland, as long as this terrorist conspiracy is dominant, who dare talk of conciliation. I … in the Imperial Parliament … ventured to invite anyone who could speak on behalf of Ireland to come and discuss any proposals. If I had given that invitation to the German Empire in the middle of the War I would have had a response; but, giving it to Ireland, there was no man dared respond. Why? They were afraid; they were intimidated.

You must break the terror before you get peace. Then you will get it. Irishmen have no real sympathy with this murder. Not a bit! They are heartily sick of the business …

We are offering Ireland not subjection, but equality. We are offering Ireland not servitude, but partnership — an honourable partnership, a partnership in the greatest Empire in the world — a partnership in that Empire at the height of its power; a partnership in that Empire in the greatest day of its glory."

Attack on Chamberlain

House of Commons
7 May 1940

• Context of speech

Although Lloyd George never held office again after 1922, there were moves to harness his immense skills. Baldwin (*qv*) toyed with the idea of bringing him into the National Government early in 1935, but this foundered on the intense hostility towards Lloyd George of several of Baldwin's colleagues, notably Neville Chamberlain (*qv*). As late as 1940 Winston Churchill (*qv*) thought of putting Lloyd George in charge of agriculture, a more important post than usual since Britain had increasingly to produce its own food.

Even this came to nothing, partly because Lloyd George was too old, partly because he was pessimistic about Britain's chances of survival and found the Blitz unnerving. (His physical timidity had tormented him in World War I, as he more than hints in the 'land fit for heroes' speech above.) But he could still hit hard in debate and although it is Leo Amery's (*see* Chamberlain) invoking Cromwell (*qv*) that is better remembered in the destruction of Chamberlain, it was Lloyd George who plunged the dagger in first.

In the Commons debate of 7 May 1940 Chamberlain called on his friends to rally to him. Then Lloyd George spoke. Sir Jock Colville (*see* Sir Winston Churchill) thought it his most forceful speech in years and describes how he held the House of Commons spellbound as he flung his arms about. Lloyd George's veiled criticisms of Baldwin foreshadowed the attack on him later in 1940 in the pamphlet 'The Guilty Men'.

❝ The greatest triumph of this extraordinary man Hitler has been that he has succeeded in putting his country into an infinitely better strategical position to wage war than his predecessors did in 1914 …

Czechoslovakia, that spear-head, aimed at the heart of Germany, broken. A million of the finest troops in Europe of a very well-educated race of free man, all gone. Such advantage as there is in Czechoslovakia, with its great lines of fortifications and its Skoda works, which turned out the finest artillery in the 1914 War, are in the hands of Hitler ...

You have a Franco-Russian Alliance, ... by which Russia was to come to the aid of Czechoslovakia if France did ... There would have been a two-front war for Germany. She knows what that means, because she had it before. That door is closed ...

With regard to our prestige, can you doubt that that has been impaired? You have only to read the friendly American paper to find out, highly friendly papers that were backing us up through thick and thin, in a country which was pro-Ally ...

There is also the fact of the state of our preparations five years ago, in 1935. In 1935 a promise of rearmament was made; in 1936 active proposals were submitted to this House and were passed without a Division. The Government said they would commit us to £1,500,000,000. If they had asked for more and had said that it was necessary, then there was no party in this House that would have challenged it. And if any party had challenged it, you had your majority.

Is there anyone in this House who will say that he is satisfied with the speed and efficiency of the preparations in any respect for air, for Army or for Navy? Everybody is disappointed. Everybody knows that whatever was done was done half-heartedly, ineffectively, without drive and unintelligently.

For three to four years I thought to myself that the facts with regard to Germany were exaggerated by the First Lord [*of the Admiralty, by now Winston Churchill*], because the then Prime Minister [*he meant Baldwin*] — not this Prime Minister — said that they were not true. The First Lord, Mr Churchill, was right about it. Then came the War.

The Prime Minister must remember that he has met this formidable foe of ours in peace and in war. He has always been worsted ... He has appealed for sacrifice. The nation is prepared for every sacrifice so long as it has leadership ... I say solemnly that the Prime Minister should give an example of sacrifice, because there is nothing which can contribute more to victory in this war than that he should sacrifice the seals of office."

'Too proud to fight'

Woodrow Wilson (1856–1924), 28th President of the USA 1913–21
Philadelphia, Pennsylvania
10 May 1915

• Biography

Academics almost never make satisfactory statesmen (bar Dr. Salazar in Portugal). They tend to be too high-minded, unworldly, cerebral and precise for the rough and tumble of politics. Woodrow Wilson was a case in point.

He first made his mark as President of Princeton, where he was an undoubted success. But even in the groves of Ivy League he had shown a pig-headed touchiness that made him take opposition personally. His tenure as Governor of New Jersey went so well that these ominous portents were forgotten. The 1912 election saw a Republican split (*see* Teddy Roosevelt) and Wilson entered the White House.

He pushed through a highly impressive body of laws, known collectively as 'the New Freedom', though in fact it involved quite a bit of restraint, albeit well-intentioned and humanitarian.

It was his winning re-election in 1916 that scuppered him, chiefly through his vote-pulling slogan 'He Kept Us Out Of The War' (coined almost as an afterthought by an over-enthusiastic supporter). Germany broadened its submarine strategy in 1917 to sink all shipping that traded with the UK, much of it American — and even the *Lusitania*, torpedoed in 1915, had had numerous American passengers. In April 1917 Wilson called on Congress to go to war with Germany, first because Germany was already warring against the US, secondly 'to make the world safe for democracy'.

He did his best to achieve the second aim by negotiating peace in Europe following the 1918 Armistice. It did not win sufficient support in the US, where the fatal isolationism of the later inter-war years already flourished. Wilson exhausted himself promoting his policy back home and suffered a stroke, obstinately rejected on America's behalf a compromise peace that might have worked and thereby ensured (if any one person can be said to have done so) that another World War would be enacted within a generation.

• Context of speech

This was delivered to an audience of newly naturalised Americans. All his life Wilson believed in his own power to get across complex ideas to ordinary people. Except on occasions of the greatest formality, such as accepting the Democratic nomination in 1912 and at state banquets and the like once he became President, he used only brief notes to refer to when speaking or none at all.

66 **Other countries depend upon the multiplication of their own native people. This country is constantly drinking strength out of new sources by the voluntary association with it of great bodies of strong men and forward-looking women. And so by the gift of the free will of independent people it is constantly being renewed from generation to generation by the same process by which it was originally created. It is as if humanity had determined to see to it that this great nation, founded for the benefit of humanity, should not lack for the allegiance of the people of the world.**

You have just taken an oath of allegiance to the United States. Of allegiance to whom? Of allegiance to no one, unless it be God. Certainly not of allegiance to those who temporarily represent this great Government. You have taken an oath of allegiance to a great ideal, to a great body of principles, to a great hope of the human race. You have said 'We are going to America', not only to earn a living, not only to seek the things which it was more difficult to obtain where you were born, but to help forward the great enterprises of the human spirit — to let man know that everywhere in the world there are men who will cross strange oceans and go where a speech is spoken which is alien to them, knowing that, whatever the speech, there is but one longing and utterance of the human heart, and that is for liberty and justice …

You cannot dedicate yourself to America unless you become in every respect and with every purpose of your will thorough Americans. You cannot become thorough Americans if you think of yourselves in groups. America does not consist of groups. A man who thinks of himself as belonging to a particular national group in America has not yet become an American, and the man who goes among you to trade upon your nationality is no worthy son to live under the Stars and Stripes …

We came to America, either ourselves or in the persons of our ancestors, to better the ideals of men, to make them see finer things than they had seen before, to get rid of things that divide, and to make sure of the things that unite. It was but an historical accident no doubt that this great country was called the 'United States', and yet I am very thankful that it has the word 'united' in its title; and the man who seeks to divide man from man, group from group, interest from interest, in the United States is striking at its very heart …

There is such a thing as a man being too proud to fight. There is such a thing as a nation being so right that it does not need to convince others by force that it is right."

The Fourteen Points

Joint Session of the US Congress
8 January 1918

• Context of speech

Wilson's Fourteen Points constituted his minimum requirements for peace with Germany.

"We entered this war because violations of right had occurred which touched us to the quick and made the life of our own people impossible unless they were corrected and the world secure once for all against their recurrence. What we demand in this war, therefore, is nothing peculiar to ourselves. It is that the world be made fit and safe to live in; and particularly that it be made safe for every peace-loving nation

which, like our own, wishes to live its own life, determine its own institutions, be assured of justice and fair dealing by the other peoples of the world as against force and selfish aggression. All the peoples of the world are in effect partners in this interest, and for our own part we see very clearly that unless justice be done to others it will not be done to us. The program of the world's peace, therefore, is our program; and that program, the only possible program, as we see it, is this:

1   Open covenants of peace, openly arrived at …

2   Absolute freedom of navigation upon the seas …

3   The removal … of … economic barriers and the establishment of … equality of trade conditions …

4   Adequate guarantees … that national armaments will be reduced to the lowest point consistent with domestic safety.

5   A free, open-minded, and absolutely impartial adjustment of all colonial claims …

6   The evacuation of all Russian territory and … settlement of all questions affecting Russia as will secure … her own political development and national policy …

7   Belgium … must be evacuated and restored …

8   All French territory should be freed and the invaded portions restored …

9   A readjustment of the frontiers of Italy should be effected along … lines of nationality.

10   The peoples of Austria-Hungary … should be accorded … autonomous development.

11   Rumania, Serbia, and Montenegro should be evacuated; occupied territories restored; Serbia accorded free and secure access to the sea; and the relations of the several Balkan states to one another determined by friendly counsel …

12   The Turkish portion of the present Ottoman Empire should be assured a secure sovereignty, but the other nationalities which are now under Turkish rule should be assured an undoubted security of life …

13   An independent Polish state should be erected which should include the territories inhabited by indisputably Polish populations …

14   A general association of nations must be formed …

In regard to these essential rectifications of wrong and assertions of right, we feel ourselves to be intimate partners of all the governments and peoples associated together against the imperialists.

We cannot be separated in interest or divided in purpose. We stand together until the end. For such arrangements and covenants we are willing to fight, and to continue to fight, until they are achieved; but only because we wish the right to prevail and desire a just and stable peace such as can be secured only by removing the chief provocations to war, which this program does remove.

We have no jealousy of German greatness, and there is nothing in this program that impairs it. We grudge her no achievement or distinction of learning or of pacific enterprise such as have made her record very bright and very enviable.

We do not wish to injure her or to block in any way her legitimate influence or power. We do not wish to fight her either with arms or with hostile arrangements of trade if she is willing to associate herself with us and the other peace-loving nations of the world in covenants of justice and law and fair dealing.

We wish her only to accept a place of equality among the peoples of the world — the new world in which we now live — instead of a place of mastery."

On German-Russian peace talks

**Leon Trotsky, *né* Lev Davidovich Brons(h)tein
(1879–1940)
Brest-Litovsk
10 February 1918**

• Biography

It is easier to keep one's name sweet in armchair revolutionary circles, which from their sedentary nature tend to be rather squeamish, if one is not in the tricky position of having actually to maintain a revolution, as opposed to preaching or starting one.

Trotsky is the nearest thing to an armchair revolutionary's revolutionary, since he lost control of events soon after the Bolsheviks had triumphed, hence retains, like Che Guevara, the romantic 'what-might-have-been' appeal.

Trotsky's appeal arose not just from his own romanticism, something he undoubtedly possessed. His doctrine of 'Permanent Revolution' predicted (and demanded) the overthrow of the existing order throughout the entire world on the heels of proletarian revolution in any one place, notably Russia in 1905, when Trotsky first formulated the doctrine.

This has particularly attracted intellectuals, such as the American men of letters Dwight Macdonald and Max Eastman, presumably in part because it was as visionary as, yet less implausible than, the withering away of the state that is the fond finale to humanity's *via dolorosa* according to orthodox Marxism. But it may also have been because the 'Permanent Revolution' doctrine seemed to sidestep the problem of how to 'make an omelette without breaking eggs', Lenin's euphemism admitting that terror is necessary to maintain revolutionary power.

Trotsky's venerators, notably Isaac Deutscher, each volume of whose biographical trilogy calls him 'prophet', seemed to think that if Trotsky rather than Stalin (*qv*) had succeeded Lenin (*qv*), the later 'excesses' of the Bolshevik experiment could have been avoided. Closer study of Trotsky's activities, facilitated by the recent opening-up of Russian archives, shows this to be a delusion.

Trotsky was famously Jewish. His father David Brons(h)tein ran counter to the Jewish stereotype, being neither bookish nor urban, but an illiterate landowner. His mother, who was from Odessa, one of Russia's liveliest centres of Jewish settlement, was true to the *Eybike Mame* (Yiddish for 'eternal mother') tradition in getting her children well educated. Trotsky was top pupil at school, and remained something of a conceited schoolboy prodigy ever after.'

He was converted to Marxism partly by Alexandra Lvovna Sokolovskaya, who became his first wife, and partly by fellow prisoners in the many gaols he occupied after his earliest seditious activities caused his arrest. He joined the Social Democrat Party, was sent to Siberia and in 1902 escaped using a bogus passport in the name of one of his gaolers, a man called Trotsky. He had numerous other aliases or *noms de plume*: Antid Oto, Arbuzov, Lvov, Neophyte, Petr Petrovich, Takhotsky, Vikentiev, L. Yanov, Yanovsky. He fled to London and collaborated with Lenin but in 1903 assumed leadership of the marginally less radical Menshevik wing of the Social Democrats in opposition to Lenin's Bolshevik one.

He was the leading figure in Russia's 1905 Revolution, becoming President of the St. Petersburg Soviet, or workers' council. On the Revolution's fizzling out he was again exiled to Siberia, again escaped and again fled abroad, this time to Vienna. He lived thereafter in Zurich, Germany, Paris and New York before returning to Russia in 1917, meanwhile beavering away at revolutionary politics and keeping himself, his second wife (if indeed he ever married her) and their children by journalism and an allowance from his father that only ceased in 1917.

Following the 1917 October Revolution he was arguably even more crucial to the Bolsheviks' survival than was Lenin. In 1918 he led the Russian team in the talks with Germany that took Russia out of World War I (*see* also Woodrow Wilson). Over the next two years he formed and led to victory in the Civil War the Red Army, commanding it across Russia's vast spaces from within an armoured train and making 'whistle-stop' speaking tours of remote spots to whip up revolutionary fervour like a radical version of American Presidential hopefuls.

He lost the long-drawn out contest with Stalin (*qv*) for the succession to Lenin. His Permanent Revolution vision proved too remote for ordinary Russians. Besides, Stalin, though greatly his intellectual inferior, was a more astute manoeuverer and Trotsky himself disdained to intrigue. In 1929 he was exported from Russia, almost as if he embodied his own Permanent Revolution doctrine, though in his case it was forcibly. He passed his remaining years in Turkey, France and Norway before ending in Mexico, where he was murdered by a Stalinist agent with what legend long had it was an ice-pick but which recently released FBI files show was a mountaineer's ice-axe.

Trotsky usually improvised his speeches, though on at least one important occasion in September 1917, involving a presentation of the Bolshevik viewpoint to a multi-party conference in Petrograd (as St. Petersburg had been named), he worked on his address in advance. He is said to have been a mannered, histrionic public speaker with an unusually resonant and clear voice. He had great variety of, and control over, his tone, ranging between honeyed cajolery and harsh, metallic, even grating, invective.

• Context of speech

The excerpt below was delivered during the negotiations to end Russia's participation on the Allied side in World War I. They lasted from December 1917 to March 1918.

66 **The task of this sub-commission ... was to state how suitable is the new border as suggested by the opposite side [*the Germans*], even if only to secure the Russian people's right of self-determination.**
We have heard the report of our representatives on the Commission ... The nations await with impatience the result ... They wonder when there will be an end to humanity's unprecedented self-destruction, brought about by the lust for power and wealth of the ruling classes in all countries.

This War has long since ceased for either side to be defensive, if it ever was. Should England retain the African colonies, Baghdad and Jerusalem, it is not a defensive war. And if Germany continues to control Belgium, Serbia, Romania, Poland and Lithuania...it is still not a defensive war, but a struggle for the division of the world.

... we want no more part in this purely imperialist War, where the wishes of the land-owning classes are openly paid for with the blood of the people. Our relationship with the imperialist governments of both sides is the same, and we are no longer willing to shed our soldiers' blood for the interests of one side over the other.

We are leading our army and our people out of the War in anticipation of what we hope will be a time when the oppressed peoples of all countries will take their fate into their own hands in the way Russia's workers have done.

Our former farm worker, currently a soldier, must return to the land that the Revolution wrested from the hands of the landowners and placed in peasant hands, so that he can till the land peacefully this spring.

Our industrial soldier must return to his shop floor to produce tools of plenty rather than tools of destruction, and together with the farmer build a new socialist economy.

We hereby notify all peoples and their governments of our intention to withdraw from the War. We issue the order fully to demobilise all armies facing the armies of Germany, Austria-Hungary, Bulgaria and Turkey. We have faith that other nations will swiftly follow our example."

Salute to the Red Army

Moscow Soviet
23 February 1922

• Context of speech

The excerpt below is from a speech commemorating the fourth anniversary of the founding of the Red Army.

"We make the anniversary of the Red Army today's date because the decree creating the Red Army was issued exactly four years ago. Actually, the Red Army was born together with the revolutionary proletariat at that...unknown hour when the first revolutionary worker took up a revolver ...

That first moment ... was the real birthday of the Red Army. Pacifists smelling of incense do not and never will understand that.

The Red Army is the organised and armed embodiment of the proletarian revolution ...

For us the army is an organised, armed section of the working class, which fights for power, takes power and defends what it has taken.

Through all its four years, the history of the Red Army has been the history of the working class in struggle. The first period of this history consisted of hasty, feverish and often helpless attempts to arm the advanced detachments of the working class. I remember how, at the time when the Brest-Litovsk negotiations broke down and German imperialism launched a new offensive, the workers of Moscow and Petrograd were seized with militant enthusiasm…

But when, after a week, we counted up the forces that we had managed to create, a miserably tiny figure emerged — not even thousands, barely hundreds.

And the whole of the first year was spent in such attempts…We built units under the blows of the enemy, we made many mistakes, we staggered between … attempts to reproduce completely what had existed earlier…and a rush to create in a very short time an army such as the world had never seen before: to turn its defects, its military naivety and ignorance, its lack of organisation into heaven knows what revolutionary advantages…

Looking back … you sometimes say to yourself 'How could we ever have conquered with the forces that we had in 1918?' Our army was numerically weak and badly organised — and if we won, it was only because this was not an 'army' in the ordinary sense of the word, but the embodiment of the revolutionary working class. Precisely because the revolution of the working class was the bearer of a new idea against the old one, its enemies were unable to withstand it…

In 1919 and 1920…we counted on our fight at the fronts merging, any day, with fronts that would stretch over the body of Europe, from us to the West…We hoped that the war we were waging would merge with the proletarian revolution in the West in the next few months, perhaps weeks.

Week followed week, month followed month — and the fourth year was upon us. The Red Army exists, but the revolution in Western Europe is developing far more slowly than we had hoped four or five years ago…

The iron chest of bourgeois society in the West is too strongly put together … When its component parts have been shattered, when it seems that just one more shove is needed and everything will fall apart, it turns out that in this stout, centuries-old structure there is still inertia enough, still sufficient conservatism…and the old edifice continues to hold out.'

On Communists joining the British Labour Party

Vladimir Ilyich Lenin, *né* Ulyanov (1870–1924)
Communist International 2nd Congress, Moscow
6 August 1920 _____

• Biography

The son of progressive parents, Lenin according to a tradition fostered by the guardians of the Marxist-Leninist faith underwent a conversion to Marxism similar to that of St. Paul to Christianity. The trigger was the execution in 1887 of his brother Alexander for conspiracy to bomb the Tsar. But Lenin chose revolution led by an élite party with himself at its head over Alexander's individualistic terrorist methods.

He was expelled from university as a result of his conversion to Marxism but then taught himself, notably classical and modern languages and law. After five years internal exile in Siberia for sedition, he migrated to Central Europe and Britain, writing quantities of revolutionary texts and taking the name Lenin, allegedly after the River Lena, in Siberia. In 1903 he became head of the Bolshevik wing of the Social Democratic Labour Party and thereafter concentrated on strengthening its organisation and faithfulness to Marxism in opposition to the heretical (and less immoderate) Menshevik element (*see* also Trotsky).

In 1917 the collapse of Tsarism caught him unawares and out of the country. But the Germans smuggled him into Russia in the hopes, eventually realised, that his anti-war stance would detach Russia from the Allies. He overthrew Russia's Provisional Revolutionary Government in October 1917 and started consolidating Bolshevik power. His methods involved terror against individuals (using the Cheka secret police, a Bolshevik creation); expropriation of property; and organisational repression, including the disbanding of an elected Constituent Assembly in which the Bolsheviks were a minority.

Even so it took three years of civil war and the temporary concession to capitalism known as the 'New Economic Policy' before Lenin's regime was secure.

He survived two assassination attempts but, partly due to the resultant wounds, suffered a series of strokes and left public life. His death may have arisen not only from the strokes but also from syphilis. He composed a testament advising the removal of Stalin (*qv*), then just beginning his rise to power. But it criticised others among the leadership, hence was suppressed. Stalin eventually succeeded Lenin in consequence.

• Context of speech

In March 1919 the Bolsheviks set up with other revolutionary socialists the Communist International, charged with promoting world revolution.

The speech excerpted below was delivered at the last session of the 2nd Congress held from 19 July to 7 August 1920. The resolution to affiliate to the British Labour Party got 58 votes for, 24 against and two abstentions. The Labour Party turned the application down. Over the next 60 years individual Communists often infiltrated the Labour Party in disguise. The final clean-out of a Marxist element was achieved by the Labour Leader Neil (now Lord) Kinnock in the 1980s.

66 **C**omrade McLaine [*William McLaine, one of two British Socialist Party delegates*] has ... **called the Labour Party the political organisation of the trade union movement** ... **I have met the same view several times ... It is erroneous ...**
Whether or not a party is really a political party of the workers does not depend solely upon a membership of workers but also upon the men that lead it, its actions and its political tactics ...

Regarded from this, the only correct, point of view, the Labour Party is a thoroughly bourgeois party, because, although made up of workers, it is led by reactionaries, and the worst kind of reactionaries at that ...

We have also heard another point of view, defended by Comrade Sylvia Pankhurst [*daughter of the suffragette agitator Emmeline Pankhurst and initially a suffragette too but by now inclining to socialism*] and Comrade Gallacher [*Willie Gallacher (1881–1965), then a Shop Stewards Movement delegate, but later Communist MP for Fife West 1935–50 and President of the British Communist Party 1956–63*] ...

Comrade Gallacher has told us here how he and his comrades have organised ... the revolutionary movement in Glasgow, ... how they gave able support to the petty-bourgeois pacifists Ramsay MacDonald [*Labour Prime Minister 1924 and 1929–31*] and [*Philip*] Snowden [*Labour Chancellor of the*

Exchequer 1924 and 1929–31; see also Sir Winston Churchill's Iron Curtain speech] when they came to Glasgow, and used this support to organise a mass movement against the war …

Comrade Sylvia Pankhurst pointed out several times that Britain needed 'Lefts'. I, of course, replied that this was absolutely true, but that one must not overdo this 'Leftism'. Furthermore she said that they were better pioneers, but for the moment were rather noisy. I do not take this in a bad sense, but rather in a good one, namely, that they are better able to carry on revolutionary agitation.

Sylvia Pankhurst also asked: 'Is it possible for a Communist Party to join another political party which still belongs [*as the Labour Party did*] to the Second International?'

… the British Labour Party is in a very special position: it is … made up of members of all trade unions, and has a membership of about four million, and allows sufficient freedom to all affiliated political parties. It thus includes a vast number of British workers who follow the lead of the worst bourgeois elements, the social-traitors …

At the same time, however, the Labour Party has let the British Socialist Party into its ranks, permitting it to have its own press organs, in which members … can freely and openly declare that the [*Labour*] party leaders are social-traitors.

This is a very original situation: a party which unites enormous masses of workers, so that it might seem a political party, is nevertheless obliged to grant its members complete latitude … In such circumstances, it would be a mistake not to join this party.

In a private talk, Comrade Pankhurst said to me: 'If we are real revolutionaries and join the Labour Party, these gentlemen will expel us.'

But that would not be bad at all. Our resolution says that we favour affiliation insofar as the Labour Party permits sufficient freedom of criticism …

In such circumstances it would be highly erroneous for the best revolutionary elements not to do everything possible to remain in such a party. Let the Thomases [*after J. H. Thomas, later a Labour Cabinet Minister*] and other social-traitors, whom you have called by that name, expel you. That will have an excellent effect upon the mass of the British workers."

Resignation speech

Sir Oswald Mosley, 6th Bt (1896–1981)
House of Commons
28 May 1930

• Biography

Given England's relatively peaceful history, bogymen based on real people are few. Richard the Lionheart's name was used by Muslim mothers to discipline fractious children in medieval Palestine. But in native nurseries Sir Oswald Mosley, alone of ogre candidates down the ages, conjures up the requisite nightmare vision.

He was born into a Midlands gentry family. His bibulous father and practical but unsophisticated mother separated when he was five, so that he was brought up by her and his father's father. Both worshipped him, hence his hubristic self-confidence.

First at Sandhurst then as a pilot in World War I he injured the same ankle twice, giving him a permanent limp. This and his womanising within the family (he allegedly bedded his first wife's two sisters and her stepmother) recall Byron (*qv*), from whose ancestor, the 1st Lord Byron, Sir Oswald's ancestor, another Oswald, had coincidentally bought one of the family estates three centuries earlier.

His later exile, self-imposed but arising from disgrace in England, recalls Byron too. Unlike Byron his memoirs survived to be published (and got reviews little less favourable than Byron's would presumably have done had they not been burnt). In his fondness for demagogic methods and leading marches he more recalls Lord George Gordon, of Gordon Riots fame, and much about Mosley suggests a late-18th century dandy-cum-political-adventurer transposed to the humdrum modern age.

He entered politics at F.E. Smith's (*qv*) suggestion, first as a Conservative MP, then as a left-leaning Independent and finally as a Labour one, becoming in 1929 a minister charged with tackling unemployment. After resigning in 1930 he founded and led first the New Party, then the British Union of Fascists (BUF) and finally the Union Movement. He must hold the British, perhaps world, record for the number of political groupings he adhered to.

His Fascism had roots in his family history, class origins, ex-soldier's camaraderie and impatience with orthodox remedies for employment, even perhaps his favourite sports (he was a fencing champion, also a useful boxer, again not unlike Byron).

He was imprisoned without trial during World War II on the grounds that he might collaborate with the Germans in any invasion, also because leading Labour politicians, notably Herbert Morrison, the Home Secretary, resented Mosley's 'betrayal' in 1930.

He stood for Parliament a few times after the War, but never won many votes. He opposed immigration to Britain and supported the repatriation of immigrants from Britain, also a united Europe.

He frequently denied that he had ever been systematically anti-semitic. But some of his public utterances in 1934, the BUF's crisis year, strongly suggest otherwise. And his marching through Jewish districts of London's East End was distinctly provocative. His first father-in-law, Lord Curzon, in 1920 observed of Mosley that he had 'a rather Jewish appearance'. The Mosley family tree shows a Lever among his ancestors, but this is not an exclusively Jewish name. On the other hand one of Sir Oswald's grandsons married an Oppenheimer, so some accommodation of Mosleys and Jewry has developed. Lord George Gordon, of whom Mosley was arguably an avatar, later converted to Judaism.

• Context of speech

Mosley was a poor orator on first entering Parliament. He tended to drone, and his voice was shrill. But through training, he became a very good one. When he had been an MP for only two years, his repeatedly denouncing the Lloyd George (*qv*) administration's repression in Ireland won considerable admiration.

Mosley's mannerisms while speaking were directly compared with those of Pitt the Elder (*qv*), his hero. His voice was harsh, but powerful enough for a parade ground. He had no need for microphones and usually disconnected them when speech-making. By the mid-1930s his oratory was first-rate, being simultaneously lucid, cogent and impassioned. He was speaking 200 nights a year, as much as one-and-a-half-hours at a time, without notes, then answering questions for up to an hour, reportedly never at a loss for words. But when he was tired a certain monotony of delivery became noticeable.

He announced his resignation from the Labour Government to Parliament on 21 May 1930. His reason was Labour's refusal to tackle unemployment seriously, a charge it is hard to deny. The 21 May speech was formal. A week later, in a debate on unemployment, he was more expansive.

"The President of the Board of Trade ... said on the 14th of May 'During the last fortnight alone £16,000,000 of new capital has been authorised or raised for overseas investment, and so I trust the process will continue.' Why? Why is it so right and proper and desirable that capital should go overseas to equip factories to compete against us, to build roads and railways in the Argentine or in Timbuctoo, to provide employment for people in those countries while it is supposed to shake the whole basis of our financial strength if anyone dares to suggest the raising of money by the Government of this country to provide employment for the people of this country?**

If those views are passed without examination or challenge the position of this country is serious indeed ... the situation which faces us is, of course, very serious. Everybody knows that; and perhaps those who have been in office for a short time know it even better. It is not, I confidently believe, irreparable, but I feel this from the depths of my being, that the days of muddling through are over, that this time we cannot muddle through. This nation has to be mobilised and rallied for a tremendous effort, and who can do that except the Government of the day?

If that effort is not made we may soon come to crisis, to a real crisis. I do not fear that so much, for this reason, that in a crisis this nation is always at its best. This people knows how to handle a crisis, it cools their heads and steels their nerves. What I fear much more than a sudden crisis is a long, slow, crumbling through the years until we sink to the level of a Spain, a gradual paralysis beneath which all the vigour and energy of this country will succumb.

That is a far more dangerous thing, and far more likely to happen unless some effort is made. If the effort is made, how relatively easily can disaster be averted. You have in this country resources, skilled craftsmen among the workers, design and technique among the technicians, unknown and unequalled in any other country in the world.

What a fantastic assumption it is, that a nation which within the lifetime of everyone has put forth efforts of energy and vigour unequalled in the history of the world, should succumb before an economic situation such as the present. If the situation is to be overcome, if the great powers of this country are to be rallied and mobilised for a great national effort, then the Government and Parliament must give a lead.

I beg the Government tonight to give the vital forces of this country the chance that they await. I beg Parliament to give that lead."

Wonders of science

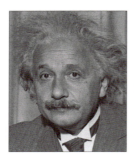

Albert Einstein (1879–1955)
Broadcast from Charlottenburg radio tower,
Berlin
22 August 1930

• Biography

Public boredom over mathematics and science is such that their male practitioners are unknown unless they come with idiosyncratic accessories (Patrick Moore's monocle or Stephen Hawking's voice-synthesiser). Female ones have to be moppet prodigies (Ruth Lawrence), outstandingly good-looking (Carol Vorderman) or provocative dressers (Baroness Greenfield's mini-skirts).

Einstein became the best known mathematician-scientist of all time not because of his theories, which few laymen understood, but through his mane of grey hair surmounting an affable teddy bear face (this at a time when short backs and sides were *de rigueur*). It helped that he was ready to clown for the cameras, witness the photo of him sticking his tongue out.

He is also the most famous exam flunk in history, his teenage failure in qualifying for a high school electrical engineering course giving hope to low test-scorers everywhere. Further, he was unsuccessful in his first efforts at academic jobs. What is less well-known is that he was a draft-dodger, to that end renouncing his German citizenship in 1896. He moved to Switzerland, worked in the Berne patent office and in his leisure hours wrote some of the most important scientific papers in history — the more remarkably since he lacked campus opportunities for discussing them.

His scientific reputation once made, he took various academic posts in Central Europe. He returned to Germany in 1914 and in 1919 won instant popular fame when the press publicised the confirmation of his theory that light would bend if subjected to gravitational pull.

He was already spending much of his time in the US when Germany went Nazi in 1933. He remained in the US thereafter. He devoted the rest of his life not just to scientific research but attempts at universal peace and fund-raising for the Hebrew University of Jerusalem. His Zionism was too weak to make him take a post there or accept the offer in 1952 of the Presidency of Israel.

• Context of speech

The occasion of the speech below was the opening of the 7th German Radio and Audio Exhibition. Einstein, who as a child had had speech problems, was a native of southern Germany and retained its accent and some of its expressions.

Einstein's belief that the radio was mostly a force for good proved over-optimistic a few years later — and in the selfsame city of Berlin — when propagandists like Goebbels and Lord Haw-Haw twisted it into a powerful instrument of war.

---

66 **L**adies **and gentlemen present (and those who are not present), when you hear the radio think also about how people have come to possess such a wonderful tool of communication. The origin of all technical achievements is the divine curiosity and speculative instinct of the working and thinking researcher as well as the constructive imagination of the technical inventor.**

Consider [*Hans Christian*] Oersted [*1777–1851, Danish physicist*], who was the first person to notice the magnetic effect of electric currents, or [*Johann Philipp*] Reis [*1834–74, German physicist*], who was the first person to make use of this effect to generate sound by using electromagnetism, or [*Alexander Graham*] Bell [*1847–1922, Scots-born, British-educated and sometime Canadian domiciled inventor but finally resident in the US, hence often claimed by Americans as one of theirs*], the first person to convert sound waves into variable electric currents with his microphone by using sensitive contacts.

Consider also Maxwell [*in full James Clerk-Maxwell (1831–79), Scottish physicist and first Professor of Experimental Physics at Cambridge*], who demonstrated the existence of electric waves by using mathematics; and Hertz [*Heinrich Rudolf (1857–94), rather than his nephew Gustav, though both were (German) physicists, the latter in addition a Nobel Laureate*], the first person to generate them, doing so with the help of a spark, and thus proving their existence.

Consider especially [*Robert von*] Lieben [*(1878–1913), a wealthy Austrian, an 'amateur' inasmuch as he never completed his formal education*], who invented a measuring instrument for electric pulses, the electric valve tube. It was also an ideal and simple instrument for generating electric waves. Think gratefully of the large number of unknown engineers who have simplified instruments of communication via radio and have adapted them to mass production in such a fashion that today they are usable by everybody.

Everybody should be ashamed who uses the wonders of science and engineering without reflecting upon them any more than a cow reflects on the botanical aspects of the plants which it eats with pleasure.

Think also about the fact that it is the engineers who make true democracy possible. They facilitate not only people's daily work but also make the works of the finest thinkers and artists accessible to the public. The pleasure of these works was till recently restricted to the privileged classes. Thus engineers wake people from their unconscious obtuseness.

The radio fulfils a unique function in the way it forges international amity. Till now nations got to know each other mostly through the distorting lens of their daily newspapers. Radio reveals them to each other clearly, and mostly as regards the friendly side of the human character. It will thus help end the feelings of mutual incomprehension that so easily turn to mistrust and hostility. In this spirit, gaze on the products of the creative impulse that this exhibition offers to the astonished senses of the visitors."

'Faith, Hope, Love and Work'

**Stanley Baldwin, 1st Earl Baldwin of Bewdley
(1867–1947)
House of Commons
16 February 1923**

• Biography

The only 20th-century Prime Minister to form three chronologically separate administrations (1923–24, 1924–29 and 1935–37), Baldwin by doing so dominated British politics between the wars. He revived his party, the Conservatives, preparing them for their long run as the 'natural party of government' (1951–64, 1970–74 and

1979–97) after his death. He won power by attracting previous Liberal supporters and even some potential Labour ones, also votes from women, then newly enfranchised. He did this through a non-partisan, pacific approach expressed in conciliatory speeches adorned with folksy touches more usual in American politicians.

He retired after clearing a constitutional hurdle of exceptional trickiness, the Abdication (*see* also Edward VIII). But he was vilified once World War II started for failing to prepare for it properly. Churchill (*qv*) even called him 'the greatest of non-statesmen'. Others among those who knew Baldwin mention characteristics like astuteness, cunning, even ruthlessness, so it is hard not to believe he possessed them in some measure, and he himself in his manoeuvres during the Abdication crisis mentions his own wiliness. To the public Baldwin's chief characteristic was straightforwardness. But the dissenting judgements deserve careful consideration.

Anti-Baldwin feeling rested partly on a belief (shared by Chamberlain (*qv*), then Chancellor of the Exchequer) that Baldwin exaggerated the electoral risk of campaigning for rearmament in 1935, hence soft-pedalled it. But at least he did not duck it altogether. And he had supported rearmament from 1934. Whether he pushed it hard enough is another matter. Lloyd George (*qv*, especially his last speech quoted) thought he hadn't. But Baldwin and he were old enemies. However, Baldwin through caution did not convince his backbenchers either, and that as early as 1936. Moreover, in the first speech excerpted below he mentions his own 'flabby' liking to agree as a good in itself, while later, in his second speech, his almost hysterical references to aerial bombardment support the contention of one of his biographers, H. Montgomery Hyde, that he was at heart a bit of a pacifist.

Academically, Baldwin's reputation has revived recently. Yet doubts about him persist, and often over his speeches, just where he supposedly shone most. Take his words to the Peace Society during his 1935 re-election campaign: 'I give you my word that there will be no great armaments'. It is argued that this did not mean no large-scale rearmament, more a denial of the former Liberal Foreign Secretary Lord Grey of Fallodon's dictum that 'great armaments lead inevitably to war' – a dictum Baldwin's audience presumably knew and accepted. But taken at face value it sounds neither honest nor courageous.

Then there is Baldwin's inept handling, not least in a speech, of the Anglo-French agreement of late 1935 conniving in Mussolini's (*qv*) invasion of Abyssinia. The aim was sensible: to free Britain in opposing Hitler, a much greater menace, especially as Baldwin doubted French co-operation if Britain opposed Mussolini (he had secret information about Mussolini's bribing the French Foreign Minister, Laval (*see* also Pope John Paul II)). Ultimately Baldwin had to repudiate the agreement and sacrifice the Foreign Secretary who had negotiated it.

Arguably his greatest mistake was letting Hitler re-militarise the Rhineland in 1936. We now know Hitler's forces had orders to withdraw if challenged. But

Baldwin 'bought' the bluff because he was acutely aware of Britain's military weakness and feared that if Hitler fell Germany would go Communist. (An odd fear: Germany's leading Communists had either been murdered by the Nazis or fled to Russia, where many were murdered by Stalin, *qv*.) Baldwin also thought Hitler's re-militarising the Rhineland removed a legitimate cause of German resentment, thus facilitating an arms-limitation agreement with Germany.

Stanley Baldwin was originally a Worcestershire iron-master. The Worcestershire element he reflected in the lyrical passages on rural life in his speeches, none more so than in his 1935 address to the Peace Society mentioned above. In most political matters he was less iron than emollient. But he could attack targets like press lords robustly enough, as in the famous remark likening their position to 'power without responsibility — the prerogative of the harlot throughout the ages'. The phrase was allegedly coined by his cousin, Rudyard Kipling.

Baldwin came late to front-rank politics, becoming President of the Board of Trade under Lloyd George (*qv*) in 1921, when in his fifties. Promoted Chancellor in 1922, he unexpectedly succeeded Bonar Law as Conservative Prime Minister in 1923. He injudiciously called an election, lost it and as a result nearly forfeited the Conservative leadership. But he won the second 1924 election, continued in office till 1929, joined Ramsay MacDonald's National Government of 1931 as Lord President of the Council and in 1935 succeeded the increasingly ineffective MacDonald as Premier.

When Baldwin first used a microphone at a public meeting he disliked it. But he quickly became a very effective broadcaster. He seemed to share his thoughts with his audience, using a conversational tone as if in the room with them. This was particularly effective in the 1926 General Strike. He was one of the first major British politicians to use his staff as speech-writers. He freely advised others on public speaking, stressing the importance of an unhurried delivery, both broadcast and in Parliament. He published five books of his own speeches. They sold in their tens of thousands. But he was not a good debater in the sense of going aggressively for the other side.

• Context of speech

Baldwin as Chancellor spoke at the opening of the parliamentary session. He had carefully prepared his speech, although it was nominally in reply to a Labour amendment, and aimed it at the nation rather than just MPs.

"One word about the speech delivered last night by the Hon. Member for Motherwell [*J.W.T. Newbold, a Communist*]. I have always been a student of history, and I learned from him several things that I had not known before. There was only one remark of his on which I wish to comment. He said that when the Labour Party had been in power, and failed, he [i.e., *the Communist Party*] was coming in.

I believe that the Hon. Member for Silvertown [*J.Jones*] expressed dissent. I am myself of that somewhat flabby nature that always prefers agreement to disagreement, and I welcome the opportunity of recording the fact that I find myself in hearty and uncompromising agreement with the Hon. Member for Silvertown.

When the Labour Party sit on these benches, we shall all wish them well in their effort to govern the country. But I am quite certain that whether they succeed or fail, there will never in this country be a Communist government, and for this reason, that no gospel founded on hate will ever seize the hearts of our people — the people of Great Britain.

It is no good trying to cure the world by spreading out oceans of bloodshed. It is no good trying to cure the world by repeating that pentasyllabic French derivative, 'proletariat'.

The English language is the richest in the world in monosyllables. Four words, of one syllable each, are words which contain salvation for this country and for the whole world. They are 'Faith', 'Hope', 'Love' and 'Work'. No government in this country today which has not Faith in the people, Hope in the future, Love for its fellow men, and which will not Work and Work and Work, will ever bring this country through into better days and better times, or will ever bring Europe through, or the world through."

'The bomber will always get through'

House of Commons
10 November 1932 _____

• Context of speech

As 1932 drew to a close the failure to reach international agreement on disarmament, plus experts' forecasts of the almost total destruction of major centres of population through aerial bombardment in any future war, combined to depress Baldwin, who was a much more sensitive man than his unassuming countryman exterior suggested.

In the speech excerpted below this all spilled out. The last paragraph in particular, though it now reads absurdly, is remarkably prophetic about the future dip in his reputation. Churchill criticised the speech for its fatalism and helplessness. The ominous statement 'the bomber will always get through' was seized on by proponents of disarmament and rearmament alike (it could be read as leading logically either to abject surrender or deterrence through mutually assured destruction, providing one re-armed). Baldwin twice tried in the following two years to put a gloss on it, but unsuccessfully.

66 **What the world suffers from ... is a sense of fear ... But in my view ... there is no greater cause of that fear than the fear of the air ... in the next war you will find that any town which is within reach of an aerodrome can be bombed within the first five minutes of war from the air ...**

I think it is well ... for the man in the street to realise that there is no power on earth that can protect him from being bombed. Whatever people may tell him, the bomber will always get through ... The only defence is in offence, which means that you have to kill more women and children more quickly than the enemy if you want to save yourselves ...

I will not pretend that we are not taking our precautions in this country. We have done it. We have made our investigations, much more quietly and hitherto without any publicity, but, considering the years that are required to make your preparations, any government of this country in the present circumstances of the world would have been guilty of criminal negligence had they neglected to make other preparations ...

I confess that the more I have studied this question the more depressed I have been at the perfectly futile attempts ... made to deal with this problem. The ... time ... wasted at Geneva ... discussing ... reduction of the size of aeroplanes ... [has] ... reduced me to despair. What would be the only result of reducing the size of aeroplanes? ... immediately every scientific man in the country will turn to making a high explosive bomb about the size of a walnut and as powerful as a bomb of big dimensions ...

If the conscience of the young men should ever come to feel with regard to this one instrument [*air-borne bombing*] that it is evil and should go, the thing will be done; but if they do not feel like that — well, as I say, the future is in their hands. But when the next war comes, and European civilisation is wiped out, as it will be and by no force more than that force, then do not let them lay blame on the old men. Let them remember that they, they principally or they alone, are responsible for the terrors that have fallen upon the earth."

On the Abdication

House of Commons
10 December 1936

• Context of speech

Immediately following Edward VIII's (*qv*) abdication, Baldwin addressed Parliament on the subject. He did so, not reading from any fair copy of a carefully drafted and meticulously revised speech, as one might expect on so momentous an occasion in constitutional history, but from scraps of paper on which he had jotted down notes back in Downing Street, many of them in the last few hours. He had even mislaid some of the scraps by the time it came to drive from Number Ten to the House of Commons, or left them behind inadvertently (accounts differ), necessitating a dash back to Number Ten to retrieve them by his Parliamentary Private Secretary.

The drama of his performance in the House was accentuated by what in a professional actor would have looked like 'business', but which in Baldwin's case were his customary fidgets. These included at first not being able to find the key to his red dispatch box, turning to a colleague in mid-sentence to confirm orally a date and groping for his loose sheets of paper on the House floor, where they had been scattered by another colleague's placing his own documents on top of Baldwin's scraps, mere 'bromo' as one observer called them. ('Bromo' was a cheap lavatory paper of the time.)

"When October came ... I was aware ... that ... a divorce case [was] coming on ... [concerning which] a difficult situation might arise later; ... I felt that ... someone should see His Majesty and warn him of the difficult situation ....

I consulted, I am ashamed to say — and they have forgiven me — none of my colleagues ...

I ... stated that I desired to see him — this is the first and only occasion on which I was the one who asked for an interview ...

I may say ... that an adviser to the Crown can be of no possible service ... unless he tells ... the truth as he sees it ... His Majesty's attitude all through has been — let me put it in this way: never has he shown any sign of offence, of being hurt at anything I have said ...

I told His Majesty that I had two great anxieties — one the effect of ... the ... criticism ... in the American press ... in the Dominions ...[,] particularly ... Canada ... [and] in this country ... I reminded him ... [that] the British monarchy is ... unique ... The Crown ... stands for far more than it ever has done ... , being ... not only the last link of Empire ... , but the guarantee in this country ... against many evils that have ... afflicted other countries ...

I ... pointed out ... that, if a verdict was given in the [divorce] case that left the matter in suspense ... that ... might be dangerous, because then everyone would be talking, and when once the press began ... a most difficult situation would arise ...

The next time I saw him was on Monday, 16th November ... By that date the decree nisi had been pronounced ... His Majesty had sent for me ... and I spoke to him ... on the question of marriage ...

I told him that I did not think that a particular marriage was one that would receive the approbation of the country. That marriage would have involved the lady becoming queen. I did tell His Majesty once that I might be a remnant of the old Victorians, but that my worst enemy would not say ... that I did not know what the reaction of the English people would be ...

I pointed out ... that the ... King's wife was different from ... the wife of any other citizen ... ; ... it was part of the price ... the King has to pay. His wife becomes queen ... ; and therefore, in the choice of a queen, the voice of the people must be heard. Then His Majesty said to me — I have his permission to state this — that he wanted to tell me something that he had long wanted to ... He said 'I am going to marry Mrs. Simpson, and I am prepared to go.' I said 'Sir, that is most grievous news and it is impossible for me to make any comment on it today.' ...

He sent for me again on Wednesday, 25th November ... a suggestion had been made ... that the King should marry, that Parliament should pass an act enabling the lady to be the King's wife without the position of queen ... my first reaction was that Parliament would never pass such a Bill ... On 2nd December the King asked me ... if I could answer his question. I gave him the reply that I was afraid it was impracticable ...

His Majesty said he was not surprised ... He took my answer with no question and he never recurred to it again ... That decision was ... formal ..., ... the only formal decision ... taken by the Cabinet until I come to ... yesterday ...

I pointed out that the ... alternatives had been narrowed and that ... he [*the King*] would be placed ... between two conflicting loyalties ... : either ... abandonment of the project on which his heart was set, and remaining as king, or ... going, and later on contracting that marriage ...

The King cannot speak for himself. The King has told us that he cannot carry ... these almost intolerable burdens of kingship without a woman at his side, and we know that. This crisis, if I may use the word, has arisen now rather than later from that very frankness of His Majesty's character which is one of many of his attractions. It would have been perfectly possible for His Majesty not to have told me ... for some months to come. But he realised the damage that might be done in the interval ... and he made that declaration to me when he did on purpose to avoid what he felt might be dangerous ... to the moral force of the Crown ... He told me his intentions and he has never wavered from them. I want the House to understand that ... not until he had fully considered ... did he make public his decision. There has been no kind of conflict in this matter. My efforts ... have been directed ... in trying to help him to make the choice which he has not made, and we have failed ... "

Christmas broadcast 1932

George V (1910–36)
By radio from Sandringham House, Norfolk
25 December 1932

• Biography

Nature had not intended George V for an innovator. He was hostile to so trivial a development as the fashion for trouser turn-ups. He was cheerfully philistine about modern art — and in public too. Yet by a quirk of history he presided over more constitutional changes than any sovereign since Charles I (*qv*), introducing some of them personally. They included diminished powers for peers; a re-branding makeover performed on his own family (from Wipper/Wettin/Saxe-Coburg-Gotha to Windsor); inventing the Order of the British Empire, which in radical fashion conferred honours on women and the middle classes; southern Ireland's secession; and the first socialist government. Then, towards the end of his reign, there came the Christmas broadcast.

Like Charles I (and Henry VIII too), George was a younger son promoted Prince of Wales after his elder brother died prematurely. He joined the Navy as a boy and remained in many ways a bluff sea-dog ever after. On land his favourite activities were stamp-collecting and shooting. (Apart from the 2nd and last Marquess of Ripon, whose 14 brace of pheasant in 60 seconds is hard to beat, he was accounted by many the best bringer-down of game-birds in the Empire.)

He was pitch-forked into the 1910 House of Lords crisis already mentioned (*see* Lloyd George) the instant he acceded. There followed in quick succession, and in addition to the other constitutional crises already mentioned, Ulster's intransigence in 1914 over Irish Home Rule, plus a related mutiny by army units near Dublin; the need to conduct World War I; the Russian Revolution (George's refusal to facilitate the emigration of his cousins the Tsar's family was long held against him); his decision not to offer the premiership to a peer in 1923, thus setting a new precedent; and his brokering the National Government in 1931. Truly a roller-coaster ride.

He held his own, surmounting each obstacle with on the whole considerable success. He failed in the no less vital, but more homely, field of family upbringing. He and his wife, Queen Mary, were too remote from their children, even by the distant standards of the day, with sad results. The eldest boy was the unsatisfactory Edward VIII (*qv*); the next, the future George VI, a stammerer; the third, Henry Duke of Gloucester, so eccentric as to seem unbalanced; the fourth, George Duke of Kent, a bisexual drug addict; the youngest, John, an epileptic.

• Context of speech

A Christmas message from the sovereign to his people via the ether was the brainwave of Sir John (later Lord) Reith, the BBC's first Director-General. In 1932, the inaugural year, the message was linked to the start of the World Service, then termed the Empire Service. George's text was written by Rudyard Kipling (*see* also Baldwin) and was broadcast live at 3 pm Greenwich Mean Time on Christmas Day 1932.

George was not particularly keen on the idea of a Christmas broadcast to begin with. But he was eventually persuaded and used a small room at Sandringham, the family's Norfolk property, as a makeshift studio.

66 **Through one of the marvels of modern science, I am enabled, this Christmas Day, to speak to all my peoples throughout the Empire. I take it as a good omen that wireless should have reached its present perfection at a time when the Empire has been linked in closer union, for it offers us immense possibilities to make that union closer still.**

It may be that our future will lay upon us more than one stern test. Our past will have taught us how to meet it unshaken. For the present, the work to which we are all equally bound is to arrive at a reasoned tranquillity within our borders, to regain prosperity without self-seeking and to carry with us those whom the burden of past years has disheartened or overborne. My life's aim has been to serve as I might towards those ends, for your loyalty, your confidence in me, has been my abundant reward.

I speak now from my home and from my heart to you all. To men and women so cut off by the snows, the deserts or the seas, that only voices out of the air can reach them; to those cut off from fuller life by blindness, sickness or infirmity; and to those who are celebrating this day with their children and their grandchildren; to all, to each, I wish a happy Christmas. God bless you."

'We have nothing to fear but fear itself'

Franklin Delano Roosevelt (1882–1945)
32nd President of the USA 1933–45
Inaugural address
4 March 1933

• Biography

The second Roosevelt President, Franklin, was only a very distant cousin of Teddy Roosevelt (*qv*) by birth. But he also married Teddy's niece, Eleanor. It was an action which, as he well knew, brought him within Teddy's orbit in a way his cousinhood would not have done.

He was a Democrat, whereas Teddy had been a Republican. And Eleanor turned out to have her own set of principles and policies, which were to the left of most Democrats' and which as First Lady she pursued as single-mindedly as Franklin did his. But his were undeniably on a larger scale, such as fighting the greatest war in all history and saving the world's biggest economy from its grimmest depression.

This allowed Franklin to outshine even cousin Teddy as President, though Teddy might well have risen to the occasion just as magnificently had he lived then. Franklin was the first and last of the multi-term Presidents — something Teddy had belatedly tried to be too, though in so maverick a fashion that he failed. But defeating first the Great Depression then the Axis Powers in World War II demanded no less. Franklin Roosevelt's 12–year presidency coincided almost exactly with Hitler's (*qv*) Third Reich, to within weeks. But it could not, bar the skilled oratory that maintained momentum, have been more different.

Franklin began his political career as Assistant Navy Secretary under Woodrow Wilson (*qv*), whose idealist influence on Franklin was to become apparent in World War II. In 1928 he was elected Governor of New York state. He had many years before contracted the polio that left him with nearly useless legs. In those days it was possible to hide such infirmities from the public — just as well, since otherwise his career might also have been crippled.

His gubernatorial success, plus the eclipse of his chief Democratic Party rival Al Smith, gave him a smooth ride to the White House in 1932. The hard part then began. His 'New Deal' policies tackled unemployment, under-investment, the un-housed and the under-fed. But it took time. Not till the end of the 1930s did industrial output overtake 1929's.

By 1945 the exhaustion of the other victor nations, not to mention the total crushing of the Axis, left America the only real world power by a huge margin. Franklin Roosevelt was among those individuals most exhausted by the struggle. He died three-and-a-half weeks before VE Day.

• Context of speech

Roosevelt's first Inaugural Address took place at a critical moment. Less than 24 hours earlier America's banks had shut their doors against investors desperate to withdraw savings. Like Stanley Baldwin (*qv*) in Britain, Roosevelt was a master not just of statesmanlike oratory before professional politicians but of the more avuncular informality desirable when radio speech-making to the masses. He could convince such audiences that he was in the room with them, indeed called a series of 30 morale-boosting broadcasts he made between 1933 and 1944 'fireside chats'.

His presidency coincided with the supremacy of radio as a broadcast medium and his ratings competed with the cream of America's popular entertainers, even Amos 'n Andy, Benny 'n Hope and Burns 'n Allen.

At Groton, his private secondary school, the other boys had reckoned Roosevelt's accent too British. Later, he relapsed into a standard upper-class New York-cum-Ivy League accent, which his latest biographer Conrad Black tells us involves a broad 'a' (*e.g.*, 'class'-'farce' not 'class'-'gas') and a frequently near-inaudible 'r'.

---

66 **This is preeminently the time to speak the truth … So, first of all, let me assert my firm belief that the only thing we have to fear is fear itself — nameless, unreasoning, unjustified terror, which paralyzes needed efforts to convert retreat into advance.**
… our common difficulties … concern, thank God, only material things. Values have shrunken to fantastic levels; taxes have risen; our ability to pay has fallen; government of all kinds is faced by serious curtailment of income; the means of exchange are frozen in the currents of trade; the withered leaves of industrial enterprise lie on every side; farmers find no markets for their produce; the savings of many years in thousands of families are gone.

More important, a host of unemployed citizens face the grim problem of existence, and an equally great number toil with little return. Only a foolish optimist can deny the dark realities of the moment.

Yet our distress comes from no failure of substance. We are stricken by no plague of locusts. Compared with the perils which our forefathers conquered because they believed and were not afraid, we have still much to be thankful for. Nature still offers her bounty and human efforts have multiplied it. Plenty is at our doorstep, but a generous use of it languishes in the very sight of the supply. Primarily this is because the rulers of the exchange of mankind's goods have failed, through their own stubbornness and their own incompetence, have admitted their failure, and abdicated. Practices of the unscrupulous money changers stand indicted in the court of public opinion, rejected by the hearts and minds of men ...

Happiness lies not in the mere possession of money; it lies in the joy of achievement, in the thrill of creative effort. The joy and moral stimulation of work no longer must be forgotten in the mad chase of evanescent profits. These dark days will be worth all they cost us if they teach us that our true destiny is not to be ministered unto but to minister to ourselves and to our fellow men.

Recognition of the falsity of material wealth as the standard of success goes hand in hand with the abandonment of the false belief that public office and high political position are to be valued only by the standards of pride of place and personal profit; and there must be an end to a conduct in banking

'Four Freedoms'

Address to the 77th US Congress
6 January 1941

• Context of speech

The first eight months of the Allied resistance to Hitler were conducted chiefly by Britain and France; the following 13, after France's collapse (*see* De Gaulle), by Britain more or less alone (*see* Sir Winston Churchill). But Franklin Roosevelt as early as 1940 shored up Britain's puny defences by trading 50 obsolescent US destroyers for British and Canadian bases in the Western Hemisphere.

Two months after the 'Four Freedoms' speech, which was technically the customary State of the Union address, he instituted Lend-Lease, a huge aid programme which was quite separate from the destroyers deal and which eventually embraced the USSR, China and (after 1944) France as well as Britain.

66 **At no previous time has American security been as seriously threatened from without as it is today** …

The United States as a nation has at all times maintained opposition — clear, definite opposition — to any attempt to lock us in behind an ancient Chinese wall while the procession of civilization went past. Today, … we oppose enforced isolation for ourselves or for any other part of the Americas … the democratic way of life is at this moment being directly assailed in every part of the world …

Therefore, as your President, performing my constitutional duty to 'give to the Congress information of the state of the Union', I find it unhappily necessary to report that the future and … safety of our country and of our democracy are overwhelmingly involved in events far beyond our borders …

In times like these it is immature — and, incidentally, untrue — for anybody to brag that an unprepared America, single-handed and with one hand tied behind its back, can hold off the whole world.

No realistic American can expect from a dictator's peace international generosity, or return of true independence, or world disarmament, or freedom of expression, or freedom of religion — or even good business … Those who would give up essential liberty to purchase a little temporary safety deserve neither liberty nor safety.

As a nation we may take pride in the fact that we are soft-hearted; but we cannot afford to be soft-headed. We must always be wary of those who with sounding brass and a tinkling cymbal preach the ism of appeasement. We must especially beware of that small group of selfish men who would clip the wings of the American eagle in order to feather their own nests …

In the future days which we seek to make secure, we look forward to a world founded upon four essential human freedoms.

The first is freedom of speech and expression — everywhere in the world.

The second is freedom of every person to worship God in his own way — everywhere in the world.

The third is freedom from want, which, translated into world terms, means economic understandings which will secure to every nation a healthy peacetime life for its inhabitants — everywhere in the world.

The fourth is freedom from fear, which, translated into world terms, means a world-wide reduction of armaments to such a point and in such a thorough fashion that no nation will be in a position to commit an act of physical aggression against any neighbor — anywhere in the world … "

Declaration of war on Japan

To the US Congress
8 December 1941

• Context of speech

The day after Japan's bombing of Pearl Harbor, the US naval base in Hawaii, Roosevelt gave the speech excerpted below. A stream of volunteers to the armed services resulted, also the collapse of isolationism.

66 **Yesterday, December 7 1941 — a date which will live in infamy — the United States of America was suddenly and deliberately attacked by naval and air forces of the Empire of Japan.**
The United States was at peace with that nation, and, at the solicitation of Japan, was still in conversation with its government and its Emperor looking toward the maintenance of peace in the Pacific.

Indeed, one hour after Japanese air squadrons had commenced bombing in the American island of Oahu, the Japanese Ambassador to the United States and his colleague delivered to our Secretary of State a formal reply to a recent American message. And, while this reply stated that it seemed useless to continue the existing diplomatic negotiations, it contained no threat or hint of war or of armed attack.

It will be recorded that the distance of Hawaii from Japan makes it obvious that the attack was deliberately planned many days or even weeks ago. During the intervening time the Japanese Government has deliberately sought to deceive the United States by false statements and expressions of hope for continued peace.

The attack yesterday on the Hawaiian Islands has caused severe damage to American naval and military forces. I regret to tell you that very many American lives have been lost. In addition, American ships have been reported torpedoed on the high seas between San Francisco and Honolulu.

Japan has ... undertaken a surprise offensive extending throughout the Pacific area ... As Commander-in-Chief of the Army and Navy I have directed that all measures be taken for our defense, that always will our whole nation remember the character of the onslaught against us.

No matter how long it may take us to overcome this premeditated invasion, the American people, in their righteous might, will win through to absolute victory ...

Hostilities exist. There is no blinking at the fact that our people, our territory and our interests are in grave danger.

With confidence in our armed forces, with the unbounded determination of our people, we will gain the inevitable triumph. So help us God.

I ask that the Congress declare that since the unprovoked and dastardly attack by Japan on Sunday, December 7 1941, a state of war has existed between the United States and the Japanese Empire."

On the Italian invasion of Abyssinia

**Haile Selassie I (1892(?)–1975),
Emperor of Ethopia 1930–36 and 1941–74
League of Nations, Geneva
30 June 1936** _____

• Biography

Like Mussolini (*qv*), his one-time conqueror, Haile Selassie was deposed after capitulating to foreign invaders, was reinstated by other foreign forces at war with the aforementioned invaders and ended the prisoner of disaffected fellow-countrymen. He may even have been murdered by such people, as Mussolini was. And his remains ended up in a location every bit as humiliating as Mussolini's, perhaps more so — interred till 1992 beneath a lavatory. At least it was an imperial palace one.

He is variously said to have been born in 1891, 1892 and even 1894, though 1892 seems the likeliest date. His father's mother was aunt to Emperor Menelik II (1889–1913) and in 1911 he strengthened his ties with the immediate imperial family by marrying a half-niece of Lij Iyasu, Menelik's grandson and briefly (1913–16) successor. When Iyasu was deposed in favour of his aunt, the Empress Zauditu, Haile Selassie was appointed Regent. He was thus effective ruler of Ethiopia long before his formal accession in 1930.

He attempted to modernise Ethiopia, but could not curb his feudal nobility. His task was hampered in any case by the Italian invasion of 1935. When the British drove the Italians from their East African possessions in 1941, they restored Haile Selassie. He had meanwhile been living in Britain. He ruled autocratically, as before, and though a 1960 coup failed he was successfully deposed in 1974. He died the next year while in the custody of the new regime, possibly through foul play.

• Context of speech

Haile Selassie had got Ethiopia into the League of Nations in 1923. To conform to the rules of his new club he announced the abolition of slavery the next year. It had been abolished often before, from as far back as the mid-19th century in fact, but had so far proved ineradicable. Pro-Italian commentators in 1935 made much of this, arguing that Mussolini was performing a civilising role similar to that of the British and French elsewhere in Africa half a century earlier.

The Italians had an air force, modern weapons and no scruples about using either, even when it was to spray the Ethiopians with toxic chemicals. They even bombed Red Cross hospital encampments. When it was clear that further resistance was useless, Haile Selassie left the country to put his case before the League. It was by now early May 1936.

In the League chamber he was at first barracked by Italian reporters in the press gallery. He made the speech in Amharic, his mother tongue. The League voted sanctions against Italy but did nothing more. It thus fell to an African autocrat from a pre-industrial civilisation to expose the uselessness of a talking-shop representing the world's most advanced nations.

---

66 **I Haile Selassie I, Emperor of Ethiopia, am here today to claim that justice which is due to my people, and the assistance promised to it eight months ago, when 50 nations asserted that aggression had been committed in violation of international treaties.** There is no precedent for a Head of State ... speaking in this assembly. But there is also no precedent for a people being victim of such injustice and being at present threatened by abandonment to its aggressor. Also, there has never before been an example of any government proceeding to the systematic extermination of a nation by barbarous means, in violation of the most solemn promises made by the nations of the earth that there should not be used against innocent human beings the terrible poison of harmful gases. It is to defend a people struggling for its age-old independence that the head of the Ethiopian Empire has come to Geneva to fulfil this supreme duty, after having himself fought at the head of his armies ...

The Italian Goverment boasts that for 14 years it has been preparing for its present conquest. It therefore recognises today that when it supported the admission of Ethiopia to the League of Nations in 1923, when it concluded the Treaty of Friendship with us in 1928, when it signed the Pact of Paris outlawing war, it was deceiving the whole world ...

I ask the 52 nations not to forget today the policy upon which they embarked eight months ago, and believing in which I directed the resistance of my people against the aggressor ... Despite the inferiority of my weapons, the complete lack of aircraft, artillery, munitions, hospital services, my confidence in the League was absolute. I thought it impossible that 52 nations, including the most powerful in the world, could be flouted by a single aggressor. Counting on the faith due to treaties, I had made no preparation for war, and that is the case with certain small countries in Europe …

What real assistance was given to Ethiopia by the 52 nations who declared the Rome Government guilty of breaching the Covenant and undertook to prevent the aggression? Has each of the state members, as it was bound to do by signing Article 15 of the Covenant, considered the aggressor as having committed an act of war against itself?

… I maintain that the problem submitted to the Assembly today is … not merely a question of settling Italian aggression. It is collective security. It is the very existence of the League of Nations. It is the confidence that each state places in international treaties. It is the value of promises made to small states that their … independence shall be respected … It is international morality that is at stake … "

Abdication broadcast

Edward VIII (Jan–Dec 1936), thereafter Duke of Windsor
Broadcast from Windsor Castle
4 December 1936

• Biography

The 1936 Abdication of Edward VIII (as it seems most convenient to call him, though his family preferred 'David' and posterity 'the Duke of Windsor') has been covered in endless books, articles and television documentaries. Yet the story is relatively simple.

A spoilt eldest son of excessively buttoned-up parents (*see* George V), but with something of the star quality that among youthful royals perhaps only Diana Princess of Wales (*qv*) has matched since, put off marrying till he was very nearly 43.

Since elegant, nice-mannered single girls get snapped up young, and since in love affairs he preferred other men's wives, he was only likely among marriageable women of his own age to find a widow or divorcee, if he found one at all. He eventually lit on a double divorcee, who was also a foreigner. Unfortunately she was the wrong kind of foreigner. Germans had supplied British royals' wives for centuries. Wallis Simpson was American.

Moreover a divorcee as queen was thought unacceptable in the industrial age, though the supposedly unenlightened Middle Ages had not minded. (Henry II's wife Eleanor was formerly Louis VII of France's.) The dreary taboo limps on today, Prince Charles having announced that when he is king his new wife Camilla will be called 'Princess of Wales'.

Edward's British subjects might just have swallowed a Queen Wallis, though no real test of public opinion was undertaken even in Britain. But the white peoples of the rest of the Empire (the 'natives' were not even rudimentarily canvassed) were deemed after superficial investigation to be implacably opposed. To marry her Edward therefore abdicated.

Was part of Wallis Simpson's attraction for Edward that through her he could break free of kingship? The question is unanswerable, though some of his actions and words hint at it. But others, particularly after he abdicated, suggest he wanted to have his cake and eat it too, *viz.*, enjoying the privileges of royal status without too many duties. There in a nutshell lay his unsuitability as king, though nobody who has not also faced reigning over a declining empire at the dawn of the mass communications age, with all the loss of privacy and restraint on action it entails, is entitled to throw stones.

• Context of speech

The idea for a broadcast to the nation by Edward seems to have originated with Wallis, who had been taken with Franklin Roosevelt's (*qv*) 'fireside chats'. But this first plan entailed broadcasting before any abdication was fixed. Worse still from the Government's point of view, in it Edward proposed appealing to 'the people' to decide the desirability of his marrying a divorcee, *i.e.*, speaking out over the heads of the politicians. On 4 December 1936 Baldwin (*qv*), Edward's Prime Minister, told him that in effect the Cabinet forbade his proposed broadcast. This seems to have decided Edward to abdicate. Cabinet ministers agreed among themselves that Edward must not broadcast (nor indeed make any other public utterance) while still king. Once he had abdicated, it was apparently agreed that he could make his broadcast.

Edward's reign technically finished on 11 December 1936 at 1.52 pm, during lunch, which he took with Winston Churchill (*qv*). He had asked Churchill round to Fort Belvedere, his camp little sham castle in Windsor Forest, to show him his farewell speech, which Churchill fine-tuned but which in every other respect Edward insisted was his own work. He also showed it to Baldwin and the Cabinet. It is probably because of this that it contains the misleading claim that there had never been any constitutional differences between them and Edward.

There was a last-minute intervention by the new King, George VI. He pointed out the inadvisability of referring to the ex-king as 'Mr Edward Windsor' (the BBC Director-General Sir John (later Lord) Reith's proposal). Instead, he suggested Edward be made a royal duke — which Edward formally was some months later. That evening he was introduced as 'His Royal Highness Prince Edward'.

> 66 **At long last I am able to say a few words of my own. I have never wanted to withhold anything, but until now it has been not constitutionally possible for me to speak.**
>
> A few hours ago I discharged my last duty as King and Emperor, and now that I have been succeeded by my brother, the Duke of York, my first words must be to declare my alliegance to him. This I do with all my heart.
>
> You all know the reasons which have impelled me to renounce the throne. But I want you to understand that in making up my mind I did not forget the country or the Empire which as Prince of Wales, and lately as King, I have for twenty-five years tried to serve. But you must believe me when I tell you that I have found it impossible to carry the heavy burden of responsibility and to discharge my duties as King as I would wish to do without the help and support of the woman I love.
>
> And I want you to know that the decision I have made has been mine and mine alone. This was a thing I had to judge entirely for myself. The other person most concerned has tried up to the last to persuade me to take a different course. I have made this, the most serious decision of my life, upon a single thought of what would in the end be the best for all.
>
> This decision has been made less difficult to me by the sure knowledge that my brother, with his long training in the public affairs of this country and with his fine qualities, will be able to take my place forthwith, without interruption or injury to the life and progress of the Empire. And he has one matchless blessing, enjoyed by so many of you and not bestowed on me — a happy home with his wife and children.

During these hard days I have been comforted by my mother and by my family. The Ministers of the Crown, and in particular Mr Baldwin, the Prime Minister, have always treated me with full consideration. There has never been any constitutional difference between me and them and between me and Parliament. Bred in the constitutional tradition by my father, I should never have allowed any such issue to arise.

Ever since I was Prince of Wales, and later on when I occupied the Throne, I have been treated with the greatest kindness by all classes, wherever I have lived or journeyed throughout the Empire. For that I am very grateful.

I now quit altogether public affairs, and I lay down my burden. It may be some time before I return to my native land, but I shall always follow the fortunes of the British race and Empire with profound interest, and if at any time in the future I can be found of service to His Majesty in a private station I shall not fail.

And now we all have a new King. I wish him, and you, his people, happiness and prosperity with all my heart. God bless you all. God Save the King."

On the Spanish Civil War

General Francisco Franco (1892–1975)
17 July 1936

• Biography

Hitler and Mussolini (*qqv*) swallowed their own bellicose propaganda and entered a major war thinking they could win it. Francisco Franco, a professional army officer, knew the odds are seldom better than 50–50: you usually either win a war or lose it. Having won power inside his own country, he sat the big one of '39–'45 out.

He was stationed in Morocco as early as 1913, was promoted number two in the Spanish Foreign Legion there in 1920 and three years later assumed full command. In 1936 it was from Morocco that he launched the assault on the mainland that by 1939 won him all Spain.

Although he triumphed in the Spanish Civil War with German and Italian aid, he was far too canny to reciprocate, apart from allowing volunteers, called the Blue Division, to fight on Hitler's Russian front in World War II. Even these he brought home in 1943, scenting disaster. True, he had in 1938 signed the Anti-Comintern Pact (an agreement between Germany, Italy and Japan directed against the USSR), but he kept Spain neutral thereafter. Franco was well aware of his southern flank's vulnerability to Allied attack; also, the Canary Islands might be taken by the Royal Navy if he antagonised Britain, and from late 1942 North Africa was coming under Allied control anyway. In the circumstances he shelved action.

Towards the end of the War he shifted to a definite pro-Allied stance. After the War he took on the formal role of Regent for life and started grooming the present King Juan Carlos as his successor.

He forged friendly relations with the US, whose anti-communism he shared. He even let the US establish four military bases in Spain, which further encouraged the Americans to counter any left-wing threat to the regime. Like Mussolini, he developed a good working relationship with the Vatican. In 1969 he formally announced that Juan Carlos would succeed him.

• Context of speech

Early in 1936 the Popular Front, a leftist coalition, was formed in Spain with a view to fighting imminent elections. The Right responded by setting up the National Front. The Popular Front subsequently got the biggest vote, but only marginally. It formed a government and in May replaced Spain's conservative president with a left-winger. Economic problems ensued.

On 17 July 1936 Franco delivered the speech below. The next day the new President installed a new premier, soon replacing him, however. Franco presently unified the right-wing anti-Republican opposition.

" Spaniards! The nation calls to her defence all those of you who hear the holy name of Spain; those in the ranks of the Army and Navy who have made a profession of faith in the service of the Motherland; and all those who swore to defend her to the death against her enemies.

The situation in Spain grows more critical every day. Anarchy reigns in most of the countryside and towns. Government-appointed authorities encourage revolts, when they do not actually lead them. Murderers use pistols and machine guns to settle their differences and treacherously to assassinate innocent people, while the public authorities fail to impose law and order.

Revolutionary strikes of all kinds paralyse the life of the nation, destroying its sources of wealth and creating hunger, forcing working men to the point of desperation. The most savage attacks are made upon national monuments and artistic treasures by revolutionary hordes who obey the orders of foreign governments, with the complicity and negligence of local authorities.

The most serious crimes are committed in the cities and countryside, while the forces that should defend public order remain in their barracks, bound by blind obedience to those governing authorities that are intent on dishonouring them.

The Army, Navy and other armed forces are the target of the most obscene and slanderous attacks, which are carried out by the very people who should be protecting their prestige. Meanwhile, martial law is imposed to gag the nation, to hide what is happening in its towns and cities and to imprison alleged political opponents."

'Peace in our time'

(Arthur) Neville Chamberlain (1869–1940)
Outside Number Ten Downing Street, London
30 September 1938 _____

• Biography

Like Baldwin (*qv*), Chamberlain, his successor as Prime Minister (1937–40), came to front-rank politics late in life and after a creditable, though not spectacularly successful, earlier career in business. Both were decent, diligent and honest men. Both were confronted abroad with someone who was none of these things: Hitler (*qv*). It would be monstrously unjust to claim Chamberlain thought throwing Hitler chunks of other people's countries would prevent him grabbing Chamberlain's own — the strategy with wolves pursuing a sled. But after Chamberlain fell from power accusations of this sort did get hurled at him. And the Czechs can hardly be blamed if they still take this attitude.

The sad thing is that Chamberlain was highly competent domestically, notably as Minister of Health 1924–29. Even as Chancellor of the Exchequer 1934–37 (a position he had also held 1923–24), he did his best to allocate the armed services decent funding. Unfortunately his best wasn't good enough. But it was in foreign policy, in which as Premier he bypassed his Foreign Secretary, that his judgement was positively flawed. Even after the War started he was ready to make concessions to any new German government, provided it dropped Hitler; its retaining other Nazis was not an insuperable handicap.

Chamberlain's then Assistant Private Secretary, Sir Jock Colville, attributed his attitude to Hitler to 'damaged vanity'. At Munich in 1938 Chamberlain had trusted Hitler's word. He afterwards told Colville that he believed Hitler had been sincere at Munich but had later changed his mind.

Chamberlain's organisational deficiencies as a wartime premier are also revealed by Colville. Chamberlain hated being bothered by business after dinner or at weekends, the latter of which he spent at Chequers (the British Prime Minister's country retreat) with no private secretary and a single telephone, situated in the pantry. He was, however, forceful, precise, unwearied and hard-working as late as April 1940, despite being 71.

When Hitler launched his May 1940 offensive, Chamberlain's position crumbled, his immediate destroyer being Lloyd George (*qv*). He died that autumn.

• Context of speech

The fate of Czechoslovakia had been decided formally between Chamberlain and Hitler at Munich on 30 September 1938. The tag 'peace with honour' had been used before, having been coined by Disraeli (*qv*) in 1878 after the Congress of Berlin. Colville reveals that re-using it was urged on Chamberlain by his wife. Its utter worthlessness as a description long haunted Chamberlain's reputation.

Chamberlain was victim of another resuscitated tag in the 7 May 1940 Parliamentary debate on the loss of Norway which finished him. Leopold Amery, soon to be Churchill's India Secretary, pointed at him and paraphrased Cromwell (*qv*): "You have sat too long here for any good you have been doing. Depart, I say, and let us have done with you. In the name of God, go!"

Chamberlain read the text below to a cheering crowd, having waved the document containing the text on stepping from his plane after returning from Germany.

66 We, the German Fuehrer and Chancellor, and the British Prime Minister, have had a further meeting today and are agreed in recognising that the question of Anglo-German relations is of the first importance for our two countries and for Europe.

We regard the agreement signed last night and the Anglo-German Naval Agreement [*signed 1935, allowing Germany a navy one-third the size of the Royal Navy, the latter to vacate the Baltic*] as symbolic of the desire of our two peoples never to go to war with one another again.

We are resolved that the method of consultation shall be the method adopted to deal with any other questions that may concern our two countries, and we are determined to continue our efforts to remove possible sources of difference, and thus to contribute to assure the peace of Europe.

My good friends, this is the second time in our history that there has come back from Germany to Downing Street peace with honour. I believe it is peace in our time."

'My patience is exhausted'

Adolf Hitler (1889–1945)
Berlin Sportspalast (athletics stadium)
26 September 1938 _____

• Biography

Like the two other major Western Eurasian landmass dictators, Napoleon and Stalin (*qqv*), Hitler was not a true native of the nation over which he came to rule, here Germany, but an outsider, being born in Austria.

Again like Stalin, the name by which he became famous was an assumed one. His father, a bastard, had originally been called Alois Schicklgruber. In changing to Hitler, which he did in 1876, Alois took a variant of the name of his mother's subsequent husband, born Johann Heidler. In addition, Adolf Hitler's mother was Johann's great-niece.

The Heidlers seem to have been of remote Czech origin. It has been plausibly suggested that the man who fathered Alois on his mother was a member of a Jewish family in Graz called Frankenberger, or conceivably Frankenreiter (though a forthcoming book on Hitlerian genealogy, due out after this one, is said not to favour the theory). Hitler may thus have been a composite of two of the very groups of humans he assaulted in his oratory.

In youth Hitler was a failed artist. In maturity, even when waging a world war at the head of a major industrial state, he kept the irregular hours of a bohemian and formulated policy capriciously rather than rationally.

He fought creditably in the German army during World War I, took control of the fledgling Nazi Party in the early 1920s and became Chancellor of Germany in 1933. Mass discontent and unemployment, national indebtedness and fear of Communism helped his rise.

Having established total Nazi control over Germany, Hitler expanded Germany's power throughout Central Europe by identical methods: bullying but specious oratory and armed force or the threat of it. Britain and France, his main Western opponents, repeatedly acquiesced till it was too late (*see* Baldwin and

Chamberlain), thus incidentally convincing Mussolini (*qv*) that Italy's interests were best served by allying with Hitler. Stalin's Russia became his ally too.

Early success in World War II went to Hitler's head. In addition to Britain, he tangled unnecessarily with Russia and America (*see* also Patton). Germany met near-total destruction in consequence and he committed suicide.

He is chiefly execrated for the murder of most of Europe's Jews, to the number roughly of 6,000,000. But he also imprisoned and had murdered gipsies, homosexuals, liberals and Communists — in short, not just political opponents, but outsiders much as he had once been.

He brought off fewer peacetime deaths than did Stalin or Mao (*qv*), neither of whom, as men of the Left, is as much reviled.

• Context of speech

The speech excerpted below, delivered towards the culmination of the Czechoslovak Crisis, contains two of Hitler's best remembered tags: 'last territorial claim' and 'my patience is exhausted'.

Through the Czechoslovak Crisis of late summer 1938 Hitler exploited Europe-wide nationalist resentment of the frontiers imposed by the Versailles Treaty ending World War I, his aim being to enlarge Germany.

The British Prime Minister Neville Chamberlain visited Hitler twice in the weeks before this speech in an attempt to avert war. But Hitler rejected his initial plan (acquiesced in by Czechoslovakia). This would have granted limited independence to the Sudetenland (the part of Czechoslovakia the Sudeten Germans lived in). Hitler wanted outright German sovereignty, disguising it under a demand for Sudeten self-determination.

Chamberlain soon accepted the self-determination demand, as did Czechoslovakia, but Hitler thereupon denounced the details as tending to delay and implied that German control must be established immediately. Chamberlain then proposed direct Czech-German talks, with Britain looking on, to arrange the Sudetenland's transfer to Germany.

The same day Hitler made the speech, he invited Chamberlain to visit him in Munich. There Britain, Czechoslovakia, France, Germany and Italy agreed some minor modifications to what was by now effectively Germany's annexing the Sudetenland. A joint Anglo-German announcement on 30 September, stating that Germany would only use peaceful matters to adjust international disputes thereafter, persuaded Chamberlain that this climb-down was worthwhile.

German troops entered the Sudetenland the next day, but World War II was postponed another year. Whether it was worth it to buy the Anglo-French alliance rearmament time has been much discussed.

"The last problem ... is the last territorial claim I have to make in Europe ... In 1918 ... Central Europe was torn in pieces and reformed by certain crazy so-called statesmen ... To this Czechoslovakia owes its existence. The Czech state began with a lie and the father of this lie was called [*Eduard*] Beneš [*1884– 1948, Czechoslovak President 1935–38 and 1946–48 and President-in-exile 1939–45*].

This Mister Beneš gave the assurance at Versailles that a Czechoslovak nation existed. He was forced to invent this lie to give the small number of his fellow-countrymen a ... fuller justification. The Anglo-Saxon statesmen, who, as always, were not very expert in geography or nationality, did not find it necessary to test Mister Beneš's assertions. Had they done so, they would have established that there is no such thing as a Czechoslovak nation, only Czechs and Slovaks, and Slovaks wanted nothing to do with Czechs.

In the end ... these Czechs annexed Slovakia. Since this state seemed unviable, three-and-a-half million Germans were absorbed, in violation of their right to and desire for self-determination. Since even that was not enough, over a million Magyars had to be added, then some Carpathian Russians and finally several hundred thousand Poles ...

Now the shameless part ... begins. This state, whose government is in the hands of a minority, obliges its other nationalities to take part in a policy that will force them one day to fire on their brothers. Mister Beneš demands of the Germans 'If I wage war against Germany, you must fire on Germans ... else you are a traitor and I will have you yourself shot.' ... I can affirm that when we occupied Austria my first order was that no Czech ... need serve in the German Army. I drove him to no conflict of conscience ...

While Mister Beneš was sneaking about the world, I as a decent German soldier did my duty. And now ... I stand against this man as a soldier defending my people.

I am grateful to Mister Chamberlain for his efforts. I have assured him that the German people desires nothing but peace ... I have further assured him that when ... the Czechs have come to terms with their other minorities — peaceably, not through oppression — I will have no further interest in the Czech state ... We want no Czechs.

But ... with regard to the Sudeten Germans, my patience is exhausted. I have made Mister Beneš an offer which is simply the carrying out of what he promised. The decision now lies with him: peace, or war ... "

Against the British holding India

Munich
8 November 1942

• Context of speech

The excerpt below was delivered three months after the 'Quit India' movement had drawn attention to Britain's delay in granting Indian independence (*see* also Gandhi). Hitler has been widely misrepresented, first as a man wholly of the far Right, second as a buffoon, third as a leader preoccupied with German and other predominantly European matters. Each view needs modifying.

Politically he was principally a demagogue, prepared to stir up trouble in whatever field helped him win power. Thus under him National Socialism, which had started out rather more socialist than, say, Lenin's (*qv*) New Economic Policy in the USSR, mutated to a chauvinistic, opportunist nihilism, reinforced by savage repression and propaganda and adorned with crackpot notions of racial purity.

But in the speech below he reverts to a near-socialist tone, inveighing as much against aristocrats such as Eden and the top-hatted capitalists of caricature as against British imperialism.

In his habits Hitler was certainly eccentric. But he constantly outwitted politicians better educated, more experienced and more steadfast in their policy than himself, not just because they underestimated the duplicity to which he could stoop but because they foolishly despised his very eccentricity, writing him off as a jumped-up drifter and dropout from a provincial lower middle-class background.

It was a forensic master-stroke to seize on Britain's possession of India, as he does here. That possession was palpably against the wishes of India's inhabitants. It was a stumbling block to Anglo-American amity. It gnawed at Britain's own liberal conscience.

Indeed, although Hitler lost the War, his needling Britain over the foppishness of an aristocratic statesman such as Eden and the injustice of Britain's holding India set in train a contempt for the old ruling class and a sense of guilt towards former subject races that is still strong in Britain today.

66 **When a few days ago, a regular snobbish, perfumed hooligan like this Mister Eden [*Anthony Eden, British Foreign Secretary 1935–38, 1940–45 and 1951–55 and Prime Minister 1955–57, created Earl of Avon 1961*] declared**

'We English have had experience in ruling', then the only thing one can say in answer is 'In ruling? In exploiting! In plundering!'
What does experience in ruling mean when, in a country which controls 40,000,000 square kilometres of the entire world, there were at the beginning of the war 2,500,000 unemployed out of a population of 46,000,000?

Where is this art of ruling, to say nothing of the art of leadership? It is no more than the lack of scruples of a robber. And when this same man then says 'We have a concern for both idealism and material worth', I reply: yes indeed they have. They have destroyed idealism everywhere, and they have grabbed and taken possession of material worth — and have always done so, moreover, by brute force alone. For over 300 years the English have oppressed and yoked and subjected nation after nation, people after people, race after race.

If they were really such brilliant rulers, then they should now be able to leave India after the Indian people have expressed their explicit desire that they do so — though they could then wait and see whether the Indians call them back again. They have been careful not to leave, although they know how to rule so wonderfully, and in this they are completely of one mind, these plunderers, whether wearing socialist cloth caps or capitalist top hats."

Let the British quit India

Mahatma Gandhi (1869–1948)
Indian National Congress committee meeting,
Bombay
8 August 1942 _____

• Biography

Do empires get the undermining they deserve? The British one governed relatively mildly, encountering mostly temperate opponents. But its masters took care to dismantle it before things got too rough, starting with India. It was Gandhi who chiefly pushed them into this, using 'moral' tactics such as non-cooperation and non-violence, rather than strenuous ones, such as the Irish approach, which involved storming post offices and shooting policemen.

In particular his fasting (nowadays called 'hunger strike'), together with brilliantly symbolic performances, notably his 'salt march' of 1930, highlighting the unfair tax on a vital preservative in India's hot climate, have set the tone for modern agitation. Here appeals to the heart via dramatic television and press photos, often over domestic issues, outweigh concrete achievement.

Gandhi was a journalist, among other callings, so understood mass concerns. He found the more visual medium of cinema puzzling (television hardly existed in his day), but he had a fine, though perhaps subconscious, grasp of how his own ultra-simple accessories of homespun loincloth, spinning wheel and 'Gandhi Cap', together with his frail and much exposed limbs, babu's spectacles and missing teeth, made the tall, resplendently uniformed sahibs look absurdly overdressed, like Ruritanian ringmasters. He had, in short, turned the British gift for understatement against its inventors.

Cynics argue that Gandhi was pushing at, if not an open, then at any rate a lightly latched door. Non-violence only succeeded because the British of his day lacked the nerve to repress opposition. (They also lacked the resources, but that has not stopped other powers futilely striving to preserve an empire.) Gandhi's tactics would never have ejected Clive of India or the Duke of Wellington in his Mahratta-busting phase.

He was born Mohandas Karamchand Gandhi, one of a family which had supplied the princely state of Porbandar with three recent prime ministers. (The 'Mahatma', meaning ultimately 'Great Soul', was bestowed later, around 1915.) He read law in London, where his vegetarianism won him friends among British progressives and simple-lifers.

Back in India his Bar practice faltered so he went to South Africa. There he started promoting Indian rights. But he supported the British Empire sufficiently to organise an Indian ambulance corps during the Boer War.

He returned to India for good during World War I, became the chief inspiration in the pro-independence body, the Indian National Congress party, and when independence did come in 1947 opposed partition between predominantly Muslim regions of the subcontinent and the predominantly Hindu ones. He was assassinated by fanatics angry at his conciliatory position towards Muslim separatism.

• Context of speech

Indian concern over just when independence was coming boiled over in the 'Quit India' agitation during World War II. By 1942 some Indians looked to the new belligerents the Japanese as possible allies against British imperialism. Not Gandhi. But he did propose non-cooperation with the Allied war effort. On 7 August 1942 an Indian National Congress Committee met in Bombay (now Mumbai). The next day it called not just for a free India but resolved that such an entity would ally with the 'United Nations' (as the Allies were then sometimes known). Gandhi thereupon delivered the speech excerpted below. The next day the British arrested him and imprisoned him for two years.

Gandhi in youth was an intensely nervous speaker. When a student in London he took elocution lessons, using as a model a speech of Pitt's (which Pitt is unclear). But this seems to have been more for social than political advancement. Towards the end of his time in Britain he was reckoned a good speaker, at any rate in vegetarian circles. It would appear that, at least when young, he prepared speeches in advance, though on one occasion, when given only five minutes to speak, he improvised.

> **I believe that in the history of the world, there has not been a more genuinely democratic struggle for freedom than ours. I read Carlyle's *French Revolution* while I was in prison, and Pandit Jawaharlal [*Nehru*, qv] has told me something about the Russian Revolution [see *also Trotsky, Lenin and Stalin*]. But it is my conviction that inasmuch as these struggles were fought with the weapon of violence they failed to realise the democratic ideal. In the democracy which I have envisaged, a democracy established by non-violence, there will be equal freedom for all. Everybody will be his own master.**

It is to join a struggle for such democracy that I invite you today. Once you realise this you will forget the differences between the Hindus and Muslims, and think of yourselves as Indians only, engaged in the common struggle for independence.

Then there is the question of your attitude towards the British. I have noticed that there is hatred towards the British among the people. The people say they are disgusted with their behaviour. The people make no distinction between British imperialism and the British people. To them, the two are one.

This hatred would even make them welcome the Japanese. It is most dangerous. It means that they will exchange one slavery for another. We must get rid of this feeling. Our quarrel is not with the British people; we fight their imperialism. The proposal for the withdrawal of British power did not come out of anger. It came to enable India to play its due part at the present critical juncture.

It is not a happy position for a big country like India to be merely helping with money and material obtained willy-nilly from her while the United Nations [*in effect the Allies*] are conducting the war. We cannot evoke the true spirit of sacrifice and valour, so long as we are not free.

I know the British Government will not be able to withhold freedom from us, when we have made enough self-sacrifice. We must, therefore, purge ourselves of hatred. Speaking for myself, I can say that I have never felt any hatred. As a matter of fact, I feel myself to be a greater friend of the British now than ever before. One reason is that they are today in distress. My very friendship, therefore, demands that I should try to save them from their mistakes.

As I view the situation, they are on the brink of an abyss. It therefore becomes my duty to warn them of their danger even though it may, for the time being, anger them to the point of cutting off the friendly hand that is stretched out to help them. People may laugh; nevertheless that is my claim. At a time when I may have to launch the biggest struggle of my life, I may not harbour hatred against anybody."

Broadcast rallying the Free French

Charles de Gaulle (1890–1970)
London, by radio
18 June 1940

• Biography

Serving in World War I taught Charles de Gaulle the value of armoured offensives bolstered by air support. He even publicised his ideas in print. Unfortunately, the man who did most to prove their effectiveness in the field was Hitler (*qv*). That was in 1940, and against the French. But de Gaulle commanded tanks too. At the Pas-de-Calais village of Caumont he on 28 May 1940 became the sole French general in that otherwise miserably conducted campaign to repulse the Boche.

At the final collapse of France in June, de Gaulle, who had been made Minister of War at the beginning of the month, set up the Free French in London. The difficulty of working with him was a torment to Churchill (*qv*). De Gaulle overcame Allied attempts to curb him. He headed France's Provisional Government from 1945 to 1946 but then withdrew into nominal retirement.

He eventually returned to government, first as Prime Minister of the Fourth Republic with unprecedentedly wide powers then as President of a new regime, the Fifth Republic, also with very wide powers.

France's reluctance wholly to give up her former colonies in North Africa was his immediate problem. De Gaulle granted independence to all France's African colonies, notably Algeria, the trickiest case of all.

He then vetoed Britain's Common Market application (*see* also Macmillan), strengthened the Franco-German *entente*, made France a nuclear power, disengaged from NATO, lent mischievous support to Quebec separatists in Canada (*see* also Trudeau) and conducted diplomatic flirtations with the USSR. He was toppled by student disturbances in Paris in 1968 which, in time-honoured French fashion, took hold nationally. Although he soon regained power, he lost a 1969 referendum which nominally proposed provincial reorganisation but which was interpreted as a vote of confidence in de Gaulle personally. He then retired, spending (to universal astonishment) a short holiday in Ireland, where it was suddenly revealed some of his ancestors came from. He had never lost this ability to surprise, as befitted a good tank commander.

• Context of speech

De Gaulle broadcast the excerpt below shortly after he had escaped from France with a handful of followers to continue the struggle against Germany, even though the rest of the French Government he had served in had been replaced by the men who were to be known as the Vichy regime and who capitulated to the Germans.

The 18th was an unfortunate date for Anglo-French relations, being the anniversary of Waterloo. It was also the date of Churchill's 'Finest Hour' speech (*qv*).

"The leaders who for many years were at the head of the French armies have formed a government. This government, alleging our armies to be undone, has agreed with the enemy to stop fighting. It is true that we were overwhelmed by the mechanised, infantry and air forces of the enemy. Infinitely more than their numbers, it was the tanks, the aeroplanes and the tactics of the Germans which made us retreat. It was the tanks, the aeroplanes and the tactics of the Germans that surprised our leaders and brought them to where they are today.

But has the last word been said? Must hope disappear? Is defeat final? No.

Believe me, I speak to you with full knowledge of the facts and tell you that nothing is lost for France. The same means that overcame us can bring us one day to victory. For France is not alone. She is not alone … She has a vast Empire behind her. She can align with the British Empire, which holds the sea and continues the fight. She can, like England, rely without limit on the immense industrial might of the United States.

This war is not limited to the unfortunate soil of our country. This war is not ended by the Battle of France. This war is a world-wide one. All the faults, all the delays, all the suffering do not prevent there from being throughout the world all the means that will be necessary one day to crush our enemies. Vanquished today by a mechanised army, we will be able to overcome them in the future by a superior mechanised army.

The destiny of the world is here. I, General de Gaulle, currently in London, invite the officers and French soldiers who find themselves on British soil or who may come here, with their weapons or without their weapons; I invite the engineers and the special workers in the armament industries who find themselves on British soil or who may come here, to put themselves in contact with me.

Whatever happens, the flame of the French Resistance must not and will not be extinguished … "

On the liberation of Paris

Hôtel de Ville (City Hall), Paris
25 August 1944 _____

• Context of speech

This excerpt is from an address to the people of Paris, made by de Gaulle when he had only arrived back in France five days earlier, having hitherto had his headquarters in Algiers. He had just assumed command of the French 2nd Armoured Division, which with various resistance units inside Paris itself liberated the capital.

There is more than one version of the speech. De Gaulle himself in his memoirs included a sentence implicitly warning the Communists in the Resistance not to make trouble. But this was cut from de Gaulle's *Discours et Messages*, which appeared in 1970, the year of his death.

There is also a longer version of the speech, recorded by the Gaullist litterateur and political writer Robert Aron (1898–1975). The 'official' version of the speech, purged, dare one say it, of the Aron-ist accretions, runs thus:

> "Why should we try to hide the emotion which we all of us, men and women, here feel? We are home once more in Paris, a Paris which is on its feet to liberate itself and which has been able to achieve it single-handed.

We should not try to conceal this profound and sacred emotion. We are living through moments which transcend the poor lives of each of us.

Paris! Outraged Paris! Broken Paris! Martyred Paris! But also liberated Paris! Liberated by the people of Paris with help from the armies of France, with the help and support of the whole of France, of France which is fighting, of the only France, the real France, eternal France.

Because the enemy which held Paris has capitulated to us, it is France that returns to Paris. She comes home bloody but resolute. She comes home wiser from the tremendous lesson she has learnt, but surer than ever of her duties and her rights.

I put duties first. I do not exclude warlike duties. The enemy totters but is not yet beaten. He remains on our soil. It will not be enough, after what has happened, if with the help of our dear and admirable allies we chase him out of our country.

We want to enter his country as we should, as conquerors. This is why the French advance guard came to Paris firing as it advanced. This is why a great French army from Italy landed in the South and is moving rapidly up the Rhône Valley. This is why our brave … Forces of the Interior will be armed with modern weapons.

It is for revenge. For revenge and justice that we shall continue to fight to the last day, until the day when victory is total and complete.

Every man here today and all who hear me elsewhere in France know that this warlike duty demands national unity.

In our present situation the nation can not allow national unity to be disrupted. The nation well knows that to conquer, to reconstruct and to be great, all Frenchmen are needed. The nation well knows that the sons and daughters of France — all the sons and daughters except for a few unhappy traitors who gave themselves over to the enemy and who are tasting or will taste the rigours of the law — yes, all the sons and daughters of France must march towards France's goal, fraternally and hand in hand.

Long live France!"

On Italy's role in World War II

Benito Mussolini (1883–1945)
Rome
10 June 1941

• Biography

While it might sound facetious to say that in Britain Sir Oswald Mosley (*qv*) gave fascism a bad name, that movement in Italy, under Mussolini at his zenith, had a pretty good one. And not just in Italy. Mussolini had come to power in 1922, well before Hitler (*qv*). Accordingly, early foreign admiration for Mussolini involved no Nazi taint. Admiring foreigners (doubtless to their embarrassment later) included Winston Churchill (*qv*), Sigmund Freud, Ramsay MacDonald, Cole Porter, George Bernard Shaw, *The Times* and Chaim Weizmann (*see* also Ben-Gurion). Franklin Roosevelt (*qv*) on becoming US President in 1933 said Mussolini was his only potential ally in trying to safeguard world peace.

As late as 1935 Mussolini's accomplishments still looked impressive, particularly as they had involved so very much less violence than Nazism in Germany or Communism in Russia. He had ended Italy's chronic parliamentary instability, squared the Vatican, drained the Pontine Marshes, suppressed the Mafia and undertaken grandiose, even useful, public works, including Europe's first motorway. He had even in 1934 faced down Hitler over Austria — the only person ever to do so in peace. (If France or Britain had achieved only that, World War II could have been averted.) Subsequently things went wrong. He invaded Abyssinia, dispelling British goodwill; drifted into Hitler's poisonous embrace; and botched World War II.

The elder son of an anti-clerical village blacksmith in Romagna, a former Papal state, he first worked as a primary schoolteacher (like many other authoritarian politicians, notably Mao, *qv*). He then became a journalist and newspaper editor before starting his Fascist movement. In those days he was a socialist, as his father had been before him, and Italian Fascism retained a strong socialist element.

Mussolini disliked Hitler, who in contrast was among Mussolini's admirers, though the admiration diminished with time. Italy declared war on the Allies in 1940 but by 1943 had had enough. King Vittorio Emmanuele III sacked Mussolini, who had never, unlike Hitler, added head of state to his other posts, and went over to the Allies. The Germans invaded Italy and made Mussolini puppet ruler of a northern enclave around Salò, on Lake Garda.

In April 1945 he fled towards Switzerland, belatedly disguising himself as a Luftwaffe corporal. He was unmasked when his wearing sunglasses on an overcast day aroused suspicion. He and his much younger mistress Clara Petacci were machine-gunned without trial. Their corpses were later hung upside-down from a girder over a petrol station in Milan. His murderers were probably Communists, both those who gave the order in Milan and the wielder(s) of the weapon(s) in the mountains.

• Context of speech

Mussolini was already an accomplished orator when only a seventeen-year-old schoolboy, being chosen to deliver a panegyric on the recently deceased composer Verdi. The speech was mentioned in the press.

He certainly had a natural gift, but he also developed it. Among his favourite books was one called *The Psychology of the Crowd*. By the time he won power he had perfected his gestures — the famous jutting jaw and broad chest thrown out for maximum effect, his hands either on his hips like a dancing master or waving in the air like a concert hall maestro, the rolling eyes with their irises entirely surrounded by whites. His voice was high-pitched, even falsetto. His choice of costume — black shirt, cravat, sash, spats, later breeches and riding boots, like a film director — set the tone for an entire political movement.

The speech excerpted below was delivered in Rome on 10 June 1941. Mussolini had numerous catastrophes to explain away after just a year of war: a failed invasion of Greece (the Germans completed it); loss entirely of Italy's East African colonies and partly of its North African one, Libya; the Italian fleet pulverised by the Royal Navy. Even France, which he had attacked after Hitler had already defeated it a year before, had only yielded the suburbs of Menton, on the Franco-Italian coastal border.

Comrades, this is a memorable, solemn day. It is just a year since our entrance into the War. A year ... during which Italian soldiers on land, sea and in the sky fought heroically, mostly on the European and African fronts ....

It was a mathematical certainty that in April ... the Italian Army would have overcome and annihilated the Greek Army. In all honesty, it must be admitted that many Greek detachments fought courageously ... however, ... the Greek Army would not have held out for six months without the aid of England. The Greek Army was fed, supplied and armed by the English. Aviation was English. Anti-aircraft and artillery also were English. No fewer than 60,000 English were in services and special groups flanking the Greek Army ...

While our Second Army of the Alps was moving down along the Dalmatian Coast with forced marches which tried the resistance of the soldiers, the Greeks, in a ruse that bore the true style of Ulysses, tried at the last minute to hold us on the Albanian frontier by offering an armistice to the Germans and not to us. They were firmly recalled by me to reason and finally surrendered unconditionally ...

The English still made a few appearances on battlefields, but, ... finding Hellenic soil too hot to for them, abandoned a dying Greece, fleeing by the usual sea route.

Collaboration ... between Germany and Italy is under way ... Ridiculous rumour-mongers who have speculated on eventual [*Italo-German*] friction or dissension, such an outcome being the product of the feeble-minded, some of whom have gone further, like the English Prime Minister [*Winston Churchill*, qv] in his useless Christmas Eve speech, are reduced to silence ... American intervention does not bother us excessively.

American intervention, if undertaken completely, would be late ... American intervention will not give victory to Britain but will prolong the War. It will not limit the area of war but will extend it to other oceans. It will change the United States regime into an authoritarian, totalitarian one in comparison with which the European forerunners — Fascist and Nazi — will feel themselves ... surpassed ...

The English have many times announced that the campaign in Italian Africa is virtually concluded. But ... they are still fighting ... [and] our ... troops are still giving the English plenty to think about ...

How long it may last cannot be known, but it is certain that resistance will be protracted to the limits of human possibility. Even the complete conquest of the [*Italian*] Empire by the English will have no decisive impact on the ending of the War.

This is a vendetta of a strictly personal character, which can have no influence on the results of a conflict that has dug an ever deeper chasm between Italy and Britain. I cannot tell you today when or how, but I affirm in the most categoric manner that ... our dead shall not go unavenged."

On British rule in India

**Sir Winston (Leonard Spencer-) Churchill
(1872–1965)
House of Commons
8 July 1920**

• Biography

Almost alone of the debaters, lawyers, parliamentarians, philosophers, politicians, pundits, revolutionaries and tyrants who throng this book, Churchill is famous more for his oratory than his specific deeds. (The sole other exception is Burke (*qv*), but really as composer of speeches rather than deliverer.) People who have never voted or attended a debate, nor could easily name Churchill's dates as a wartime Prime Minister (they are 1940–45), yet cock an ear when a recording emits in those instantly recognisable slurred tones the evocative tags 'blood, toil, tears and sweat', 'we shall fight them on the beaches …', 'this was their finest hour' or 'Never in the field of human conflict …'.

There is a fifth tag usually associated with a speech of Churchill's: 'Iron Curtain'. But it was not properly his. It was first used of Germany corralling the Belgians behind the German lines in 1914 by Elisabeth Queen of the Belgians (herself a German). It got extended to Russia in 1920 by Ethel Snowden, wife of the Labour politician Philip (*see* also Lenin), and was seized on in 1945 to rouse the shreds of German public opinion against the Soviet menace by the Nazi propaganda boss Dr. Goebbels.

Churchill was lucky as an orator in having radio at his disposal. Lucky, too, in that nightly the people of wartime Britain clustered round their sets at home or in pubs, air-raid shelters, messes and clubs to 'listen in', as it was then called — not just to broadcasts of his parliamentary speeches, though they were the gems, but to the Nine o'clock News, which kept them more prosaically informed of how the terrible conflict was proceeding.

He was one of the last major politicians to concoct his own material, though even there his secretary Sir Jock Colville admits to authorship of the less important addresses in Churchill's second administration (1951–55), having become so attuned to his master's idiosyncrasies of expression that he could counterfeit them.

These idiosyncrasies exploited many of the more gloriously recondite terms in Fowler's *English Usage* such as anaphora, asyndeton and chiasmus, while not neglecting the more shopworn forensic devices, *e.g.*, the iterated, even reiterated, synonym. The results were *tours de force*, harking back beyond the baroque masters of 18th-century public address such as Pitt the Elder (*qv*), almost to the king of mannerist prose himself, Sir Thomas Browne.

Fancy phrases would have got Churchill nowhere without a down-to-earth diction. But even then his eloquence did not bewitch everybody, and as can be seen in the piece on Lloyd George, the latter was thought the better platform orator. Demosthenes (*see* Pitt the Elder) was said to have practised speaking with a pebble in his mouth, though this may have been an 'obturator', or primitive tooth filling. Apocalyptic-sounding cinema voice-overs today are credited with a 'gravelly' delivery. Churchill sounded as if shifting his words across an entire shingle beach, pounded by a spring tide of potent liquor. This his hefty actual intake of whisky and champagne certainly promoted, if it did not cause.

He deliberately, hence derisively, mispronounced Teutonisms, *e.g.*, 'Nazzy' for 'Nazi', though his French accent was atrocious merely by nature. Too much is sometimes made of his original speech impediments such as the lisp and stammer. These have been so common among great orators as arguably to spur, rather than curb, improved performance.

Winston, eldest son of Lord Randolph Churchill (*qv*), was born at Blenheim Palace, seat of their ancestors the Dukes of Marlborough. Educated at Harrow, where he did better academically than he liked us to believe, then Sandhurst, he was first a cavalry officer in the Sudan then a war correspondent and prisoner of the Boers in South Africa before entering domestic politics as MP for Oldham in 1900.

At that stage he was a Unionist, in practice Conservative. In 1904 he joined the Liberals, rising to Home Secretary and, during World War I, First Lord of the Admiralty. From 1915 to 1917, following the disastrous Gallipoli campaign, which he had promoted, he fought on the Western Front. In 1917 he joined Lloyd George's (*qv*) Coalition as Minister of Munitions, becoming Secretary of State for War and Air in 1919. He lost his seat in 1922.

In 1924 he re-entered Parliament as MP for Epping, this time as a 'Constitutionalist'. He supported the Conservatives, however (the only major party he never joined was Labour), and under Baldwin (*qv*) was Chancellor of the Exchequer from 1924 to 1929.

Most of the 1930s he spent out of office. But he was far from inactive. He warned in numerous speeches of the growing menace of Hitler (*qv*). He wrote popular history books, employing a sonorous prose style as lucrative as it was individual. He painted in a sub-impressionist idiom and was an active bricklayer, being sufficiently professional to win a union card.

When World War II began he became First Lord of the Admiralty again. He succeeded Chamberlain (*qv*) as Prime Minister in May 1940 and as Conservative leader five months later. He steered Britain through the rest of the War with a mixture of stirring oratory; huge personal magnetism that captivated even senior military men apprehensive of his erratic grasp of strategy; warm friendship with America, his mother's country, and its then President Franklin Roosevelt (*qv*); and muted distrust of Stalin's (*qv*) Russia, with which he nonetheless made common cause against Nazi Germany.

Defeated in the 1945 general election, he yet helped prepare the West for the Cold War with his Iron Curtain speech (*qv* below). His second premiership was marred by a stroke, though this was concealed from the public. He was reluctant to relinquish office, having conceived an avuncular *tendresse* for the young Queen (*see* Elizabeth II), rather like Lord Melbourne's with the young Queen Victoria, though without the hint of the lubricious that one detects with Melbourne. He was eventually persuaded to retire in 1955. On his death he was given a state funeral, a privilege accorded only a handful of other national heroes.

• Context of speech

On 8 July 1920 the Amritsar Massacre in India (details of which are covered below) came up for discussion in the House of Commons. The brutality involved did much to destroy British prestige in India. Churchill, as Secretary of State for War, had responsibility for handling the matter in Parliament. The original speech was punctuated by various interjections from other MPs.

66 **Collisions between troops and native populations have been painfully frequent in the melancholy aftermath of the Great War** …

But there are certain broad lines by which … an officer in such cases should be guided. First of all, … is the crowd attacking anything or anybody? … Are they trying to force their way forward to the attack …? …

The second question is this: is the crowd armed? … By armed I mean armed with lethal weapons … 'I was confronted', says General Dyer, 'by a revolutionary army.' What is the chief characteristic of an army? Surely it is that it is armed. This crowd was unarmed … there is another test … I mean the doctrine that no more force should be used than is necessary to secure compliance with the law …

If … there are guides of a positive character, there is surely one guide which we can offer them of a negative character … I mean a prohibition against what is called 'frightfulness' … the inflicting of great slaughter or massacre upon a particular crowd of people, with the intention of terrorising not merely the rest of the crowd, but the whole district or the whole country …

These observations … lead me to the specific circumstances of the fusillade at the Jallianwallah Bagh … The crowd was unarmed, except with bludgeons. It was not attacking anybody or anything. It was holding a seditious meeting. When fire had been opened upon it to disperse it, it tried to run away. Pinned up in a narrow place considerably smaller than Trafalgar Square, with hardly any exits, and packed together so that one bullet would drive through three or four bodies, the people ran madly this way and the other. When the fire was directed upon the centre, they ran to the sides. The fire was then directed to the sides. Many threw themselves down on the ground; the fire was then directed down on the ground. This was continued for 8 to 10 minutes …

Finally, when the ammunition had reached the point that only enough remained to allow for the safe return of the troops, and after 379 persons, which is about the number gathered together in this Chamber today, had been killed, and when most certainly 1,200 or more had been wounded, the troops, at whom not even a stone had been thrown, swung round and marched away ...

We have to make it absolutely clear, some way or another, that this is not the British way of doing business. I shall be told that it 'saved India'. I do not believe it for a moment. The British power in India does not stand on such foundations. It stands on much stronger foundations ...

Our reign in India or anywhere else has never stood on the basis of physical force alone, and it would be fatal to the British Empire if we were to try to base ourselves only upon it. The British way of doing things ... has always meant and implied close and effectual co-operation with the people of the country. In every part of the British Empire that has been our aim, and in no part have we arrived at such success as in India, whose princes spent their treasure in our cause, whose brave soldiers fought side by side with our own men, whose intelligent and gifted people are co-operating at the present moment with us in every sphere of government and of industry ... "

On the start of World War II

House of Commons
3 September 1939

• Context of speech

The day Britain declared war on Germany, Churchill spoke in the House of Commons. The words as yet lack the full force of his famous broadcast set pieces, but the style is developing.

"We must not underrate the gravity of the task which lies before us or the temerity of the ordeal, to which we shall not be found unequal. We must expect many disappointments, and many unpleasant surprises, but we may be sure that the task which we have freely accepted is one not beyond the compass and the strength of the British Empire and the French Republic.

The Prime Minister [*Chamberlain*, qv] said it was a sad day, and that is indeed true, but at the present time there is another note which may be present, and that is a feeling of thankfulness that, if these great trials were to come upon our Island, there is a generation of Britons here now ready to prove itself not unworthy of the days of yore and not unworthy of those great men, the fathers of our land, who laid the foundations of our laws and shaped the greatness of our country.

This is not a question of fighting for Danzig [*modern Gdansk, the Baltic port in Poland that Hitler used to pick a quarrel with Poland over*] or fighting for Poland. We are fighting to save the whole world from the pestilence of Nazi tyranny and in defence of all that is most sacred to man. This is no war of domination or imperial aggrandisement or material gain; no war to shut any country out of its sunlight and means of progress. It is a war, viewed in its inherent quality, to establish, on impregnable rocks, the rights of the individual, and it is a war to establish and revive the stature of man.

Perhaps it might seem a paradox that a war undertaken in the name of liberty and right should require ... surrender for the time being of so many of the dearly valued liberties and rights. In these last few days the House of Commons has been voting dozens of Bills which hand over to the executive our most dearly valued traditional liberties. We are sure that these liberties will be in hands which will not abuse them, which will use them for no class or party interests, which will cherish and guard them, and we look forward to the day, surely and confidently we look forward to the day, when our liberties and rights will be restored to us, and when we shall be able to share them with the peoples to whom such blessings are unknown."

'Blood, toil, tears and sweat'

House of Commons
13 May 1940

• Context of speech

In spring 1940 the inactive 'Phoney War' of the preceding winter ended. Hitler launched his offensive in the West, overrunning Denmark, Norway and the Low Countries.

The disaster threatening Britain engulfed the Prime Minister, Chamberlain, who resigned on 10 May. He was replaced by Churchill. There was solid opposition to Churchill's taking over, mostly in old-fashioned Conservative circles, and when on 13 May he entered the House of Commons to make the speech below, Chamberlain got more cheers. Churchill's chief supporters in the Commons at that point were among the Labour members.

The speech delivered, Churchill's prestige rose. But Colville, the Private Secretary who Churchill had acquired from Chamberlain three days earlier and who soon became devoted to his new master, thought it no more than 'a brilliant little speech'. This now sounds patronising, but probably reflects contemporary parliamentary opinion.

> **On Friday evening last I received His Majesty's commission to form a new Administration. It was the evident wish and will of Parliament and the nation that this should be conceived on the broadest possible basis and that it should include all parties ... I have completed the most important part of this task. A War Cabinet has been formed of five Members, representing, with the Opposition and Liberals, the unity of the nation. The three party Leaders have agreed to serve, either in the War Cabinet or in high executive office ...**
>
> To form an Administration of this scale and complexity is a serious undertaking in itself, but it must be remembered that we are in the preliminary stage of one of the greatest battles in history, that we are in action at many other points in Norway and in Holland, that we have to be prepared in the

Mediterranean, that the air battle is continuous and that many preparations ... have to be made here at home.

In this crisis I hope I may be pardoned if I do not address the House at any length today. I hope that any of my friends and colleagues, or former colleagues, who are affected by the political reconstruction, will make allowance, all allowance, for any lack of ceremony with which it has been necessary to act. I would say to the House, as I said to those who have joined this government: 'I have nothing to offer but blood, toil, tears and sweat.'

We have before us an ordeal of the most grievous kind. We have before us many, many long months of struggle and of suffering. You ask, what is our policy? I can say: It is to wage war, by sea, land and air, with all our might and with all the strength that God can give us; to wage war against a monstrous tyranny, never surpassed in the dark, lamentable catalogue of human crime.

That is our policy. You ask, what is our aim? I can answer in one word: It is victory, victory at all costs, victory in spite of all terror, victory, however long and hard the road may be; for without victory there is no survival. Let that be realised; no survival for the British Empire, no survival for all that the British Empire has stood for, no survival for the urge and impulse of the ages, that mankind will move forward towards its goal. But I take up my task with buoyancy and hope. I feel sure that our cause will not be suffered to fail among men. At this time I feel entitled to claim the aid of all, and I say: 'Come then, let us go forward together with our united strength.' "

'Fight them on the beaches'

House of Commons
4 June 1940

• Context of speech

Three weeks after the preceding speech, it was clear that France was about to collapse, though de Gaulle's (*qv*) joining the French Government was still 24 hours in the future and Churchill was at pains still to speak of the Anglo-French alliance. But his main emphasis to Parliament was that Britain now stood to all intents and purposes by itself.

> ❝ I have, myself, full confidence that if all do their duty, if nothing is neglected and if the best arrangements are made, as they are being made, we shall prove ourselves once again able to defend our Island home, to ride out the storm of war and to outlive the menace of tyranny, if necessary for years, if necessary alone.
>
> At any rate, that is what we are going to try to do. That is the resolve of His Majesty's Government — every man of them. That is the will of Parliament and the nation.
>
> The British Empire and the French Republic, linked together in their cause and in their need, will defend to the death their native soil, aiding each other like good comrades to the utmost of their strength.
>
> Even though large tracts of Europe and many old and famous states have fallen or may fall into the grip of the Gestapo and all the odious apparatus of Nazi rule, we shall not flag or fail.
>
> We shall go on to the end, we shall fight in France, we shall fight on the seas and oceans, we shall fight with growing confidence and growing strength in the air, we shall defend our Island, whatever the cost may be, we shall fight on the beaches, we shall fight on the landing grounds, we shall fight in the fields and in the streets, we shall fight in the hills; we shall never surrender, and even if, which I do not for a moment believe, this Island or a large part of it were subjugated and starving, then our Empire beyond the seas, armed and guarded by the British Fleet, would carry on the struggle, until, in God's good time, the New World, with all its power and might, steps forth to the rescue and the liberation of the Old.❞

'Their finest hour'

House of Commons
18 June 1940

• Context of speech

By now all pretence as to the continuation of the French forces as allies against Germany was at an end, though coincidentally it was on this day that de Gaulle made his speech rallying the Free French outside France and the less-free French at home who still hankered after liberty.

"In what way has our position worsened since the beginning of the War? It has worsened by the fact that the Germans have conquered a large part of the coastline of Western Europe, and many small countries have been overrun by them ... During the first four years of the last war the Allies experienced nothing but disaster and disappointment ... : one blow after another, terrible losses, frightful dangers. Everything miscarried ...

During that war we repeatedly asked ourselves ... 'How are we going to win?' and no one was able ever to answer it with much precision, until at the end, quite suddenly, quite unexpectedly, our terrible foe collapsed before us, and we were so glutted with victory that in our folly we threw it away ...

However matters may go in France ... we in this Island ... will never lose our sense of comradeship with the French people ... and if final victory rewards our toils they shall share the gains, aye, and freedom shall be restored to all. We abate nothing of our just demands; not one jot or tittle do we recede. Czechs, Poles, Norwegians, Dutch, Belgians have joined their causes to our own. All these shall be restored.

What General Weygand [*1867–1965, appointed in May 1940 — too late to make a difference — as commander of the Allied armies in France*] called the Battle of France is over.

I expect that the Battle of Britain is about to begin. Upon this battle depends the survival of Christian civilisation. Upon it depends our own British life, and the long continuity of our institutions and our Empire. The whole fury and might of the enemy must very soon be turned on us.

Hitler knows that he will have to break us in this Island or lose the war. If we can stand up to him, all Europe may be free and the life of the world may move forward into broad, sunlit uplands.

But if we fail, then the whole world, including the United States, including all that we have known and cared for, will sink into the abyss of a new Dark Age made more sinister, and perhaps more protracted, by the lights of perverted science.

Let us therefore brace ourselves to our duties, and so bear ourselves that, if the British Empire and its Commonwealth last for a thousand years, men will still say 'This was their finest hour.' "

'The Few'

House of Commons
20 August 1940

• Context of speech

Churchill had the prophet's ability not just to foresee an episode but to capture it in a telling phrase. He had already in the 18 June speech above mentioned the 'Battle of Britain'. It commenced on 15 August following (Feast of the Assumption of the Blessed Virgin Mary, in medieval times the protectress of England, of which there was a cult as 'the Dowry of Mary'). The fiercest fighting took place in the fortnight of 24 August–6 September, after which the Luftwaffe increasingly abandoned attacks on British airfields to bomb civilians.

> **Almost a year has passed since the war began, and it is natural for us, I think, to pause on our journey at this milestone and survey the dark, wide field ... Although this war is in fact only a continuation of the last, very great differences in its character are apparent. In the last war millions of men fought by hurling enormous masses of steel at one another. 'Men and shells' was the cry, and prodigious slaughter was the consequence ...**
>
> The British casualties in the first 12 months of the Great War amounted to 365,000. In this war, I am thankful to say, British killed, wounded, prisoners and missing, including civilians, do not exceed 92,000, and of these a large proportion are alive as prisoners of war ...
>
> There is another more obvious difference from 1914. The whole of the warring nations are engaged, not only soldiers, but the entire population, men, women and children. The fronts are everywhere. The trenches are dug in the towns and streets. Every village is fortified. Every road is barred. The front line runs through the factories. The workmen are soldiers with different weapons but the same courage ...
>
> Hitler is now sprawled over Europe. Our offensive springs are being slowly compressed, and we must resolutely and methodically prepare ourselves for the campaigns of 1941 and 1942. Two or three years are not a long time, even in our short, precarious lives. They are nothing in the history of the nation, and when we are doing the finest thing in the world, and have the honour to be the sole champion of the liberties of all Europe, we must not grudge these years ... as we toil and struggle through them ...

The road to victory may not be so long as we expect. But we have no right to count upon this. Be it long or short, rough or smooth, we mean to reach our journey's end ...

Our people are united and resolved, as they have never been before. Death and ruin have become small things compared with the shame of defeat or failure in duty.

We cannot tell what lies ahead. It may be that even greater ordeals lie before us. We shall face whatever is coming to us. We are sure of ourselves and of our cause and that is the supreme fact which has emerged in these months of trial.

Meanwhile, we have not only fortified our hearts but our Island. We have rearmed and rebuilt our armies in a degree which would have been deemed impossible a few months ago. We have ferried across the Atlantic, in the month of July, thanks to our friends over there, an immense mass of munitions of all kinds, cannon, rifles, machine-guns, cartridges and shell, all safely landed without the loss of a gun or a round. The output of our own factories, working as they have never worked before, has poured forth to the troops.

The whole British Army is at home. More than 2,000,000 determined men have rifles and bayonets in their hands tonight and three-quarters of them are in regular military formations. We have never had armies like this in our Island in time of war. The whole Island bristles against invaders, from the sea or from the air ...

Our Navy is far stronger than it was at the beginning of the war ... The merchant tonnage under the British flag, after a year of unlimited U-boat war, after eight months of intensive mining attack, is larger than when we began.

We have, in addition, under our control at least 4,000,000 tons of shipping from the captive countries which has taken refuge here or in the harbours of the Empire. Our stocks of food of all kinds are far more abundant than in the days of peace and a large and growing programme of food production is on foot.

Why do I say all this? Not assuredly to boast; not assuredly to give the slightest countenance to complacency. The dangers we face are still enormous, but so are our advantages and resources.

I recount them because the people have a right to know that there are solid grounds for the confidence which we feel, and that we have good reason to believe ourselves capable ... of continuing the war 'if necessary alone, if necessary for years' ...

The great air battle which has been in progress over this Island for the last few weeks has recently attained a high intensity. It is too soon to attempt to assign limits either to its scale or to its duration. We must certainly expect that greater efforts will be made by the enemy than any he has so far put forth ...

It is quite plain that Herr Hitler could not admit defeat in his air attack on Great Britain without sustaining most serious injury. If, after all his boastings and blood-curdling threats and lurid accounts trumpeted round the world of the damage he has inflicted, of the vast numbers of our Air Force he has shot down, so he says, with so little loss to himself; if after tales of the panic-stricken British crushed in their holes cursing the plutocratic Parliament which has led them to such a plight; if after all this his whole air onslaught were forced after a while tamely to peter out, the Fuehrer's reputation for veracity of statement might be seriously impugned. We may be sure, therefore, that he will continue as long as he has the strength to do so, and as long as any preoccupations he may have in respect of the Russian Air Force allow him to do so. ...

The enemy is, of course, far more numerous than we are. But our new production already, as I am advised, largely exceeds his, and the American production is only just beginning to flow in. It is a fact, as I see from my daily returns, that our bomber and fighter strength now, after all this fighting, are larger than they have ever been. We believe that we shall be able to continue the air struggle indefinitely and as long as the enemy pleases, and the longer it continues the more rapid will be our approach, first towards that parity, and then into that superiority in the air, upon which in a large measure the decision of the war depends.

The gratitude of every home in our Island, in our Empire, and indeed throughout the world, except in the abodes of the guilty, goes out to the British airmen who, undaunted by odds, unwearied in their constant challenge and mortal danger, are turning the tide of the World War by their prowess and by their devotion. Never in the field of human conflict was so much owed by so many to so few ... "

To the Allies

St James's Palace, London
12 June 1941

• Context of speech

At midday a meeting of Allied Representatives convened in the Picture Gallery at St. James's Palace. Ten nations took part: Belgium, Czechoslovakia, the Free French,

Greece, Luxembourg, The Netherlands, Norway, Poland, the United Kingdom and Yugoslavia. Only Ethiopia was unrepresented, no native of that country of sufficient importance being in Britain. Churchill addressed them and Colville describes how Churchill shook his finger at the microphone as if it had been Hitler himself.

66 **Here before us on the table lie the title deeds of ten nations or states whose soil has been invaded and polluted and whose men, women and children lie prostrate or writhing under the Hitler yoke ...**
Here we meet while from across the Atlantic Ocean the hammers and lathes of the United States signal in a rising hum their message of encouragement and their promise of swift and ever-growing aid.

What tragedies, what horrors, what crimes has [*sic*] Hitler and all that Hitler stands for brought upon Europe and the world! The ruins of Warsaw, of Rotterdam, of Belgrade are monuments which will long recall to future generations the outrage of unopposed air bombing applied with calculated scientific cruelty to helpless populations ...

But far worse than these visible injuries is the misery of the conquered peoples. We see them hounded, terrorised, exploited. Their manhood by the million is forced to work under conditions indistinguishable in many cases from actual slavery. Their goods and chattels are pillaged or filched for worthless money. Their homes, their daily life are pried into and spied upon by the all pervading system of secret political police which, having reduced the Germans themselves to abject docility, now stalks the streets and byways of a dozen lands. Their religious faiths are affronted, persecuted or oppressed in the interest of a fanatic paganism devised to perpetuate the worship and sustain the tyranny of one abominable creature. Their traditions, their culture, their laws, their institutions, social and political alike, are suppressed by force or undermined by subtle, coldly planned intrigue.

The prisons of the continent no longer suffice. The concentration camps are overcrowded. Every dawn German volleys crack. Czechs, Poles, Dutchmen, Norwegians, Yugoslavs and Greeks, Frenchmen, Belgians, Luxemburgers make the great sacrifice for faith and country. A vile race of Quislings — to use a new word which will carry the scorn of mankind down the centuries [*Vidkun Quisling (1887–1945) was Hitler's puppet Prime Minister of occupied Norway*] — is hired to fawn upon the conqueror, to collaborate in his designs and to enforce his rule upon their fellow countrymen while grovelling low themselves. Such is the plight of once glorious Europe and such are the atrocities against which we are in arms ...

Hitler, with his tattered lackey, Mussolini (*qv*), at his tail and Admiral Darlan [*Vichy* (*see* de Gaulle) *representative in North Africa, who nonetheless, whether genuinely or tactically, collaborated with the Allies following their landings there in 1942 but was soon assassinated*] frisking by his side, pretends to build out of hatred, appetite and racial assertion a new order for Europe. Never did so mocking a fantasy obsess the mind of mortal man …

Hitler may turn and trample this way and that through tortured Europe. He may spread his course far and wide and carry his curse with him. He may break into Africa or into Asia. But it is here, in this island fortress, that he will have to reckon in the end. We shall strive to resist by land and sea.

We shall be on his track wherever he goes. Our air power will continue to teach the German homeland that war is not all loot and triumph. We shall aid and stir the people of every conquered country to resistance and revolt. We shall break up and derange every effort which Hitler makes to systematise and consolidate his subjugations. He will find no peace, no rest, no halting place, no parley. And if, driven to desperate hazards, he attempts invasion of the British Isles, as well he may, we shall not flinch from the supreme trial. With the help of God, of which we must all feel daily conscious, we shall continue steadfast in faith and duty till our task is done … "

On determination

Harrow School
29 October 1941

• Context of speech

Although Churchill was not shy about mentioning his education at Harrow, he considered Eton good enough for his own son, the wayward Randolph. Given that the father he so reverenced, Lord Randolph (*qv*), had also been to Eton, he may simply have thought it gave one better instruction, without necessarily being the better school. (Before World War I, certainly, and perhaps after it, boys who were thought too stupid for Eton were often packed off to Harrow.) At any rate, Churchill often went down to Harrow to participate in the boys' autumnal singing of school songs, notably 'Forty Years On'. In 1941 he gave one of his more memorable speeches at one of these gatherings.

66 **Almost a year has passed since I came down here at your Head Master's kind invitation ... to cheer myself and cheer the hearts of a few of my friends by singing some of our own songs ... when I was here last time we were quite alone, desperately alone, and we had been so for five or six months. We were poorly armed ... We had the unmeasured menace of the enemy and their air attack still beating upon us, and you yourselves had had experience of this attack; and I expect you are beginning to feel impatient that there has been this long lull with nothing particular turning up.**

But we must learn to be equally good at what is short and sharp and what is long and tough. It is generally said that the British are often better at the last. They do not expect to move from crisis to crisis. They do not always expect that each day will bring up some noble chance of war. But when they very slowly make up their minds that the thing has to be done and the job put through and finished, then, even if it takes months — if it takes years — they do it ...

But for everyone, surely, what we have gone through in this period — I am addressing myself to the School — surely from this period of ten months, this is the lesson:

Never give in. Never give in. Never, never, never, never — in nothing, great or small, large or petty — never give in, except to convictions of honour and good sense. Never yield to force. Never yield to the apparently overwhelming might of the enemy.

We stood all alone a year ago, and to many countries it seemed that our account was closed, we were finished. All this tradition of ours, our songs, our school history, this part of the history of this country, were gone and finished and liquidated.

Very different is the mood today. Britain, other nations thought, had drawn a sponge across her slate. But instead our country stood in the gap. There was no flinching and no thought of giving in. And by what seemed almost a miracle to those outside these Islands, though we ourselves never doubted it, we now find ourselves in a position where I say that we can be sure that we have only to persevere to conquer.

You sang here a verse of a school song; you sang that extra verse written in my honour, which I was very greatly complimented by and which you have repeated today. But there is one word in it I want to alter. (I wanted to do so last year, but I did not venture to.) It is the line 'Not less we praise in darker days'.

I have obtained the Head Master's permission to alter 'darker' to 'sterner'. 'Not less we praise in sterner days'.

Do not let us speak of darker days. Let us speak rather of sterner days. These are not dark days. These are great days — the greatest days our country has ever lived. And we must all thank God that we have been allowed, each of us according to our stations, to play a part in making these days memorable in the history of our race."

To the Canadian Parliament

Ottawa
30 December 1941

• Context of speech

Once the US entered the War following Pearl Harbor (*see* Franklin Roosevelt), Churchill went to Washington to co-ordinate US-British policy. He addressed a joint session of Congress on 26 December, remarking that had his father rather than mother been American he 'might have got here on my own'. He then went on to Canada, where he addressed its Parliament.

"We did not make this war. We did not seek it. We did all we could to avoid it. We did too much to avoid it. We went so far at times in trying to avoid it as to be almost destroyed by it when it broke upon us. But that dangerous corner has been turned, and with every month and every year that passes we shall confront the evil-doers with weapons as plentiful, as sharp and as destructive as those with which they have sought to establish their hateful domination …

The peoples of the British Empire may love peace. They do not seek the lands or wealth of any country, but they are a tough and hardy lot. We have not journeyed all this way across the centuries, across the oceans, across the mountains, across the prairies, because we are made of sugar candy.

Look at the Londoners, the Cockneys. Look at what they have stood up to. Grim and gay with their cry 'We can take it' and their war-time mood of 'What is good enough for anybody is good enough for us.' We have not asked that the rules of the game should be modified. We shall never descend to the German and Japanese level, but if anybody likes to play rough we can play rough too. Hitler and his Nazi gang have sown the wind; let them reap the whirlwind …

… We plunged into this war all unprepared because we had pledged our word to stand by the side of Poland, which Hitler had feloniously invaded, and in spite of a gallant resistance had soon struck down. There followed those astonishing seven months which were called on this side of the Atlantic the 'phoney' war. Suddenly the explosion of pent-up German strength and preparation burst upon Norway, Denmark, Holland and Belgium. All these absolutely blameless neutrals, to most of whom Germany up to the last moment was giving every kind of guarantee and assurance, were overrun and trampled down. The hideous massacre of Rotterdam, where 30,000 people perished, showed the ferocious barbarism in which the German Air Force revels when, as in Warsaw and later Belgrade, it is able to bomb practically undefended cities.

On top of all this came the great French catastrophe. The French Army collapsed, and the French nation was dashed into utter and, as it has so far proved, irretrievable confusion. The French Government had at their own suggestion solemnly bound themselves with us not to make a separate peace … But their generals misled them. When I warned them that Britain would fight on alone whatever they did, their generals told their Prime Minister and his divided Cabinet 'In three weeks England will have her neck wrung like a chicken.' Some chicken. Some neck … "

On Victory in Europe

Broadcast from Number Ten Downing Street, London
8 May 1945

• Context of speech

At 2.41 am on 8 May 1945 the War in Europe formally ended. The date was christened 'VE (*ie*, Victory in Europe) Day'. (The War in the Far East ended four months later, being commemorated by the expression 'VJ (Victory in Japan) Day'.)

"**My dear friends, this is your hour. This is not victory of a party or of any class. It is a victory of the great British nation as a whole. We were the first, in this ancient Island, to draw the sword against tyranny. After a while we were left all alone against the most tremendous military power that has been seen. We were all alone for a whole year.**

There we stood, alone. Did anyone want to give in? Were we down-hearted? The lights went out and the bombs came down … So we came back after long months from the jaws of death, out of the mouth of Hell, while all the world wondered.

When shall the reputation and faith of this generation of English men and women fail? I say that in the long years to come not only will the people of this island but of the world, wherever the bird of freedom chirps in human hearts, look back to what we have done and they will say 'do not despair, do not yield to violence and tyranny, march straightforward and die, if need be, unconquered.' … A terrible foe has been cast on the ground and awaits our judgment and our mercy.

But there is another foe who occupies large portions of the British Empire, a foe stained with cruelty and greed — the Japanese. I rejoice we can all take a night off today and another day tomorrow. Tomorrow our great Russian allies will also be celebrating victory and after that we must begin the task of rebuilding our hearth and homes, doing our utmost to make this country a land in which all have a chance, in which all have a duty. And we must turn ourselves to fulfil our duty to our own countrymen, and to our gallant allies of the United States who were so foully and treacherously attacked by Japan. We will go hand and hand with them. Even if it is a hard struggle we will not be the ones who will fail."

'The Iron Curtain'

Westminster College, Fulton, Missouri
5 March 1946

• Context of speech

Though this has become known as the 'Iron Curtain' speech, Churchill himself entitled it 'The Sinews of Peace'. It is a phrase that is all but forgotten, so for once his prophetic powers had failed him (perhaps being out of office occluded his second sight).

66 **I come to the crux of what I have travelled here to say. A shadow has fallen upon the scenes so lately lit by the Allied victory. Nobody knows what Soviet Russia and its Communist international organisation intends [*sic*] to do in the immediate future, or what are the limits, if any, to their expansive and proselytising tendencies.**

I have a strong admiration and regard for the valiant Russian people and for my wartime comrade Marshal Stalin [*qv*]. There is deep sympathy and goodwill in Britain — and I doubt not here also — towards the peoples of all the Russias and a resolve to persevere through many differences and rebuffs in establishing lasting friendships …

From Stettin in the Baltic to Trieste in the Adriatic an iron curtain has descended across the Continent. Behind that line lie all the capitals of the ancient states of Central and Eastern Europe. Warsaw, Berlin, Prague, Vienna, Budapest, Belgrade, Bucharest and Sofia, all these famous cities and the populations around them, lie in what I must call the Soviet Sphere, and all are subject in one form or another, not only to Soviet influence but to a very high and, in some cases, increasing measure of control from Moscow …

In front of the Iron Curtain which lies across Europe are other causes for anxiety … in a great number of countries, far from the Russian frontiers and throughout the world, Communist Fifth Columns are established and work in complete unity and absolute obedience to the directions they receive from the Communist centre …

These are sombre facts for anyone to have to recite on the morrow of a victory gained by so much splendid comradeship in arms and in the cause of freedom and democracy; but we should be most unwise not to face them squarely while time remains ...

From what I have seen of our Russian friends and allies during the War, I am convinced that there is nothing for which they have less respect than for weakness, especially military weakness. For that reason the old doctrine of a balance of power is unsound. We cannot afford ... to work on narrow margins, offering temptations to a trial of strength. If the Western Democracies stand together ... no one is likely to molest them. If, however, they become divided or falter in their duty ... then indeed catastrophe may overwhelm us all ... ”

Riposte to Churchill's Iron Curtain speech

Joseph Stalin, *né* **Iosif/Josef Vissarionovich Djugashvili/Dzhugashvili (1878–1953) 14 March 1946**

• Biography

The two chief culprits in the seven-decade state-run crime spree otherwise called the Soviet experiment were Lenin (*qv*) and Stalin. Both operated under aliases. Their love of nicknames (Stalin also used 'Koba') is shared by gangsters, and it is gangsters that in the last resort such men most resemble, however much more exalted the Bolsheviks' ultimate vision than mobster *omertà*. Stalin's primacy among his henchmen in particular rested on a network of favours owed and returned; fear; 'respect' (real and feigned); blackmail; and shared criminal guilt — even irregular cash gifts doled out from a war chest, though gross corruption in the Soviet leadership dates only from his later years.

Stalin was from Georgia, a savage semi-Asiatic land finally absorbed by Russia as late as the year of his birth, which he later falsified as 1879, perhaps to quell doubts over his paternity. Banditry and vendettas flourished in Georgia, shaping Stalin's political methods, as his 20,000,000 to 30,000,000 slaughtered victims testify (a precise corpse count is impossible). He may have been a Tsarist police informer in youth. He certainly funded his early sedition by outright law-breaking, chiefly armed robbery. He remained a revolutionary all his life, whether grabbing power, wielding it or crushing threats to it (some real, the rest — perhaps most — imagined).

The utopian aim of the Soviet experiment — the 'omelette' of Lenin's imagery (*see* Trotsky) — remained largely untasted by the masses. The latter had to be content with the broken egg-shells, seasoned by appetisers such as universal education and a basic welfare system. Meanwhile the means to the revolutionaries' end were not just born in criminality but remained mired in it.

Stalin joined the Bolshevik Central Committee in 1912. During the 1917 Revolution and ensuing Civil War he and Trotsky were Lenin's chief lieutenants. He became Party General Secretary in 1922 and increasingly its leader following Lenin's death. By 1941, when Hitler (*qv*) invaded, Stalin had ousted Trotsky, destroyed many comrades from revolutionary days, crushed the peasantry, industrialised Russia at breakneck speed (though the necks were other people's) and executed much of his officer corps, endangering Russia's very survival.

Hitler's invasion followed two years of a Hitler–Stalin pact during which the two men dismembered Poland. (Britain's guaranteeing Poland's integrity, the official reason Chamberlain (*qv*) declared war in 1939, was thus degraded to a petulant, specifically anti-German gesture, since honouring the guarantee properly would have meant declaring war on the USSR too.) Stalin long refused to believe Hitler would attack him, less from trust than from obstinate adherence to a pact of his own forging — irresponsibility which was itself criminal in that it eventually multiplied Russian casualties.

But Stalin successfully rallied his people and through their heroic sacrifices, Western *matériel* (often ungraciously accepted and seldom mentioned afterwards), Hitler's folly and some good generals played the largest part of any of the World War II Allies in defeating Nazism. Conversely, he declared war on Japan only on 8 August 1945, an action now thought to have been what brought Japan's surrender within days, more so than America's atomic bombs. But America had done most of the fighting against Japan since 1941, so that Stalin's claim to have accomplished the same against Germany (*see* the speech below) was special pleading, though technically accurate.

• Context of speech

Stalin's riposte to Churchill's 'Iron Curtain' speech tried to equate Churchill's 'English-speaking peoples' theme to racism. It is a device we have already encountered with Hitler (*qv*) and it foreshadowed the colossally expanded use of 'racist' today as a label which, once fixed on someone, destroys his or her reputation even among moderate people. Hitler's and Stalin's role in fashioning this weapon should be better known.

As a speaker Stalin, unlike Trotsky, lacked fire. He was unpolished. But his accomplices preferred their Stalin speeches that way. Or said they did.

“Mister Churchill now stands in the position of a fire-brand of war. And Mister Churchill is not alone here. He has friends not only in England but also in the United States of America.

In this respect, one is reminded remarkably of Hitler and his friends. Hitler began to set war loose by announcing his racial theory, declaring that only people speaking the German language represent a fully valuable nation. Mister Churchill begins to set war loose, also by a racial theory, maintaining that only nations speaking the English language are … called upon to decide the destinies of the … world.

The German racial theory brought Hitler and his friends to the conclusion that the Germans, as the only fully valuable nation, must rule over other nations. The English racial theory brings Mister Churchill and his friends to the conclusion that nations speaking the English language … should rule over the remaining nations of the world ….

As a result of the German invasion, the Soviet Union has irrevocably lost in battles with the Germans, and also during the German occupation and through the expulsion of Soviet citizens to German slave labour camps, about 7,000,000 people [*this was the official figure then; later, Soviet propagandists realised the publicity value of a much higher toll and started quoting 20,000,000*]. In other words, the Soviet Union has lost in men several times more than Britain and the United States together.

It may be that some quarters are trying to push into oblivion these sacrifices of the Soviet people which ensured the liberation of Europe from the Hitlerite yoke.

But the Soviet Union cannot forget them. One can ask, therefore, what can be surprising in the fact that the Soviet Union, in a desire to ensure its security for the future, tries to ensure that these countries have governments whose relations to the Soviet Union are loyal? …

Mister Churchill evades the truth when he speaks of the growth of the influence of the Communist parties in Eastern Europe …. The growth of the influence of Communism cannot be considered accidental. It is a normal function. The influence of the Communists grew because during the hard years of Fascism in Europe, Communists showed themselves reliable, daring and self-sacrificing fighters against Fascist regimes.

Mister Churchill is sometimes reminiscent in his speeches of an aristocrat dealing with common people from small houses, patting them on the shoulder in a lordly manner and pretending to be their friend. But these people are not so simpleminded as might first appear. Common people, too, have their opinions and their own politics. And they know how to stand up for themselves.

It is they, millions of these common people, who have voted Mister Churchill and his party out in England, giving their votes to the Labour Party. It is they, millions of these common people, who have isolated the reactionaries in Europe and the collaborators with Fascism, and have showed a preference for Left-wing democratic parties."

To US GIs before D-Day

George S(tuart) Patton (1885–1945)
Stourport-on-Severn, Worcestershire
5 June 1944

• Biography

When told that James Wolfe (1727–59), the taker of Quebec, was mad, George III said he wished the man would bite some of his other generals. Outstanding military commanders are often a little unbalanced. Patton was about as outstanding as any in history when it came to combat. Unfortunately he was a liability in modern warfare, where democratic belligerent nations can sustain more damage — with public opinion, where it really matters — through a general's unbridled tongue than by setbacks in the field.

Like other tank commanders of his generation, Patton started as a cavalry officer, being involved in a 1916 operation to capture the Mexican bandit Pancho Villa. His first tank action was in Flanders in September 1918. He then returned to peacetime soldiering back in the USA, serving with Eisenhower (*qv*), a close friend, and lobbying Washington for more armoured units.

During World War II he commanded the US Army Western Task Force in the Morocco landings of 1942, imposing some badly needed discipline; the 7th Army in the 1943 Sicily invasion; and, most famously, the 3rd Army in the 1944 Normandy landings and beyond. Far beyond; by May 1945 he had reached western Czechoslovakia.

But he was impetuous, slapping a couple of soldiers while in Sicily for what he considered cowardice. Had Eisenhower, formerly his junior, not by now been his commanding officer (a leap-frogging that itself reflected Patton's tactlessness), it might have ruined him. At least his ferocious reputation made him a useful decoy. He was kept in Sicily; the Germans inferred a landing in southern France. He was sent to Egypt; they suspected a Balkan thrust. He was made commander of a phantom army group in Britain; Hitler (*qv*) assumed the Allies would invade Europe via Calais.

His talent was appreciated not just by Hitler but by Stalin (*qv*), who reckoned even the Red Army could not have matched Patton's drive across Northern France, also von Rundstedt, Patton's opponent in the Ardennes in 1944 and a man as critical of Hitler as Patton was of Allied pusillanimity.

Patton alone of the Western generals seems to have grasped the importance of speed, in this respect resembling Julius Caesar (*see* Marc Antony), another military genius who addressed his troops with great coarseness. In his 1944–45 thrust towards Germany Patton outflanked strong defences, forcing the enemy to scuttle backwards or be trapped. Eisenhower and Montgomery, mindful of the politicians at home, Allied rivalries in the field and the bad press ensuing from any extra-bloody engagement, advanced more cautiously. Again the Germans withdrew, but steadily, hence more damagingly.

Patton was shaping up as the chief critic of the Soviet presence in Europe when he was killed following a car crash seven months after VE Day. Oddly enough, it was occasioned by a lorry-driver's unexpected left turn, just as Patton himself had in one of his most brilliant manoeuvres swung his 3rd Army north to take pressure off the 101st Airborne Division locked up in Bastogne, in eastern Belgium, just after repulsing von Rundstedt's Ardennes offensive.

• Context of speech

Patton extemporised his speeches, not even using notes. He was unapologetic about his coarse language, maintaining that it was the best way to get his message across to the average soldier. Mind, he added, it had to be eloquent coarseness. An earlier version of the speech excerpted below was delivered to the 6th Armored Division on 31 May 1944. Technically Patton was a poor orator: self-conscious and with a shrill voice. But as early as the 1942 North African campaign men liked serving under him, not because he was affable but because they would more probably survive than with a 'nicer' man.

---

66 **Only two percent of you right here today would die in a major battle. Death must not be feared. Death, in time, comes to all men. Yes, every man is scared in his first battle. If he says he's not, he's a liar** ...

There are four hundred neatly marked graves somewhere in Sicily. All because one man went to sleep on the job. But they are German graves, because we caught the bastard asleep before they did ...

Don't forget, you men don't know ... I'm here ... I'm not supposed to be commanding this Army. I'm not even supposed to be here in England. Let the first bastards to find out be the goddamned Germans. Some day I want to see them raise up on their piss-soaked hind legs and howl 'Jesus Christ, it's the Goddamned Third Army again and that son-of-a-fucking-bitch Patton.'

We want to get the hell over there. The quicker we clean up this goddamned mess, the quicker we can take a little jaunt against the purple-pissing Japs and clean out their nest, too ...

Sure, we want to go home. We want this war over with. The quickest way to get it over with is to go get the bastards who started it. The quicker they are whipped, the quicker we can go home. The shortest way home is through Berlin and Tokyo. And when we get to Berlin I am personally going to shoot that paper-hanging son-of-a-bitch Hitler ...

I don't want to get any messages saying 'I am holding my position'. We are not holding a goddamned thing. Let the Germans do that. We are advancing constantly and we are not interested in holding onto anything, except the enemy's balls. We are going to twist his balls and kick the living shit out of him all of the time ... We are going to go through him like crap through a goose ...

From time to time there will be some complaints that we are pushing our people too hard. I don't give a good goddamn about such complaints. I believe in the old and sound rule that an ounce of sweat will save a gallon of blood. The harder we push, the more Germans we will kill. The more Germans we kill, the fewer of our men will be killed. Pushing means fewer casualties. I want you all to remember that.

There is one great thing that you men will all be able to say after this war is over and you are home once again. You may be thankful that twenty years from now when you are sitting by the fireplace with your grandson on your knee and he asks you what you did in the great World War II, you won't have to cough, shift him to the other knee and say, 'Well, your Granddaddy shoveled shit in Louisiana.' No, sir, you can look him straight in the eye and say 'Son, your Granddaddy rode with the Great Third Army and a Son-of-a-Goddamned-Bitch named Georgie Patton!' ... "

To troops before Agincourt

Laurence Olivier (1907–89)
Shakespeare (1564–1616),
Henry V, Act IV, Scene 3

• Biography

Some explanation is necessary for reintroducing Shakespeare so late in an oratorical anthology arranged broadly by when the composer of the oration lived. The reason is Olivier's use of the Henry V speech before Agincourt, not in its original form as a rebuke to Henry's cousin the Earl of Westmoreland, but as a pep talk to the troops *à la* Patton (*qv*). The analogy is a close one. Both the King and Patton aim to encourage cross-Channel invaders from England who will do battle against a strongly entrenched enemy on the mainland of Europe, specifically in northern France.

Laurence Olivier was himself of French extraction, though his Protestant ancestors had emigrated following Louis XIV's harrying of Protestants in the late 17th century. In England the Oliviers produced numerous clerics, a profession where declamation is an essential skill.

Olivier rose rapidly in his profession. By the 1930s he was one of a handful of leading Shakespearian actors. In World War II he served in the Fleet Air Arm. He had already taken flying lessons while working in Hollywood and liked to draw a parallel between flying and acting, in particular the need to balance humility and confidence. In addition, he had already played a test pilot (in *Q Planes* (1938)).

As a real airman he was a liability. As a screen hero he shone. The Government sponsored the film of *Henry V*. It was released on 12 July 1944, five-and-a-half weeks after the Normandy Landings. It was set in Normandy (the taking of Harfleur) and the Picardy-Upper Normandy borders (the site of Agincourt). As the credits roll, the following legend appears: 'To the Commandos and Airborne Troops of Great Britain this film is dedicated, the spirit of whose ancestors it has been [*sic*] humbly attempted to recapture in some ensuing scenes.' Not only is it a shockingly ungrammatical sentence; one wonders why the other units in the British forces are not included.

• Context of speech

Olivier had already broadcast the speech below, first in a radio performance called 'Into Battle' in May 1942 then in a radio adaptation of the entire play. Once the film was given the go-ahead he was appointed to direct. The Agincourt scene was shot in Co. Wicklow, in Ireland, then a neutral state (and not, under De Valera, outstandingly benevolently neutral either). Moreover, the extras, particularly the French cavalrymen, were recruited from the Irish equivalent of Britain's Home Guard. But of all these ironies, the richest is the way rain hampered the shooting, since historically it was rain that turned the battlefield to a bog, enabling the English foot soldiers and archers to immobilise then destroy the French heavy infantry and horse — the Panzer units of their day.

Once released, *Henry V* outlasted the War, running till June 1945. The following spring it was released in the US and won Olivier an Oscar, not just for his acting but for producing and directing it. A knighthood followed in 1947 and a peerage in 1970. He is still the only actor ever ennobled. A recording of the speech was played at his memorial service. It is pointless to try and describe his speaking style since it varied so much with each character he played, though his clarity was always first-rate. Sad to say, his attempt at a speech of his own devising in his maiden effort in the House of Lords reads archly and convolutedly. Its language was so purple that had it been a complexion one would have diagnosed imminent syncope. Still, purple was Olivier's favourite colour. And it may be that his delivery overcame the poor content, as a good actor's should.

66 **WESTMORELAND: Oh that we now had here but one ten thousand of those men in England that do no work today.**

HENRY V: What's he that wishes so?
My cousin Westmoreland? No, my fair cousin,
If we are marked to die, we are enow [*enough*]
To do our country loss; and if to live,
The fewer men, the greater share of honour.
God's will! I pray thee, wish not one man more.
By Jove, I am not covetous for gold,
Nor care I who doth feed upon my cost;
It yearns me not if men my garments wear;
Such outward things dwell not in my desires.
But if it be a sin to covet honour,

I am the most offending soul alive.
No, faith, my coz [*cousin*], wish not a man from England.
God's peace! I would not lose so great an honour
As one man more, methinks, would share from me
For the best hope I have. Oh do not wish one more!
Rather proclaim it, Westmoreland, through my host,
That he which hath no stomach to this fight,
Let him depart; his passport shall be made
And crowns for convoy put into his purse.
We would not die in that man's company
That fears his fellowship to die with us.
This day is called the feast of Crispian.
He that outlives this day, and comes safe home,
Will stand a tip-toe when the day is named,
And rouse him at the name of Crispian.
He that shall live this day, and see old age,
Will yearly on the vigil feast his neighbours,
And say 'To-morrow is Saint Crispian'.
Then will he strip his sleeve and show his scars,
And say 'These wounds I had on Crispin's day.'
Old men forget, yet all shall be forgot,
But he'll remember with advantages
What feats he did that day. Then shall our names
Familiar in his mouth as household words,
Harry the King, Bedford and Exeter,
Warwick and Talbot, Salisbury and Gloucester,
Be in their flowing cups freshly remembered.
This story shall the good man teach his son;
And Crispin Crispian shall ne'er go by,
From this day to the ending of the world,
But we in it shall be remembered;
We few, we happy few, we band of brothers;
For he today that sheds his blood with me
Shall be my brother; be he ne'er so vile [*low-born*];
This day shall gentle [*make more aristocratic*] his condition,
And gentlemen in England now a-bed
Shall think themselves accursed they were not here,
And hold their manhoods cheap whiles any speaks

On the A-Bomb

Emperor Hirohito of Japan (1926–89)
Tokyo
14 August 1945

• Biography

Sovereigns defeated in either of the two World Wars usually lost their thrones, even when they had conducted war moderately. The Japanese Emperor in 1945 kept his. How? Many of his fighting men had behaved every bit as swinishly as their Axis partners from Hitler's (*qv*) Germany. Prisoners-of-war of the Japanese and others they maltreated, for instance the 'comfort women', had as much cause for bitterness as concentration camp inmates towards the Nazis in Europe.

The reasoning of Douglas MacArthur, the Allied Supreme Commander occupying Japan following Hirohito's surrender in August 1945, was that by maintaining the monarchy he could avoid a struggle to impose order that would probably cost a huge number of lives over and above those already expended in combat. Even as it was, hot-head Japanese youths, real diehards, made various attacks on symbolic locations in Tokyo and Yokohama following the broadcast excerpted below, including a threat to the Imperial Palace, where among other things they butchered the Imperial Guard Division's general in command.

Over in Europe, Victor Emmanuel II of Italy failed to salvage his throne, even though he had sacked Mussolini (*qv*) and ditched Hitler for the Allies. And if the reverence-for-the-head-of-state conditions in Japan had been matched in Germany — where support for the Nazis was indeed pretty solid even at the end — it is inconceivable that the Allies would have retained Hitler on the same grounds as held good with Hirohito.

So Hirohito was lucky to be an emperor, so remote from ordinary people, whether his subjects the Japanese or the American conqueror MacArthur, that *not* deposing him and trying him for war crimes was actually considered viable.

For he was not quite the helpless victim of protocol over Japan's original decision to make war that would have justified such kid-glove treatment. How could such a figure have been, if the reverence accorded him so exceeded that of western democracies for their leaders, whether elected presidents or constitutional sovereigns? If your prestige is that great, you necessarily influence decision-making.

Hirohito was born in 1901 and succeeded his long-decrepit father Yoshihito in 1926, having been Regent since 1921. His grandfather the Emperor Meiji had been Japan's first constitutional sovereign, but was nonetheless supreme head of the armed forces. In 1928 and 1936 Hirohito, who inherited both roles, asserted himself against the militarist elements in his government and armed forces. But for the most part he was a diffident ruler, absorbed in marine biology, much as Louis XVI in pre-revolutionary France tinkered with locks.

He made dissenting noises against his ministers' most aggressive decisions, on one occasion by reciting a poem, an eccentric form of protest in itself but in this case so obliquely worded as to be quite exceptionally ineffectual. He was frequently incomprehensible in this sort of way, his general absent-mindedness even taking the form of forgetting to do up his fly-buttons. It was only when his Prime Minister in January 1945 urged immediate peace that he jibbed, though by spring he was convinced a negotiated peace was inevitable. His continuing the war till August in the hope that a late success would soften the Allies' terms cost Japan an extra one-and-a-half million deaths, to say nothing of the Allies' losses.

But he survived. He renounced his divine status as emperor — itself proof that he can't have been divine, for real gods have no choice in the matter. He endorsed MacArthur's new constitution, which committed Japan to peace. He embarked on a meet-the-people tour of the length and breadth of Japan that by 1950 established his mortal, and constitutional, status.

• Context of speech

Unfortunately, he wasn't initially very contrite, as may be seen below. The occasion was his broadcast to his subjects on 14 August 1945, which he delivered in tears. It was the first time the vast majority of his subjects had heard his voice and some of the youthful hot-head element already mentioned thought it bogus, stormed the imperial palace and lost over thirty of their number killed.

---

66 **We have ordered Our Government to communicate to the Governments of the United States, Great Britain, China and the Soviet Union that Our Empire accepts the provisions of their joint declaration [*that broadcast on 27 July 1945 demanding unconditional surrender*]** ...

We declared war on America and Britain out of Our sincere desire to ensure Japan's self-preservation and the stabilisation of East Asia, it being far from Our thoughts either to infringe upon the sovereignty of other nations or to embark upon territorial aggrandisement.

But now the war has lasted for nearly four years. Despite the best that has been done by everyone — the gallant fighting of the military and naval forces, the diligence and assiduity of Our civil servants and the devotion of Our 100,000,000 people — the war situation has developed not necessarily to Japan's advantage, while the general trends of the world have all turned against her interests.

Moreover, the enemy has begun to employ a new and most cruel bomb, the power of which to do damage is, indeed, incalculable, taking the toll of many innocent lives. Should We continue to fight, it would not only result in an ultimate collapse and obliteration of the Japanese nation, it would also lead to the total extinction of human civilisation.

Such being the case, how are We to save the millions of Our subjects or to atone Ourselves before the hallowed spirits of Our imperial ancestors? This is the reason why We have ordered the acceptance of the provisions of the joint declaration of the powers ...

The thought of those officers and men as well as others who have fallen in the field of battle, those who died at their posts on duty, or those who met otherwise with death and all their bereaved families, pains Our heart night and day.

The welfare of the wounded and the war sufferers and of those who have lost their home and livelihood is the object of Our profound solicitude. The hardships and sufferings to which Our nation is to be subjected hereafter will certainly be great ...

Beware most vigilantly of any outbursts of emotion that may engender needless complications, of any fraternal contention and strife that may create confusion, lead you astray and cause you to lose the confidence of the world.

Let the entire nation continue as one family from generation to generation, ever firm in its faith in the imperishable nature of its divine fatherland, and mindful of its heavy burden of responsibilities, and the long road before it. Unite your strength in such a way that you are dedicated to future reconstruction. Cultivate the ways of rectitude and nobility of spirit, and work with resolution so that you may enhance the innate glory of the Imperial State and keep pace with the progress of the world."

Apology for Japan's waging war

Drafted 1948 but never delivered

• Context of speech

Three years after the War Hirohito had become more aware of his part in it. He came close to making a real apology, and one couched in personal terms. It seems to have been composed by Michiji Tajima, a leading courtier though only recently appointed to the post. Its use of an exclusively imperial pronoun, superior even to the royal 'We' in English, has been cited as evidence that Hirohito personally commissioned the speech.

It was never delivered, however, and the document containing it was not discovered till 2003. But Hirohito did make another kind of public gesture dissociating himself from the leading politicians who had started the war. After Hideki Tojo, Japan's wartime Prime Minister, and other top war criminals were included among the dead commemorated at a leading shrine in Tokyo in 1978, Hirohito stopped paying his respects there. His successor Akihito has gone much further, expressing regret for Japanese wartime misdeeds in China, Korea and Southeast Asia when on visits to those places. In 2006 he went as far as to state that royal families everywhere should campaign against war. Hirohito's draft apology runs thus:

"**For more than twenty years after my enthronement, I constantly endeavoured to do my duty. However, I could not change the current of the times, [we] lost good relations with our neighbours and fought with great powers, which ultimately led to miserable defeat in war and brought about the terrible disaster we experience now.**
I am burning with the flame of anguish. I am deeply ashamed of my immorality. I do not have peace of mind. Thinking of the nation, I do not know what to do with the heaviness of the burden I bear."

'The Forgotten People'

Sir Robert (Bob) Gordon Menzies (1894–1978)
Broadcast to Australians
22 May 1942

● Biography

Few Australian politicians have been as well-known in Britain as Menzies. This was partly because of his Anglophilia, partly because of his longevity as Australia's Prime Minister (1949 to 1966) – but mostly because he thought of himself as British. A fourth reason was his fervent monarchism. It won him a Knighthood of the Thistle from the Queen (*see* Elizabeth II), an honour the more heartfelt since it is in her personal gift, not just a bauble she hands out on the say-so of whoever is British Prime Minister.

It was certainly appreciated by Menzies, whose quoting 'I did but see her passing by/And yet I love her till I die' about the Queen on her first visit to Australia in 1954 is now seen there by many as either too familiar or too unctuous and in any case as ludicrously over the top. Whether, in any case, the Queen would have been quite so free with the Thistle had she known how much Menzies's memory would come to be reviled by leftist Australians as a red-baiter is an interesting question. As also is to what extent this signal mark of royal favour helped undermine the monarchy's reputation for impartiality there, though it survived the 1999 referendum by a comfortable but not spectacular 55% to 45% vote (*see* also Howard).

Menzies was initially a barrister and entered politics through his involvement with a case concerning the balance between state and federal power. Just five years after winning election to Australia's Federal parliament he was Prime Minister, having done much to form the new United Australia Party (UAP), of which he had become leader.

He followed Britain in declaring war on Germany in 1939, and managed to bring Australia's other politicians with him on this. But he was anxious to focus on the Japanese threat in the Pacific rather than disperse Australians to the European or North African theatres. His Anglophilia was always tempered by annoyance over the way Britain frequently took Australian compliance with its wishes for granted.

In 1941 his lack of support both within his own party and nationally led to his resigning the premiership. The UAP's weakness moved him to take the chief role in founding towards the end of the War the Liberal Party.

In 1949 he and his new party won overwhelmingly in elections to the House of Representatives (the lower house of Australia's legislature). He had recently become converted to a feeling in his party that Communist domestic subversion was not only widespread but as dangerous as the external threat to peace by the USSR. His 1950–51 anti-Communist legislation was harsh, breached the legal principle of presumed innocence and was struck down by the High Court. But a defection by a Soviet diplomat and a split between strongly anti-Communist leftists and those better disposed to Communism allowed him to retain power. Defence considerations in the eastern Pacific drew him closer to the US and Australia got involved in the Vietnam War.

• Context of speech

The subject of it was incorporated in a book of collected speeches, *The Forgotten People and Other Studies in Democracy* (Sydney 1943). Menzies claimed never to use notes, reckoning he had more impact speaking impromptu, while the risks of saying something he would later regret were minimal.

66 **The time has come to say something of the forgotten class — the middle class — those people who are constantly in danger of being ground between the upper and the nether millstones of the false war; the middle class who, properly regarded, represent the backbone of this country** ...

I must define what I mean when I use the expression 'middle class' ... salary-earners, shopkeepers, skilled artisans, professional men and women, farmers and so on ... They are for the most part unorganised and un-selfconscious. They are envied by those whose benefits are largely obtained by taxing them. They are not rich enough to have individual power. They are taken for granted by each political party in turn. They are not sufficiently lacking in individualism to be organised for what ... these days we call 'pressure politics' ...

The middle class provides more than any other the intellectual life which marks us off from the beast; the life which finds room for literature, for the arts, for science, for medicine and the law ...

The case for the middle class is the case for a dynamic democracy as against the stagnant one. Stagnant waters are level, and in them the scum rises. Active waters are never level: they toss and tumble and have crests and troughs; but the scientists tell us that they purify themselves in a few hundred yards …

If the motto is to be 'Eat, drink and be merry, for tomorrow you will die, and if it chances you don't die, the State will look after you; but if you don't eat, drink and be merry and save, we shall take your savings from you', then the whole business of life would become foundationless.

Are you looking forward to a breed of men after the War who will have become boneless wonders? Leaners grow flabby; lifters grow muscles …

What really happens to us will depend on how many people we have who are of the great and sober and dynamic middle class — the strivers, the planners, the ambitious ones. We shall destroy them at our peril."

On freedom of speech

Broadcast to Australians
19 June 1942

• Context of speech

The month after 'The Forgotten People' speech, Menzies turned to the intellectual conditions under which the War was having to be fought, though he had more sense than to put it like that.

"Speaking last year, President [*Franklin D.*] Roosevelt (*qv*), in discussing the things at stake in this war, made use of an expression — 'The Four Freedoms' — which has now found currency in most of our mouths …

Tonight … I take … freedom of speech and expression, which connotes also freedom of thought …

Let us ... remember that the ... essence of freedom is that it is freedom for others as well as ... ourselves: freedom for people who disagree with us as well as for our supporters; freedom for minorities as well as for majorities ...[,] a conception which is not born with us but which we must painfully acquire. Most of us have no instinct at all to preserve the right of the other fellow to think what he likes about our beliefs and say what he likes about our opinions ...

All things considered, the worst crime of Fascism and its twin brother, German National Socialism, is their suppression of free thought and free speech. It is one of the many proofs that, with all their cleverness, they are primitive and reactionary movements. One of the first actions of the Nazis in Germany was to regiment the newspapers by telling them exactly what they could print. The result was that newspaper controversy came to an end, since all sang the same tune. When I was in Berlin in 1938 I mentioned this phenomenon to a high German official of the Foreign Office and, with about the one gleam of humour that I encountered on that visit, he replied that he thought it quite a good idea, since it saved buying more than one newspaper.

As you probably know, I am one who has in recent years had a severe battering from many newspapers, but I am still shocked to think that intelligent men, in what they believe to be a free country, can deny to the newspapers or to critics of any degree the right to batter at people or policies whom they dislike or of whom they disapprove ...

There are Fascist tendencies in all countries — a sort of latent tyranny. And they exist ... in radical as well as in conservative quarters. Suppression of attack, which is based upon suppression of really free thought, is the instinctive weapon of the vested interest ...

You will agree that I speak as one with some practical — occasionally painful — experience, when I say that the arrow of the critic is never pleasant and is sometimes poisoned. Much criticism is acutely partisan or actually unjust. But every man engaged in public affairs must sustain it with a good courage and a cheerful heart. He may, if he can, confute his critic, but he must not suppress him. Power is apt to produce a kind of drunkenness, and it needs the cold douche of the critic to correct it ... "

On freedom of the press

Broadcast to Australians
26 June 1942

• Context of speech

This was another in Menzies's summer 1942 series of radio talks..

> **he press … devotes a good deal of space to discussing public men. They will, I am sure, have no objection to the process being, for once, courteously reversed.**
I have never been able to accept the idea that newspapers have some detached existence apart from that of the human beings who conduct them. Newspapers are … business enterprises, … gathering and selling news and advertisements, and seasoning the whole with topical comment and criticism …

The editor or controller of the newspaper has a perfect right to criticise, to praise, or to blame, according to the personal opinion of his proprietor, or the joint opinion of his directors or shareholders …

But his right of free thought and free speech is one which … is equally subject to the laws of defamation.

Every good newspaper will admit that you do not purchase any special privilege to defame when you acquire … a newspaper; nor do you … purchase a privilege to criticise beyond that enjoyed by other citizens. You merely secure a wider audience and, properly considered, shoulder greater responsibilities …

If the *Daily Thunderer*, with half a million readers, libels me, irreparable harm is done to me, because people impute to the *Thunderer* a sort of unearthly wisdom and uncommon knowledge which induces some of them to say 'It must be true. I read it in the paper.' Or, more fatuously still, 'where there's smoke, there's fire.'

If the Press, then, is to see its function in modern society aright, it will dwell on its responsibilities … as well as upon its rights …

There is another tendency among some newspapers to depart from the old and good journalistic tradition. That tradition was to report fairly and without comment; and, separately, to criticise … bitterly. The public mind was informed by the reporter and persuaded by the leader-writer.

But there is today a perceptible tendency to mingle report with comment …

Reporting of this kind is not reporting at all. It is misleading; it can confer no privilege and excite no respect. That last observation is important. A critic, to carry weight, must be respected. For a man to be respected he must respect others …

If our diet is to become one of half-truths and prejudice and unfounded comment, either in Parliament or the press, we shall become slaves.

In time of war these questions, far from disappearing, become particularly acute. The power of censorship offers great temptation to political administrators. The eagerness of millions of people for the latest news, and perhaps excitement, and the natural tendency to look for scapegoats after every defeat offer temptations to the press.

It is unfortunate that both Parliament and press cannot regard themselves as engaged in a vital joint enterprise in which each must be fearless but restrained; in which each is looked to for good judgement; in which each should look to discharge its own function without seeking to control or discredit the other. In this way authority and freedom would show that they could march side by side to a battle where both must win if either is to survive."

Dedication to her people

Elizabeth II (1952–)
21st birthday radio broadcast from
Cape Town
21 April 1947 _____

• Biography

If nature did not intend George V for an innovator, nor did it intend his granddaughter the Queen for the most continuously photographed, filmed, recorded and generally scrutinised person in the world. And 'continuously' here means over a period of 55 years of her reign, following the earlier 26 of her 'pre-reign' youth. Diana (*qv*), her daughter-in-law, was in comparison a mere nine-days wonder.

The Queen would have preferred a life in the country with lots of dogs and horses. We know this because she once said so. One of the ways in which her senior realm, Britain, has changed for the worse as far as she is concerned is the way Windsor, her weekend retreat from urban duties, has become all but swallowed by Greater London and assailed by aircraft noise. Balmoral is too remote for use except in the long summer–early autumn break. Even then it can prove alarmingly far away from the capital, as the crisis following Diana's death showed. This restricts the Queen's genuinely rural retreats to Sandringham, in Norfolk.

One might think that the depths of Norfolk at Christmas-time would be the one moment you could put your feet up. It may be for other members of her family; not for the Queen. That is what duty means: even Christmas Day one is 'on' it. So it is appropriate that the two speeches here deal respectively with the self-dedication that lies at the heart of her sense of duty and the Coronation at which that dedication to duty was cemented by an oath-taking.

• Context of speech

At its most basic level the South African tour of 1947 gave the Royal Family, particularly the King, George VI, something like a holiday, one that was needed following the War and its austere aftermath. It also showed them to an economically important part of the Empire, as it was still — just — correct to call it. Further, South Africa had given valuable wartime help both in manpower and as a staging post for shipping. A thank-you was clearly due.

Among those who heard the speech excerpted below was the young Mandela, who later remarked how impressive it was and how it showed what a leader the Queen would be.

66 **On my twenty-first birthday [*when in those days one legally came of age*] I welcome the opportunity to speak to all the peoples of the British Commonwealth and Empire, wherever they live, whatever race they come from, and whatever language they speak. Let me begin by saying 'thank you' to all the thousands of kind people who have sent me messages of good will ...**

As I speak to you today from Capetown I am six thousand miles from the country where I was born. But I am certainly not six thousand miles from home. Everywhere I have travelled in these lovely lands of South Africa and Rhodesia [*now Zambia and Zimbabwe*] my parents, my sister and I have been taken to the heart of their people and made to feel that we are just as much at home here as if we had lived among them all our lives ...

Although there is none of my father's subjects from the oldest to the youngest whom I do not wish to greet, I am thinking especially today of all the young men and women who were born about the same time as myself and have grown up like me in the terrible and glorious years of the Second World War.

Will you, the youth of the British family of nations, let me speak on my birthday as your representative? Now that we are coming to manhood and womanhood it is surely a great joy to us all to think that we shall be able to take some of the burden off the shoulders of our elders who have fought and worked and suffered to protect our childhood.

We must not be daunted by the anxieties and hardships that the War has left behind for every nation of our Commonwealth. We know that these things are the price we cheerfully undertook to pay for the high honour of standing alone, seven years ago, in defence of the liberty of the world ...

If we all go forward together with an unwavering faith, a high courage, and a quiet heart, we shall be able to make of this ancient Commonwealth, which we all love so dearly, an even grander thing ... than it has been in the greatest days of our forefathers.

To accomplish that we must give nothing less than the whole of ourselves. There is a motto which has been borne by many of my ancestors — a noble motto, 'I serve'. Those words were an inspiration to many bygone heirs to the Throne when they made their knightly dedication as they came to manhood.

I cannot do quite as they did. But through the inventions of science I can do what was not possible for any of them. I can make my solemn act of dedication with a whole Empire listening. I should like to make that dedication now. It is very simple.

I declare before you all that my whole life whether it be long or short shall be devoted to your service and the service of our great imperial family to which we all belong."

First Christmas broadcast

Sandringham House, Norfolk
25 December 1952 _____

• Context of speech

This was the first Christmas broadcast of the Queen's reign. Until 1957 Christmas broadcasts were transmitted by BBC radio, from 1957 to 1996 by BBC TV (except for 1969, when there was no Christmas broadcast at all since there had been a TV documentary on the Royal Family that year). Since 1997 the BBC and ITN (Independent Television News) have taken it in biennial turns, each doing a two-year stint.

> **Each Christmas, at this time, my beloved father broadcast a message to his people in all parts of the world. Today I am doing this to you, who are now my people.**
> As he used to do, I am speaking to you from my own home, where I am spending Christmas with my family …
>
> Most of you to whom I am speaking will be in your own homes, but I have a special thought for those who are serving their country in distant lands far from their families. Wherever you are, either at home or away, in snow or in sunshine, I give you my affectionate greetings, with every good wish for Christmas and the New Year.
>
> At Christmas our thoughts are always full of our homes and our families …
>
> But we belong, you and I, to a far larger family. We belong, all of us, to the British Commonwealth and Empire, that immense union of nations, with their homes set in all the four corners of the earth. Like our own families, it can be a great power for good — a force which I believe can be of immeasurable benefit to all humanity.
>
> My father, and my grandfather before him, worked all their lives to unite our peoples ever more closely, and to maintain its ideals which were so near to their hearts. I shall strive to carry on their work.
>
> Already you have given me strength to do so. For, since my accession ten months ago, your loyalty and affection have been an immense support and encouragement. I want to take this Christmas Day, my first opportunity, to thank you with all my heart.

Many grave problems and difficulties confront us all, but with a new faith in the old and splendid beliefs given us by our forefathers, and the strength to venture beyond the safeties of the past, I know we shall be worthy of our duty …

At my Coronation next June, I shall dedicate myself anew to your service. I shall do so in the presence of a great congregation, drawn from every part of the Commonwealth and Empire, while millions outside Westminster Abbey will hear the promises and the prayers being offered up within its walls, and see much of the ancient ceremony in which Kings and Queens before me have taken part through century upon century.

You will be keeping it as a holiday; but I want to ask you all, whatever your religion may be, to pray for me on that day — to pray that God may give me wisdom and strength to carry out the solemn promises I shall be making, and that I may faithfully serve Him and you, all the days of my life.

May God bless and guide you all through the coming year."

'Tryst with Destiny'

Jawaharlal ('Panditji', or 'Scholar') Nehru (1889–1964)
Indian Independence Day
14 August 1947

• Biography

It has often proved difficult for a national leader to maintain democracy, or resist the temptation to overthrow it, after winning independence from a colonial power. In Africa democracies have tumbled like ninepins. India is different. Yet a prime ministerial dynasty has dominated it for much of the period since 1947, a dynasty that was founded, however unwittingly, by Nehru. His daughter Indira Gandhi — no relation of Mahatma Gandhi (*qv*) — was India's Prime Minister from 1966 till 1977 and again from 1980 till her assassination by her own guards in 1984. Indira's son Rajiv Gandhi succeeded her as Prime Minister till 1989 but in 1991 was assassinated too. And Rajiv's widow Sonia Gandhi leads Nehru's old Indian National Congress party.

Like Mahatma Gandhi, his mentor in many ways, Nehru trained as a barrister, agitated for independence and was jailed by the British. He even discarded western clothes for such homespun accessories as the Gandhi Cap. But he differed sharply from Gandhi over India's future. Gandhi envisaged a simple agrarian existence. Nehru, impressed by the Soviet experiment though critical of Stalin's (*qv*) repression, believed in industrialisation through state planning.

Following independence in 1947, he was India's prime minister and foreign minister till his death. His problems included tension with Muslim Pakistan, including a quarrel over Kashmir, and his achievements were not without their high-handed element, notably the absorption of the princely states and the overrunning of the Portuguese colony of Goa. His biggest crisis was an invasion by the Chinese in 1962.

To cope with this he requested Western aid. But in foreign affairs generally he had tried to steer a middle way between the West and the Soviet Bloc by making India a leader of what was called the Non-Aligned nations.

• Context of speech

Indian independence at last became a reality on 14 August 1947. Nehru ushered it in with the speech excerpted here, his most famous one. He usually extemporised his speeches, even when making several a day.

---

    66 **Long years ago we made a tryst with destiny, and now the time comes when we shall redeem our pledge, not wholly or in full measure, but very substantially. At the stroke of the midnight hour, when the world sleeps, India will awake to life and freedom** …

Freedom and power bring responsibility. The responsibility rests upon this Assembly [*the Constituent Assembly, convened in New Delhi*], a sovereign body representing the sovereign people of India. Before the birth of freedom we endured all the pains of labour and our hearts are heavy with the memory of this sorrow …

On this day our first thoughts go to the architect of this freedom, the Father of our Nation [*Gandhi*, qv], who, embodying the old spirit of India, held aloft the torch of freedom and lit up the darkness that surrounded us. We have often been unworthy followers of his and have strayed from his message, but not only we but succeeding generations will remember this message and bear the imprint in their [*sic*] hearts of this great son of India, magnificent in his faith and strength and courage and humility. We shall never allow that torch of freedom to be blown out, however high the wind or stormy the tempest.

Our next thoughts must be of the unknown volunteers and soldiers of freedom who, without praise or reward, have served India even unto death.

We think also of our brothers and sisters who have been cut off from us by political boundaries, and who unhappily cannot share at present in the freedom that has come.

We have hard work ahead. There is no resting for any one of us till we redeem our pledge in full, till we make all the people of India what destiny intended them to be. We are citizens of a great country on the verge of bold advance, and we have to live up to that high standard. All of us, to whatever religion we may belong, are equally the children of India, with equal rights, privileges and obligations. We cannot encourage communalism or narrow-mindedness, for no nation can be great whose people are narrow in thought or in action ... "

On the imminent foundation of Israel

David Ben-Gurion (1886–1973)
1st Prime Minister of Israel
Elected Assembly of Palestine Jewry
2 October 1947

• Biography

Zionism, the movement to re-establish a Jewish nation in Palestine, was the work chiefly of three men. They were Theodore Herzl (1860–1904), its founding father;

Chaim Weizmann (1874–1952; *see* also Mussolini), urbane draughtsman of its blueprint, as it were, also its promoter among the British, though he also became Israel's first President; and lastly David Ben-Gurion, the hard-nosed on-site project manager (to continue the metaphor), who got Israel up and going and who then led it for most of its first 18 years. Sadly, he clashed with Weizmann.

Ben-Gurion's original name was Gruen or Grün. The name Ben-Gurion he borrowed from a hero of the 1st-century Jewish revolt against Rome. He came from Płońsk, about 40 miles northwest of Warsaw. In 1906 he joined other Jewish migrants in Palestine, then still part of the Turkish Empire. After deportation in 1916 as an undesirable alien, though he had urged loyalty to Turkey as best promoting Zionism, he returned to Palestine two years later attached to the British forces, recent British success in Palestine having by now convinced him that Turkey would lose the War.

He rose through the secretariat of the Histadrut (General Federation of Jewish Labour) to a position of pre-eminence. He turned the Histadrut into a major economic force, representing it in the World Zionist Organization and Jewish Agency and becoming chairman of both in 1935.

On the formation of Israel in 1948 he became its first Prime Minister, also Defence Minister. He retired in 1953 but made a comeback in 1955, first as Defence Minister then as Prime Minister. He recognised West Germany, a hard decision given Hitler's (*qv*) Jewish extermination programme a decade earlier.

Ben-Gurion became famous for combining sober realism with proselytising fervour. As a youth in Poland he was already an able polemicist. In a 1905 debate at Płońsk he represented Poale(i) Zion ('Workers of Zion'), a Marxist-Zionist group, against a famous Warsaw orator Shmulik the Bundist (the Jewish Bund [League] fought for Jewish rights within the Russian Empire and scorned Zionism). His earthy analogies and entertaining anecdotes *à la* Ronald Reagan (*qv*) delighted his provincial audience. Shmulik's socialist aridities flopped.

Conversely, when Ben-Gurion in America during World War I delivered impassioned speeches purely about Zionism, they flopped, even though the listeners were Jewish groups, whereas his schmaltzier rival Alexander Chashin thrived through discussing literature and life back in Europe as well. At this time Ben-Gurion said 'I hardly believe in the power of orators.' Evidently he was a debater rather than monologueist, performing best when up against opponents.

• Context of speech

The state of Israel was founded just over seven months after his speech.

"**Political developments have swept us on to a momentous parting of the ways — from Mandate [*the British administration of Palestine, initiated after World War I*] to independence .... Security is our chief problem. I do not minimise the virtue of statehood even within something less than all the territory of the Land of Israel on either bank of the Jordan. But security comes unarguably first** ...

Recent upsets and upheavals in Palestine, in the Middle East and in the wide world, and in British and international politics as well, magnify it from a local problem of current safety into Zionism's hinge of destiny ...

Just think of the new factors ... : the anti-Zionist policy pursued by the Mandatory Government [i.e., *the British, who frustrated mass immigration by Jews even before World War II for fear of antagonising the Arab states bordering Palestine, and who after World War II, to the still greater fury of Ben-Gurion and his followers, tried to prevent much of what was left of European Jewry from reaching Palestine*] during the past ten years, the obliteration of European Jewry with the willing aid of the acknowledged leader of the Palestine Arabs, the establishment of an Arab League active and united only in combating Zionism, [*Ernest*] Bevin's [*British Foreign Secretary 1945–51*] ugly war against the Jews, the crisis in Britain and its political and economic aftermath, the creation of armed forces in the neighbouring states, the intrusion of the Arab Legion. And not a single Jewish unit exists ...

It is the duty of this Assembly to decide upon a defence scheme that will gear our economy, our public life and our education to instant needs. There is the possibility, how near in time I cannot say, but very real, that we may be sucked into a political vacuum. Politics, predominantly, abhor a vacuum. If we do not fill it, others will. Let us, once for all, slough the fancy that others may run our errand, as Britain promised twenty-seven years ago ...

You had to be purblind ten years ago not to see that the Mandate was disintegrating, the Mandate as we came specifically to interpret it in Palestine: a form of administration deputed by the nations to facilitate Jewish entry and settlement for so long as the Jews themselves could not stand alone in their homeland and conduct the work of government by right of majority ...

Now final judgement is passed by the United Nations and the Mandatory [*Britain*]. The Mandate is to end. That is the common denominator uniting majority and minority ... and dispelling the friction between the Council of the United Nations and the British Government. No one can predict how things will go in the General Assembly. It may not decide at all, but one thing is certain: the Mandate is doomed, not just the British Mandate, but the principle ... "

On Yugoslavia's split with the USSR

Tito, *né* Josip [Joseph] Broz (1892–1980)
1952 _____

• Biography

However brutal and tyrannical the Yugoslav Communists (accounts of their murdering opponents at the close of World War II make distinctly unpleasant reading), they deserve half a cheer out of three. Theirs was the only Soviet Bloc regime to break with Stalin (*qv*). They did this under their leader, Marshal Tito. (He was long known by this vainglorious military rank and the single name he apparently adopted in 1934, possibly following a stay in Italy, where it is the modern version of the Latin 'Titus'.)

Yugoslavia got away with defying Stalin in a way other Soviet Bloc countries could not since it lacked a common border with Russia, hence could less easily be invaded. But this only partly detracts from Tito's achievement. And as he developed his independence, eventually joining the other Non-Aligned countries (*see* also Nehru), he made Yugoslavia one of the less disagreeable Communist countries to live in, if no paradise.

He started life as a mechanic (before World War I he was at one point a test driver for Daimler motor cars). During World War I, in which he served with the Austro-Hungarian army, he was captured by the Russians. He took a minor part in the Russian Revolution but soon returned to what was now Yugoslavia. He rose in the Yugoslav Communist Party, adhering faithfully to the Moscow line, till World War II, when Axis forces invaded Yugoslavia and he set up the Partisans, Communist guerrillas who fought not just the invaders but non-Communist Yugoslav resistance elements. Tito's Partisans persuaded the Allies they were the most effective fighters against the Germans, won western Allied aid and initially maintained good relations with the USSR.

In 1948 Tito's refusal to toe the Stalin line got him expelled from the Cominform (bloc of Soviet-leaning regimes). Thereafter he established an ever more independent and, as time went on, a relatively free Yugoslavia, even going so far as to give republics in a new Yugoslav federal structure a degree of autonomy. Towards the end of his life nationalist tensions in Yugoslavia obliged him to quell dissent, and a decade after his death Yugoslavia fell apart.

• Context of speech

Tito gave the following speech in 1952.

66 **The roots of the present state of affairs in the world go back to the imperialist method applied at Teheran, Yalta [*locations of summit meetings involving the UK, US and USSR leadership*], Moscow and Berlin during the War, when an attempt was first made to solve international problems.**
No one in this country or in the world was surprised when at Teheran, Yalta, Moscow and Berlin the Western powers approached the solution of world problems in their accustomed way. But for all who credited the rumour that the USSR was the protector of little peoples, this came as a real moral blow, as the first strong doubts about the Soviet Union and the justice of Moscow's policy.

From Teheran to this day, Moscow has flaunted its imperialist majesty. Today we can boldly assert that the whole of Soviet foreign policy — setting aside ordinary propaganda tricks like their alleged struggle for peace and so forth — has been such as to contribute greatly to present international tension.

It was Moscow, was it not, who created colonies in the heart of Europe where there had once been independent states like Czechoslovakia, Poland, Hungary, Rumania, Bulgaria and so on? Not to mention the enslavement of the Baltic countries back before the War.

The USSR has pushed North Korea into an aggressive war so as to bring South Korea under its sway while letting others get their hands dirty. In saying this I do not in the least diminish the responsibility of the Western powers. They are just as responsible for the situation in Korea since the war began in 1950. This Korean War — which could turn into a world conflict — results from a division into spheres of interest."

On the Allies' oppression of Germany

Konrad Adenauer (1876–1967)
Berne, Switzerland
23 March 1949 _____

• Biography

From 1918 to 1933 the Weimar Republic governed Germany. It was always weak, which was why Adenauer avoided national politics then. The Nazis persecuted him nonetheless. They deprived him of his provincial government post in 1933 and imprisoned him both in 1934 and 1944.

To the Western Allies who in 1945 controlled what was to become West Germany he was that rarest of jewels, a 'good' German. He became at the Americans' invitation Cologne's mayor a second time but was sacked by a local British Military Government officer a few months later. This proved a boon, catapulting him into national politics. He assumed the leadership of the Christian Democratic Union, West Germany's newly founded centre-right party, and became Chancellor of West Germany in 1949, holding the post till 1963.

• Context of speech

By 1949 the Four Powers who controlled Germany (France, the UK, the USA and USSR) were in disagreement.

Adenauer delivered his speech on 23 March 1949, some months before elections to West Germany's first Bundestag (parliament). His criticism of the Allies was courageous at a time when West Germany had everything to lose from non-compliance with its foreign masters.

By the speech he established himself as the German people's principal spokesman. It was delivered at a session of the Inter-Parliamentary Union — one reason it was so noticed. The post-War Germans were delighted that someone had at last stuck up for them. It helped win Adenauer the Chancellorship, and with it the joint leadership of Western Continental Europe for the next decade and a half.

66 **The world has seen the formation of two power-groups. On one side there is the group … led by the United States of America and united in the Atlantic Pact. This group defends the values of Christian and Western civilization, freedom and true democracy. On the other side there is Soviet Russia with her satellites.**

The line dividing these two groups … runs right down the centre of Germany. Twenty million Germans live under Soviet rule, about 43 million in the orbit of the Atlantic bloc.

The … Germans in the … Atlantic bloc possess the most important mineral deposits and the greatest European industrial potential. But this area, the three Western zones of Germany, is in a state of disorder that is in the long run untenable. Even today a very considerable part of these 43 million live in such abject housing conditions, such a state of legal bondage as may have been imaginable in the Balkans a hundred years ago but would hardly have been thought possible in Central Europe for centuries.

It is impossible to understand the present condition of Germany without a brief survey of what happened after 1945. The unconditional surrender of the German armed forces in May 1945 was interpreted by the Allies to mean a complete transfer of governmental authority to their hands.

This interpretation was wrong in international law. By it the Allies in practice took on an impossible task … They could not have solved this task with the best will in the world. There was bound to be failure and this failure damaged the prestige of the Allies in Germany.

It would have been wiser if the Allies had, after a short intermediate period … , let the Germans order their own affairs and had stuck to supervision only. Their attempt to govern this large disorganized country from outside … was bound to fail. It brought about a rapid economic, physical, and psychological disintegration of the Germans which could have been avoided.

Intentions such as had once been manifested in the Morgenthau Plan [*suggesting Germany be broken up and reduced to a pre-industrial economy*] played their part. This continued until the Marshall Plan [*whereby the US aided war-torn Western Europe*] brought the turning point. The Marshall Plan will remain for all time a glorious page in the history of the United States of America. But the change was very slow and the economic, physical, moral and political decline of Germany which had begun with the unconditional surrender took great efforts to reverse."

Checkers speech

**Richard M(ilhous) Nixon (1913–94),
37th President of the USA 1969–74
TV broadcast
23 September 1952**

• Biography

The only US President ever to resign (and he did so only under threat of
impeachment), Nixon has as a result featured continuously in popular demonologies.
A more mature examination reveals his great gifts and achievements. The latter he
was not slow to list in his resignation speech below.

    Against that has to be set not just his involvement in the original Watergate
burglary (*see* context of second speech below) but his long-drawn out though ultimately
futile attempt to conceal it. In the process he effectively committed an obstruction of
justice, though he was never tried for this. As President he definitely in 1969, without
Congress's approval, bombed Cambodia, a country with which the US was not at war.
This to many people was a much worse crime than anything to do with Watergate,
though some authorities argue that the constitutional aspect is a grey area.

    Nixon trained as a lawyer but soon entered politics, first as a Republican
Member of the House of Representatives (1947–51) then as a Senator (1951–53). In
both roles he denounced left-leaning rival politicians.

    After having been Eisenhower's Vice-President (1953–61), he very narrowly lost
the 1960 presidential election to John F. Kennedy (*qv*). There were blatant electoral
irregularities but Nixon declined, or was persuaded to decline, to call for an
investigation due to the tense state of American-Soviet relations, an example of
magnanimity very untypical of Nixon generally. In 1962 he lost a California
gubernatorial election and despairingly told the media 'you won't have Richard
Nixon to kick around any more', in effect retiring from politics.

    America's disastrous showing in Vietnam revived his career. He won the 1968
presidential election, negotiated a face-saving withdrawal from Vietnam, initiated the
SALT (Strategic Arms Limitations Talks) negotiations with Russia and diplomatic
relations with China and brought off a peace agreement between Israel and its opponents

Egypt and Syria. Domestically he more or less completed the racial integration of public (*i.e.*, state-run) schools in the Southern states. This is an undeniably impressive record.

He came to grief over Watergate, as mentioned below. By the time of his death his very considerable achievements were recognised by the more thoughtful conservative politicians and opinion-formers in America and Europe.

• Context of speech

By mid-September 1952 that year's presidential campaign was in full swing, with polling day only eight weeks away. The Republican candidate, Eisenhower, had chosen Nixon, then a first-term Senator, as his running mate. On 18 September the *New York Post* revealed that some businessmen had topped up Nixon's senatorial salary of $15,000 a year [*£3,000 a year then, or over £580,000 today*] with a clandestine fund to the tune of some $18,000 [*then equivalent to about £3,600, or over £700,000 today*].

The Republican campaign was not going so well that Eisenhower would be likely to overlook this, though he had put Nixon on his ticket in the first place to placate the Republican right. Nonetheless, there was a real risk to Nixon that he might be dropped. On 23 September he took to the airwaves to defend himself, arguing among other things that the businessmen had received no special favours from him in return. Television was a new medium then, but he is reckoned to have reached about 60,000,000 viewers.

66 **My fellow Americans, I come before you tonight as a candidate for the vice-presidency and as a man whose honesty and integrity has [*sic*] been questioned …** I'm sure that you have read the charge, and you've heard it, that I, Senator Nixon, took $18,000 from a group of my supporters …

Not one cent of the $18,000 or any other money of that type ever went to me for my personal use. Every penny of it was used to pay for political expenses that I did not think should be charged to the taxpayers of the United States …

The taxpayers shouldn't be required to finance items which are not official business …

Well, then the question arises, you say 'Well, how do you pay for these and how can you do it legally?' And there are several ways that it can be done, incidentally, and it is done legally in the United States Senate and in the Congress. The first way is to be a rich man. I don't happen to be a rich man, so I couldn't use that one.

Another way that is used is to put your wife on the pay roll. Let me say, incidentally, that my opponent, my opposite number for the vice-presidency on the Democratic ticket, does have his wife on the pay roll and has had her on his pay roll for the past ten years. Now let me just say this: that's his business, and I'm not critical of him for doing that. You will have to pass judgment on that particular point …

And so now, what I am going to do — and incidentally, this is unprecedented in the history of American politics — I am going at this time to give to this television and radio audience a complete financial history, everything I've earned, everything I've spent, everything I owe …

First of all, we've got a house in Washington which cost $41,000 [*then about £8,000, or well over £1.5m today*] and on which we owe $20,000 [*then about £4,000, or over £770,000 today*]. We have a house in Whittier, California, which cost $13,000 [*then about £2,600, or well over £500,000 today*] and on which we owe $3,000 [*then about £600, or over £165,000 today*]. My folks are living there at the present time …

I should say this, that Pat [*Nixon's wife*] doesn't have a mink coat, but she does have a respectable Republican cloth coat [*a hit at sitting President Truman, whose administration had been sullied by allegations of bribery involving mink coats*]. And I always tell her that she'd look good in anything …

We did get something, a gift after the election … It was a little cocker spaniel dog, … black and white spotted. And our little girl Tricia, the six-year-old, named it Checkers.

And you know, the kids, like all kids, love the dog and I just want to say this right now, that regardless of what they say about it, we're going to keep him … "

Resignation as President

Broadcast from The White House
8 August 1974

• Context of speech

After winning re-election as President in November 1972, Nixon soon got into trouble over a breaking and entering operation against Democratic offices at the Watergate Hotel in Washington, DC, back in June of that year. It had not even been necessary because his victory at the polls was in the event so huge. It fairly soon emerged that the incident involved some of his leading assistants. Slowly, over two years, evidence emerged implicating Nixon, both ever more deeply and in a way that eroded his general popularity, by revealing his tendency to foul language and paranoia.

"**Throughout the long and difficult period of Watergate, I have felt it was my duty to persevere, to make every possible effort to complete the term of office to which you elected me.**

In the past few days, however, it has become evident to me that I no longer have a strong enough political base in the Congress to justify continuing that effort ...

I have never been a quitter. To leave office before my term is completed is abhorrent to every instinct in my body. But as President, I must put the interest of America first.

Therefore, I shall resign the Presidency effective at noon tomorrow. Vice-President Ford will be sworn in as President at that hour in this office ...

I shall leave this office with regret at not completing my term, but with gratitude for the privilege of serving as your President for the past five and a half years. These years have been a momentous time in the history of our nation and the world ...

We have ended America's longest war ... We have unlocked the doors that for a quarter of a century stood between the United States and the People's Republic of China ... In the Middle East, 100 million people in the Arab countries, many of whom have considered us their enemy for nearly 20 years, now look on us as their friends ... Together with the Soviet Union we have made the crucial breakthroughs that have begun the process of limiting nuclear arms ... We have opened ... new relations with the Soviet Union ...

When I first took the oath of office as President five and a half years ago, I made this sacred commitment, to 'consecrate my office, my energies, and all the wisdom I can summon to the cause of peace among nations.' I have done my very best in all the days since to be true to that pledge. As a result of these efforts, I am confident that the world is a safer place today, ... and that all of our children have a better chance than before of living in peace rather than dying in war ...

To have served in this office is to have felt a very personal sense of kinship with each and every American. In leaving it, I do so with this prayer: May God's grace be with you in all the days ahead."

Denunciation of Stalin

Nikita Sergeyevich Khrushchev (1894–1971)
CPSU 20th Congress, Moscow
25 February 1956 _____

• Biography

Stalin's (*qv*) Ukrainian boss during World War II, and as such getting almost as much blood on his hands as did his master, Khrushchev nonetheless went some way to relaxing the ferocious regime he took over on Stalin's death a decade later. Further, he was the first senior Soviet figure to call Stalin's brutal methods in question, though prudently waiting till he was in the top post himself to do so.

He was brought down by very much the same sort of harebrained scheme as Stalin had occasionally tried out. In Khrushchev's case this was the Virgin Lands development. But Khrushchev lacked Stalin's ruthlessness in pushing it to a satisfactory conclusion, meanwhile murdering his critics among the leadership or shifting the blame onto others when things went wrong. As a result he was in 1964 overthrown.

Khrushchev came to Stalin's notice through the latter's second wife, Nadya Alliluyeva. At the 17th Party Congress in 1934 he was elected to the Central Committee. In 1935 he became the Moscow city number two boss, as which he got constructed the deep and splendid metro system which even now impresses tourists and which was to serve as effective air raid shelters in World War II. In 1939 he was elevated to the Politburo.

As Soviet leader in the 1950s and early 1960s he formulated the doctrine of Peaceful Co-Existence with the West. Sad to say, he is nowadays according to Russian opinion polls the most reviled Soviet leader after Mikhail Gorbachev, whereas Stalin is viewed positively or very positively by half the population. Presumably that is why Stalin's mass murdering (effected with Khrushchev's help) was accepted so readily.

• Context of speech

The address excerpted below was made to a closed session of the CPSU (Communist Party of the Soviet Union).

The way it was disseminated in the West is almost as interesting as its being delivered at all. A British journalist, one of a handful of Western reporters then resident in Moscow, was approached by an acquaintance who he suspected was with the KGB [*Committee for State Security, successor to the NKVD* (see *below*)]. This acquaintance gave him a précis of the speech just as he was about to take a holiday abroad and suggested he file the story in London.

The journalist was pretty sure this was done on the orders of Khrushchev himself, with whom the journalist had developed reasonably good relations through regular meetings at press receptions and the like. Khrushchev in this regard was far more of a mixer than his predecessors among the Soviet leadership. The speech had to be disseminated clandestinely since the CPSU Central Committee had decided never to publish it formally.

The shock of Khrushchev's denouncing Stalin, even to hardened CPSU cadres, was so severe that many fainted. The Polish Communist boss Bolesław Bierut, an unreformed Stalinist, read a transcript a few weeks later and died of a heart attack. Such men reacting like maiden aunts reaching for the smelling salts on hearing a risqué story would be funny if the history behind it all were not so grim.

The speech paved the way for the Hungarian Uprising later in 1956, quite possibly also the Sino-Soviet split from 1960 on and certainly the *perestroika* (restructuring) policies of Mikhail Gorbachev, who in 1956 was a fledgling CPSU member. The text of the speech was not published in the USSR till 1988, on the eve of the system's collapse.

❝ Stalin acted not through persuasion, explanation and patient cooperation but by imposing his ideas and demanding absolute submission to them. Whoever opposed them or tried to put forward a point of view of his own was doomed to removal from the leadership, followed by moral and physical destruction ...

Stalin originated the concept of an enemy of the people [*actually it existed at least as far back as the French Revolution*]. The term automatically made it unnecessary to prove that anyone engaged in public controversy was guilty of ideological error. It made possible the cruellest repression, violating all norms of revolutionary legality, against anyone who in any way disagreed with Stalin …

The concept of an enemy of the people actually eliminated the possibility of any kind of ideological debate or even the expression of one's views on this or that issue, even views of a common sense character. The only proof of guilt required — one that was against all norms of modern legal principle — was the confession of the accused himself; and, as subsequent investigations have proved, confessions were obtained through physical pressure against the accused …

The Commission [*of Inquiry*] has become acquainted with a huge amount of material in the NKVD [*chief Soviet secret police organisation between 1934 and 1954*] archives. It has become apparent that many activists who in the period 1937–38 were branded as enemies were actually never enemies, spies, wreckers and so on, but were always honest Communists … Often, no longer able to bear barbaric torture, they confessed to all kinds of grave and unlikely crimes.

Lenin (*qv*) used severe methods only in the most necessary cases, when the exploiting classes were still in existence and were vigorously opposing the revolution …

Stalin, on the other hand, used extreme methods and mass repression at a time when the revolution was already victorious … It is clear that here Stalin showed in a whole series of cases his intolerance, his brutality and his tendency to the abuse of power. Instead of proving his political correctness [*used here without irony, unlike in the West today*] and mobilising the masses, he often chose the path of repression and physical annihilation, not only against actual enemies, but also against individuals who had committed no crimes against the Party and the Soviet Government."

'Imperialism a paper tiger'

Mao Zedong (formerly known as Mao Tse Tung) (1893–1976)
1 December 1958

• Biography

Mao was by far the nastiest of the 20th-century monsters in human form (*see* also Hitler and Stalin). Nastiest? Surely so mild an epithet is an understatement? Ah, but mass murder (in Mao's case an all-time record of 70,000,000 peacetime deaths according to his most recent biographer) is an occupational by-product of despots. His personal habits were more individual. They took the form of never brushing his teeth and not taking a bath for a quarter of a century. The many girls procured for him by his secret police chief, Kang Sheng, suffered most from this.

He was also the most capricious, even downright silly, of despots, given to fatuously impractical policies much as a student addict of radicalism with no experience of hard reality might be. In a rational world Mao would have had no impact outside the class room (he started life as a primary school master), or at most the local tavern debating club. But the 20th century was not a rational one. He was even for a time feted in the West.

He was one of the first members of the Chinese Communist Party. Breaking with the Chinese Nationalists in the 1930s, he evacuated his followers from China's Nationalist-dominated coastal areas to the remote Northwest. Known as the 'Long March', this established an independent power base, though only after desertions, lost battles and purges of any dissident followers that may have diminished his forces by as much as 90 percent. The starry-eyed account by Mao's dupe at the time, the American journalist Edgar Snow, is now discredited.

Later Mao patched things up with the Nationalists but after World War II turned on them and in 1949 won control of all mainland China.

He sought to industrialise China in the programme called the 'Great Leap Forward', decreeing gigantic agricultural communes, tens of thousands-strong, and forcing on his people such schoolboy contraptions as back-yard steel furnaces.

Professional economic tools like statistics and budgets bored him. The Great Leap Forward turned out the Gigantic Belly Flop; 30,000,000 are reckoned to have died of famine. Told that his subjects were forced to eat leaves, Mao guffawed.

In 1960 he took a back seat while other clearer minds tried to clean up the mess. From 1966 to 1976 Mao struck back against them through the 'Cultural Revolution', calling them 'capitalist roaders' for such modest measures as wage differentials. The destruction followed of an entire generation's education.

An eternal student revolutionary type, even down to his filthy bodily state, this incompetent, narcissistic practitioner of the sort of thing that even Lenin dubbed 'infantile leftist disorder' died in 1976.

• Context of speech

It was delivered at Wuchang during a meeting of the Chinese Communist Party Politburo on 1 December 1958.

> " **All reactionaries are paper tigers. In appearance, the reactionaries are terrifying, but in reality, they are not so powerful**.
>
> Just as there is not a single thing in the world without a dual nature … so imperialism and all reactionaries have a dual nature — they are simultaneously real tigers and paper tigers.
>
> In the past … the slave-owning class, the feudal landlord class and the bourgeoisie were vigorous, revolutionary and progressive — they were real tigers.
>
> But in time, because their opponents — the slave class, the peasant class and the proletariat — grew in strength and struggled more and more fiercely, these ruling classes changed into their opposites … changed into paper tigers …
>
> The reactionary, backward-looking, decaying classes retained this dual nature even in their last life-and-death struggle against the people …. On the one hand, they were real tigers: they devoured people … by the millions and tens of millions. The cause of the people went through a period of difficulties and hardships, and along the road there were many twists and turns …
>
> Were these not living tigers, iron tigers, real tigers? Nevertheless, in the end they changed into paper tigers, dead tigers and bean-curd [i.e., 'milksop'] tigers. These are historical facts. Have people not seen or heard about these facts? There have indeed been thousands and tens of thousands of them! Thousands and tens of thousands! …

'Winds of change'

**Harold Macmillan, 1st Earl of Stockton
(1894–1986)
Capetown
3 February 1960**

• Biography

Macmillan was not the last of the patrician Conservative Prime Ministers (Sir Alec Douglas Home has that questionable distinction), nor indeed by birth very patrician. But he came to typify the breed. He did so by a number of superficial accessories. There was his OE tie, a typically bogus adorment in that he'd been miserable at Eton and left early, also his game-bird shooting in plus fours – a splendid gift to the satirists who flourished in his last years of power and still more so to the Labour Party, whose attacks on 'grouse moor Toryism' still resonate, particularly as David Cameron (*qv*) has been known to enjoy a bang or two with a twelve-bore. There were his constant classical allusions, one of which appears in the speech excerpted below. It was as if Macmillan, often dubbed an 'actor manager', was more a casting director uncertain whether to assign himself the country squire role or bufferish don one in an Aldwych farce.

The real Macmillan was rather darker. His domineering American mother began his emotional emasculation. His chronically unfaithful wife Lady Dorothy finished the job. She was aunt of the 11th Duke of Devonshire, who Macmillan gave government jobs to — a case of cronyism even Tony Blair (*qv*) at his most back-scratching has never contemplated. The long affair she started in 1929 with the maverick Conservative MP Bob Boothby may have contributed to Macmillan's nervous breakdown in 1931.

And Macmillan was actually rather left-wing. His first constituency, Stockton (whence he borrowed his title on ennoblement), was an inter-war unemployment hell-hole. This tormented him. Concern over providing jobs contributed to his inflationary policies as Chancellor of the Exchequer and Prime Minister.

During World War II he became Minister Resident in the Mediterranean theatre. Here he adroitly handled de Gaulle (*qv*) and the Americans. He also presided over the repatriation and in many cases forcible deportation of prisoners of war to Russia and Yugoslavia, where Stalin and Tito (*qqv*) had many of them murdered. True, he had no say in the original decision, nor its execution. But the plea 'I voss chust orders obeyink' saved no Nazi apparatchiks' necks at Nuremberg. Macmillan's survived, long entwined by a Brigade of Guards tie, his other favourite item of haberdashery, when his OE one was at the dry cleaner's.

Between 1951 and 1954 as Minister of Housing he fulfilled his party's pledge to build 300,000 houses a year, though many considered it over-ambitious, both intrinsically and as distorting the general economy. After some months as Defence Secretary (1954–55), when Churchill's (*qv*) meddling proved irksome, and a few more as Foreign Secretary, when the new Premier Eden also interfered, he became Chancellor. Though Macmillan handled matters ineptly during the Suez Crisis (when in 1956 Britain, France and Israel conspired to invade Egypt, alienating America), he succeeded Eden the following year.

Initially his premiership went well. He renewed friendship with America, his mother's ancestry helping there. His ascendancy in Parliament and his party was considerable. He timed the 1959 election beautifully. But he neglected trade union reform, failed to get Britain into the Common Market and was beset by several sex and spying scandals. He did, however, play a useful part in negotiating the 1963 nuclear test ban treaty.

In autumn 1963 he resigned precipitately over an enlarged prostate, handling the succession to the premiership in such a way that the Conservatives looked high-handed, secretive, devious, manipulative, undemocratic and, finally, rather ridiculous. Years later he embarrassed his distant successor as premier, Margaret Thatcher (*qv*), by likening her privatisations to 'selling the family silver'. He has often been compared with Disraeli (*qv*) for his wit, histrionic manner and panache-cum-social conscience. But Disraeli underneath his studied insouciance was relatively serious, whereas Macmillan under his had a distinctly frivolous streak.

Unless you count what Auberon Waugh called the 'phantom' growth on John Major's upper lip, Macmillan is so far the last premier to have sported a moustache.

• Context of speech

Macmillan spent more time than was wise on foreign and what were then called 'colonial' matters, given Britain's domestic problems. At least he assessed African nationalism accurately. This was more than his party's right-wingers were capable of. They founded the Monday Club to commemorate the speech excerpted below, which was delivered on a Monday.

"Ever since the break up of the Roman Empire one of the constant facts of political life in Europe has been the emergence of independent nations. They have come into existence over the centuries in different forms, different kinds of government, but all have been inspired by a deep, keen feeling of nationalism, which has grown as the nations have grown.

In the 20th century, and especially since the end of the War, the processes which gave birth to the nation states of Europe have been repeated all over the world. We have seen the awakening of national consciousness in peoples who have for centuries lived in dependence upon some other power. Fifteen years ago this movement spread through Asia. Many countries there, of different races and civilisations, pressed their claim to an independent national life.

Today the same thing is happening in Africa, and the most striking of all the impressions I have formed since I left London a month ago is of the strength of this African national consciousness. In different places it takes different forms, but it is happening everywhere.

The wind of change is blowing through this continent, and whether we like it or not, this growth of national consciousness is a political fact. We must all accept it as a fact, and our national policies must take account of it.

Well, you understand this better than anyone. You are sprung from Europe, the home of nationalism. Here in Africa you have yourselves created a free nation, a new nation. Indeed in the history of our times yours will be recorded as the first of the African nationalists. This tide of national consciousness which is now rising in Africa is a fact, for which both you and we and the other nations of the western world are ultimately responsible.

For its causes are to be found in the achievements of western civilisation, in the pushing forwards of the frontiers of knowledge, the applying of science to the service of human needs, in the expanding of food production, in the speeding and multiplying of the means of communication and perhaps above all and more than anything else in the spread of education. As I have said, the growth of national consciousness in Africa is a political fact, and we must accept it as such.

That means, I would judge, that we've got to come to terms with it. I sincerely believe that if we cannot do so we may imperil the precarious balance between the East and West on which the peace of the world depends."

Inaugural

John ('Jack') F(itzgerald) Kennedy (1917–63)
35th President of the USA 1961–63
Washington, DC
20 January 1961

• Biography

He was not the youngest ever US President. Teddy Roosevelt (*qv*) still holds that record. But Jack Kennedy was easily the most youthful — a rather different thing. Further, he and his elegant wife actually managed for a time to make the presidency chic, or 'hip' as the jargon of the day had it.

What kind of President he would have been in the long run can never be known. He was assassinated too soon — one thousand days, roughly, from his Inauguration, a figure which lends a passage in his Inaugural speech (*see* below) an uncanny prescience.

And in health terms he was not sprightly, even if youthful. He had a chronically bad back. Sexually, he was almost too 'hip', sleeping with as many women as possible, often several times a day. He and a Mafia mobster at one point shared the same doxy.

He was the son of a millionaire, his consequent lack of trader skills arguably handicapping him in negotiations when president. His father, Joe Kennedy, if he did not quite 'buy' him the presidency, certainly festooned the path to the White House with dollar bills. After being a Member of the House of Representatives (1947–53), then Senator from Massachusetts (1953–60), Jack Kennedy narrowly defeated Nixon (*qv*) in 1960.

He inherited, hence carelessly endorsed, the 'Bay of Pigs' scheme to overthrow Castro (*qv*) in Cuba in 1961. But over that selfsame island of Cuba he made a comeback in 1962, forcing Khrushchev (*qv*) to remove Soviet missiles recently stationed there. This had the immediate effect of curbing Khrushchev's riskier moves in international affairs and in the longer term contributed to his downfall. Domestically Kennedy started the civil rights legislative programme which his successor, Lyndon Johnson, successfully concluded, but also, again in foreign affairs, started the American involvement in Vietnam whose escalation destroyed Johnson. His last achievement before his assassination in Dallas on 22 November 1963 was the 1963 Test Ban Treaty. It is doubtful if he could have capped this, however much longer he might have lived.

• Context of speech

The 'youth' theme in the excerpt below was deliberate. The outgoing President, Eisenhower, was the oldest then to have held the office.

" **L**et the word go forth from this time and place, to friend and foe alike, that the torch has been passed to a new generation of Americans — born in this century, tempered by war, disciplined by a hard and bitter peace, proud of our ancient heritage — and unwilling to witness or permit the slow undoing of those human rights to which this nation has always been committed, and to which we are committed today at home and around the world.**

Let every nation know, whether it wishes us well or ill, that we shall pay any price, bear any burden, meet any hardship, support any friend, oppose any foe in order to assure the survival and the success of liberty.

This much we pledge — and more. To those old allies whose cultural and spiritual origins we share, we pledge the loyalty of faithful friends. United, there is little we cannot do in a host of cooperative ventures. Divided, there is little we can do — for we dare not meet a powerful challenge at odds and split asunder.

To those new states whom we welcome to the ranks of the free, we pledge our word that one form of colonial control shall not have passed away merely to be replaced by a far more iron tyranny. We shall not always expect to find them supporting our view. But we shall always hope to find them strongly supporting their own freedom — and to remember that, in the past, those who foolishly sought power by riding the back of the tiger ended up inside.

To those peoples in the huts and villages across the globe struggling to break the bonds of mass misery, we pledge our best efforts to help them help themselves ... If a free society cannot help the many who are poor, it cannot save the few who are rich.

... to those nations who would make themselves our adversary, we offer not a pledge but a request: that both sides begin anew the quest for peace, before the dark powers of destruction unleashed by science engulf all humanity in planned or accidental self-destruction ...

So let us begin anew — remembering on both sides that civility is not a sign of weakness, and sincerity is always subject to proof. Let us never negotiate out of fear. But let us never fear to negotiate.

Let both sides explore what problems unite us instead of belaboring those problems which divide us.

Let both sides, for the first time, formulate serious and precise proposals for the inspection and control of arms — and bring the absolute power to destroy other nations under the absolute control of all nations.

Let both sides seek to invoke the wonders of science instead of its terrors. Together let us explore the stars, conquer the deserts, eradicate disease, tap the ocean depths and encourage the arts and commerce.

Let both sides unite to heed in all corners of the earth the command of Isaiah — to 'undo the heavy burdens ... and to let the oppressed go free.' ...

All this will not be finished in the first 100 days. Nor will it be finished in the first 1,000 days, nor in the life of this Administration, nor even perhaps in our lifetime on this planet. But let us begin ...

Now the trumpet summons us again — not as a call to bear arms, though arms we need; not as a call to battle, though embattled we are — but a call to bear the burden of a long twilight struggle, year in and year out, 'rejoicing in hope, patient in tribulation' — a struggle against the common enemies of man: tyranny, poverty, disease and war itself ...

And so, my fellow Americans: ask not what your country can do for you — ask what you can do for your country ... "

'Ich bin ein Berliner'

June 1963

• Context of speech

The excerpt below was delivered in late June 1963 on the first leg of a five-country tour of Western Europe to boost NATO members' morale. The Berlin Wall had been built by the East Germans two years before. It was an attempt both to stop an exodus of their more enterprising citizens to the West and to cow the West Berliners.

66 **Two thousand years ago the proudest boast was '*civis Romanus sum*.' Today, in the world of freedom, the proudest boast is '*Ich bin ein Berliner*.' I appreciate my interpreter translating my German!**

There are many people in the world who really don't understand, or say they don't, what is the great issue between the Free World and the Communist World. Let them come to Berlin. There are some who say that Communism is the wave of the future. Let them come to Berlin. And there are some who say in Europe and elsewhere we can work with the Communists. Let them come to Berlin. And there are even a few who say that it is true that Communism is an evil system, but it permits us to make economic progress. *Lass' sie nach Berlin kommen*. Let them come to Berlin.

Freedom has many difficulties and democracy is not perfect, but we have never had to put a wall up to keep our people in, to prevent them from leaving us …

I know of no town, no city, that has been besieged for 18 years that still lives with the vitality and the force, and the hope and the determination of the city of West Berlin. While the wall is the most obvious and vivid demonstration of the failures of the Communist system, for all the world to see, we take no satisfaction in it, for it is, as your Mayor has said, an offense not only against history but an offense against humanity, separating families, dividing husbands and wives and brothers and sisters, and dividing a people who wish to be joined together.

What is true of this city is true of Germany — real, lasting peace in Europe can never be assured as long as one German out of four is denied the elementary right of free men, and that is to make a free choice. In 18 years of peace and good faith, this generation of Germans has earned the right to be free, including the right to unite their families and their nation in lasting peace, with good will to all people. You live in a defended island of freedom, but your life is part of the main. So let me ask you as I close, to lift your eyes beyond the dangers of today, to the hopes of tomorrow, beyond the freedom merely of this city of Berlin, or your country of Germany, to the advance of freedom everywhere, beyond the wall to the day of peace with justice, beyond yourselves and ourselves to all mankind.

Freedom is indivisible, and when one man is enslaved, all are not free. When all are free, then we can look forward to that day when this city will be joined as one and this country and this great Continent of Europe in a peaceful and hopeful globe. When that day finally comes, as it will, the people of West Berlin can take sober satisfaction in the fact that they were in the front lines for almost two decades.

All free men, wherever they may live, are citizens of Berlin, and, therefore, as a free man, I take pride in the words '*Ich bin ein Berliner*.' "

On the Bay of Pigs

Fidel Castro (1926–)
President of Cuba 1976–2006
Havana
19 April 1961

• Biography

If leaders of one-party states had doyens the way diplomats do, Castro would fit the bill. He has been in power the longest of the world's politicians, elected or unelected. He has also been the target of attempts to take him out by the world's leading power, the US, more often than has any other thorn in its side. This is not just because his revolutionary island of Cuba is only 90 miles south of the American mainland, but through its three decades as a Soviet-subsidised outpost of socialism in the Western Hemisphere. Following the USSR's collapse he has opened Cuba to tourists. But its economy is pitiful.

He was born to a self-made planter by a maid who had worked for the planter and his first wife and who may only have married the planter after Castro's birth. He went to a Jesuit school then became a law student at Havana University, soon plunging into student politics, where he made a name as organiser and public speaker.

On graduating he practised law. He also took to journalism. In 1952 he ran for the Cuban Congress but Fulgencio Batista, who had been Cuba's President from 1940 to 1944, staged a coup before polling started. Castro led a rising the next year, it failed and he was imprisoned. Released under an amnesty in 1955, he started a guerilla movement in the mountains of eastern Cuba. It triumphed in 1959.

He was not originally a Communist or Marxist, but soon declared his conversion to the latter doctrine and increasingly brought Communists into his government. This, and his attacking US business interests in Cuba, caused the US to sponsor an invasion by Cuban exiles in 1961. It failed and Castro turned to the USSR, both for economic assistance and support against the US.

Castro's early successes in education, health care and housing came at the cost of freedom and consumer satisfaction. Housing is, in 2007, in urgent need of updating in any case. His past triumphs overseas, where in Angola and the Horn of Africa Cuban troops exported revolution in a way that Trotsky (*qv*) never could, now seem of historical interest only, given the end of the Cold War. And Castro's personal antipathy to homosexuality and prudishness over women's emancipation look plain bigoted.

• Context of speech

Castro's early oratory was pompous, mannered and allusive, though he was thought a good speaker (Latinate languages like Spanish, make English oratory in comparison sound almost slangy.) Since taking power he has tended to instruct his listeners rather than work them up to action, though he has got ever longer-winded. But he has tried to establish a rapport with audiences, often improvising answers to shouted comments from the crowd so that a dialogue gets going. His voice is somewhat high-pitched, though his almost Stakhanovite oratory output (1–4 hours long twice a week for 30 years) would make most people sound hoarse.

Two years to the day after the 19 April 1961 invasion of Cuba in the Bay of Pigs (specifically two beaches), Castro commemorated it in a speech at the Chaplin Theatre in Havana. (Charlie Chaplin, being a leftist, was not tarred with the Yanqui imperialist brush.)

"This date will always be of great importance in our Revolution's history. It was for our country and our Revolution a decisive battle. It has not been the only decisive battle of the Revolution. It may not even be the last, though I hope it will be.** But it was the last of a series of battles ... fought as part of the Revolution. The preceding battles made the revolution possible. The Battle of Playa Girón [*one of the two beaches already mentioned*] ... confirmed it ...

Because the Battle was over in 72 hours, the danger can be underestimated ... Those who organised the invasion are not fools. In their political grasp they do not shine; in social matters they are inept. But militarily they are by no means novices ...

Most of you recall that after the Revolution triumphed we found ourselves with a few tanks — some of them antiquated Shermans, others English Comets. We have not yet found out why Señor Batista did not use them to fight with, since those tanks were found in the old Columbia camp, today Ciudad Libertad [*Freedom City*]. And I recall there were also some armoured cars and some very light tanks, which by today's standards look like toys, called General Stuarts.

There was an enormous variety of weapons, and also various aeroplanes. But as you know, all that equipment needs constant repair. It needs spare parts, especially when raw recruits must be trained. When the Revolution triumphed we did not have one single tank warfare expert. We did not have a single artilleryman. And as for fighter pilots ...

We had no technicians, and since our soldiers in many cases had never even seen a tank, the tanks were rapidly wearing out. Our equipment after a few months was practically — or would practically have been — unserviceable.

Our enemies were already preparing their expedition, and we decided to acquire some weapons, starting in Europe, bought from a Belgian factory. Our enemies tried to prevent our arming ... Because the arms factory at the beginning resisted their pressure, they resorted to sabotage. That was how a ship came to explode at our docks just as unloading began.

Since then we have unloaded no one knows how many hundreds of ships ... and what a coincidence — what a coincidence! — not one of those ships has exploded. The ship that exploded came from a Western European country where CIA agents work freely. When investigations indicated there had been sabotage, the imperialists denied it. As you will recall, to see if there was any possibility of the explosion having been an accident, several crates were even dropped from an aeroplane. It proved impossible to get them to explode, but that did not stop the imperialists denying their part in it all ...

Our people awoke one dawn under attack at various points by planes that bore Cuban markings — an unprecedentedly piratical and contemptible act, as well as being cowardly and treacherous. We next saw what our enemies … publicised … in the world press. What did they say? That Yankee planes equipped by them and organised by them had attacked Cuba from Central American bases? No! When we charged that Yankee planes had attacked Cuba, they said it was untrue and that the planes were Cuban planes that had rebelled …

Today, 19 November, is fundamentally — that is, April; I do not know why November came out there — 19 April; the date is not in the least important. The significance of the day will never be forgotten by us. It is a day fundamentally for gathering together the comrades of the revolutionary armed forces, and that is why we have seen those comrades fill a large part of this theatre. But it is not a day for the comrades of the armed forces alone. It belongs to all the people."

'I have a dream'

The Rev. Martin Luther King, Jr. (1929–68)
Lincoln Memorial, Washington, DC
August 1963

• Biography

Politically active clerics are unknown in mainland Britain, even though, or perhaps because, senior bishops of the Established Church have automatic seats in the upper house of the legislature. (The Rev. Ian Paisley, who is in any case very much not a cleric of the Established Church, only became known outside Northern Ireland after its separate legislature was done away with.)

In America things are very different. There, where significantly men (and women) of God are still called 'preachers', several have changed the face of national politics within living memory: Billy Graham, Martin Luther King, Jesse Jackson (*qv*) and Al Sharpton. Three of these, however, have been black and have been active in what for want of a better phrase one can only call racial politics. The leading figure among them was King.

He was precocious both in religion and politics, also in the matter of international recognition: ordained at nineteen, National Association for the Advancement of Colored People (NAACP) executive committee member at 25, a Nobel Peace Laureate aged 35 (then the youngest ever). Alas, he was also one of the youngest martyrs of post-war times, being assassinated when only 39.

He became a national figure aged 26 when in December 1955 he organised a boycott (*see* also Parnell) of buses in Montgomery, Alabama, after a black woman got convicted of flouting the local ordinance that black people generally should sit at the back of buses, the front seats being reserved for whites, and should stand if whites needed a seat. The boycott lasted over a year, cost the local bus company nearly two-thirds of its revenue and resulted in the ordinance being declared unlawful by the US Supreme Court.

Aged only 28, King next became President of the Southern Christian Leadership Conference. This, despite its sectarian name, was inspired in its creed of non-violence by Gandhi (*qv*). From then till the mid-1960s, when the Vietnam War started competing for national attention, the Civil Rights movement, of which King was the best-known leader, dominated American domestic politics.

His assassination occurred when in comparison with his earlier causes he had got involved in a parochial, even bathetic, issue, to wit a garbage-handlers 'and sewage-processors' strike. It was triggered when two black garbage-handlers were killed by the crusher mechanism in their garbage truck and bad weather got black sewage-disposal workers sent home without pay while their white brothers still drew wages. It nonetheless encapsulated every bit as dramatically as the bus boycott of thirteen years earlier the disgraceful treatment of blacks in the world's foremost democracy.

• Context of speech

In August 1963 a quarter of a million people converged on Washington, DC, to demonstrate for the implementing of civil rights which were nominally in every American's possession already. King's speech paved the way for the passing of the Civil Rights Act the following year.

In June 2006 an early handwritten draft of the speech was among a collection of King's papers bought for $32m (£16m in 2007 terms) by Atlanta worthies for conserving at King's old college, Morehouse.

"Let us not wallow in the valley of despair. I say to you today my friends — so even though we face the difficulties of today and tomorrow, I still have a dream.

It is a dream deeply rooted in the American dream. I have a dream that one day this nation will rise up and live out the true meaning of its creed: 'We hold these truths to be self-evident, that all men are created equal.'

I have a dream that one day on the red hills of Georgia the sons of former slaves and the sons of former slave-owners will be able to sit down together at the table of brotherhood.

I have a dream that one day even the state of Mississippi, a state sweltering with the heat of injustice, sweltering with the heat of oppression, will be transformed into an oasis of freedom and justice.

I have a dream that my four little children will one day live in a nation where they will not be judged by the color of their skin but by the content of their character.

I have a dream today.

I have a dream that one day down in Alabama, with its vicious racists … one day right there in Alabama little black boys and black girls will be able to join hands with little white boys and white girls as sisters and brothers.

I have a dream today. I have a dream that one day every valley shall be exalted, and every hill and mountain shall be made low, the rough places will be made plain, and the crooked places will be made straight, and the glory of the Lord shall be revealed and all flesh shall see it together.

This is our hope. This is the faith that I go back to the South with. With this faith we will be able to hew out of the mountain of despair a stone of hope. With this faith we will be able to transform the jangling discords of our nation into a beautiful symphony of brotherhood. With this faith we will be able to work together, to pray together, to struggle together, to go to jail together, to stand up for freedom together, knowing that we will be free one day …

And so let freedom ring from the prodigious hilltops of New Hampshire. Let freedom ring from the mighty mountains of New York. Let freedom ring from the heightening Alleghenies of Pennsylvania.

Let freedom ring from the snow-capped Rockies of Colorado. Let freedom ring from the curvaceous slopes of California. But not only that; let freedom ring from Stone Mountain of Georgia. Let freedom ring from Lookout Mountain of Tennessee. Let freedom ring from every hill and molehill of Mississippi — from every mountainside.

Let freedom ring. And when this happens, and when we allow freedom to ring — when we let it ring from every village and every hamlet, from every state and every city, we will be able to speed up that day when all of God's children — black men and white men, Jews and Gentiles, Protestants and Catholics — will be able to join hands and sing in the words of the old Negro spiritual: 'Free at last! Free at last! Thank God Almighty, we are free at last!' "

'Rivers of blood'

J(ohn) Enoch Powell (1912–98)
Midland Hotel, Birmingham
20 April 1968

• Biography

Enoch Powell held Cabinet office for only 15 months in a 37-year career as MP. Yet he achieved more than most Cabinet Ministers of a decade's standing, more even than many Prime Ministers.

He began the dispelling of the illusion that budget deficits and money-printing maintain employment. His insistence that his concern over immigration was fundamentally patriotic attracted mass working-class support as no other right-of-centre politician has done since universal suffrage came in. He frustrated Harold Wilson's 1968 attempt to reform the House of Lords. He helped topple two administrations, one of them his own leader Edward Heath's in 1974, the other Jim Callaghan's in 1979. His doctrines were so all-embracing, and had such coherence and logic, that they got called Powellism. No other modern politician has been commemorated in this way bar Margaret Thatcher (*qv*) with 'Thatcherism' — and she adopted many of Powell's ideas to do so.

In his classical learning, grasp of modern languages, huge moral authority and poetic leanings Powell recalls Gladstone (*qv*). But he was a better prophet. Gladstone merely resembled one (the Old Testament sort) when in his denunciatory moods. Unfortunately Powell's prophecies, like the Trojan sibyl Cassandra's, did not convince the state's decision-makers, though the twin Trojan Horses that have eroded the 'British way of life' have been less immigration than (a) American 'culture' and (b) bureaucratic European meddling. He is best remembered for the speech below, which certainly many ordinary people thought hit the nail on the head. Yet its climax, where in effect he said copious immigration would have grossly sanguinary consequences, has proved a misjudgement, notwithstanding the odd riot.

After an early career as an academic, he served in World War II as a supremely competent staff officer in the Middle East then India. His love of India alone should absolve him of the absurd charge of racism.

He entered Parliament as Conservative MP for Wolverhampton South-West in 1950. By 1957 he was Financial Secretary to the Treasury. Here he opposed inflation, converting his boss the Chancellor of the Exchequer but not Macmillan (*qv*), whose failure to back the Treasury team obliged them to resign.

He was Health Minister from 1960 to 1963 but resigned when Lord Home succeeded Macmillan. Under Heath as Tory leader his Conservative loyalties waned, especially over Heath's sacrificing British parliamentary sovereignty for European Community membership.

This, Heath's 1972 U-turn over wage restraint and his calling the February 1974 election on a 'who governs Britain?' cry ended Powell's Conservative adherence altogether. Conservatives blamed him for their defeat. From October 1974 till 1987 he was Ulster Unionist MP for Down South, as which for a time he persuaded his fellow Unionists to support Labour's minority government. Although he influenced Margaret Thatcher, he never rejoined the Conservatives, especially after the 1985 Anglo-Irish Agreement, which he thought betrayed the Union.

• Context of speech

The date of the speech, 20 April, was Hitler's (*qv*) birthday, as was soon pointed out by the kind of people who enjoy childish point-scoring.

It seems probable that Powell had overlooked this. But he can hardly have overlooked the assassination of Martin Luther King (*qv*) a little more than two weeks earlier. Indeed, this is probably what he had in mind when he mentioned 'that tragic and intractable phenomenon ... the other side of the Atlantic' immediately after the famous quotation involving blood. He was open to a charge of want of taste, however, a charge given extra force by the unnecessarily lurid figure of speech which forms a coda to the excerpt given here.

And as an experienced politician, he should have known how easily colourful words in a speech get wrenched out of context and blight the rest of your career. Something like that happened, for although he at no point uttered the words 'Rivers of Blood', this is what the speech has come to be entitled in popular memory.

The next day Heath sacked him from the Shadow Cabinet for alleged racialism. Two days after that over 2,000 London dockers struck in sympathy with Powell. Hundreds marched to Westminster to oppose Labour's Race Relations Bill. Powell's continued working-class following helped Heath win the 1970 election.

66 **In 15 or 20 years, on present trends, there will be in this country three and a half million Commonwealth immigrants and their descendants ... That is the official figure given ... by the ... Registrar General's Office. There is no comparable official figure for the year 2000, but it must be in the region of five to seven million, approximately one-tenth of the whole population ... Whole areas, towns and parts of towns across England will be occupied by sections of the immigrant and immigrant-descended population ...**

We must be mad, literally mad, as a nation to be permitting the annual inflow of some 50,000 dependants, who are for the most part the material of the future growth of the immigrant-descended population. It is like watching a nation busily engaged in heaping up its own funeral pyre.

The Conservative Party's policy is that all who are in this country as citizens should be equal before the law and that there shall be no discrimination or difference made between them by public authority ... This does not mean that the immigrant and his descendant should be elevated into a privileged or special class or that the citizen should be denied his right to discriminate in the management of his own affairs between one fellow-citizen and another ...

Those who ... demand legislation as they call it 'against discrimination' ... have got it exactly and diametrically wrong. The discrimination and the deprivation, the sense of alarm and of resentment, lies [*sic*] not with the immigrant population but with those among whom they have come and are still coming. This is why to enact legislation of the kind before Parliament at this moment is to risk throwing a match onto gunpowder ...

The other dangerous delusion ... is summed up in the word 'integration'. To be integrated into a population means to become for all practical purposes indistinguishable from its other members. Now, at all times, where there are marked physical differences, especially of colour, integration is difficult though, over a period, not impossible …

Now we are seeing the growth of positive forces acting against integration, of vested interests in the preservation and sharpening of racial and religious differences, with a view to the exercise of actual domination, first over fellow-immigrants and then over the rest of the population …

For these dangerous and divisive elements the legislation proposed in the Race Relations Bill is the very pabulum they need to flourish. Here is the means of showing that the immigrator communities can organise to consolidate their members, to agitate and campaign against their fellow citizens, and to overawe and dominate the rest with the legal weapons which the ignorant and the ill-informed have provided. As I look ahead, I am filled with foreboding; like the Roman, I seem to see the River Tiber foaming with much blood…"

Against separatist terrorists

(Joseph Philippe) Pierre (Yves) Elliott Trudeau
(1919–2000)
Broadcast to Canadian nation
16 October 1970

• Biography

Canada and its Prime Ministers were long seen as worthy but dull, and in one or two Prime Ministerial cases not all that worthy. In 1968, the year of so many other exciting events around the world, this changed. Trudeau became Prime Minister, putting his country squarely — and trendily – on the Sixties map.

As can be seen from his names, Trudeau culturally straddled the long-standing gulf between Anglophone and Francophone Canadians. He himself was bilingual, his father being French and his mother Scots-French. He was also a lawyer, initially an academic one but also a former Minister of Justice, as which he legalised homosexuality and made divorce easier.

Sad to say, he could not as Prime Minister maintain the trendiness sufficiently to keep in tow his wife Margaret, who became for a while the world's most famous prime ministerial spouse. She was too friendly with Castro, Ted Kennedy (brother of John F. Kennedy, *qv*) and the Rolling Stones guitarist Ronnie Wood. Trudeau consorted with Castro also, but in more statesmanlike fashion. The Trudeaux eventually divorced.

• Context of speech

On 5 October 1970, hence the entire episode being called the 'October Crisis', members of a cell of a separatist terrorist group, the Front de Libération du Québec (FLQ), kidnapped a British diplomat, James Cross. When their conditions for his release were not met, members of another FLQ cell kidnapped on 10 October Quebec's Labour Minister, Pierre Laporte.

It soon began to look as if the Cross cell and the Laporte one had different aims, or at any rate different degrees of determination. It later transpired that the Laporte cell acted precipitately after hearing news of Cross's kidnapping. They had made no preparations, and after taking Laporte to a makeshift lair even lacked money for food. Laporte treated them and himself to a barbecue chicken meal.

Meanwhile troops were called out. The authorities' determination to resist the demands varied in intensity. Trudeau commented in a broadcast interview 'Yes, well there are a lot of bleeding hearts around who just don't like to see people with helmets and guns. All I can say is, go on and bleed, but it is more important to keep law and order in the [*sic*] society than to be worried about weak-kneed people ... I think the [*sic*] society must take every means at its disposal to defend itself against the emergence of a parallel power which defies the elected power in this country and I think that this goes to any distance.'. On being asked just how far he would go, he said 'Well, just watch me.'

On 16 October 1970 he broadcast the speech excerpted below. Laporte was found dead on 18 October, either murdered in cold blood or killed trying to escape. On 3 December Cross was freed in a police raid on his captors' lair. Five FLQ members of the Cross cell were given safe conduct to Cuba, but eventually returned to Canada and were given prison sentences. Members of the Laporte cell also received prison sentences, two of them life ones for Laporte's murder.

66 **I** **am speaking to you at a moment of grave crisis** ...
The governments of Canada and Quebec have been told by groups of self-styled revolutionaries that they intend to murder in cold blood two innocent men unless their demands are met. The kidnappers claim they act ... to draw attention to ... social injustice ...

They want ... the police to offer up as a sacrificial lamb a person whom they assume assisted in the lawful arrest and proper conviction of certain of their criminal friends.

They also want money. Ransom money ...

They demand the release from prison of 17 criminals, and the dropping of charges against six other men, all of whom they refer to as 'political prisoners' ...

Three are convicted murderers; five others were jailed for manslaughter; one is serving a life imprisonment after having pleaded guilty to numerous charges related to bombings; another has been convicted of 17 armed robberies; two were once paroled but are now back in jail awaiting trial on charges of robberies ... deciding whether to release ... these criminals is ... a responsibility ... the Government will discharge according to law ...[:] the safety of the hostages is without question the responsibility of the kidnappers ... Nothing that either the Government of Canada or the Government of Quebec has done or failed to do ... could possibly excuse any injury to either of these two innocent men. The guns pointed at their heads have FLQ fingers on the triggers ... Should there be harm done to these men, the Government promises unceasing pursuit of those responsible ...

In order to save the lives of Mr Cross and Mr Laporte, we have engaged in communications with the kidnappers.

The offer of the Federal Government to the kidnappers of safe conduct out of Canada to a country of their choice in return for the delivery of the hostages has not yet been taken up, neither has the offer of the Government of Quebec to recommend parole for the five prisoners eligible for parole.

This offer of safe conduct was made only because Mr Cross and Mr Laporte might be able to identify their kidnappers and to assist in their prosecution. By offering the kidnappers safe exit from Canada, we removed from them any possible motivation for murdering their hostages ...

If a democratic society is to continue to exist, it must be able to root out the cancer of an armed, revolutionary movement that is bent on destroying the very basis of our freedom. For that reason the Government, following ... requests of the Government of Quebec and the City of Montreal for urgent action, [has] decided to proclaim the War Measures Act ... to permit the ... weight of Government to be brought ... to bear on ... persons advocating or practicing violence [for] ... political ends ...

The criminal law as it stands is simply not adequate to deal with systematic terrorism.

The police have therefore been given certain extraordinary powers ... [They] include the right to search and arrest without warrant, to detain suspected persons without the necessity of laying specific charges immediately, and to detain persons without bail.

These are strong powers and I find them as distasteful as I am sure do you. They are necessary, however, to permit the police to deal with persons who advocate or promote the violent overthow of our democratic system. In short, I assure you that the Government recognises its grave responsibilities in interfering in certain cases with civil liberties, and that it remains answerable to the people of Canada for its actions. The Government will revoke this proclamation as soon as possible ... "

'The lady's not for turning'

Margaret Hilda Thatcher, Baroness Thatcher (1925–)
Conservative Party Conference, Brighton
10 October 1980

• Biography

Britain's first and so far only woman Prime Minister, Margaret Thatcher, like Hillary Clinton (*qv*), has often been more cordially loathed by her enemies than adored by her fans — though fans, not just supporters, she certainly has had. The loathing is something top female politicians seem to attract, for example Indira Gandhi (*see* Nehru) and, in Sri Lanka, Mrs. Bandaranaike.

Margaret Thatcher did more to roll back the state than any other Conservative leader since the state became predominant in people's lives. She cut the trades unions down to size, seized back the Falklands, privatised whole swathes of British industry, clawed back overgenerous British payments to Brussels, slashed taxes, exposed public health and state education to market forces, tripped a mutual admiration *pas de deux* with Reagan (*qv*) and faced down the Soviet Union. But even all that does not explain her enemies' personal antipathy. And the enemies were not all on the Left. She had her detractors among the highest in the Conservative Party. She was brought down by members of her own Cabinet.

• Context of speech

Its most memorable phrase was 'the lady's not for turning'. This was a play on *The Lady's Not for Burning* (first performed 1948), the title of a play — the other sort — by the now all-but-forgotten verse dramatist Christopher Fry.

It was designed to emphasise that there would be no U-turn *à la* Ted Heath's in 1972 (*see* also Enoch Powell). This was not just a tilt at Heath, notorious though was his distaste for Margaret Thatcher, his successor. Margaret Thatcher's Cabinet was still stuffed with 'wets' left over from the Conservatives' craven past, unemployment was high and despite Enoch Powell there were plenty of voices urging her to go over-budget or print money to palliate it.

The words were by Margaret Thatcher's chief speech-writer Sir Ronnie Millar, himself a playwright. And the phrase was, to borrow an expression from the theatre, an instant hit.

66 **There are many things to be done to set this nation on the road to recovery, and I do not mean economic recovery alone, but a new independence of spirit and zest for achievement.**

It is sometimes said that because of our past we, as a people, expect too much and set our sights too high. That is not the way I see it. Rather it seems to me that ... our ambitions have steadily shrunk. Our response to disappoint-ment has not been to lengthen our stride but to shorten the distance to be covered. But with confidence in ourselves and in our future what a nation we could be! ...

And a great nation is the voluntary creation of its people — a people composed of men and women whose pride in themselves is founded on the knowledge of what they can give to a community of which they in turn can be proud.

If our people feel that they are part of a great nation and they are prepared to will the means to keep it great, a great nation we shall be, and shall remain. So, what can stop us from achieving this? What then stands in our way? The prospect of another winter of discontent? I suppose it might.

But I prefer to believe that ... we are coming, slowly, painfully, to an autumn of understanding. And I hope that it will be followed by a winter of common sense ...

To those waiting with bated breath for that favourite media catchphrase, the 'U' turn, I have only one thing to say. 'You turn if you want to. The lady's not for turning.' I say that not only to you but to our friends overseas and also to those who are not our friends...

This afternoon I have tried to set before you some of my most deeply held convictions and beliefs. This Party, which I am privileged to serve, and this Government, which I am proud to lead, are engaged in the massive task of restoring confidence and stability to our people...

If we were to fail, that freedom could be imperilled. So let us resist the blandishments of the faint hearts; let us ignore the howls and threats of the extremists; let us stand together and do our duty, and we shall not fail."

'Evil empire'

Ronald Reagan (1911–2004)
40th President of the USA 1981–89
British Houses of Parliament
8 June 1982

• Biography

Did Reagan win the Cold War? He himself is supposed to have said so. Many people thought it was he who had. Clearly other world leaders had contributed, notably John Paul II, but also, albeit obliquely, Khrushchev (*qqv*). Nonetheless, even if Reagan was lucky in being in the right position, the Presidency, at the right time, the late 1980s, he deserves a good deal of the credit.

His rise in American politics owed much to his opponents' underestimating him. Reagan's strength as President lay precisely in the ignorance, laziness and lack of sophistication imputed to him by critics. He sat back, getting plenty of rest (he was only weeks away from his 70th birthday when inaugurated) and delegating widely. He never lost sight of a very few major principles. But he was too nice for a chief executive. His sacking of at least one subordinate was on his wife Nancy's orders; on another occasion she did the sacking herself.

Chief of the few major principles he kept in focus was the wickedness of Communism and the concomitant need for its destruction. It had been around so long that more 'professional' politicians in the West tended to regard it as rather like bad weather — something you just shrug your shoulders and put up with. Not Reagan.

He had been a Hollywood actor, the 'Erroll Flynn of the B movies' as he self-deprecatingly put it. (He was good at self-deprecation, not on the whole a very American trait.) He thus knew the value not just of presentation but of exposition (establishing the background of a plot), pithy scripts, cutting to the action — stuff as vital to effective politics as to film-making. He had also been an effective trade unionist negotiator as President of the Screen Actors Guild, even leading a successful six-month strike in 1959. (In the late 1940s he was rather left-wing.) And as an old FBI informer he knew something of the value of covert surveillance. If anyone had bothered to examine these aspects of his past, they might have been better prepared for him.

He first came to Republicans' attention in 1964, when he supported their reactionary presidential nominee Barry Goldwater. He then won election as Governor of California and in 1980 defeated the discredited sitting President Jimmy Carter. He survived an assassination attempt, slashed taxes, spent heavily on armaments and did little, if anything, to curb substantial corruption at the heart of his administration.

Although he won re-election in 1984 by one of the most overwhelming majorities ever, the corruption culminated in a scheme by underlings to sell arms to Iran in exchange for Iran's releasing American hostages, the resulting arms sale revenue being channelled to help opponents of the Communist-dominated Nicaraguan government. This breached both the Administration's policy of refusing to bargain over hostages and Congress's ban on helping the Nicaraguan rebels. But Reagan's prestige was such that the charges rolled off him like oil off Teflon, invented as a spin-off of the space programme and a metaphor to describe Reagan's immunity to mud-slinging.

• Context of speech

This, famous for its alliterative twin disyllables 'evil empire', officially did not feature in a Reagan speech till the following year, when he spoke to the National Association of Evangelicals at Orlando, Florida.

The fact is, officials cut the 'evil empire' phrase out of the script for the Parliament speech — not once, but twice, Reagan having had it re-inserted after the first excision. Reagan was far too old a hand to lie down under this sort of back office bossiness and in the end just added his pet phrase orally. The 'official' Parliamentary speech runs thus:

> 66 **We're approaching the end of a bloody century plagued by a terrible political invention – totalitarianism ... Yet optimism is in order ... From Stettin on the Baltic to Varna on the Black Sea, the regimes planted by totalitarianism have had more than thirty years to establish their legitimacy. But none – not one regime – has yet been able to risk free elections. Regimes planted by bayonets do not take root ...**
>
> Historians looking back at our time will note the consistent restraint and peaceful intentions of the West. They will note that it was the democracies who

refused to use the threat of their nuclear monopoly in the Forties and early Fifties for territorial or imperial gain.

Had that nuclear monopoly been in the hands of the Communist world, the map of Europe — indeed, the world — would look very different today. And certainly they will note it was not the democracies that invaded Afghanistan or suppressed Polish Solidarity [*see* John Paul II] or used chemical and toxin warfare in Afghanistan and Southeast Asia.

If history teaches anything, it teaches self-delusion in the face of unpleasant facts is folly. We see around us today the marks of our terrible dilemma — predictions of doomsday, anti-nuclear demonstrations, an arms race in which the West must, for its own protection, be an unwilling participant. At the same time we see totalitarian forces in the world who seek subversion and conflict around the globe to further their barbarous assault on the human spirit. What, then, is our course? Must civilisation perish in a hail of fiery atoms? Must freedom wither in a quiet, deadening accommodation with totalitarian evil [*this was probably the place where he substituted the words 'evil empire'*]? ...

And one of the simple but overwhelming facts of our time is this: of all the millions of refugees we've seen in the modern world, their flight is always away from, not toward the Communist world. Today on the NATO line, our military forces face east to prevent a possible invasion. On the other side of the line, the Soviet forces also face east to prevent their people from leaving ... "

On the Challenger space shuttle disaster

Broadcast from Oval Office
28 January 1986

• Context of speech

The explosion of the space shuttle Challenger early in 1986 shook America's self-confidence. Space exploration had seemed as if it was becoming as safe as air travel. Suddenly it was brought home that it wasn't. At 5 pm Eastern Time, mere hours after the disaster, Reagan, a specialist in nurturing America's self-confidence, broadcast live from the Oval Office on nationwide radio and television. To students of presidential oratory his words about feeling the astronauts' families' loss are interesting as prefiguring the 'I feel your pain' theme of Bill Clinton's oratory [see Hillary Clinton].

> 66 **I'd planned to speak to you tonight ... on the state of the Union, but the events of earlier today have led me to change those plans. Today is a day for mourning and remembering. Nancy and I are pained to the core by the tragedy of the shuttle Challenger. We know we share this pain with all of the people of our country. This is truly a national loss ...**
>
> We mourn seven heroes: Michael Smith, Dick Scobee, Judith Resnik, Ronald McNair, Ellison Onizuka, Gregory Jarvis and Christa McAuliffe. We mourn their loss as a nation together.
>
> For the families of the seven, we cannot bear, as you do, the full impact of this tragedy. But we feel the loss, and we're thinking about you so very much. Your loved ones were daring and brave ... They had a hunger to explore the universe and discover its truths. They wished to serve, and they did. They served all of us ...
>
> They, the members of the Challenger crew, were pioneers ...
>
> The future doesn't belong to the fainthearted; it belongs to the brave. The Challenger crew was pulling us into the future, and we'll continue to follow them.
>
> I've always had great faith in and respect for our space program, and what happened today does nothing to diminish it. We don't hide our space program. We don't keep secrets and cover things up. We do it all up front and in public. That's the way freedom is, and we wouldn't change it for a minute. We'll continue our quest in space. There will be more shuttle flights and more shuttle crews and, yes, more volunteers, more civilians, more teachers in space. Nothing ends here; our hopes and our journeys continue ...
>
> There's a coincidence today. On this day 390 years ago, the great explorer Sir Francis Drake (qv) died aboard ship off the coast of Panama. In his lifetime the great frontiers were the oceans, and an historian later said 'He lived by the sea, died on it, and was buried in it.' Well, today we can say of the Challenger crew: Their dedication was, like Drake's, complete ... "

'Tear down this wall!'

Brandenburg Gate, West Berlin
12 June 1987

• Context of speech

By the late 1980s Gorbachev's *glasnost* ('openness') and *perestroika* [*see* also Khrushchev] policies were beginning to suggest that the Soviet 'system' was undertaking major internal reform. Reagan's huge expenditure on arms, troublesome though it was going to be for the US economy through massive budget deficits, was proving even more of a strain on the USSR. Reagan aimed the speech excerpted below as much at the Soviet Bloc as at his immediate audience, perhaps even more so. Two years afterwards the Berlin Wall was indeed dismantled.

"**Our gathering today is being broadcast throughout Western Europe and North America. I understand that it is being seen and heard as well in the East. To those listening throughout Eastern Europe, I extend my warmest greetings and the good will of the American people. To those listening in East Berlin, a special word: although I cannot be with you, I address my remarks to you just as surely as to those standing here before me. For I join you, as I join your fellow countrymen in the West, in this firm, this unalterable belief: *Es gibt nur ein Berlin* ['There is only one Berlin'].**

Behind me stands a wall that encircles the free sectors of this city, part of a vast system of barriers that divides the entire continent of Europe. From the Baltic, south, those barriers cut across Germany in a gash of barbed wire, concrete, dog runs, and guard towers. Farther south, there may be no visible, no obvious wall. But there remain armed guards and checkpoints all the same … Yet it is here in Berlin where the wall emerges most clearly — here, cutting across your city, where the news photo and the television screen have imprinted this brutal division of a continent upon the mind of the world.

Standing before the Brandenburg Gate, every man is a German, separated from his fellow men. Every man is a Berliner, forced to look upon a scar …

Where four decades ago there was rubble, today in West Berlin there is the greatest industrial output of any city in Germany ... Where a city's culture seemed to have been destroyed, today there are two great universities, orchestras and an opera, countless theaters, and museums. Where there was want, today there's abundance ... From devastation, from utter ruin, you Berliners have, in freedom, rebuilt a city that once again ranks as one of the greatest on Earth ...

And now the Soviets themselves may, in a limited way, be coming to understand the importance of freedom. We hear much from Moscow about a new policy of reform and openness. Some political prisoners have been released. Certain foreign news broadcasts are no longer being jammed. Some economic enterprises have been permitted to operate with greater freedom from state control ... We welcome change and openness; for we believe that freedom and security go together, that the advance of human liberty can only strengthen the cause of world peace.

There is one sign the Soviets can make that would be unmistakable, that would advance dramatically the cause of freedom and peace. General Secretary Gorbachev, if you seek peace, if you seek prosperity for the Soviet Union and Eastern Europe, if you seek liberalization – Come here to this gate! Mr Gorbachev, open this gate! Mr Gorbachev, tear down this wall! ... "

On a free Poland

**Pope John Paul II (1920–2005)
'The Great', *né* Karol Wotyła
(reigned 1978–2005)
Gniezno, Poland
3 June 1997**

• Biography

The only memorable *mot* by Stalin (*qv*) was his contemptuous 'How many divisions has the Pope?' He put it to the then French Foreign Minister Pierre Laval, a future

Nazi collaborator (like Stalin), when discussing an anti-German alliance in 1935. Laval, already collaboration-minded, had proposed as part of the alliance a Soviet-Vatican concordat.

No jibe in history has backfired more spectacularly. An ex-seminarian like Stalin should have appreciated the power of belief systems better. When Communism collapsed in the late 1980s, it was through its practitioners' loss of faith. John Paul II arguably did more than anyone else to cause that collapse.

He was born in Poland, a nation which, with Ireland, is the truest European daughter of the Church, though neither country then had produced a pope. (The Irish still haven't.)

Unlike Stalin, whose only regular employment was very briefly as a meteorologist, Karol Wotyła had by the time he found his vocation held several 'ordinary' jobs: messenger boy, quarryman, factory worker. He therefore knew the proletariat. By the 1980s few top Communists did. Their remoteness from the class they claimed to represent contributed to their downfall.

Karol Wotyła was far from remote. For a start, he took part in sports: skiing, jogging, playing goalie at football. His fitness probably saved him when on 13 May 1981 he was shot by a would-be assassin. (The date was the anniversary of Our Lady of Fatima's manifestation in Portugal, as John Paul pointed out; secularists should note that it was also the anniversary of Stalin's *mot* to Laval.)

His love of the drama and playwright's skills made him a superb communicator — not through the somewhat baroque pageants of papal tradition (in 1978 he refused a full coronation), but through 'working' vast audiences in direct speech and gesture.

He was ordained priest in 1946, promoted Bishop in 1958 then Archbishop of Kraków in 1963, became a Cardinal in 1967 and as the compromise candidate succeeded John Paul I in October 1978. He was conservative over family matters such as abortion and divorce, but innovative in the very many saints he made. He travelled extremely widely, his polyglot talents smoothing his path.

The immediate cause of what in Italy has been declared a KGB [*see* also Khrushchev] attempt on his life, the 1981 shooting by a Turk whose immediate controllers were the Bulgarian secret service, was his visit to Poland in 1979 and the support he gave to the founding in 1981 of Solidarity, the Polish workers' movement.

The bogusness of Communist claims to represent workers had been revealed before, notably over the 1953 East German uprising. This time revolt occurred in an intensely Catholic country. And outside support came not from easily discredited sources of mere hot air, such as American radio, but from a native Pole, who knew by experience how to baffle a police state, who was in nobody else's pocket and who headed the largest Christian church on earth.

The best testimony to John Paul's role in defeating Communism comes from the former Soviet leader Mikhail Gorbachev, who admitted that without him it would have been impossible. The next best is that of General Wojciech Jaruzelski, architect of martial law in Poland (the regime's only solution to Solidarity if a Soviet invasion was to be avoided). He allegedly termed John Paul 'the detonator' of the final collapse of the Communist regime, which occurred in 1989.

• Context of speech

The speech excerpted below was delivered on John Paul's pastoral visit to Poland on the millennial anniversary of the death of St. Adalbert, the man who brought Christianity to Poland.

66 **Deeply impressed upon my memory is the meeting in Gniezno in June 1979, when, for the first time, the Pope, a native of Kraków, was able to celebrate the Eucharist on the Hill of Lech, in the presence of the unforgettable Primate of the Millennium, the whole Polish Episcopate and many pilgrims not only from Poland but also from the neighbouring countries.**

Today, eighteen years later, we should return to that homily in Gniezno, which in a certain sense became the programme of my pontificate. But first of all it was a humble reading of God's plans, linked with the final twenty-five years of our millennium. I said then: 'Is it not Christ's will, is it not what the Holy Spirit disposes, that this Polish Pope, this Slav Pope, should at this precise moment manifest the spiritual unity of Christian Europe? We know that the Christian unity of Europe is made up of two great traditions, of the West and of the East ... Yes, it is Christ's will, it is what the Holy Spirit disposes, that what I am saying should be said in this very place and at this moment in Gniezno.'

From this place there flowed forth at that time the power and strength of the Holy Spirit. Here reflection on the new evangelisation began to take shape in concrete terms. In the meantime great changes took place, new possibilities arose, other people appeared on the scene. The wall which divided Europe collapsed. Fifty years after the Second World War began, its effects ceased to ravage the face of our continent. A half century of separation ended, for which millions of people living in Central and Eastern Europe had paid a terrible price ...

Dear brothers and sisters, after so many years I repeat the same message: a new openness is needed. For we have seen, at times in a very painful way, that the recovery of the right to self-determination and the growth of political and economic freedom is not sufficient to rebuild European unity. How can we not mention here the tragedy of the nations of the former Yugoslavia, the drama experienced by the Albanian people and the enormous burdens felt by all the societies which have regained their freedom and with great effort are liberating themselves from the yoke of the Communist totalitarian system?

Can we not say that after the collapse of one wall, the visible one, another, invisible wall was discovered, one that continues to divide our continent — the wall that exists in people's hearts? It is a wall made out of fear and aggressiveness, of lack of understanding for people of different origins, different colour, different religious convictions; it is the wall of political and economic selfishness, of the weakening of sensitivity to the value of human life and the dignity of every human being. Even the undeniable achievements of recent years in the economic, political and social fields do not hide the fact that this wall exists. It casts its shadow over all of Europe. The goal of the authentic unity of the European continent is still distant. There will be no European unity until it is based on unity of the spirit … "

'Keep hope alive'

The Rev. Jesse Louis Jackson, _né_ Burns (1941–)
Democratic National Convention,
Atlanta, Georgia
19 July 1988

• Biography

Since Martin Luther King's (_qv_) death the leading black US civil rights campaigner has been Jesse Jackson. He met King in 1965 when they both took part in a march at Selma, Alabama, to register black voters. King put him in charge of the Southern Christian Leadership Conference's Chicago operation to get blacks there more jobs, an aim Jackson fulfilled by organising boycotts (_see_ also Parnell) of businesses reluctant to employ or otherwise do business with blacks.

From 1979 Jesse Jackson became increasingly active abroad. Through personal appeals to foreign leaders, some of whom he established friendship with, chiefly President Assad of Syria, he pulled off notable coups in getting US prisoners of war and other detainees released. Among them were a US Navy pilot in Syria in 1983, 22 civilians in Cuba in 1984 and three more US servicemen in what had formerly been Yugoslavia in 1999.

He ran for the Democratic nomination for President in both 1984 and 1988, winning respectively three-and-a-half million votes, five primaries and 450 Convention delegates and nearly seven million votes, 11 primaries and 1,200 Convention delegates. In 1988 he garnered a 55 percent vote in the Michigan Democratic Caucus, briefly pulling into the lead among Democratic presidential hopefuls in terms of delegates pledging support. His support declined soon afterwards.

• Context of speech

Jackson has reworked the 'Keep hope alive!' tag many times since, notably in rallying Democrats against George W. Bush (*qv*) in the 2000 and 2004 presidential elections.

"When I look out at this convention, I see the face of America: red, yellow, brown, black and white. We are all precious in God's sight – the real rainbow coalition ... You see me on TV, but you don't know the me that makes me, me. They wonder, 'Why does Jesse run?' because they see me running for the White House. They don't see the house I'm running from.

I have a story. I wasn't always on television. Writers were not always outside my door ... You see, I was born of a teen-age mother, who was born of a teen-age mother.

I understand. I know abandonment, and people being mean to you, and saying you're nothing and nobody and can never be anything.

I understand. Jesse Jackson is my third name. I'm adopted. When I had no name, my grandmother gave me her name. My name was Jesse Burns 'til I was 12. So I wouldn't have a blank space, she gave me a name to hold me over. I understand when nobody knows your name. I understand when you have no name.

I understand. I wasn't born in the hospital. Mama didn't have insurance. I was born in the bed at [the] house. I really do understand. Born in a three-room house, bathroom in the backyard, slop jar by the bed, no hot and cold running water. I understand. Wallpaper used for decoration? No. For a windbreaker. I understand. I'm a working person's person. That's why I understand you whether you're black or white. I understand work. I was not born with a silver spoon in my mouth. I had a shovel programmed for my hand ...

Call you outcast, low down, you can't make it, you're nothing, you're from nobody, subclass, underclass; when you see Jesse Jackson, when my name goes in nomination, your name goes in nomination.

I was born in the slum, but the slum was not born in me. And it wasn't born in you, and you can make it.

Wherever you are tonight, you can make it. Hold your head high; stick your chest out. You can make it. It gets dark sometimes, but the morning comes. Don't you surrender!

Suffering breeds character, character breeds faith. In the end faith will not disappoint.

You must not surrender! You may or may not get there but just know that you're qualified! And you hold on, and hold out! We must never surrender!! America will get better and better.

Keep hope alive. Keep hope alive! Keep hope alive! On tomorrow night and beyond, keep hope alive! ... ”

'Let freedom reign'

Nelson Rolihlahla Mandela (1918–)
President of South Africa 1994–99
Inauguration, Pretoria (recently renamed
Tshanwe)
10 May 1994

• Biography

In the late 1980s South Africa's apartheid regime buckled under international business boycotting and demographics; whites were 21 percent of the population in 1936, down to 16 percent by 1980 and forecast as falling to under ten percent by 2010. In 1990 the new President of South Africa F.W. de Klerk released from prison Nelson Mandela, best known of the leaders of the African National Congress (ANC). The ANC, South Africa's chief anti-apartheid organisation before its banning, was legalised.

Mandela was a lawyer by profession and an aristocrat by birth. The two circumstances gave him the confidence, his first day on Robben Island (South Africa's Alcatraz), to threaten a bullying prison warder with being hauled to court if he, Mandela, was subject to any disciplinary indignity not mentioned in official regulations, in this case having to run from the landing stage up to the cell-block.

He joined the ANC in 1942, helping to increase its membership and its effectiveness by non-violent but drastic methods such as boycotts (*see* also Parnell), strikes, civil disobedience and non-cooperation (*see* also Gandhi). Later still he turned to armed insurrection and by 1990 had been in prison for 17 years.

Within one year he was elected President of the resuscitated ANC and within another three President of South Africa. Despite the problems of recreating South Africa in a new form (some of which problems have arisen from his rash choice of second wife Winnie, who he subsequently divorced), he has remained cheerful, with his massive integrity intact, even after stepping down to retire in June 1999.

• Context of speech

Those who watched the inauguration on television may recall how, when the crowd got so exultant they started dancing about, Mandela essayed a graceful boogie or two up on the podium. What other world leaders could have carried that off without looking either a populist prat or a condescending stuffed shirt?

66 **We, the people of South Africa, feel fulfilled that humanity has taken us back into its bosom; that we, who were outlaws not so long ago, have today been given the rare privilege to be host to the nations of the world on our own soil ...**

We have triumphed in the effort to implant hopes in the breasts of the millions of our people. We enter into a covenant that we shall build the society in which all South Africans, both black and white, will be able to walk tall, without any fear in their hearts, assured of their inalienable right to human dignity — a rainbow nation at peace with itself and the world ...

We dedicate this day to all the heroes and heroines in this country and the rest of the world who sacrificed in many ways and surrendered their lives so that we could be free. Their dreams have become reality. Freedom is their reward.

We are both humbled and elevated by the honour and privilege that you, the people of South Africa, have bestowed on us, as the first President of a united, democratic, non-racial and non-sexist South Africa, to lead our country out of the valley of darkness.

We understand it still that there is no easy road to freedom. We know it well that none of us acting alone can achieve success. We must therefore act together as a united people, for national reconciliation, for nation-building, for the birth of a new world. Let there be justice for all. Let there be peace for all. Let there be work, bread, water and salt for all ...

Never, never and never again shall it be that this beautiful land will again experience the oppression of one by another and suffer the indignity of being the skunk of the world.

Let freedom reign. The sun shall never set on so glorious a human achievement. God bless Africa. Thank you."

'Time and Space'

Diana Princess of Wales, *née* Lady Diana Spencer (1961–97)
Royal Geographical Society, South Kensington, London
12 June 1997

• Biography

Despite the incarnations listed above, her impact was so huge that the 'Diana' alone is instantly recognisable. Of who else in history can that be said — whose forename has not been so unusual as to give the game away (thus excluding 'Elvis', etc.)?

Her marriage to the Prince of Wales made her a star. But it was the rocky course of it that made her a superstar. When the divorce finally came, the Buckingham Palace apparatchiks quaintly announced that her 'HRH' would be taken away from her. As damp squib excommunications go, this recalls the Pope's absolving Elizabeth I's (*qv*) subjects of their allegiance on the eve of the Armada.

For Diana had a knack of upstaging everyone she came in contact with. Not just her husband, but even his family. Although it was the folks in the big house at the end of the Mall who had conferred the position and substantive titles on her, one was reminded of Jack Kennedy (*qv*), who when visiting France with his wife in 1961 told the Paris Press Club 'I am the man who accompanied Jacqueline Kennedy to Paris ...'

When Diana posed in front of the Taj Mahal for her famous 1992 statement to the world that her marriage was over, all the more telling because it was pictorial rather than textual, it was the Taj Mahal that fell into the background. Like Norma Desmond, she was big; it was royals, and royal palaces, that got small.

• Context of speech

In January 1997 Diana went to Angola, where a civil war had been crackling away for nearly a quarter of a century, causing by its end in 2002 some 500,000 deaths.

She was accompanied by a BBC film crew and, among a swarm of other journalists, the *Daily Telegraph*'s veteran columnist Lord ('Bill') Deedes. In Angola she was relatively unknown, so when she won admiration for her gestures of concern it had little to do with her status.

Once back in London she gave the speech excerpted below. Four months after her death on 31 August following, a ban on landmines was signed by 122 countries in Ottawa. By late 2005 signatory countries totalled 154, though China, India, Pakistan, Russia and the US (all, coincidentally or otherwise, nuclear powers) were not among them.

66 **The mine is a stealthy killer. Long after conflict is ended, its innocent victims die or are wounded singly, in countries of which we hear little. Their lonely fate is never reported. The world, with its many other preoccupations, remains largely unmoved by a death roll of something like 800 people every month ... Those who are not killed outright — and they number**

another 1,200 a month — suffer terrible injuries and are handicapped for life.

I was in Angola in January with the British Red Cross — a country where there are 15 million landmines in a population ... of 10 million ... Some people chose to interpret my visit as a political statement. But it was not. I am not a political figure. As I said at the time, ... my interests are humanitarian ... During my days in Angola, I saw at first hand three aspects of this scourge. In the hospitals of Luanda, the capital, and Huambo, scene of bitter fighting not long ago, I visited some of the mine victims who had survived, and saw their injuries.

I am not going to describe them, because in my experience it turns too many people away from the subject. Suffice to say, that when you look at the mangled bodies, some of them children, caught by these mines, you marvel at their survival. What is so cruel about these injuries is that they are almost invariably suffered where medical resources are scarce ...

This emergency medical care, moreover, is only the first step back to a sort of life. For those whose living is the land, loss of an arm or leg is an overwhelming handicap which lasts for life ...

Angola is full of refugees ... The refugee turns towards home, often ignorant of conditions in his homeland. He knows of mines, but homeward bound, eagerness to complete the journey gets the better of him. Or he finds mines on what was once his land, and attempts to clear them ... These mines inflict most of their casualties on people who are trying to meet the elementary needs of life. They strike the wife, or the grandmother, gathering firewood for cooking. They ambush the child sent to collect water for the family ...

There are said to be around 110 million mines lurking somewhere in the world. And over a third of them are to be found in Africa ...

Even if the world decided tomorrow to ban these weapons, this terrible legacy of mines already in the earth would continue to plague the poor nations of the Globe ...

One of my objectives in visiting Angola was to forward the cause of those, like the Red Cross, striving in the name of humanity to secure an international ban on these weapons ...

But for this generation in much of the developing world, there will be no relief, no relaxation ... mines cast a constant shadow ... Resettlement of refugees is made more hazardous. Good land is put out of bounds. Recovery from war is delayed. Aid workers themselves are put at risk. I would like to see more done for those living in this 'no man's land' ... between the wrongs of yesterday and the urgent needs of today ... "

'The People's Princess'

(An)T(h)ony Charles Lynton Blair (1953–)
Trimdon, Co. Durham
1 September 1997 _____

• Biography

It is too early to say whether Blair was the worst prime minister of modern times — say the two centuries since Addington, Pitt the Younger's (*qv*) successor. But he was undoubtedly the most disappointing, perhaps of all time. For in ten years, with hefty parliamentary majorities and a feeble Opposition, he notched up just one-and-a-half real achievements: freeing interest rates from government control and — so far — a solid-looking settlement in Northern Ireland.

The other achievements conceded him even by hostile press commentators, namely city academies and early improvement in primary schools (not, however, sustained), must be set against the entire field of education. There they are dwarfed by entrance qualifications abased to near dunce level, curricula 'trendified' to the point of incoherence, test questions pared down to pub quiz reductionism and exam passes scattered like confetti. This is Caucus Race teaching, where everyone gets a prize for fear of hurt feelings otherwise.

The positive demerits of Blair's premiership abound: mercenary malleability (notably withdrawing a ban on tobacco sponsorship in motor-racing following a hefty payment to party funds); cronyism (jobs to old flatmates); personal mendacity (his own Chancellor, Gordon Brown (*qv*), in 2004 said he could not now believe anything Blair might say); obsequiousness towards President Bush's (*qv*) foreign policy (even if one generously concedes that the actual justice of the Iraq War is debatable); inadequately supplying the troops he sent on campaign (bad boots, skimped equipment maintenance); and obsession with meeting paper targets at the expense of solid performance (crime reduction, surgical operations), said targets being jiggled to accommodate tardy or simply inadequate execution.

To the accusation that Blair brought about the greatest encroachment on personal liberty since emergency laws in both world wars, the only defence is that his administration was too incompetent to be capable of so complex a task. But he presided over it (both the encroachment and the incompetence). As regards his 'presidential' style of governing, the sidelining of Parliament had already been set in train by EC legislation. But he also politicised the civil service, or ignored it in favour of getting chums like Lord Levy to implement policy. Then there were his questionable methods of funding his party, again involving Lord Levy. The latter's qualifications for conducting Middle East peace negotiations were not immediately apparent ever, but still less so if he was likely to take time off to rattle the collecting box. All this was so far from 'New' Labour, or indeed anything else modern, that it harked back to the 18th century, when jobbery, placemen, patronage and kinship networks were the rule.

The one thing truly modern was Blair's communication technique. He relied on journalists and their methods: press release, *démenti*, leak, monitoring of opponents' statements, swift rebuttal of criticism, briefing, counter-briefing, distracting attention from bad results by media stunts. Parliamentary debate to endorse his plans he often sidestepped. Instead, he elevated the fourth estate to first place. But journalists are no better at running a country than politicians are at writing readable prose.

• Context of speech

Four months into his premiership, Blair had to cope with the death of Diana (*qv*), being woken up in the middle of the night to digest the news while weekending in his constituency of Sedgefield, Co. Durham. He was at first uncertain as to whether it was his place to make any statement at all. But the Queen (*see* Elizabeth II) told him that no member of the Royal Family was planning to. This colossal misjudgement, along with the Queen's protocol quibble of refusing initially to fly the Buckingham Palace flag at half-mast, for a moment looked like dealing the monarchy a blow it would never recover from.

Blair jotted down suitable phrases for a speech on scraps of paper, only assembling them into a coherent whole 20 minutes before delivery. This curiously *ad hoc* process over a prime minister's speech on a royal crisis had occurred before with Baldwin (*qv*) at the time of the Abdication.

The phrase 'the People's Princess' was originally thought to have been dreamt up by Alastair Campbell, Blair's Press Secretary and *éminence grise*. Recently Blair himself has claimed authorship.

"**I am utterly devastated. The whole of our country, all of us, will be in a state of shock and mourning. Diana was a wonderful, warm and compassionate person who people, not just in Britain, but throughout the world, loved and will mourn as a friend. Our thoughts and prayers are with her family, in particular with her two sons, and with all of the families bereaved in this quite appalling tragedy.**

I feel like everyone else in this country today — utterly devastated. Our thoughts and prayers are with Princess Diana's family — in particular her two sons, two boys — our hearts go out to them. We are today a nation, in Britain, in a state of shock, in mourning, in grief that is so deeply painful for us.

She was a wonderful and warm human being. Though her own life was often sadly touched by tragedy, she touched the lives of so many others in Britain — throughout the world — with joy and with comfort. How many times shall we remember her, in how many different ways, with the sick, the dying, with children, with the needy, when, with just a look or a gesture that spoke so much more than words, she would reveal to all of us the depth of her compassion and her humanity.

How difficult things were for her from time to time, surely we can only guess at — but the people everywhere, not just here in Britain but everywhere, they kept faith with Princess Diana, they liked her, they loved her, they regarded her as one of the people.

She was the People's Princess and that's how she will stay, how she will remain in our hearts and in our memories forever ...

She seemed full of happiness, full of life, she was great fun to be with and she was an unusual but a really warm character and personality and I will remember her personally with very great affection. I think the whole country will remember her with the deepest affection and love and that is why our grief is so deep today. Thank you.

I should say to you I have already spoken to The Queen and the Prince of Wales."

Valedictory

Trimdon Labour Club, Sedgefield, Co. Durham
10 May 2007

• Context of speech

On the same date in May on which Churchill (*qv*) became Prime Minister Blair gave his farewell speech. The turn-out, a predominantly elderly one, totalled a little over a hundred. He came down to earth from the heavens in an executive jet and after the speech re-ascended into them, like the *deus ex machina* of classical drama. One reporter (from the *Daily Telegraph*) thought he seemed close to tears. Another (from the *Daily Mail*) recorded his lip as quivering.

The speech, with its fuzzy logic, absurdities ('give the impossible a go'), almost petulant insistence on his own righteousness, mild religiosity, condescension to tradition (including the tradition of his own party) and elevation of conviction above reasoning, perfectly illustrates Tony Blair's inadequacies. Early in his premiership the *Spectator* called him a snake oil salesman. Revivalist preacher would have been closer to the mark. He converted many, but pulling off the hard bit, the Second Coming, was beyond him.

> "**There is a judgment to be made on my premiership. And in the end that is for you, the people, to make** …
>
> Now in 2007, you can easily point to the challenges, the things that are wrong, the grievances that fester.
>
> But go back to 1997. Think back. No, really, think back. Think about your own living standards then in May 1997 and now …
>
> There is only one government since 1945 that can say all of the following: 'More jobs, fewer unemployed, better health and education results, lower crime and economic growth in every quarter' — this one.
>
> But I don't need a statistic. There is something bigger than what can be measured in waiting lists or GSCE results or the latest crime or jobs figures …
>
> This is a country today that for all its faults, for all the myriad of unresolved problems and fresh challenges, is comfortable in the 21st century, at home in its own skin, able not just to be proud of its past but confident of its future.

I don't think Northern Ireland would have been changed unless Britain had changed, or the Olympics won if we were still the Britain of 1997.

As for my own leadership, ... right at the outset one thing was clear to me. Without the Labour Party allowing me to lead it, nothing could ever have been done.

But I knew my duty was to put the country first ...

What I had to learn, however, as prime minister was what putting the country first really meant. Decision-making is hard. Everyone always says: 'Listen to the people.' The trouble is they don't always agree ...

In government, you have to give the answer — not *an* answer, *the* answer. And, in time, you realise putting the country first doesn't mean doing the right thing according to conventional wisdom or the prevailing consensus or the latest snapshot of opinion.

It means doing what you genuinely believe to be right. Your duty is to act according to your conviction ...

Sometimes, as with the completely unexpected, you are alone with your own instinct ... some things I knew I would be dealing with. Some I thought I might be. Some never occurred to me on that morning of 2 May 1997 when I came into Downing Street for the first time.

Great expectations not fulfilled in every part, for sure. Occasionally people say, as I said earlier, 'They were too high, you should have lowered them.'

But, to be frank, I would not have wanted it any other way. I was, and remain, as a person and as a prime minister, an optimist. Politics may be the art of the possible — but at least in life, give the impossible a go.

So of course the vision is painted in the colours of the rainbow, and the reality is sketched in the duller tones of black, white and grey. But I ask you to accept one thing. Hand on heart, I did what I thought was right.

I may have been wrong. That is your call. But believe one thing if nothing else. I did what I thought was right for our country ...

The British are special. The world knows it. In our innermost thoughts, we know it. This is the greatest nation on earth.

It has been an honour to serve it. I give my thanks to you, the British people, for the times I have succeeded, and my apologies to you for the times I have fallen short. Good luck."

Funeral speech on Diana

Charles Edward Maurice Spencer
9th Earl Spencer (1964–)
Westminster Abbey
6 September 1997

• Biography

There has long been a convention that funeral speeches say *'de mortuis nil nisi bonum'*, or 'nothing about the dead other than what is nice'. Thus the panegyric in Europe (*see* Pericles) and the eulogy in America. With obituaries, there is a recent tendency to mention the subject's 'warts', and as a result they have become not just more truthful but a lot more interesting. Lord Spencer's contribution to this trend was in 1997 to give the funeral oration itself more bite, with an open attack on the media and a veiled one on the Royal Family.

This went beyond Marc Antony's (*qv*) undermining Brutus and the other conspirators. The Royal Family sat before Spencer as he spoke, down among the congregation. They could no more get up and leave Westminster Abbey than could the dead princess vacate her coffin. It was a reminder that Spencer's illustrious ancestor John Duke of Marlborough, a biography of whom he has written, was no great respecter of royalty either, first deserting James II then intriguing against James's successor, William III, and with none other than James, by now an exile.

• Context of speech

Diana's funeral was held on 6 September 1997. London was sombre that day, though the sun shone. Four million people are said to have descended on the capital (other sources say one million). One million of them lined the route the cortège took from Kensington Palace before the funeral and thousands assembled in and around Parliament Square for the funeral itself, which was held in Westminster Abbey.

After Elton (now Sir Elton) John performed a recycled 1973 pop song of his, 'Candle in the Wind', what sounded like far-off rain was heard by the congregation in the Abbey. It was the crowd outside applauding. Some inside the Abbey started applauding too, but soon stopped. Then Spencer spoke.

Afterwards, there was more applause, this time general both inside and outside the Abbey. Princes William and Harry joined in. Even the Prince of Wales was observed patting his thigh in a typically diffident gesture of muted approval. Clapping in churches had once been 'not done'. Another remnant of protocol was being breached by the dead princess in her coffin (*see* also Blair).

Journalists covering the event reported that support for Spencer among the crowds was overwhelming, despite his hit at the Royal Family. The Queen (*see* Elizabeth II) was said to be 'disappointed' by Spencer's not paying more tribute to Diana's faith, gifts and achievements. The disappointment was interpreted by some journalists as anger.

Spencer claims he composed the speech in two hours, and, more bizarrely, that on giving a read-through of it to his sister's coffin well before the funeral, he heard a whisper of satisfaction from the coffin. When delivering it at the funeral he spoke at first directly to the occupant of the coffin, only later addressing the congregation.

66 **Today is our chance to say thank you for the way you brightened our lives, even though God granted you but half a life** ...

There is a temptation to rush to canonise your memory. There is no need to do so. You stand tall enough as a human being of unique qualities not to need to be seen as a saint. Indeed to sanctify your memory would be to miss out on the very core of your being, your wonderfully mischievous sense of humour, with a laugh that bent you double.

... But your greatest gift was your intuition ... This is what underpinned all your other wonderful attributes. And if we look to analyse what it was about you that had such a wide appeal, we find it in your instinctive feel for what was really important ...

Diana explained to me once that it was her innermost feelings of suffering that made it possible for her to connect with her constituency of the rejected ...

For all the status, the glamour, the applause, Diana remained throughout a very insecure person at heart, almost childlike in her desire to do good for others so she could release herself from deep feelings of unworthiness of which her eating disorders were merely a symptom.

... The last time I saw Diana was on July the First, her birthday, in London, when, typically, she was not taking time out to celebrate her special day with friends, but was guest of honour at a special charity fundraising evening. She sparkled, of course, but I would rather cherish the days I spent with her in March, when she came to visit me and my children at our home in South Africa. I am proud that, apart from when she was on display meeting President Mandela [*qv*], we managed to … stop the … paparazzi from getting a single picture of her. That meant a lot to her.

Those were days I will always treasure. It was as if we had been transported back to our childhood when we spent such an enormous amount of time together — the two youngest in the family.

Fundamentally she had not changed at all from the big sister who mothered me as a baby, fought with me at school and endured those long train journeys between our parents' homes with me at weekends.

… There is no doubt that she was looking for a new direction in her life at this time. She talked endlessly of getting away from England, mainly because of the treatment that she received at the hands of the newspapers …

She would want us today to pledge ourselves to protecting her beloved boys William and Harry from a similar fate, and I do this here Diana on your behalf. We will not allow them to suffer the anguish that used regularly to drive you to tearful despair.

And beyond that, on behalf of your mother and sisters, I pledge that we, your blood family, will do all we can to continue the imaginative way in which you were steering these two exceptional young men so that their souls are not simply immersed by duty and tradition, but can sing openly as you planned …

William and Harry, we all care desperately for you today. We are all chewed up with the sadness at the loss of a woman who was not even our mother. How great your suffering is, we cannot even imagine.

I would like to end by thanking God for the small mercies he has shown us at this dreadful time. For taking Diana at her most beautiful and radiant and when she had joy in her private life. Above all, we give thanks for the life of a woman I am so proud to be able to call my sister, the unique, the complex, the extraordinary and irreplaceable Diana, whose beauty, both internal and external, will never be extinguished from our minds."

On the centenary of Australia's federation

John Winston Howard (1939–)
Australian House of Representatives,
Melbourne
10 May 2001

• Biography

The last three British Prime Ministers (Major, Blair (*qv*) and Brown (*qv*)) got there respectively after only 11 years in Parliament, no years in any office and ten years in high office but none in any lower one. John Howard in Australia is a reminder that such rapid progress to the top is unusual. On the other hand his apprenticeship in junior posts has been an exceptionally long one.

Originally a suburban solicitor, and always mindful of both the importance and vulnerability of small businesses, Howard entered the Australian House of Representatives in 1974. He was made Minister for Business and Consumer Affairs the very next year and moved up to Cabinet rank as Treasurer (equivalent to Chancellor of the Exchequer in Britain) two years after that. His party affiliations he recounts in the speech excerpted below.

After becoming Prime Minister in 1996 he cut government debt, sold off state-owned industries, restricted trade union power, introduced a tax on consumption and curbed firearms ownership, the last measure following the massacre of no fewer than 35 victims by a gun-toting maniac in Tasmania.

Although himself a monarchist, Howard recognised the force of republican sentiment in Australia and in 1998 initiated a debate over it.

• Context of speech

Australia became independent of Britain in 1901. On the occasion of the Centenary of Federation sitting of the Australian House of Representatives, Howard addressed it. His reputation in Parliament is as a debater rather than deliverer of set-piece speeches. Not surprisingly, since in the excerpt below the only time he comes alive is in reaction to hecklers.

66 It is proper on an occasion such as this that all of us who have gathered in Melbourne have honoured the traditions of the two sides of politics from which we come. As it happened, the centenary of the first meeting of the federal parliamentary Labor caucus occurred on the eve of the centenary of the first sitting of the Commonwealth Parliament. I congratulate the Australian Labor Party on its 100 years of existence. I do not necessarily wish it unbounded goodwill for the future, but in that spirit of generosity [*here some of his audience interrupted him*] — gee, this is a lot cosier, Mr Speaker — in this spirit of generosity that ought to pervade [*sic*] on an occasion like this, I do congratulate it on lasting 100 years. I will say no more about the future.**

Might I also take the opportunity to record my deep pride and admiration for the contribution made to the life of this nation by the party that I am proud to lead, the Liberal Party of Australia, founded by the great Robert Gordon Menzies [*qv*], who went on to become the longest serving Prime Minister in Australia's history. I record its contribution and I record the contribution also made by the National Party of Australia and by its predecessors the National Country Party and the Country Party — essentially the same manifestation — and in that the great contribution that both of those parties have made to representing the people of rural and regional Australia …

All history in a way is something of a judgment of good against evil, of triumph versus failure; but, if you look at the balance sheet of Australian history especially over the last 100 years, it has been one of great progress, of heroic achievement, of great democratic institutions and of a great open-hearted people who have been prepared to risk and to give all to defend what they hold dear. We have built in this nation of ours a society of which we can all be justly proud, a society to which people from all around the world have contributed, a society which is a model of cohesion, compassion and decency and one in which we should express undiminished faith and hope for the next 100 years."

To troops about to invade Iraq

Tim Collins (1960–)
Fort Blair Mayne, Northern Kuwait
19 March 2003 _____

• Biography

Has any single speech outside politics won such fame for its deliverer, so swiftly and with such dramatic results for his career, as with Tim Collins? Its dissemination around the world was due to the press, which was later to try and crucify Collins (though not, be it said, in the same newspaper).

Collins, of mixed Dubliner and Belfast Presbyterian parentage, first joined the Royal Signals, did a stint with the SAS (Special Air Service) and was then made commanding officer of 1 R Irish (the 1st Battalion Royal Irish Regiment).

In May 2003, two months after the speech below, Collins was charged with atrocities while in Iraq. He was later cleared and won libel actions against two Sunday newspapers, to whom officialdom had leaked details of the Army internal inquiry. Collins left the Army in disgust in 2004. He has subsequently made a living as a journalist, author and public speaker.

• Context of speech

On 19 March 2003 he addressed about 800 soldiers of his regiment, part of the forces about to invade Iraq. He spoke off the cuff, without even notes. Through Sarah Oliver, of the *Mail on Sunday*, he became a national, perhaps even world, figure. George W. Bush (*qv*) is said to have a copy of the speech mounted on his office wall.

> **66 W**e go to liberate, not to conquer. We will not fly our flags in their country. We are entering Iraq to free a people and the only flag which will be flown in that ancient land is their own. Show respect for them.

There are some who are alive at this moment who will not be alive shortly. Those who do not wish to go on that journey, we will not send. As for the others, I expect you to rock their world. Wipe them out if that is what they choose. But if you are ferocious in battle, remember to be magnanimous in victory.

Iraq is steeped in history. It is the site of the Garden of Eden, of the Great Flood and the birthplace of Abraham. Tread lightly there.

You will see things that no man could pay to see — and you will have to go a long way to find a more decent, generous and upright people than the Iraqis. You will be embarrassed by their hospitality, even though they have nothing.

Don't treat them as refugees, for they are in their own country. Their children will be poor. In years to come they will know that the light of liberation in their lives was brought by you.

If there are casualties of war, then remember that when they woke up and got dressed in the morning they did not plan to die this day. Allow them dignity in death. Bury them properly and mark their graves.

It is my foremost intention to bring every single one of you out alive. But there may be people among us who will not see the end of this campaign. We will put them in their sleeping bags and send them back. There will be no time for sorrow.

The enemy should be in no doubt that we are his nemesis and that we are bringing about his rightful destruction. There are many regional commanders who have stains on their souls and they are stoking the fires of hell for Saddam. He and his forces will be destroyed by this coalition for what they have done. As they die, they will know their deeds have brought them to this place. Show them no pity.

It is a big step to take another human life. It is not to be done lightly. I know of men who have taken life needlessly in other conflicts. I can assure you they live with the mark of Cain upon them.

If someone surrenders to you, then remember they have that right in international law and ensure that one day they go home to their family. The ones who wish to fight, well, we aim to please.

If you harm the regiment or its history by over-enthusiasm in killing or in cowardice, know it is your family who will suffer. You will be shunned, unless your conduct is of the highest — for your deeds will follow you down through history. We will bring shame on neither our uniform or our nation.

[referring to Saddam Hussein's biological and chemical weapons] It is not a question of if, it's a question of when. We know he has already devolved the decision to lower commanders, and that means he has already taken the decision himself. If we survive the first strike, we will survive the attack.

As for ourselves, let's bring everyone home and leave Iraq a better place for us having been there. Our business now is north."

'Axis of Evil'

George Walker Bush (1946–)
43rd President of the USA 2001–
State of the Union address to the US Congress
29 January 2002

• Biography

Many US presidents have been related to each other, though often pretty remotely. The presidency is now getting positively dynastic, first with a father–son succession, currently with the possibility of a husband–wife one (*see* Hillary Clinton). The father and son are George Herbert Walker Bush, President 1989–93, and his second son, another George — 'Dubya' as he is known, and as it will be handier to call him to avoid confusion.

Dubya barely won the 2000 presidential election, and then only because he took Florida, which his brother Jeb governed and where incompletely processed voting slips further tainted his victory. Accordingly his presidency started on a somewhat partisan note, much as it looks like ending. On the following 11th of September terrorists spectacularly destroyed the World Trade Center in New York. Known, from America's expressing dates month-first, as '9/11' (and coincidentally the national emergency phone number there), the episode dominated Dubya's entire presidency.

Though Iraq's involvement in 9/11 was uncertain, he successfully invaded it in 2003, toppling its repellent dictator Saddam Hussein. He then got stuck, unable to control the country, while corruption there swallowed $9 billion of US aid money. If he withdrew, US prestige suffered and the Middle East became even more unstable. If he sent more troops, he risked antagonising American public opinion, which was increasingly against the venture.

Iraq, doubling of the national debt and the Senate's blocking Bush's Bill to give America's 12 million or so illegal immigrants citizenship have led to charges that Bush is the worst President ever. His forging good relations with India is a plus, however. His attempts, though frustrated by his own party's senators, to legalise kangaroo military tribunals and torture of prisoners of war have disgusted even conservatives. The chief victim of all this politically is brother Jeb, otherwise the Republicans' ideal presidential candidate in 2008. The beneficiaries look likely to be Giuliani (*qv*) directly, and indirectly Hillary Clinton or Obama (*qv*) if Giuliani cannot beat whichever of them is the Democratic candidate.

• Context of speech

Bush was notably inarticulate in campaigning during the 2000 presidential election. Catachreses tumbled from his lips almost as readily as in Britain with Tony Blair's (*qv*) in-house clown and nominal Number Two, John Prescott. Having won the election, Bush improved, even before Inauguration. Was his pre-poll tongue-tied state just nerves, then? Conceivably. More probably he sensed that Americans mistrust fluency. (In the 1997 movie *The Devil's Advocate*, Al Pacino gives the game away that he is Satan by his command of foreign languages; nowhere but in America could the cloven hoof take polyglot form.)

Once President, Bush relied increasingly on the best speech-writer in the business: Michael Gerson. He is said to have used Gerson's talents before becoming President, but if so the best was yet to come. Gerson coined the 'Axis of Evil' tag quoted below. Gerson left Bush's employ in mid-2006. Bush's stock has been plummeting ever since.

66 **North Korea is a regime arming with missiles and weapons of mass destruction, while starving its citizens.** Iran aggressively pursues these weapons and exports terror, while an unelected few repress the Iranian people's hope for freedom.

Iraq continues to flaunt its hostility toward America and to support terror…This is a regime that has already used poison gas to murder thousands of its own citizens, leaving the bodies of mothers huddled over their dead children. This is a regime that agreed to international inspections then kicked out the inspectors. This is a regime that has something to hide from the civilized world.

States like these, and their terrorist allies, constitute an axis of evil, arming to threaten the peace of the world. By seeking weapons of mass destruction, these regimes pose a grave and growing danger. They could provide these arms to terrorists, giving them the means to match their hatred…

We will work…to deny terrorists and their state sponsors the materials, technology and expertise to make and deliver weapons of mass destruction…

We'll be deliberate, yet time is not on our side. I will not wait on events while dangers gather. I will not stand by as peril draws closer and closer. The

United States of America will not permit the world's most dangerous regimes to threaten us with the world's most destructive weapons.

Our war on terror is well begun, but it is only begun. This campaign may not be finished on our watch, yet it must be and it will be waged on our watch...

If we stopped now, leaving terror camps intact and terror states unchecked, our sense of security would be false ... History has called America and our allies to action, and it is both our responsibility and our privilege to fight freedom's fight.

Our first priority must always be the security of our nation ... My budget supports three great goals for America: we will win this war, we will protect our homeland, and we will revive our economy.

September 11 brought out the best in America and the best in this Congress...Now Americans deserve to have this same spirit directed toward addressing problems here at home.

I am a proud member of my party. Yet as we act to win the war, protect our people and create jobs in America, we must act first and foremost not as Republicans, not as Democrats, but as Americans.

It costs a lot to fight this war. We have spent more than a billion dollars a month — over $30 million a day — and we must be prepared for future operations...

Our men and women in uniform deserve the best weapons, the best equipment and the best training — and they also deserve another pay raise. My budget includes the largest increase in defense spending in two decades, because while the price of freedom and security is high, it is never too high. Whatever it costs to defend our country, we will pay ... "

'We have more work to do'

Barack Hussein Obama (1961–)
Keynote address at the Democratic
Convention, Boston
26–29 July 2004 _____

• Biography

Unlike Hillary Clinton (*qv*), his main rival for the 2008 Democratic presidential
nomination, Obama opposed the Iraq war back in 2002, when he was an Illinois state
senator. In 2006 he became US Senator from Illinois. He sketches his background in
the speech excerpted below. In addition, he studied at Harvard Law School then
worked as a Chicago civil rights lawyer and academic before entering politics.

He is a cannier campaigner than the speech's wholesome vision suggests. Early
in 2007, he said he saw Hillary as ally rather than competitor – this after her camp
felt obliged to deny originating the lie that Obama once attended a radical Islamic
school. A Hillary-supporter admitted that nobody wanted to be seen attacking
Obama just then. Obama thus triumphed three ways: cleared of the Islamic 'slur' and
patently 'nicer' than Hillary, who may have authorised the 'slur' anyway. (Or maybe
Insight, the right-wing periodical that published the story, traded on Hillary's
reputation and set her up.)

As the 2007 spring turned to summer, however, Obama's relatively slack grasp
of public policy hampered his challenging Hillary in the opinion polls. Both did well
in celebrity endorsements. Just as medieval claimants to a throne sought
ecclesiastical support, so now a presidential hopeful needs the blessing of Hollywood,
which virtually constitutes an extra pillar of the Constitution, up there with the
Supreme Court and Electoral College. Conversely Obama could not immediately win
black activists' endorsements, and even when he did, only drew level with Hillary in
that regard. Unkind commentators ascribed this to jealousy by older black activists
towards the new kid, who in any case is the product of voluntary immigration to
America, not the fettered kind their ancestors underwent centuries ago.

• Context of speech

Delivered in 2004 just after the Democrats had chosen John Kerry as their presidential candidate, the speech excerpted below made Obama a national figure. In the run-up to the 2008 election he has continued to stress his similarity, in lack of experience, to Lincoln (*qv*), thus turning a handicap into an advantage. In his second book of autobiography he calls his style of communicating sometimes 'rambling, hesitant and overly verbose', apparently unaware that 'verbose' means overly stuffed with words already. His voice has been described variously as a 'sombre' and as a 'conversational' baritone.

66 **On behalf of the great state of Illinois — crossroads of a nation, land of Lincoln, let me express my deep gratitude for the privilege of addressing this convention. Tonight is a particular honor for me because, let's face it, my presence on this stage is pretty unlikely.**

My father was … born and raised in a small village in Kenya. He grew up herding goats, went to school in a tin-roof shack …

Through hard work and perseverance my father got a scholarship to study in a magical place, America …

While studying here my father met my mother …

Her father worked on oil rigs and farms through most of the Depression. The day after Pearl Harbor, my grandfather signed up … , joined Patton's [*qv*] army, marched across Europe. Back home my grandmother raised a baby and went to work on a bomber assembly line. After the war, they … moved … to Hawaii, in search of opportunity …

My parents … would give me an African name, Barack, or 'blessed', believing that in a tolerant America your name is no barrier to success …

And I stand here today grateful for the diversity of my heritage …

I stand here knowing that … in no other country on earth is my story even possible.

Tonight, we gather to affirm the greatness of our nation … ; our pride is … summed up in a declaration made over 200 years ago: 'We hold … that all men are created equal … that they are endowed … with certain inalienable rights, that among these are life, liberty and the pursuit of happiness.'

That is the true genius of America, a faith … that we can tuck in our children at night and know that they are fed and clothed and safe from harm; that we can say what we think, write what we think, without hearing a sudden knock on the door; that we can have an idea and start our own business without paying a bribe; that we can participate in the political process without fear of retribution; and that our votes will be counted – or at least, most of the time.

This year, in this election, we are called to reaffirm our values ...

And fellow Americans, Democrats, Republicans, independents, I say to you tonight, we have more work to do ...

Now, don't get me wrong, the people I meet in small towns and big cities and diners and office parks, they don't expect government to solve all of their problems. They know they have to work hard to get ahead ...

Go into any inner-city neighborhood, and folks will tell you that government alone can't teach kids to learn.

They know that parents have to teach, that children can't achieve unless we ... turn off the television sets and eradicate the slander that says a black youth with a book is acting white ...

People don't expect ... government to solve all their problems. But they sense, deep in their bones, that with just a slight change in priorities, we can make sure that every child in America has a decent shot at life and that the doors of opportunity remain open to all. They know we can do better. And they want that choice ... alongside our famous individualism, there's another ingredient in the American saga, a belief that we are all connected as one people.

If there's a child on the south side of Chicago who can't read, that matters to me, even if it's not my child.

If there's a senior citizen somewhere who can't pay for their prescription and having to choose between medicine and the rent, that makes my life poorer, even if it's not my grandparent.

If there's an Arab-American family being rounded up without benefit of an attorney or due process, that threatens my civil liberties.

It is that fundamental belief ... I am my brother's keeper, I am my sister's keeper, that makes this country work ... "

At 2004 Republican Convention

Rudolph (Rudy) William Giuliani (1944–)
30 August 2004 _____

• Biography

Judging from opinion polls at the time of going to press, Giuliani remains the leading contender for the Republican presidential nomination in 2008, also the sole Republican who really might beat Hillary Clinton (*qv*). These two strengths would normally go together. But Republicans, increasingly faith-based rather than rational, do not always choose the strongest candidate, more the one they feel cosiest with.

They find Giuliani liberal. He's pro-gun control. He accepts abortion and homosexual marriage. He's on his third wife, having dumped his second very publicly as part of a press conference. True, his marriage to his first wife was annulled, she being a cousin; technically, his third's really his second. But evangelicals don't cotton to annulment; it's a Catholic thing, and young Rudy was not just a choir boy (with 'soprano' relatives, according to one biography), he nearly became a priest.

In a February 2007 opinion poll, otherwise suitable presidential candidates who were in their third marriage proved only marginally less unpopular than atheists, homosexuals and septuagenarians and less popular than Mormons, women, Jews, blacks and Catholics in that order. This is a pity, since Giuliani has that ability, rare among politicians, to rib himself. When his 'third' wife was criticised, he told her attackers in spring 2007 to 'show a little decency', adding 'There's plenty to attack me about. Please do it' and observing that his wife was 'a civilian, to use the old Mafia distinction.'

Rudy Giuliani trained as a lawyer. He later took law posts in Washington under Presidents Ford and Reagan (*qv*), the latter of whom he has praised extensively in his 2007 campaigning while barely mentioning President Bush (*qv*). He then returned to New York, his birthplace, and became Mayor, the first Republican to control Gotham since John Lindsay in the 1960s. He slashed crime rates by 57 or 64 percent (accounts differ) — and murder ones by a whopping 67 or 70 percent (accounts differ there too). His big break came with the 9/11 World Trade Center destruction in 2001. Bush was initially nowhere to be seen. Giuliani took centre stage, exuded authority, and in so doing put down his marker for the White House.

• Context of speech

The excerpt below was part of Giuliani's address to the Republican National Convention in New York on 30 August 2004.

" **I remember — I remember the days following September 11th when we were no longer Republicans or Democrats, but we were Americans. We were determined to do everything, everything that we could to help the victims, to rebuild our city and to disable our enemies.**

I remember President Bush coming here on September 14, 2001, and lifting the morale of our rescue workers by talking with them and embracing them and staying with them much longer than was planned.

In fact — in fact, if you promise to keep this between us — because, I mean, I could get in trouble for this. But I get in trouble all of the time. I was Mayor of New York. It is my opinion that when President Bush came here on September 14, 2001, the Secret Service was not really happy about his remaining in the area so long. With buildings were still unstable, with fires raging below ground of 2,000 degrees or more, there was good reason for their concern.

Well, the President remained there. And talked to everyone, to the firefighters, to the police officers, the health care workers, the clergy. But the people that I believe — this is my opinion now from observing it — that the people that spent the most time with him were our construction workers.

Now, New York construction workers are very special people. I'm sure this is true all over America where you come from, but I know the ones in New York really well. And they were real heroes that day, like many others.

But I have to tell you, they're big. They are really big. They have arms that are bigger than my legs. And they have opinions that are bigger than their arms.

So every time the President would go up to one of them, they would hold his hand a little bit longer. And they would give him advice. I think like his Cabinet, Mr Vice President, gives him advice.

They would like tell him in their own language exactly what he should do with the terrorists.

I can't repeat — after all, this is the Republican Convention. I can't repeat what they said, but one of them really got the President's attention. The President really bonded with him. They sort of hit it off. And the guy's giving him this long explanation of exactly what he should do. And when the man finished, President Bush said in a rather loud voice, 'I agree.'

At this point, all of the people kind of looked at this guy, all of his buddies. And can you imagine — I mean, you're a construction worker, and all your buddies say — and the President says, 'I agree.'

The guy went up in his own estimation from his 6 feet to about 6' 10. He lost total control of himself. Forgot who he was dealing with. He leaned over. He grabbed the President of the United States in this massive bear hug, and he started squeezing him.

And the Secret Service agent standing next to me, who wasn't happy about any of this, instead of running over and getting the President out of this grip, puts his finger in my face and he says to me 'If this guy hurts the President, Giuliani, you're finished.'

I didn't know what to say. I was kind of shook when the — and I said — the only thing I could think of, and it's the moral of the story, I said 'But it would be out of love.' … "

On abortion

Hillary Rodham Clinton (*née* Rodham, later Hillary Clinton; 1947–)
To New York State Family Planning Providers
24 January 2005

• Biography

The loathing women politicians generate has been mentioned already (*see* Margaret Thatcher). It may arise from misogyny, though the worst misogynists can be women.

It may arise from the difficulty women in positions of power have in emanating authority rather than bossiness.

With Hillary Clinton there is also her personality. It comes across as cold, self-righteous, rancorous and excessively insincere, even for a politician. Her exaggerated facial contortions alone suggest falsity. Even when she tries to be ingratiating she grates. Take her recently adopted faux cornpone accent when campaigning below the Mason-Dixon Line, as if reprising Hattie McDaniel's 'Mammy' in *Gone with the Wind.* This is either embarrassing or offensively patronising, depending on your ethnicity.

Americans have already endured eight years of Hillary in the White House, but without the privilege of voting her there. For the Clintons' 1992 sales pitch, 'buy one, get one free', cut both ways. One could envisage exasperated Democrats saying 'we may have voted for Bill, but in spite of, not because of, Hill.' Republicans and Ross Perot-supporters didn't even have that consolation.

Then there is the question of how much Hillary was involved in husband Bill's iniquities – or committed her own. Take the shady Whitewater development in Arkansas, over which, plus missing billing records from her law firm, she feared she might be indicted. There was Hillary's alleged hiring of Jerry Parks, an Arkansas gumshoe, to snoop on Bill with a view to divorce proceedings should he duck a presidential bid in 1992. Parks was later murdered. Coincidence?

Once in the White House, Hillary botched the clean-up of its Travel Office, America's healthcare overhaul and even meat-and-potatoes tasks like entertaining efficiently. And not through stupidity, for she is bright, but through lack of judgement — the quality a president needs above all. It's all very well sarcastically saying you could have stayed home and baked cookies, provided you're a healthcare wizard in lieu. If you're not, but you can't organise a cookie cookout either, you're pretty darn useless.

Hillary's spokesmen retort that she has learnt from her mistakes. Well she's 60 this year. Isn't that a bit late to get things right? This is all subjective stuff, however. More damaging professionally, since she's now a Senator, is the charge that she voted for invading Iraq in 2002, when it was popular, but is desperately backtracking now it's not.

Her line goes 'if we knew then what we know now ... I wouldn't have voted that way.' A recent book by two *New York Times* reporters alleges she never read the National Intelligence Estimate on Iraq before voting. Maybe she read it later. She certainly followed Barack Obama (*qv*) in voting against funding the troops there — but after dispatching them. So how would troops fare, sent there but unsupported? Luckily Hillary can work miracles. She made a $100,000 profit over cattle futures back in Arkansas. With skills like that, if she becomes President she could be her own Agriculture or Treasury Secretary.

• Context of speech

Abortion is one of the most divisive topics in America. The Right broadly deplores it, usually on religious grounds. The Left broadly defends it, on the grounds of 'a woman's right to choose'. Hillary used to be unequivocally pro-choice. Recently she sang a different tune:

> **I believe we can all recognize that abortion in many ways represents a sad, even tragic choice to many, many women ... This decision is a profound and complicated one; a difficult one, often the most difficult that a woman will ever make. The fact is that the best way to reduce the number of abortions is to reduce the number of unwanted pregnancies in the first place ...**

Now back when the National Campaign was getting off the ground, I actually came to New York City and gave a speech ... challenging the media to ... use its power to send strong, clear messages to teenagers to be responsible. Back then I used the phrase 'teenage celibacy' over and over. Of course, no one talks about 'teenage celibacy' anymore, but the message remains relevant and necessary today. I think it's a synonym for abstinence.

... Research shows that the primary reason that teenage girls abstain is because of their religious and moral values. We should embrace this — and support programs that reinforce the idea that abstinence at a young age is not just the smart thing to do, it is the right thing to do. But we should also recognize what works and what doesn't work, and to be fair, the jury is still out on the effectiveness of abstinence-only programs ...

Yes we do have deeply held differences of opinion about the issue of abortion. I for one respect those who believe with all their hearts and conscience that there are no circumstances under which any abortion should ever be available. But that does not represent even the majority opinion within the anti-abortion community .... Those in the pro-choice community who have fought so hard for so many years ... believe just as strongly the point of view based on experience and conscience that they have come to. The problem I always have is, what is the proper role of government in making this decision? ...

There is no reason why government cannot do more to educate and inform and provide assistance so that the choice guaranteed under our Constitution either does not ever have to be exercised or only in very rare circumstances. But we cannot expect to have the kind of positive results that all of us are hoping for to reduce the number of unwanted pregnancies and abortions if our government refuses to assist girls and women with their health care needs, a comprehensive education and accurate information.

So my hope now, today, is that whatever our disagreements with those in this debate, that we join together to take real action to improve the quality of health care for women and families, to reduce the number of abortions and to build a healthier, brighter more hopeful future for women and girls in our country and around the world ... "

Conservative leadership bid

David Cameron (1966–)
Conservative Party Conference, Blackpool
4 October 2005

• Biography

The topsy-turvy nature of modern British politics is nowhere better illustrated than in Cameron's career. Although quite possibly the next Prime Minister, this is despite the terrible handicap of education first at Eton then Oxford, where, as if his toff background wasn't bad enough already, he got caught on camera striking a proud pose in a Bullingdon Club tail coat. It has become one of the great images of arrogance of recent times, more striking, because Cameron in it shows snootier deportment, even than Prince Harry's Afrika Korps fancy dress *faux pas* in 2005.

But in today's Britain, which in this respect resembles Mao's (*qv*) Cultural Revolution China, a toff who purges himself of his blue blood through humiliation can get rehabilitated. Cameron has dutifully been photographed in eco-trainers refashioned from old fireman's trousers doing 'community' work, also in cycling helmet pedalling his green way to power. True, that a chauffeur-driven car has followed behind with his paperwork or second pair of shoes has not helped, though the media's calling it 'chauffeur-driven' is way below the belt. Would a driverless out-of-control vehicle have improved matters?

The topsy-turviness doesn't stop there. The physical handicap of Cameron's eldest son, which one would hesitate to mention except that Cameron himself lets it be known so often, is one of his strongest assets. For the 'I feel your pain' syndrome that Reagan (*qv*) touched on 20 years ago is now dominant. If you are unlucky enough to have no pain, people won't feel for you, so you appear 'out of touch' and — the final wickedness — un-caring.

Cameron's critics completely miss the point when they stress his lack of experience of the 'real world'. His past PR and television involvement *are* the real world, politically speaking. Menial occupations – hewing wood and drawing water – are for peasants in fairy tales.

For the Age of Enlightenment – in which Hans Christian Andersen and the Brothers Grimm disseminated said fairy tales – is over. The Age of Entitlement has replaced it. Here rights rise above duties, sentiment and self-absorption win out over sense and self-improvement.

• Context of speech

The speech excerpted below is what won Cameron the leadership when the actual contest took place. The Party under Michael Howard had diminished Blair's (*qv*) majority in the general election of May 2005. But it still lost, and for the third time running. Howard, its fourth leader in eight years, arranged a protracted two-month leadership campaign to succeed him that gave Cameron, his protégé, the optimum chance.

After the speech, which he delivered without notes, Cameron attended an obscure drinks function that would normally have attracted few. Suddenly it got crowded. Party members, and more importantly journalists, turned up in force to meet the new star. Few people could recall just what it was he had said. That, however, is modern power.

> ❝I joined this party because I love my country. I love our character. I love our people, our history, our role in the world. This is the only party that understands, and is proud of, what we have been and who we are.**
>
> I joined this party because I believe in freedom. We are the only party believing that if you give people freedom and responsibility, they will grow stronger and society will grow stronger.

I joined this party because I believe in aspiration. This party, the Conservative Party, is the only party that wants everybody to be a somebody — a doer, not a done-for ...

Everyone knows that our economy needs lower and simpler taxes. Who's standing in the way? The great tax-riser and complicator, Gordon Brown [qv].

Everyone knows that business needs deregulation to compete with China and India. Who is standing in the way? The great regulator and controller, Gordon Brown ...

There's one thing Gordon Brown fears more than anything else: a Conservative Party that has the courage to change. So let's give him the fright of his life.

There are some people who say all we've got to do is wait for the economy to hit the rocks, for Gordon Brown to be more leftwing than Blair [qv]; all we need is one more heave.

I think that's a pathetic way for a great party to behave. One more heave means one more defeat. I don't want to hang around and wait till something turns up. Do you?

Some say, hit Labour harder and the electorate will come to their senses. I say that's rubbish. People know that Labour have failed; they want to know how we will succeed. I don't want to let them down. Do you?

Some say that we should move to the right. I say that will turn us into a fringe party, never able to challenge for government again. I don't want to let that happen to this party. Do you?

We don't just need new policies or presentation or organisation, or even having a young, passionate, energetic leader — though come to think of it, that might not be such a bad idea.

We've got to recognise that we're in third place amongst under-35s, that we've lost support amongst women, that public servants no longer think we're on their side, that the people with aspirations who swept Margaret Thatcher to power have drifted away from our party ...

So let's build together a new generation of Conservatives. Let's switch a new generation on to Conservative ideas. Let's dream a new generation of Conservative dreams.

There is a new generation of social entrepreneurs tackling this country's most profound social problems.

There is a new generation of businessmen and women who are taking on the world, creating the wealth and opportunity for our future.

We can lead that new generation. We can be that new generation, changing our party to change our country. It will be an incredible journey. I want you to come with me ... "

Nobel Literature Prize acceptance

Harold Pinter (1930–)
Börssalen (video projection hall), Swedish
Academy, Stockholm
7 December 2005

• Biography

Until well into the 20th century a major speech in a serious play and a rousing one in politics were pretty similar: lofty language, high-flown appeals to noble sentiments, hyperbole and other tricks of rhetoric, solid construction and reasonable length. After World War II politicians at least paid lip service to this tradition, though in practice often descending to advertising copy journalese and intellectual sleight of hand.

'High-brow' drama, in Pinter's hands among others, but chiefly his, diverged much further. Tension was developed through misunderstood exchanges, implied rather than explicit plot developments, demotic dialogue shaped not by interlocutors but by the current speaker's train of thought, often a rambling or repetitive one. Even pauses. The last of these is Pinter's special trademark, though he skilfully deploys the others too.

He is not unmindful of the declamatory 'great tradition', though almost comically condescending about it. In a 2002 interview he said: '… language leads us … politically … into all sorts of fields. It's the rhetoric which does that, and sometimes it works. It works in the sense that when Churchill in the War said, "We will fight them on the …" you know, beaches and all that, I suppose the British public needed such a thing at the time, and it was quite useful — I suppose. I think it was.'

Comically? Yes, because although Pinter started as a very apolitical playwright, outflanked in public debate by the more engagé Angry Young Men, he is now so politically overwrought as to seem an Angry Old One. Yet politically he is not taken seriously. Partly this is because he is thought to take himself too seriously. But his abandoning traditional oratory in favour of oblique devices, though a perfectly legitimate literary strategy, weakens his political message. For what is mannah to the masses is still prime corn (*see* among others Thatcher, Reagan, Jesse Jackson). Pinter cannot cut it — the corn. He can be a funny playwright. What he cannot have wanted to be was a bit of a joke.

He was born to second-generation immigrant Jews in London's East End, though bar his bar mitzvah he has not been observant. Further back his ancestors seem to have come from Odessa. (*See* also Trotsky, who Pinter resembles in, nowadays, having more money than is good for his radical credentials, also a fondness for aliases, namely 'David Baron' and 'Pinta' [*sic*].) The 'Pinter' may be of Sephardic origins, however (*i.e.*, from the Iberian Peninsula).

He refused to do military service in 1948, citing pacifism. This, however commendable ethically, already suggests political eccentricity bordering on myopia. Pacifists, particularly those in 1948 (the year of the Berlin Airlift, Israel's foundation (*see* Ben-Gurion) and Tito's (*qv*) break with Stalin, *qv*), survived because others bore arms on their behalf.

Pinter briefly trained at RADA, Britain's leading drama school, and became an actor. He is a good one, among very few who can pull off a traditional English aristocrat, witness his Sir Thomas Bertram in the 1999 film of *Mansfield Park* (*see* also Wilberforce).

His first play, *The Room*, was put on in 1957. *The Birthday Party* followed in 1958, folding after a week amid bad notices from the *Guardian*, *The Times* and Milton Shulman in the *Evening Standard*. But the leading critic of the day, Harold Hobson, praised it in the *Sunday Times*. By 1960 Pinter was established as one of Britain's chief playwrights.

Nearly half a century later there are those who find his early work dated. Certainly the preoccupation of 1950s 'high-brow' dramatists like Pinter and Samuel Beckett with tramp figures and rootlessness seems excessively 'of-its-time', though tramps and scarce accommodation are today as prevalent as ever. Pinter's real thematic strength, this author would argue, is less existential menace (product chiefly of the post-war neurosis over atomic annihilation) than the evergreen phenomenon of adultery. This is something Pinter knows a lot about, if his uncle-by-marriage the novelist Anthony Powell is any authority.

Pinter's political preoccupations, which have burgeoned since his marriage to the middle-brow historian Lady Antonia Fraser, involve an almost visceral hatred of America where he is nonetheless revered by the theatre-going public, to the near exclusion of all else. This lop-sided approach also weakens him politically.

Samuel Beckett is a major literary influence on him (also, like Pinter, a very competent cricketer). Pinter is particularly interesting on how Beckett once spotted a weakness in a play script of Pinter's that nobody else noticed till rehearsals began.

• Context of speech

After Pinter won the 2005 Nobel Prize for Literature he pre-recorded an acceptance speech. Its peroration consisted of an attack on the US. The bit here describes his literary technique.

66 **I have often been asked how my plays come about. I cannot say. Nor can I ever sum up my plays, except to say that this is what happened. That is what they said. That is what they did.**

Most of the plays are engendered by a line, a word or an image. The given word is often shortly followed by the image. I shall give two examples of two lines which came right out of the blue into my head, followed by an image, followed by me.

The plays are *The Homecoming* and *Old Times*. The first line of *The Homecoming* is 'What have you done with the scissors?' The first line of *Old Times* is 'Dark.'

In each case I had no further information.

In the first case someone was obviously looking for a pair of scissors and was demanding their whereabouts of someone else he suspected had probably stolen them. But I somehow knew that the person addressed didn't give a damn about the scissors or about the questioner either, for that matter.

'Dark' I took to be a description of someone's hair, the hair of a woman, and was the answer to a question. In each case I found myself compelled to pursue the matter. This happened visually, a very slow fade, through shadow into light.

I always start a play by calling the characters A, B and C.

In the play that became *The Homecoming* I saw a man enter a stark room and ask his question of a younger man sitting on an ugly sofa reading a racing paper. I somehow suspected that A was a father and that B was his son, but I had no proof. This was however confirmed a short time later when B (later to become Lenny) says to A (later to become Max), 'Dad, do you mind if I change the subject? I want to ask you something. The dinner we had before, what was the name of it? What do you call it? Why don't you buy a dog? You're a dog cook. Honest. You think you're cooking for a lot of dogs.' So since B calls A 'Dad' it seemed to me reasonable to assume that they were father and son. A was also clearly the cook and his cooking did not seem to be held in high regard. Did this mean that there was no mother? I didn't know. But, as I told myself at the time, our beginnings never know our ends.

'Dark.' A large window. Evening sky. A man, A (later to become Deeley), and a woman, B (later to become Kate), sitting with drinks. 'Fat or thin?' the man asks. Who are they talking about? But I then see, standing at the window, a woman, C (later to become Anna), in another condition of light, her back to them, her hair dark.

It's a strange moment, the moment of creating characters who up to that moment have had no existence. What follows is fitful, uncertain, even hallucinatory, although sometimes it can be an unstoppable avalanche. The author's position is an odd one. In a sense he is not welcomed by the characters. The characters resist him, they are not easy to live with, they are impossible to define. You certainly can't dictate to them. To a certain extent you play a never-ending game with them, cat and mouse, blind man's buff, hide and seek. But finally you find that you have people of flesh and blood on your hands, people with will and an individual sensibility of their own, made out of component parts you are unable to change, manipulate or distort … "

On nine years of Labour government

(James) Gordon Brown (1951–)
Labour Party Conference, Manchester
25 September 2006

• Biography

Understudying a star is difficult. Ten long years Gordon Brown waited in the wings for Tony Blair (*qv*) — once the *jeune premier* of British politics but with time more a candidate for Denville Hall — to dry, get the bird or stumble into the pit. Anything, provided Brown got his break. But with Blair slower to hang up his grease paint than Marlene Dietrich, Brown seemed confined to what showbiz jargon calls the deuce spot.

Reprising a star turn is worse. Though Blair, like many stars, increasingly just 'was' rather than doing anything, he dominated British politics. Can Brown match that? His antipathy to Blair goes way back, but he will not want to seem a flop in comparison. At least Brown is familiar to today's public. Other Chancellors-promoted-Premier, *e.g.*, Baldwin (*qv*), were often unknowns.

Brown's 'Euro-scepticism' looks encouraging. In autumn 1997 he formulated the 'Five-Tests' benchmark for Britain's joining the Euro. It was not cleared with Blair first. A Blair aide, allegedly Alastair Campbell, riposted shortly before the 2001 election that Brown had 'psychological flaws'. Brown's brooding mien and volcanic rages support this. He once tore papers from a colleague's grasp, tongue-lashing a nearby civil servant. He once lifted another colleague by his jacket lapels, screaming at him — over welfare changes. Brown's finger on the nuclear button may not be itchy but could be 'twitchy'. At least when Blair invaded Iraq it was in collusion with others.

As Chancellor, Brown started prudently. But even his first budget in 1997 raided pension funds, with disastrous results. His later performance deteriorated, though till near the end he kept inflation low. He ignored Treasury experts generally, was even absent at crucial junctures, such as the long-running tax credits fiasco; sold over half Britain's gold reserves in 1999 at a depressed price, swiftly through mismanagement driving it still lower. In 2001–06 he increased Britain's indebtedness by over £130 billion. Treasury mandarins, the Civil Service's elite, reckon him intelligent but bad at handling more than one subject at a time.

• Context of speech

Brown's speeches, following alleged voice coaching, have recently sounded less harsh in tone, though his content still creaks (too many statistics, the same joke again and again). His boastfulness and anxiety to justify himself suggest insecurity. The more bizarre images, *e.g.* 'our prudence' and the mountain metaphor (*see* below), do indeed suggest psychological flaws, so perhaps Campbell (if it was he) did not err. In autumn 2006 Brown published his collected speeches. Celebrity 'endorsements' included a superbly non-committal one by Mandela (*qv*).

In the best-known divvying up of a national polity at a dinner table since Gillray's 'Plumb Pudding' cartoon of Pitt the Younger and Napoleon (*qqv*) partitioning the globe, Brown at the Granita restaurant in Islington in 1994 allegedly wangled the reversion, fixed for Blair's second term, of running Britain. In September 2006 (when Brown did not deny the Granita story, though twice offered the opportunity), he was seen as endorsing a move concocted in another restaurant, this time a 'curry house', to force Blair to announce his departure within 12 months. The slavish, but surely insincere, praise of Blair in the speech excerpted below — embarrassingly like encomia on the 'Dear Leader' in North Korea — should be seen against that background.

66 **L**et me begin by addressing one point directly.
I've worked with Tony Blair for almost ten years as Chancellor — the longest relationship of any Prime Minister and Chancellor in British history.

And it has been a privilege for me to work with and for the most successful ever Labour leader and Labour Prime Minister.

Building New Labour and winning three elections, he recognised what we must never forget, that we must always be in tune with the aspirations, at all times on the side, of the British people.

And in the time we've been MPs — working together for more than 23 years — I believe that we have real achievements together.

But it's hardly surprising that as in any relationship there have been times when we've differed. And where over these years differences have distracted from what matters I regret that, as I know Tony does too …

And Tony, you taught us something else — and once again you saw it right, you saw it clearly and you saw it through; that the world did change after September 11. That no one can be neutral in the fight against terrorism and that we — Britain — have new international responsibilities to discharge.

And let us be clear: the renewal of New Labour will be founded on that essential truth — the need for global co-operation in the fight against terrorism, never anti-Americanism, recognising that the values of decent people everywhere are for liberty, democracy and justice not just for ourselves but for everyone, not least for the poorest countries and peoples of the world …

Whether it is building social justice at home, the advances in peace in Northern Ireland, resolution in the face of terrorism and [*sic*] leadership on Africa, let us today applaud the immense national and international contribution, as Leader and Prime Minister, of Tony Blair …

Our prudence yes, she'll always be around, was and is for a purpose …

And don't let Conservatives tell you it hasn't made a difference — higher school results, lower waiting times, more police on the beat and the longest sustained fall in child poverty and pensioner poverty since records began.

So as a party and a government we have climbed a huge mountain.

But we must now climb many more and even more challenging mountains ahead.

The next ten years will be even more demanding.

And because the challenges are quite different, the programme for governing will be different."

Bibliography

Basler, Roy L., *Abraham Lincoln: His Speeches and Writings* (Cleveland, Ohio, 1946)

Carlyle, Thomas, *The Letters and Speeches of Oliver Cromwell* (London, 1904)

Collins, Christopher, ed., *Thatcher: Complete Public Statements 1945–1990* (Oxford, 2000)

Copeland, Lewis, ed., *The World's Great Speeches* (London, 1942)

Fox, Charles James, *The Speeches of the Right Honourable Charles James Fox in the House of Commons* (VI vols., London, 1815)

George-Brown, Lord, selected and ed., *The Voice of History: Great Speeches of* [sic] *the English Language* (London, 1979)

Harris, Robin, ed., *The Collected Speeches of Margaret Thatcher* (London, 1997)

Hayward, John, ed., *Silver Tongues* (London, 1937)

Hazlitt, William, *The Eloquence of the British Senate* (London, 1808)

Hitler, Adolf, *The Speeches of Adolf Hitler 1922–1939* (Oxford, 1942)

Hutton, A. W. and H. J. Cohen, ed., *The Speeches and Public Addresses of the Right Hon. W. E. Gladstone, with Notes and Introductions* (X vols., London, 1892–94)

MacArthur, Brian, ed., *The Penguin Book of Historic Speeches* (London 1995) and *The Penguin Book of Twentieth-Century Speeches* (London, 2000)

Peel, Sir Robert, *The Speeches of the Right Honourable Sir Robert Peel, Bart., Delivered in the House of Commons* (IV vols., London, 1853)

Peterson, Houston, ed., *A Treasury of the World's Greatest Speeches* (New York, 1954)

Pitt the Younger, William, *The Speeches of the Right Honourable William Pitt in the House of Commons* (IV vols., London, 1806)

Rhodes R. James, ed., *Winston S. Churchill: His Complete Speeches, 1897–1963* (VIII vols., London, 1974)

Scotland, Andrew, selected and ed., *The Power of Eloquence: a treasury of British speech* (London, 1961)

Sebag Montefiore, Simon, (introduction), *Speeches that Changed the World* (London, 2005)

Thierry, R., ed., *The Speeches of the Right Honourable George Canning, with a Memoir of His Life* (VI vols., London, 1828)

Zevin, B. D., ed., *Nothing to Fear: The Selected Addresses of Franklin Delano Roosevelt 1932–1945* (1946)